TERRORISM, WAR AND INTERNATIONAL LAW

The Ashgate International Law Series

Series Editor: Alex Conte, OECD, Paris

The Ashgate International Law Series brings together top-quality titles, principally in the area of public international law but also in private international law, under the label of a single international series. Each title represents work which is the result of high-level research, aimed at both the professorial and postgraduate academic market as well as the expert practitioner.

Also in the series

A Dual Approach to Ocean Governance
The Cases of Zonal and Integrated Management
in International Law of the Sea
Yoshifumi Tanaka
ISBN 978 0 7546 7170 1
e-ISBN 978 07546 90269

Terrorism, War and International Law

The Legality of the Use of Force Against Afghanistan in 2001

MYRA WILLIAMSON
The University of Waikato, New Zealand

ASHGATE

Published by
Ashgate Publishing Limited
Wey Court East
Union Road
Farnham
Surrey, GU9 7PT
England

Ashgate Publishing Company
Suite 420
101 Cherry Street
Burlington
VT 05401-4405
USA

www.ashgate.com

British Library Cataloguing in Publication Data
Williamson, Myra
Terrorism, war and international law : the legality of the use of force against Afghanistan in 2001. - (The Ashgate international law series)
1. Intervention (International law) - History 2. War (International law) - History 3. Terrorism - Prevention
4. War on Terrorism, 2001-- Law and legislation
5. Afghanistan - Politics and government
I. Title
341.5'84

Library of Congress Cataloging-in-Publication Data
Williamson, Myra.
Terrorism, war, and international law : the legality of the use of force against Afghanistan in 2001 / by Myra Williamson.
p. cm. -- (Ashgate international law series)
Includes index.
ISBN 978-0-7546-7403-0 -- ISBN 978-0-7546-9425-0 (ebook)
1. Intervention (International law)--History. 2. War (International law)--History. 3. Terrorism--Prevention. 4. War on Terrorism, 2001---Law and legislation. 5. Afghanistan--Politics and government. I. Title.

KZ6368.W55 2009
958.104'7--dc22

2008047425

Reprinted 2010

ISBN 978-0-7546-7403-0
e-ISBN 978-0-7546-9425-0

Mixed Sources
Product group from well-managed forests and other controlled sources
www.fsc.org Cert no. SA-COC-1565
© 1996 Forest Stewardship Council
FSC

Printed and bound in Great Britain by
MPG Books Ltd, Bodmin, Cornwall.

Contents

Preface

This work examines the international law pertaining to the use of force by states, in general, and to the use of force in self-defence, in particular. The main question addressed here is whether it was lawful for the United States, the United Kingdom and their allies to use force against al Qaeda, the Taliban and Afghanistan, on 7 October 2001.

The focus is not only on this specific use of force, but also on the changing nature of conflict, the definition of terrorism and on the historical evolution of limitations on the use of force, from the League of Nations until 2008. In the two chapters (Chapters 4 and 5) which trace the recent developments in international law, five inter-related themes are highlighted: developments in the limitations on the resort to force generally, the use of force in self-defence, pre-emptive self-defence, the use of forcible measures short of war, and the use of force in response to non-state actors. The historical analysis includes a particular emphasis on understanding the meaning of the phrase, 'inherent right of self-defence', a right which was preserved by Article 51 of the United Nations' Charter. The analysis is then applied to the use of force against Afghanistan beginning on 7 October 2001. Following the terrorist attacks of 11 September 2001, the US and the UK notified the United Nations Security Council of their resort to force in self-defence under Article 51. Each element of Article 51 is thus analysed and the conclusion reached is that there are significant doubts as to the lawfulness of that decision to employ force. In addition to the self-defence justification, other possible grounds for intervention are also examined, such as humanitarian intervention, Security Council authorisation and intervention by invitation.

This book challenges the common assumption that the use of force against Afghanistan was an example of states exercising their inherent right to self-defence. It proposes that this particular use of force, if left unchallenged, would lead to an expansion of the right of self-defence which would ultimately hinder rather than enhance international peace and security. The work draws on recent examples, in Chapter 7, such as the use of force against Iraq in 2003, against Lebanon in 2006 and against Syria in 2007, to illustrate the point that the use of force against Afghanistan, if left to stand unchallenged, could become a dangerous precedent for the use of force in self-defence in the future.

In writing this book I have drawn upon, *inter alia*, material which I presented in a paper at the Cortona Colloquium 2007, hosted by the Comune di Cortona in Italy. I would like to thank the Giangiacomo Feltrinelli Foundation, and particularly the members of the Scientific Committee of the Colloquium, for inviting me to participate, thereby giving me the opportunity to discuss some of my ideas with a group of wonderful scholars from around the world. I would especially like to thank Sara Benjamin, Professor Danilo Zolo, Professor Gustavo Gozzi, Judge Flavia Latanzi and the Director of the Foundation, Chiara Daniele, for their assistance and contributions to my thoughts on some of the issues discussed in this work.

I would also like to thank a number of people at the University of Waikato in Hamilton, New Zealand, including the former Dean of the School of Law, Professor John Farrar, Professor Alexander Gillespie, Associate Professor Claire Breen and Professor Margaret Bedggood for their ongoing advice and support. I would like to thank the law librarians in the University of Waikato Law Library for their research support with this project, especially Law Librarian Kay Young and Library Assistant Emma Pooley. I also need to thank Computer Consultant Dan Taylor for sharing his computer expertise and for providing technical assistance.

I would like to express my gratitude to all the individuals at Ashgate Publishing who have played a role in bringing this work to press, including the Commissioning Editor, Alison Kirk, Elaine Couper, Nikki Dines and Patrick Cole, as well as the anonymous reviewer. Their comments, advice and patience were most appreciated.

Finally, I would like to thank my family for their enduring support which has been invaluable in assisting me to complete this work. In seeing this project through to completion, I have relied on the support of my husband, Adnan Otari, my children Gassune and Zinedeen, my sister, Evelyn Williamson, and, most of all, my parents, Duncan and Gretta Williamson, who have helped me in more ways than I can possibly acknowledge.

Myra Williamson
School of Law,
The University of Waikato,
New Zealand
February 2009

List of Abbreviations

ABC	Australian Broadcasting Corporation
AJIL	*American Journal of International Law*
ASIL	American Society of International Law
Bevans	Bevans, Charles I. (ed.), *Treaties and Other International Agreements of the USA 1776–1949*
Brooklyn J. Int'l L.	*Brooklyn Journal of International Law*
BSP	British and Foreign State Papers
BYIL	*British Yearbook of International Law*
Cal. W. Int'l L.J.	*California Western International Law Journal*
CCM	Convention on Cluster Munitions
Cd	Command Papers (UK)
Chi. J. Int'l L.	*Chicago Journal of International Law*
Cornell Int'l L.J.	*Cornell International Law Journal*
COSIMO	Conflict Simulation Model
COW	Correlates of War Project
CTS	Parry's Consolidated Treaty Series
DRV	Democratic Republic of Vietnam
Duke J. Comp. & Int'l L.	*Duke Journal of Comparative and International Law*
ECOMOG	ECOWAS Military Observer Group
ECOWAS	Economic Community of Western African States
EJIL	*European Journal of International Law*
EU	European Union
FAA	Federal Aviation Administration
Fletcher F. World Aff.	*The Fletcher Forum of World Affairs*
FTO	Foreign Terrorist Organization
GAOR	General Assembly Official Records (UN)
Harv. J.L. & Pub. Pol'y	*Harvard Journal of Law and Public Policy*
Hastings Int'l & Comp. L. Rev	*Hastings International and Comparative Law Review*
HCT	Hertslet's Commercial Treaties
HMSO	Her Majesty's Stationery Office
Hous. J. Int'l L.	*Houston Journal of International Law*
ICJ	International Court of Justice

ICJ Rep	International Court of Justice Reports
ICLQ	*International and Comparative Law Quarterly*
ICTY	International Criminal Tribunal for the Former Yugoslavia
IIS	Iraqi Intelligence Service
ILM	International Legal Materials
ILR	International Law Reports
JCSL	*Journal of Conflict and Security Law*
KOSIMO	Conflict Simulation Model
LNOJ	*League of Nations Official Journal*
LNTS	League of Nations Treaty Series
Martens	Martens, G.F. de, *Noveau recueil général des traits*, 2nd Series
MEPV	Major Episodes of Political Violence
Mich Law Rev	*Michigan Law Review*
NAC	North Atlantic Council
NATO	North Atlantic Treaty Organization
NSA	National Security Agency (US)
NSC	National Security Council (US)
NSS	National Security Strategy (US)
OAS	Organisation of American States
OAU	Organisation of the African Union
P	Parliamentary Papers (UK)
PACE	Parliamentary Assembly of the Council of Europe
PCIJ	Publications of the Permanent Court of International Justice
PLO	Palestine Liberation Organization
QUTLJJ	*Queensland University of Technology Law and Justice Journal*
Rec. des Cours	*Recueil des cours de l'Academie de droit international*
RIAA	Reports of International Arbitral Awards
SCOR	Security Council Official Record
SCR	Security Council Resolution
Trócaire Dev. R.	*Trócaire Development Review*
UAE	United Arab Emirates
UCDP	Uppsala Conflict Data Project
UK	United Kingdom
UNCIO	UN Conference on International Organization
UNGA	United Nations General Assembly
UNSC	United Nations Security Council
UNTS	United Nations Treaty Series

US	United States of America
USSR	United Soviet Socialist Republic
Va. J. Int'l L.	*Virginia Journal of International Law*
Val. U.L. Rev	*Valparaiso University Law Review*
Vand. J. Transnat'l L.	*Vanderbuilt Journal of Transnational Law*
Wash. U.J.L. & Pol'y	*Washington University Journal of Law and Policy*
Yale J. Int'l L.	*Yale Journal of International Law*
Yrbk. ILC	*Yearbook of the International Law Commission*

For ourselves, we shall not trouble you with specious pretences – either of how we have a right to our empire because we overthrew the Mede, or are now attacking you because of wrong that you have done us – and make a long speech which would not be believed; and in return we hope that you, instead of thinking to influence us by saying that you did not join the Lacedaemonians, although their colonists, or that you have done us no wrong, will aim at what is feasible, holding in view the real sentiments of us both; since you know as well as we do that right, as the world goes, is only in question between equals in power, while the strong do what they can and the weak suffer what they must.

Thucydides, *The History of the Peloponnesian War*, Book V, Chapter XVII

For my mum and dad,
Margaret Elizabeth ('Gretta') Williamson
and
Duncan Williamson

Chapter 1
Introduction

According to Thucydides, a delegation from Athens, then at the height of its powers, told the conquered inhabitants of the small island of Melos that right was only in question between equals in power. The Athenian delegation reportedly said that 'the strong do what they can and the weak suffer what they must'.[1] A thousand years later, those sentiments were also cited by Grotius in the opening passages of *De Jure Belli ac Pacis*.[2] The Athenian concept of imperialism is now supposedly outdated, in an age when the United Nations' (UN) Charter upholds the rights of independent and equal sovereign states. Modern states have agreed to be bound by the UN Charter and are supposed to refrain from the use or threat of force in their relations with one another, unless the use of force is either sanctioned by the UN Security Council, or they are acting in self-defence.

Did the United States of America (US) and the United Kingdom (UK) act lawfully when they employed force against Afghanistan on 7 October 2001? States are permitted to use force in individual or collective self-defence. That is a right which is preserved by Article 51 of the UN Charter. That provision has been interpreted in different ways by states, scholars and judges. The reference to an 'inherent' right of self-defence in Article 51 implies that a right existed before the UN Charter came into being, thus necessitating an historical inquiry. This book is not only concerned with the lawfulness of the use of force against Afghanistan; it is also concerned with the broader picture which encompasses inter-connected issues regarding terrorism, war and international law.

The analysis begins in Chapter 2 with a broad sketch of the changing nature of conflict. That chapter examines the evolving nature of threats faced by states, including the progression from large-scale inter-state conflict to smaller-scale, intra-state conflict, as well as the increasingly significant threat posed by non-state actors. Chapter 3 moves away from conflict generally to terrorism in particular. It analyses the origins of both the concept and the term 'terrorism' and it traces

---

1 Thucydides, *The Complete Writings of Thucydides: The History of the Peloponnesian War*, Book V, Chapter XVII, para 89 (Crawley, R. trans.) (New York: Everyman's Library, 1951) at 301. A passage with similar meaning appears in Book VI: 'Besides, for tyrants and imperial cities nothing is unreasonable if expedient …': ibid., Book VI, Chapter XX, para 85 at 350.

2 Grotius, H., *The Law of War and Peace (De Jure Belli ac Pacis)*, Prologomena (Loomis, L. trans.) (Roslyn, New York: Walter J. Black, 1949) at para 3: 'On most men's lips are the words of Euphemus, quoted by Thucydides, that for a king or a free city nothing is wrong that is to their advantage.'

historical and contemporary attempts to define it. In Chapters 4 and 5 the focus shifts towards the limitations on the resort to force which have evolved across two 'epochs' of international law. In Chapter 4 the period from 1919 to 1944 is analysed to understand what the 'inherent' right to self-defence mentioned in Article 51 may mean. In Chapter 5 the developments that have occurred from 1945 until the present are discussed. Throughout Chapters 4 and 5 the focus is on tracing the evolution of legal limitations on the use of force through five distinct lenses: the use of force generally, the use of force specifically in self-defence, pre-emptive self-defence,[3] forcible measures short of war, and the use of force by, and in response to, non-state actors. What is apparent from the historical inquiry is that the current international law regarding the resort to force has not arisen out of a vacuum and that modern interpretations must have regard to historical antecedents.

In Chapter 6 the international law on the resort to force is applied to the facts of the 2001 intervention in Afghanistan. Although the use of force against Afghanistan was roundly justified on the grounds of self-defence, the analysis therein shows that serious doubts can be raised as to whether it was a lawful use of

3 The terms 'pre-emptive self-defence' and 'anticipatory self-defence' are used interchangeably in this book to refer to the concept of a state using force before an armed attack has occurred. This approach is consistent with the observation that 'pre-emptive', 'preventive' and 'anticipatory' are terms commonly used to refer to the same concept, although there is some degree of inconsistency between scholars: some use one term to the exclusion of the others, whilst others prefer to use the terms interchangeably: see, *inter alia*, Byers, M., *War Law* (London: Atlantic Books, 2005), 72–81; Gray, C., 'A New War for a New Century? The Use of Force Against Terrorism After September 11, 2001', in Eden, P. and O'Donnell. T. (eds) *September 11, 2001 – A Turning Point in International and Domestic Law?* (New York: Transnational Publishers, 2005), 107–13; Maogoto, J., *Battling Terrorism* (Aldershot: Ashgate, 2005), 5–7 and 111–37; Gardam, J., *Necessity, Proportionality and the Use of Force by States* (Cambridge: Cambridge University Press, 2004), 146–7; Gray, C., *International Law and the Use of Force*, 2nd edn (Oxford: Oxford University Press, 2004), 95 and also chapter 6; Karoubi, M., *Just or Unjust War – International Law and Unilateral Use of Armed Force by States at the Turn of the 20th Century* (Aldershot: Ashgate, 2004), 204; Brownlie, I., *Principles of International Law*, 6th edn (Oxford: Oxford University Press, 2003), 701–2; Shaw, M., *International Law* 5th edn (New York: Cambridge University Press, 2003), 1028–30; Franck, T., *Recourse to Force – State Action Against Threats and Armed Attacks* (Cambridge; New York: Cambridge University Press, 2002), 97–108; McCormack, T., *Self-Defense in International Law – The Israeli Raid on the Iraqi Nuclear Reactor* (New York: St Martin's Press, 1996), 122 ff; Arend, A. and Beck, R., *International Law and the Use of Force* (USA and Canada: Routledge, 1993), 71–80. For examples of where an intentional distinction *is* drawn between the concepts of 'anticipation' and 'pre-emption', see Anton, D., Mathew, P. and Morgan, W., *International Law – Cases and Materials* (South Melbourne: Oxford University Press, 2005), 545; and also O'Connell, M. 'The Myth of Preemptive Self-Defense', *ASIL Presidential Task Force on Terrorism* (Washington, DC: ASIL, 2002). For further discussion of this issue, see Chapter 5, 'Pre-emptive Self-defence' and Chapter 6, 'Pre-emptive Self-defence'.

force. In particular, concerns are raised as to whether there was an 'armed attack' that triggered the Article 51 UN Charter right of self-defence; whether the right to respond forcefully had expired by the time that the invasion began; whether responsibility for the terrorist attacks was adequately attributed to the targets of the military action and whether the customary law elements of the right of self-defence, such as necessity, proportionality and immediacy, were satisfied. Chapter 6 also addresses whether other grounds for intervention could potentially have been relied upon, such as humanitarian intervention, Security Council authorisation and intervention by invitation. The purpose of Chapter 6 is to discuss all aspects of the justifications for resorting to force against Afghanistan to determine whether any of those grounds, or potential grounds, were satisfied. The analysis suggests that this use of force may have had more in common with the ideals of Athenian imperialism than the rule of law embodied in the UN Charter.

In Chapter 7, the concluding chapter, some general comments are offered on the current status of the law regarding the resort to force, and self-defence in particular. Chapter 7 attempts to forecast the implications of accepting that the use of force against Afghanistan was lawful. Reference is made to the use of force against Iraq in 2003 and Lebanon in 2006 as further examples of the way in which militarily powerful states are able to impose their will and their interpretations of international law on less powerful states, thereby weakening the effectiveness of legal limitations on the recourse to force.

It will become evident that the historical perspective is an important aspect of the analysis undertaken herein. As Robert Ago has noted, international law is not a new phenomenon; any scholar who seeks to understand current relations between states without appreciating the historical nexus is bound to be misled.[4] In the context of the law regarding the resort to force, connections between the past and the present, and the present and the future, are ignored at our peril. Studying the history of inter-state relations may provide us with lessons which are useful: 'ancient realities may help us to appreciate how dangerous it is to persist in certain errors of judgment.'[5]

4 Ago, R. 'The First International Communities in the Mediterranean World' (1982) 53 *BYIL* 213.

5 Ibid.

Chapter 2
The Changing Nature of Conflict

Introduction

This text is principally concerned with the use of force in self-defence, especially when that force is used in response to terrorism. As noted in Chapter 1, this text is particularly concerned with the use of force by the United States and its allies against Afghanistan in response to the terrorist attacks that occurred on 11 September 2001.

Before proceeding to an examination of that central issue in Chapter 6, it is necessary to reflect on the state of armed conflict that existed prior to the events of 11 September 2001 and on some post-9/11 trends. There is currently a virtual presumption that we now live in different times, with a heightened level of conflict and a heightened consciousness of the threat posed by international terrorism. It has become a cliché to speak about the 'post-September 11 world', implying that fundamental and irreversible changes in the global political and legal landscape have occurred. The objective of this chapter is to measure the extent to which we are living in a new, post-September 11 era. It also aims to place the events that are at the heart of this text into a political and historical context by examining how armed conflict has evolved.

This chapter consists of three parts. First, historical trends in armed conflict are briefly examined. Secondly, trends in modern armed conflict are traversed and the question as to whether the world is more or less violent today than in the past is addressed, together with some observations regarding the ways in which conflict has changed in type and intensity. A small selection of conflict data sets is analysed to identify conflict trends and answer questions such as whether there are a greater or lesser number of conflicts than there used to be; whether conflicts are more or less destructive than they used to be; and what factors differentiate modern conflicts from earlier ones. Thirdly, there is an examination of the threat posed to international peace and security by non-state actors, and in particular by acts of terrorism.[1] Since terrorism is an integral part of the text, it is necessary to touch upon terrorism *trends*, since significant changes may have implications for the way that states respond, and particularly for the international law that constrains states' resort to force in response to acts of terrorism. The third part of this chapter seeks to answer questions such as whether acts of terrorism are more prevalent today than in the past, whether acts of terrorism result in a greater or lesser number of casualties and the extent to which terrorism poses a threat to international peace

1 The issue of how 'terrorism' should be defined is discussed in Chapter 3.

and security. For the purposes of effecting change in international law, it is useful to know whether the events of 11 September, and the subsequent use of force against Afghanistan, were isolated incidents, the beginning of a new era, or merely the continuation of an already established one. Understanding trends in conflict and terrorism may help to explain why force was used against Afghanistan and whether it can be justified.[2] Furthermore, at a time when so many presume that the world was changed forever on 11 September 2001, it is important to consult raw data on conflict and terrorism to determine the extent to which global peace and security have been affected. By examining empirical data to trace conflict and terrorism trends, a rational and objective foundation will be set for more controversial assertions in later chapters.

Historical Trends in Armed Conflict: A Brief History of Conflict Research

Research into the causes and patterns of conflict has a long history. Quincy Wright is widely regarded as the pioneer in this field. His famous work on the causes and patterns of war, *The Study of War*, was first published in 1942, during World War II. A parallel has been drawn between his book and Hugo Grotius' *De Jure Belli ac Pacis* or *On the Law of War and Peace*, which appeared in 1625 during the Thirty Years War. As Grotius' book became a basis for the study of what later became known as 'international law', so Quincy Wright's book marks the beginning of what has become known as 'peace research' or 'conflict research'.[3]

Wright's research was based largely on the wars that occurred in the period from approximately 1480 to 1940. Although constrained by the time in which it was written, many of Wright's observations seem equally relevant today. He reflected on the reasons why war has come, through the generations, to be regarded by a majority of the population as a problem:[4] 'Because the world is getting smaller, because changes occur more rapidly, because wars are more destructive, and because peoples are more impressed by the human responsibility for war, the recurrence of war has become a problem for a larger number of people.'

Wright acknowledged that the intensity of war[5] may be measured by the frequency of battles, campaigns or wars.[6] These military incidents may in turn be measured according to the absolute number of combatants engaged, to the number engaged relative to the supporting population, to the absolute number of

---

2 The legal issues surrounding the use of force against Afghanistan in 2001 are discussed in Chapter 6.

3 Deutsch, K., 'Preface to the Second Edition', in Wright, Q., *A Study of War* (Chicago and London: The University of Chicago Press, 1965).

4 Ibid., 5.

5 Wright provides a definition for 'war' in both the legal and material sense, ibid., 8–13.

6 See Wright's definition of a 'battle', ibid., 102.

battle casualties of various types (killed, wounded, prisoners), or to the number of casualties relative either to the number of combatants or to the number of the supporting population.[7] In terms of categorising a conflict as worthy of inclusion in a study, Wright pondered over whether one should place in the same category civil wars between factions of the same civilization, and imperial wars between groups from different civilizations. He questioned the temporal and spatial limitations that should be adopted in a statistical tabulation of military incidents and accepted that there was insufficient data to allow him to include every battle or war between civilised peoples since civilisation began. He concluded that it would not be illuminating to 'lump together' in a single tabulation conflicts that occurred in Egyptian, Mesopotamian, Chinese, Indian and Mayan civilisations. If regular trends or fluctuations in war and peace existed, then it seemed probable to Wright that they must be relative to groups of people in more or less continuous contact with one another, that is, to a civilisation.[8]

In addition to the difficulties of defining an area of study within which conflict trends may be analysed, another early researcher identified the problem of obtaining accurate statistics on which to base a study.[9] The difficulty of obtaining accurate statistics remains a problem which affects even the latest research into conflict trends, such as that carried out jointly by the Department of Peace and Conflict Research at Uppsala University and the International Peace Research Institute (PRIO). The researchers in the project known as the Uppsala Conflict Data Project (UCDP) observed the need for more accurate casualty statistics in order to study the severity of war, and in particular its human cost.[10]

A brief history of conflict research shows that conflict data statistics must be read on the understanding that regardless of whether they relate to the ancient or the recent past, the selections which researchers make will naturally affect the outcome of their study. Conflict researchers are usually careful to point out the limitations of their research and to explain their subjective choices in selecting data for inclusion. These factors must be borne in mind when drawing conclusions about conflict trends.

---

7 Ibid., 218.

8 Ibid., 103.

9 Samuel Dumas commented on the difficulties in compiling accurate statistics due to an absence of records, errors of estimation and falsification of statistics: see Dumas, S. and Vedel-Petersen, K. *Losses of Life Caused by War* (Oxford: Clarendon Press, 1923).

10 For instance, the number of casualties in the Chechen War is estimated in the UCDP as 30,000 to 60,000 and the number of civilian deaths in Rwanda in 1994 as 500,000 to 800,000: Gleditsch, N., Wallensteen, P., Eriksson, M., Sollenberg M. and Strand, H., 'Armed Conflict 1946–2001: A New Dataset' (2002) 39 (5) *Journal of Peace Research* 615 at 625–6.

The History of War – Wright's Four Stages

Wright divided the history of war into what he described as four very unequal stages dominated respectively by animals, primitive men, civilised men and men using modern technology.[11] The first two stages (prehuman/animal warfare and primitive warfare, respectively) are of limited assistance in the present context given the remoteness in time and the scarcity of evidence presently available.[12] It is Wright's third and fourth stages which are of greater relevance here.

Historical warfare Wright's third stage of warfare began in the valleys of the Nile and the Euphrates, 6,000–10,000 years ago; in the valleys of the Indus and Yellow Rivers 4,000–5,000 years ago, and in Peru and Mexico around 3,000–4,000 years ago. Evidence of the nature of war in this period is to be found in contemporaneous and older writings; in inscriptions of a descriptive, chronological and analytical nature, and in archaeological remains.[13] A study of warfare in this period is more relevant to the present inquiry, as it concerns warfare between or within the literate civilisations from Egypt to Mesopotamia to the age of discovery in the fifteenth century – a span of over 6,000 years.[14] Although trends in modern conflict may be related to conflict in this period, the main difficulty with making any comparison is the dearth of reliable information. Wright acknowledged that even when records of the battles and wars exist, data as to the number of participants and casualties is unreliable.[15]

Despite these difficulties, one trend observed was that conflict tended to occur *between* different civilisations rather than *within* civilisations. In a comprehensive study of battles that occurred between 500 BCE and 1500 AD, most battles fell into the inter-civilisation category.[16] Another study reached a similar finding, although the study was confined to far fewer battles.[17] In comparing successive civilisations during this period, Wright concluded that there was a trend towards larger armies, both absolutely and in proportion to the population. Secondly, war tended to become absolutely and relatively more costly, both in life and wealth. Thirdly, military activity tended to become more concentrated, with longer peace intervals between wars. Fourthly, wars tended to become more extended in space with fewer places of safety and more inconvenience to civilians. Fifthly,

11 Wright, supra n. 3 at 30.

12 For an account of this period, see Wright, supra n. 3 at 53–101.

13 Ibid., 31.

14 Legal, moral and philosophical attempts to limit the resort to force during this period are discussed below in Chapters 4 and 5.

15 See Wright, supra n. 3 at 101–65.

16 Harbottle, T., *Dictionary of Battles from the Earliest Date to the Present Time* (London: Swan Sonnenschein & Co. Ltd, 1904), in Wright, supra n. 3 at 120.

17 Creasy, E., *The Fifteen Decisive Battles of the World: From Marathon to Waterloo* (London: R. Bentley, 1851), in Wright, supra n. 3 at 104–20.

war became ideologically and legally more distinct from peace and tended to be regarded as more abnormal and more in need of rational justification.[18] Finally, he noted that the changes in war on the whole tended to favour defensive rather than offensive operations.[19]

Modern warfare (1480–1940) Wright's fourth and final stage began with the invention of printing in the fifteenth century, followed by the voyages from Western Europe establishing continuous contacts between the centres of civilisation in Europe, the Near East, the Americas and the Far East. The increased availability of source material means that more detailed analysis of conflict patterns is possible. In Wright's study of modern warfare from 1480 to 1940, he discussed four conflict trend variables: spatial, temporal, quantitative and qualitative.

With regard to *spatial variability*, he noted that the majority of battles involved 'great' (powerful) states, rather than small states.[20] The same conclusion was reached in a study of the proportion of war years in the history of states.[21] The latter study showed that between 1480 and 1940, the 'great' states averaged twice as many wars as the smaller states, although the wars of the smaller states tended to last longer.

Trends in *temporal variability* varied, depending on the type of conflict. Battles became more prolonged;[22] but the duration of wars fluctuated.[23] There was a tendency throughout most of the period (1480–1940) for wars to occur approximately every 50 years, with every alternate period of concentration being more severe. Some authors attributed this cycle to the passage of two generations[24]

18 This is a point borne out by the analysis presented in Chapter 4.

19 See Wright, supra n. 3 at 120–21.

20 For example, from 1480 to 1940, there were about 2,600 important battles involving European states. Of those battles, France participated in 42 per cent; Austria-Hungary in 34 per cent; Germany (Prussia) in 25 per cent; Great Britain and Russia each in about 22 per cent; Turkey in 15 per cent; Spain in 12 per cent; the Netherlands in 8 per cent; Sweden in 4 per cent and Denmark in 2 per cent.

21 'It is the stronger nations since 1700 that have devoted the most time to war ... Spain, Turkey, Holland and Sweden were active in warfare at the same period that they were politically great': Woods, F. and Baltzly, A., *Is War Diminishing?* (Boston: Houghton-Mifflin, 1915) in Wright, supra n. 3 at 221–2.

22 During the seventeenth century, 96 per cent of battles lasted for a day or less; in the eighteenth century the figure was 93 per cent; in the nineteenth century 84 per cent, and in the twentieth century only 40 per cent: ibid., 223–4.

23 The average duration of participation in a war by the 11 principal European powers from 1450 to 1930 was 2.5 years. The average varied little from the fifteenth to the eighteenth centuries but wars were exceptionally short in the nineteenth century (1.4 years) and exceptionally long in the early years of the twentieth century (four years): ibid., 225–7.

24 This theory suggests that the warrior does not wish to fight again himself and prejudices his son against war, but the grandsons are taught to think of war as romantic:

whilst others attributed it to the cycle of business.[25] One researcher explained it on the basis that 'a long and severe bout of fighting confers immunity on most of those who have experienced it'.[26] After a decade or two, the immunity apparently faded and the next generation was likely to enter war with enthusiasm.[27]

Quantitative trends showed that the size of armies tended to increase, both absolutely and in proportion to the population.[28] After World War I, the military and naval establishments diminished but this trend was reversed with vigour in the increasing state of tension that prevailed after 1931. Throughout the period, the trend was towards an increase in the duration of battles, in the number of battles in a war year and in the total number of battles during a century. The number of battles within a war also tended to increase. There was also an upward trend in the number of belligerents in a war, in the rapidity with which a war spread and in the area covered by a war.[29] An upward trend was also observed regarding the costs of war in human and economic terms, both absolutely and relative to the population. However, the proportion of persons engaged in battles who were killed tended to decline.[30]

The trend may have been towards a decrease in battlefield casualties, but due to the fact that an increasing proportion of the population was engaged in the armies, and that the number of battles tended to increase, the overall effect was an increase in the number of *total* casualties as a result of modern warfare.[31] One researcher,

Spengler, O., *The Decline of the West* (Atkinson, C., trans.) (New York: Alfred A. Knopf, 1932), ibid., 230.

25 Stimson, R., 'The War System', *Conferences on the Cause and Cure of War* (New York: National Committee on the Cause and Cure of War, 1933): <http://www.worldcat.org/oclc/2659784>, ibid., 230.

26 Richardson, L., quoted in Blainey, G., *The Causes of War* (Melbourne: Sun Books, 1973) 6.

27 Ibid.

28 In the sixteenth century, armies seldom reached over 20,000–30,000. In the seventeenth century, armies often reached 50,000–60,000. In the eighteenth century, armies increased greatly in size, with Napoleon having as many as 200,000 men in battles: Wright, supra n. 3 at 232–3.

29 'The number of participants in a war has tended to increase from 2 or 3 in the sixteenth and seventeenth centuries to 3 or 4 in the nineteenth and twentieth centuries, thus suggesting that wars spread more easily today than formally – a natural result of the development of transport and communications.': ibid., 238–41.

30 During the Middle Ages, 30–50 per cent of those engaged in a battle were killed or wounded; in the sixteenth century, the number was around 40 per cent of the defeated side; in the seventeenth, eighteenth and nineteenth centuries, the numbers fell to around 20 per cent, 15 per cent and 10 per cent respectively; in the twentieth century, it was about 6 per cent: ibid., 241–2.

31 The percentage of the French population killed or wounded in battles from 1630–39 was 0.09 per cent. This figure rose steadily until it peaked in the years 1910–19, when it was 5.63 per cent. A similar trend, although with lower figures, was observed in Great Britain: ibid., 658–63, Tables 54, 55 and 56.

who estimated the number of war casualties per 1,000 members of the population, found that from the twelfth to the twentieth century, there was a steady increase in the number of war casualties in European countries when compared with the total population.[32] Along with the rise in the *human* cost, there was also an upward trend in the *material* cost. There is agreement amongst researchers that war became increasingly costly to governments in direct financial burdens as well as in indirect losses from misdirection of productive resources.[33]

Finally, regarding *qualitative trends*, Wright observed that war became 'less functional, less intentional, less directable and less legal'.[34] The warlike states increasingly led their nations to a more complete organisation of the state's resources, economy, opinion and government for war, even in times of peace. Wright's assessment that war became less easy to localise and 'materially more destructive and morally less controllable'[35] is supported by the work of modern scholars.[36] Kaldor notes that at the turn of the century, the ratio of military to civilian casualties in wars was eight to one. By 1999, that ratio had been almost exactly reversed: in the wars of the 1990s, the ratio of military to civilian casualties was approximately one to eight.[37]

Modern Conflict Data

This part of the chapter examines conflict trends in the twentieth and twenty-first centuries. One of the difficulties in assessing conflict trends is directly attributed to the lack of official data.[38] Since the UN does not collect data on armed conflicts, privately funded research institutes are the sole source of contemporary conflict data sets.[39] According to the Stockholm International Peace Research Institute

---

32 In Europe, per 1,000 population, there were two casualties in the twelfth century, five in the thirteenth century, eight in the fourteenth century, ten in the fifteenth century, 37 in the seventeenth century, 33 in the eighteenth century, 15 in the nineteenth century and 54 in the first 15 years of the twentieth century: Sorokin, P., *Social and Cultural Dynamics: A Study of Change in Major Systems of Art, Truth, Ethics, Law and Social Relationships* (Boston: Porter Sargent, 1957), ibid., 656, Appendix XX, Table 51.

33 For the monetary costs of recent conflicts, see, *inter alia*, the Stockholm International Peace Research Institute (SIPRI) Yearbooks.

34 Wright, supra n. 3 at 248.

35 Ibid.

36 For example, Kaldor, M., *New and Old Wars – Organized Violence in a Global Era* (Cambridge: Polity Press, 1999).

37 Ibid., 7–8. For analysis of the way in which war affects civilians, see Mack, A. (ed), *Human Security Report 2005 – War and Peace in the 21st Century* (2005): <http://www.humansecurityreport.info/HSR2005_PDF/Part1.pdf> at 3 June 2008.

38 Mack, supra n. 37 at 18.

39 Ibid., 18–20. Note that the UN utilises the research undertaken by some of the projects discussed here. The UCDP, for example, focuses some of its research specifically

(SIPRI), there are currently 16 reputable English-language conflict data projects producing information on various aspects of conflict.[40] Some projects focus on the *patterns of conflict occurrence*, others on the causes and processes of conflict, the costs of conflict and conflict early warning. For present purposes, it is projects that fall into the first of those categories that are particularly relevant. The projects discussed here are the Correlates of War (COW), the Uppsala Conflict Data Project (UCDP), the Major Episodes of Political Violence (MEPV), and the Conflict Simulation Model (KOSIMO).[41] Before examining their findings, a brief description of their respective objectives and coverage is provided below.[42] Most of these projects determine whether a conflict should be included in a data set by creating a threshold for the number of people that are killed in a conflict. Variations in definitions, purposes and coding rules can lead to significant divergence on basic parameters, such as the number, frequency, duration and dispersal of armed conflict, a factor which must be kept in mind when comparing data.[43]

Correlates of War Project[44]

The Correlates of War (COW) is a study of the conditions associated with the outbreak of war, as well as the conditions surrounding militarised disputes.[45] Inter-state conflict is the special focus of this project, with emphasis on conflicts that involve the threat, use or display of force. Intra-state and extra-state conflicts are also studied. Currently, the project includes data from 1816 to 1997.[46] One of the problems of relying on the COW data is its definition of 'inter-state war'. Before including a conflict, it stipulates that there be sustained combat between the regular forces of two or more members of the international system and that there be a total of *at least 1,000 battle-related fatalities* in any one year. This relatively high threshold has the effect of excluding some conflicts, which it may seem intuitively

on the UN's involvement in armed conflict, and that research has been used in various UN reports; see: <http://www.pcr.uu.se/research/UCDP/ucdp_projects/UN_in_Armed_Conflicts_Wallensteen.htm> at 3 June 2008.

40 See the SIPRI website on conflict data sets: <http://www.sipri.org/contents/conflict/conflictdatasets.html/view?searchterm=conflict%20data%20sets> at 3 June 2008.

41 There is a slight overlap between some of the conflict data in this part and the conflict data referred to in the preceding part of this chapter because Wright's analysis was based on data up to and including 1940, whereas at least one of the modern conflict data projects (COW) uses data which dates to 1816.

42 A description of all 16 data sets is available in *SIPRI Yearbook 2002* (2002) at 88–96.

43 Ibid., 81 and 96.

44 There were previously two projects, the COW and COW2, but in November 2005 the COW2 was renamed and changed back to the 'Correlates of War' project.

45 See the COW website for a description of the project: <http://www.correlates of war.org> at 3 June 2008.

46 COW Inter-State War Data, 1816–1997 v. 3: ibid.

reasonable to include in a data set of armed conflict.[47] For example, the Basque conflict has not accumulated enough deaths to qualify for inclusion, nor had the Northern Ireland conflict, which had claimed more than 3,000 casualties but did not qualify under the COW threshold of more than 1,000 deaths in a single year.[48]

Uppsala Conflict Data Project (UCDP)[49]

The Uppsala Conflict Data Project (UCDP) was originally based on data from the post-Cold War period to include conflicts that occurred between 1989 and 2001, but it has been extended and is updated on a yearly basis so that it currently includes data for the entire post-World War II period from 1946 to 2007.[50] The main point of distinction between the COW project and the UCDP is in the latter's lower threshold requirement for inclusion. An 'armed conflict' is defined in the UCDP as a contested incompatibility that concerns government and/or territory where the use of armed force between two parties (at least one of which is the government of a state) results in *at least 25 battle-related deaths* in one calendar year.[51] This is a much lower threshold than the COW's requirement of 1,000 deaths in a single year and it allows for the inclusion of lower-intensity conflicts. The UCDP divides its data on armed conflicts into two levels of intensity: minor armed conflicts[52] and war.[53] A possible disadvantage is that it only reaches back to 1946, whereas the COW data dates from 1816. However, extending analysis of conflict occurrence over long periods raises the issue of whether the theoretical explanations are equally reasonable for the whole period and whether variables such as the 'degree of democracy' or 'economic development' mean the same thing across the entire period.[54] The UCDP data is widely cited and is regarded by

---

47 Gleditsch et al., supra n. 10 at 617–19.

48 The threshold that 1,000 deaths occur in a *single year* is set for extra-systemic (also known as extra-state war), which is defined as 'sustained armed combat between a state member of the international system and a non-system-member political entity outside its territorial boundaries'.

49 Based at the Department of Peace and Conflict Research at Uppsala University, in Uppsala, Sweden, UCDP, see: < http://www.pcr.uu.se/database/> at 3 June 2008.

50 The UCDP data has been published in the SIPRI Yearbooks since 1988 and in the *Journal of Peace Research* since 1993.

51 See the UCDP Codebook: <http://www.pcr.uu.se/database/definitions_all.htm> at 3 June 2008. See also Gleditsch et al., supra n. 10 at 618–19.

52 Between 25 and 999 battle-related deaths in a given year: UCDP/PRIO Armed Conflict Database Codebook Version 4, 2007 see: <http://www.pcr.uu.se/publications/UCDP_pub/UCDP_PRIO_Codebook_v4-2007.pdf> at 3 June 2008.

53 At least 1,000 battle-related deaths in a given year: ibid.

54 Gleditsch et al., supra n. 10 at 617–18.

some as the most comprehensive single source of information on contemporary global political violence.[55]

Major Episodes of Political Violence (MEPV)[56]

The Major Episodes of Political Violence (MEPV) project categorises all episodes of major political violence of any type in the 'contemporary period', from 1946 to 2006.[57] Categories include all forms of inter-state, intra-state and inter-communal warfare. The MEPV draws upon 16 sources of conflict data, including the COW, the UCDP, the SIPRI Yearbooks, as well as from its own researchers.[58] The MEPV is the only data set discussed here that does not require a state to be an antagonist in order for a violent conflict to be included: the MEPV includes conflicts such as inter-communal violence, which the other data sets would exclude by definition.[59] The MEPV findings are incorporated into a biannual report[60] on global trends in violent conflict, produced by the Center for International Development and Conflict Management (CIDCM).[61]

---

55 Mack, supra n. 37 at 20. The UCDP is also cited by the United Nations, 'A More Secure World: Our Shared Responsibility', Report of the Secretary-General's High Level Panel on Threats, Challenges and Change (2004).

56 It is located at the Center for Systemic Peace at the University of Maryland in the United States, MEPV <http://members.aol.com/CSPmgm/warlist.htm> at 3 June 2008.

57 Ibid.

58 Ibid.

59 The MEPV data includes civil intra-state, ethnic intra-state and international event inter-state conflicts in its study of 'major armed conflicts'.

60 CIDCM reports were published in 2001, 2003 and 2005. An executive summary of the latest report, Peace and Conflict 2008, is available at: <http://www.cidcm.umd.edu/pc/executive_summary/pc_es_20070613.pdf> at 3 June 2008.

61 CIDCM <http://www.cidcm.umd.edu> at 3 June 2008.

Conflict Simulation Model (KOSIMO)[62]

Unlike the other three conflict data sets, the Conflict Simulation Model (KOSIMO or COSIMO 1) uses qualitative rather than quantitative parameters for variables.[63] The justification for adopting a purely qualitative definition was to allow for the inclusion of non-violent conflicts that have not led to battle deaths, but, in the eyes of the participants, have the potential to escalate into a violent conflict. The KOSIMO definition also excludes all non-national, constitutional, criminal and economic conflicts.[64] The KOSIMO database contains 693 political conflicts from 1945 to 1999 and is based on published material from American and European conflict researchers. Each conflict in the data set is coded with 28 variables.[65] Although this comprehensive coding of each conflict is valuable, the KOSIMO database's usefulness is limited to the extent that it relies on existing databases and it ends in 1999.[66]

In summary, researchers have produced several conflict data sets which can assist in answering questions such as whether conflict is more prevalent today than it was in the past, and to what extent conflict has changed and continues to evolve in terms of, *inter alia*, type, location, frequency and intensity. The four conflict data sets utilised here relate to the periods 1816–1997 (COW); 1946–2007 (UCDP); 1946–2006 (MEPV) and 1945–1999 (KOSIMO). The discussion below

62 The COSIMO, originally 'KOSIMO', project is located at the Heidelberg Institute for International Conflict Research, see <http://www.hiik.de/en/kosimo/kosimo1.html> at 3 June 2008. Note that the first version of the database, now referred to on the Heidelberg Institute website as 'COSIMO 1', comprises data on national and international conflicts from 1945 to 1998, prepared under the direction of Professor Dr Frank Pfetsch. The methodology used for the first database differs from that used in the new database, known as 'COSIMO 2', recently renamed as CONIS (Conflict Information System) which is yet to be published: see <http://www.hiik.de/en/kosimo/kosimo2.html> at 3 June 2008. This text retains the acronym 'KOSIMO' rather than the updated 'COSIMO I', since the former is easily identifiable in the literature. For a summary of the KOSIMO objectives and findings, see Pfetsch, F. and Rohloff, C., 'Kosimo: A Databank on Political Conflict' (2000) 37 (3) *Journal of Peace Research* 379.

63 'Conflict' is defined as: 'the clashing of overlapping interests around national values and issues (independence, self-determination, borders and territory, access to or distribution of domestic or international power); *the conflict has to be of some duration and magnitude* of at least two parties (states, groups of states, organizations or organized groups) that are determined to pursue their interests and win their case. At least one party is the organized state' (emphasis added): Pfetsch and Rohloff, ibid., 386.

64 Ibid.

65 Ibid.

66 See n. 62.

focuses solely on post-1946 trends due to the availability and comparability of reliable data.[67]

Conflict Trends: Post-World War II

Some general trends regarding the total number of conflicts, conflict type and conflict intensity can be observed by examining the findings of the data projects. According to the UCDP,[68] there was a total of 228 armed conflicts from 1946 to 2004 in 148 locations across the world.[69] The latest data from the UCDP[70] shows that there were 232 conflicts in the slightly longer period from 1946 to 2006.[71] The highest total number of armed conflicts in a single year was recorded in 1991 and 1992, with 51 active conflicts.[72]

The severity of violence reached in a conflict has been divided into two (formally three) categories by the UCDP: minor intensity and war.[73] The number of conflicts that reached the level of *war* rose steadily throughout the 1950s, 1960s, 1970s and 1980s and peaked around 1992.[74] From 1991 to 1992 (52 wars each year) onwards there was a sharp decline, followed by a slight rise in 1998–99 and then a further decline since 2000. The lowest number of wars per year was recorded in 2005 and 2006, with five active wars in each of those years.[75] Conflicts of 'minor intensity' peaked in 1994 and have dropped to 27 per year in both 2005 and 2006.[76] In 2006,

---

67 Trends in the post-1946 period are emphasised because three of the four data sets use 1945/1946 as a starting point.

68 Note that the UCDP has a much lower threshold for inclusion than the COW data sets, requiring only 25 annual battle-related deaths, as opposed to the COW's requirement for at least 1,000.

69 Harbom, L. and Wallensteen, P., 'Armed Conflict and Its International Dimensions 1946–2003' (2005) 42 (5) *Journal of Peace Research* 623.

70 The UCDP regularly updates its conflict data; see UCDP, 'Latest versions of data', available at: <http://www.pcr.uu.se/research/UCDP/data_and_publications/datasets.htm> at 3 June 2008.

71 See UCDP, 'Conflicts by region 1946–2006', available at: <http://www.pcr.uu.se/research/UCDP/graphs/region_only.pdf> at 3 June 2008.

72 Harbom and Wallensteen, supra n. 69. See also UCDP, 'Active conflicts by conflict type 1946–2006', available at: <http://www.pcr.uu.se/research/UCDP/graphs/type_year.pdf> at 3 June 2008.

73 A 'minor' armed conflict would require at least 25 battle-related deaths per year, but less than 1,000 during the course of the conflict, and 'war' would require at least 1,000 battle-related deaths per year. For information about the removal of the intermediate category, see the UCDP/PRIO Armed Conflict Codebook.

74 Note that the other three conflict data projects discussed here provide different figures for the total number of conflicts due to the different definitions adopted by each project and the years over which the project spans.

75 Harbom, L. and Wallensteen, P., 'Armed Conflicts 1989–2006' (2007) 44 (5) *Journal of Peace Research* 623.

76 Ibid., 624.

the latest year for which published data from the UCDP is available, there was a total of 32 active armed conflicts around the world, a relatively low figure that has remained constant for the past three years.[77] Despite small variations in exact figures, these trends are confirmed by other studies.[78]

There are at least three results from the latest UCDP data concerning post-World War II conflict trends which might give rise to optimism and which ought not to be overlooked. First, for the three years from 2004 to 2006 inclusive, there were *no interstate wars* whatsoever.[79] Second, in the last two years (2005 and 2006), *no new conflicts* were initiated.[80] Third, throughout the 2000s, fewer minor conflicts have been escalating into wars, suggesting that the international community appears to be able to prevent armed conflict from escalating.[81]

Location Europe was the main location for conflict prior to 1946, but it has been superseded by Africa, Asia and the Middle East in the post-1946 era. Although it is common to classify conflicts by region, the method by which the data is presented can lead to misleading impressions of the size and location of the zones of peace and the zones of conflict. For instance, a list of countries in conflict could portray the entire country of Russia as being involved in conflict, due to the Chechnya War. A more realistic picture of the zones of conflict emerges by plotting the conflicts by their actual location on a map of the world. That has been done by two researchers who have used UCDP data to trace the geographical location of conflicts from 1946 to 2000.[82] Three general zones of conflict are evident: one covers Central America, the Caribbean and South America; the second zone reaches from East Central Europe through to the Balkans, the Middle East and includes India and Indonesia; whilst the third zone is Africa, and spans virtually the entire continent.[83] This is obviously a significant change from the locations of conflict in the pre-1946 period when conflict was largely concentrated in the European region.

From 1989 to 2000, the number of armed conflicts in all the major regions of the world declined, or at worst, remained the same. The number of conflicts in Europe peaked in 1993 at ten; in the Middle East the peak was in 1991, 1992 and 1993 with seven; in Asia the number of armed conflicts peaked in 1992 at 20; and in Africa the peak occurred in 1992 with 15. The number of armed conflicts in

---

77 Ibid.

78 See, for instance, Marshall, M. and Gurr, T. *Peace and Conflict 2005 – A Global Survey of Armed Conflicts, Self-Determination Movements and Democracy* (College Park, Maryland: Center for International Development and Conflict Management (CIDCM), 2005): <http://www.systemicpeace.org/PC2005.pdf> at 11 ff. Their statistics show that total warfare peaked in the late 1980s but societal warfare peaked in about 1992.

79 Harbom and Wallensteen, supra n. 75 at 624.

80 Ibid.

81 Ibid., 625.

82 Buhang, H. and Gates, S., 'The Geography of Civil War' (2002) 39 (4) *Journal of Peace Research* 417.

83 Ibid., 423, see Figure 2.

the Americas peaked much earlier, in 1989, with eight.[84] By 2000, the number of conflicts had decreased in all of those regions.[85]

Research shows that there is a connection between conflict location and violence. The KOSIMO data shows that in Europe and America, non-violent conflicts outnumbered violent conflicts from 1945 to 1995.[86] However, in the Middle East/Maghreb, Sub-Saharan Africa and Asia/Oceania regions, the opposite was true.[87] Thus, Europe and the Americas have not only experienced less conflict *per se* than other regions, but also the conflicts that occurred in the latter regions were more likely to be non-violent.

In 2006, the latest UCDP figures show that the 32 active armed conflicts were situated in 23 locations and they mainly involved states in Asia (15 conflicts)[88] and Africa (nine conflicts).[89] There were relatively few ongoing conflicts in the Americas (two)[90] and Europe (one).[91] The data underlines the distinction between pre-1946 and post-1946 conflict: a discernible and permanent shift has occurred away from Europe towards Asia and Africa.[92]

---

84 Wallensteen, P. and Sollenberg, M., 'Armed Conflict 1989–2000' (2001) 38 (5) *Journal of Peace Research* 632, see Table III.

85 In 2000 the corresponding figures were: Europe (one), Middle East (three), Asia (14), Africa (14) and the Americas (one). These comparisons show that in the latter half of the 1990s, the number of conflicts declined in all regions. However, the same two regions – Asia and Africa – were leading the statistics at both the beginning and the end of the period: ibid.

86 In Europe, there were 75 non-violent conflicts versus 28 violent conflicts; in 'America' there were 56 non-violent conflicts versus 46 violent conflicts: see KOSIMO <http://www.hiik.de/en/kosimo/kosimo.htm≥ (accessed at 14 November 2006).

87 In the Middle East/Maghreb, there were 54 non-violent conflicts versus 113 violent conflicts; in Sub-Saharan Africa there were 43 non-violent conflicts versus 102 violent conflicts; and in Asia/Oceania there were 58 non-violent conflicts versus 86 violent conflicts: ibid.

88 Harbom and Wallensteen, supra n. 75 at 629–32, Appendix 1 'Armed Conflicts Active in 2006'. The UCDP data shows that of the 15 conflicts in Asia, 13 were of minor intensity and two were wars. 'Minor intensity' means that there were at least 25 battle-related deaths in any given year but fewer than 1,000. 'War' means that there were at least 1,000 battle-related deaths in any year.

89 Ibid. Of the nine conflicts active in Africa, seven were of minor intensity and two were wars.

90 Ibid. The Americas were experiencing two conflicts in 2006, both of which were coded as minor: in Colombia between the government and FARC and ELN, and in the United States between the government and al Qaeda.

91 Ibid. The UCDP records only one active conflict in Europe, between the Russian government and the Republic of Chechnya. That conflict was coded as 'minor'.

92 For the entire post-World War II period, the UCDP shows that the most conflicts occurred in Africa (74), ahead of Asia (68), followed by the Middle East and Europe (both 32) and the Americas (26): UCDP, 'Charts and Graphs', available at: <http://www.pcr.uu.se/research/UCDP/graphs/charts_and_graphs.htm> at 3 June 2008.

Frequency A study of the 432 international crises that occurred from the end of World War I to 2001 has shown that the frequency of international crises declined by nearly half in the first decade after the end of the Cold War.[93] This sharp reduction in the number of international crises is explained in part by the decline in power of the Soviet Union in the late 1980s, culminating in its disintegration into 15 independent states, coupled with the emergence of the US as the sole dominant military power.[94] The two states that triggered the most crises in the post-1989 period were Iraq and Pakistan with five and two crises respectively.[95] This was a marked change from the previous era in which states such as Africa, Libya, Israel, Rhodesia/Zimbabwe (and also Pakistan) were prominent. Not only were there fewer crises, with fewer triggering actors, but also international crises were fundamentally different in the post-Cold War era as compared with the previous four decades. Protracted conflicts characterised 61 per cent of all crises in the earlier era, but only 50 per cent of post-Cold War international crises. Decisive outcomes are less common in post-1989 crises but an encouraging trend is that the international community has attempted to resolve twice as many conflicts by mediation than in the earlier post-World War II decades.[96]

Recent figures show that between 2001 and 2005, 11 wars have been suspended or repressed (four in 2001, six in 2002 and one in 2003).[97] During the same period, only five new wars have broken out (two in 2001, one in 2002 and two in 2003).[98] According to the UCDP, during the past two years for which data is available (2005 and 2006) *no new conflicts* erupted.[99] The recent trend points towards the initiation of fewer new conflicts, but the continuation of entrenched conflicts which are becoming protracted and more difficult to solve.[100]

Type of conflict The most obvious trend in the post-1946 period has been the significant increase in the number of internal conflicts, especially when compared to the decrease in inter-state conflicts. The UCDP data confirms that internal/intra-state conflict has become the dominant form of conflict in the latter years of the

---

93 International Crisis Behaviour Project, cited by Wilkenfeld, J., 'International Crises' in *Peace and Conflict 2003*, CIDCM, Maryland, February 2003 at 43.

94 Ibid., 43.

95 Iraq: Gulf War 1990–91, Bubiyan 1991, Iraq Deployment in Kuwait 1994, UNSCOM I 1997–98 and UNSCOM II 1998; Pakistan: Kargil 1999 and the India Parliament Attack 2001: ibid., 44.

96 Mediation characterised only 30 per cent of earlier crises but was used by the international community in attempting to resolve international crises in 60 per cent of post-Cold War crises: ibid., 45.

97 Marshall and Gurr, supra n. 78 at 12 and Appendix Table 11.1.

98 Two new conflicts broke out in 2001 (al Qaeda's attack on the US and the US's punitive attack on Afghanistan); one conflict in 2002 (Ivory Coast) and two in 2003 (the US invasion of Iraq and an ethnic war in Darfur): ibid.

99 Harbom and Wallensteen, supra n. 75 at 624–5.

100 Ibid.

post-World War II era. The UCDP identifies three types of conflict: intra-state, inter-state and internationalised intra-state.[101] The trends for these three types of conflict over the period 1989–2006 may be summarised as follows. *Inter-state* conflicts remained low throughout this period but it is noteworthy that there were *no* inter-state conflicts recorded in 2004, 2005 and 2006 and a total of seven for the entire period.[102] By contrast, *intra-state* conflicts peaked in 1991 with 50 conflicts that year, and they thereafter decreased steadily to the period-low of 25 conflicts in 2003 followed by a slight rise in the past two years. There was a total of 89 intra-state conflicts across the entire period.[103] The third type of conflict, *internationalised intra-state*, followed a slightly erratic pattern, reaching a peak in 2005 (with six conflicts), and a total of 26 for the entire period.[104] In summary, there has been a clear *downward trend* since 1991–92 in the overall number of conflicts. The lowest overall number of conflicts for the 1989–2006 period was experienced in 2003, when there were 29 active conflicts.[105]

The data from the MEPV project confirms the UCDP's findings. It classifies conflicts as either civil-intra-state,[106] ethnic-intra-state[107] or international event-state.[108] In the post-1946 period, the overwhelming majority of conflicts were civil-intra-state or ethnic-intra-state, rather than international event-state. It may be confidently concluded that in the post-war era, the predominant form of conflict has been intra-state, rather than inter-state.

Number of casualties The post-1946 trend has been towards fewer conflicts and fewer casualties per conflict. According to the COW data, there were 3,333,669 battle-related deaths recorded in the post-1946 inter-state conflicts. Given that the post-1946 period measured by the COW Project is 51 years, this equates on average to 65,366 deaths per year: far fewer than in the pre-1946 period.[109] Conflicts in the post-1946 era have become less destructive if measured solely in terms of battle-related deaths. Estimating the number of casualties per conflict is arguably more difficult in the post-1946 era than in the pre-1946 era due to the increasing

101 Inter-state armed conflict occurs between two or more states; intra-state conflict occurs between the government of a state and internal opposition groups; and internationalised internal armed conflict occurs between the government of a state and internal opposition groups, with intervention from other states in the form of troops: see Harbom and Wallensteen, supra n. 75 at 632, 'Definitions'.

102 Ibid., 624, Table II.

103 Ibid.

104 Ibid.

105 Ibid.

106 Involving rival political groups.

107 Involving the state agent and a distinct ethnic group.

108 Involving two or more states, but may represent a distinct polity resisting foreign domination.

109 There were on average 218,658 deaths per year due to inter-state conflict in the pre-1946 period.

difficulty of determining estimates of 'directly related' deaths. The distinction between combatants and non-combatants has grown increasingly obscure as less formal civil conflict interactions predominate. The MEPV data shows that there is a trend towards lower total 'battlefield' deaths in the latter decades of the post-war period. Whereas in the early post-war years it was not unusual to find deaths in the hundreds of thousands, and even millions, that has become the exception in the last two decades of the twentieth century and the early twenty-first century.[110]

The fact that wars have become less deadly is a point also stressed in the *Human Security Report 2005*. It is estimated that World War I killed 1–3 million people per year on the battlefield and that World War II averaged 3–4 million battle deaths per year. Since the end of the Korean War, the annual global battle toll has never again reached even half a million.[111] When global battlefield deaths are measured per thousand of the world's population (rather than in absolute numbers), it is apparent that conflicts in the 1990s were only one-third as deadly as in the 1970s.[112] The decline in battle deaths may be attributed to the changing nature of conflict: today's wars are predominantly low-intensity or 'minor' intensity, intra-state conflicts rather than large-scale inter-state wars involving huge armies and heavy conventional weapons. Although estimating battle deaths is an important measure of the human costs of war, it does not take into account the numbers killed indirectly, such as through the collapse of a society's economy and its infrastructure: there is no global trend data available on indirect deaths.[113]

Probability of conflict Throughout the latter part of the post-World War II period, there has been a rapidly increasing number of independent states. Assuming that all nations are equally likely to become involved in a conflict, a higher number of countries should logically produce a higher overall frequency of conflict. The recent decline in the number of armed conflicts after the end of the Cold War, together with the increase in the number of states, has brought the probability of any single country being in conflict in a given year to a low level corresponding to the end of the 1950s, and lower than at any time during the Cold War.[114] Thus, the overall risk of a state being embroiled in conflict has dramatically declined.[115]

Fewer conflicts, greater complexity, highly protracted One of the most notable features of modern intra-state conflict is their complexity: there is typically

110 See the MEPV website, supra n. 56. From 1945 to 1975, there were many conflicts where the number of deaths was 100,000 or greater, whereas from 1976 to 2005, conflicts with extreme numbers of deaths were infrequent.

111 Mack, supra n. 37 at 29.

112 Ibid., 30, see Figure 1.8.

113 Ibid., 31.

114 Gleditsch et al., supra n. 10 at 621.

115 Ibid.; see also Mack, supra n. 37 at 23.

a diversity of warring parties and multiple grievances.[116] The number of states involved in the same conflict remains high, perhaps affecting the ability of parties to end conflicts through victory or peace agreements. There has been a significant increase in the number of actors involved in post-1989 conflicts. More than 80 state actors, two regional organisations[117] and at least two multinational coalitions[118] have been parties to those conflicts. In addition, more than 200 non-governmental parties have been involved, to reach a total of approximately 300 actors involved in the conflicts that occurred between 1989 and 2000 alone.[119] This proliferation of actors probably accounts for the difficulties in ending the post-1989 conflicts and has led some researchers to conclude that this trend projects a 'bleak future'.[120] Aside from greater complexity, the other notable feature of the conflicts currently in existence is that they are often highly protracted. The latest data from the UCDP shows that out of the 32 armed conflicts in existence in 2006, 11 had been active for more than ten consecutive years, and many of the remaining 21 had been going for over ten years, then experienced a lull of a year or two, only to restart again.[121] Thus, although conflict has declined, the conflicts that remain are complex, typically involve multiple actors and often have a long history. This is significant because in such entrenched conflicts, 'the warring parties are more likely to pursue maximalist goals and show little interest in negotiation'.[122]

Conclusion

Armed conflict has decreased significantly in the post-Cold War era, both in the numbers of states affected by major armed conflict and in overall magnitude. The general magnitude of global warfare has decreased by over 50 per cent since peaking in the mid-1980s, falling by the end of 2002 to its lowest level since the early 1960s.[123] Inter-state wars have become increasingly uncommon since the UN collective security system was established following World War II. The 1990 Iraq invasion of Kuwait and the subsequent 1991 US-led Gulf War were perhaps the 'only unambiguous inter-state wars during the post-Cold War era'.[124]

Prior to World War II, most conflicts were international in character, involving massive armies and massive casualties, with most wars being fought mainly

116 See *SIPRI Yearbook 2005* at 88–96, citing the examples of Burundi and Colombia. See also Harbom and Wallensteen, supra n. 75.

117 The North Atlantic Treaty Organisation (NATO) and ECOMOG.

118 In the 1991 Gulf War and in the war between the government of Afghanistan and the Taliban.

119 Wallensteen and Sollenberg, supra n. 84 at 633–4.

120 Ibid., 634.

121 Harbom and Wallensteen, supra n. 75 at 625.

122 Ibid.

123 Marshall and Gurr, supra n. 78.

124 Ibid., 13.

on European soil. Most fatalities were the combatants themselves, rather than civilians, and the technological innovations in the creation of new weapons systems were underdeveloped. Conflicts since 1946 have been mainly driven by internal, ethno-national clashes, and inter-state wars have given way to the increasing incidence of intra-state wars. Civilian casualties have gained greater prominence in these internal conflicts and civilian populations have been affected to a much greater extent, especially with the blurring of distinctions between combatants and civilians and the technological developments of more lethal weaponry. A disparity has also arisen between the number of civilians killed in conflicts and the number of soldiers killed. Shaw has noted that the 'relegitimation of war' has been due in part to the very small number of fatalities within the Western armed forces when compared to civilian fatalities in conflicts such as in Afghanistan.[125]

While the data suggests that both the numbers and intensity of conflict are decreasing, there remains a large number of states in transition, so-called 'anocracies'.[126] There was a threefold jump in the number of 'anocracies' from 16 in 1985 to 47 in 2002. There may be an increase in conflict in those states because research suggests that 'anocracies' are highly transitory regimes, with over 50 per cent experiencing a major regime change within five years, and they are much more vulnerable to new outbreaks of armed societal conflict.[127] Furthermore, they are about six times more likely than democracies and two and a half times more likely than autocracies to experience new outbreaks of societal wars.[128] The overall trends in conflict since World War II can be summarised as follows. Warfare is far less deadly in the twenty-first century than it has been in the past. Fewer wars are fought and fewer people die in those wars. The number of battle deaths has decreased steadily since the 1950s; the 1990s was the least violent decade since the end of World War II.[129] Inter-state warfare has decreased steadily since the end of World War II, especially since the 1970s. The incidence of intra-state warfare rose steadily after World War II, until peaking in 1992, but since then, it has also been in a steep decline.[130] An entire category of warfare, extra-state or colonial wars has virtually disappeared. In the past decade, 95 per cent of conflicts have taken place

---

125 Shaw, M., 'Risk-Transfer Militarism, Small Massacres and the Historic Legitimacy of War' (2002) 16 (3) *International Relations* 343.

126 Marshall, M. and Gurr, T., *Peace and Conflict 2003 – A Global Survey of Armed Conflicts, Self-Determination Movements and Democracy* (2003) available at: <http://www.cidcm.umd.edu/publications/publication.asp?pubType=paper&id=2> at 8 January 2009, at 17 and 19. 'Anocracies' are described as a middling category rather than a distinct form of governance. They are countries whose governments are neither fully democratic nor fully autocratic. They sometimes result from failed attempts to greater democracy, as in, for example, Algeria, Angola, Cambodia and Haiti.

127 Ibid., 17.

128 Ibid.

129 Mack, supra n. 37 at 17.

130 Ibid., 22.

within states, not between them.[131] The nature of conflict has changed, especially since the demise of colonialism and the end of the Cold War, and the evidence shows that it currently poses a far lesser threat to global peace and security than it once did.[132]

Non-state Actors

Overview

One aspect of the changing nature of conflict is the asymmetric threat posed by non-state actors, especially those engaged in 'international terrorism'. The inherent problem in discussing terrorism statistics is that each study uses a different definition, which in turn impacts upon the figures and can render meaningful analysis impossible.[133] Issues concerning the definition of the term 'terrorism' are addressed in Chapter 3. A brief summary of terrorism trends is attempted in this chapter without delving too far into the definitional issue.

Terrorism is not a new phenomenon – it is as old as humanity, since brutal violence has long been used as a tool for making strong, and unforgettable, political statements.[134] One study of international terrorism trends has found that incidents have fallen significantly in the post-Cold War period, after two decades (during the 1970s and 1980s) of showing no signs of abatement.[135] Although the number of incidents has dropped dramatically, trans-national/international terrorism still poses a significant threat because each incident is almost 17 per cent more likely to result in death or injuries compared with the previous two decades, and inflicting massive civilian casualties is often the main objective.[136]

---

131 Ibid., 18.

132 For analysis of the main reasons for the decrease in warfare, see Mack, supra n. 37, Part V.

133 For example, the controversial US Department of State's statistics on terrorism in the report *Patterns of Global Terrorism 2003*. The US Department of State claimed that the 2003 total of 190 terrorist acts was the lowest since 1969 and that terrorist attacks had decreased by 45 per cent between 2001 and 2003. However, two academics used the same statistics and found that there had been a 36 per cent increase: see Krueger, A. and Laitin, D., '"Misunderestimating" Terrorism', September/October 2004, *Foreign Affairs* and see discussion infra.

134 Marshall and Gurr, supra n. 78 at 62.

135 Enders, W. and Sandler, T., 'Is Transnational Terrorism Becoming More Threatening?' (2000) 44 (3) *Journal of Conflict Resolution* 307. That study defines terrorism as 'the premeditated use or threat of use of extranormal violence or brutality by subnational groups to obtain a political, religious, or ideological objective through intimidation of a large audience, usually not directly involved with the decision making'.

136 Ibid., 307–8.

The dramatic fall in the number of terrorist incidents after the Cold War is said to be due to reduced state sponsorship, increased efforts to thwart terrorism and the demise of many leftist groups. Even though international terrorism is less common than it was during the Cold War years, there is apparently a perception that it poses an even greater risk to lives and property.

Terrorism Trends: Pre-1919

The historical precursors to the modern 'terrorists' could arguably be traced to antiquity. An analysis of the term 'pirate', perhaps the first non-state actors to use force against a state, and a historical survey of their practices from antiquity through to the present, would be an interesting place to begin any study of terrorism trends. However, a discussion and comparison of their practices and objectives with those of the modern 'terrorist' is beyond the ambit of this text. A more recent precursor would arguably be the anarchists who terrorised Europe during the latter years of the nineteenth century into the early years of the twentieth. Between 1881 and the end of the nineteenth century, a number of heads of state were either assassinated or targeted for assassination by members of the anarchist movement.[137] European governments, at first on a national level and then at an international level, 'struggled to forge weapons that might control and suppress what was then perceived as society's fiercest and most intractable enemy, *anarchist terrorism*'.[138]

Delegates from European states met at the highly secretive International Conference of Rome for the Social Defense Against Anarchists in 1898.[139] The Conference's final protocol defined anarchism as, 'any act that used violent means to destroy the organization of society'.[140] It also included a provision whereby states agreed to extradite persons who had attempted to kill or kidnap a sovereign or head of state. Prompted by the assassination of US President McKinley by an anarchist in 1901, a second anti-anarchist conference was held in St Petersburg in 1904. Ten

---

137 Between March 1892 and June 1894 eleven dynamite explosions occurred in Paris, killing nine people. Bombs were also exploded in Spain, France and Italy. President Carnot of France was stabbed to death in 1894; Spanish Prime Minister Canovas was assassinated by shooting in 1897; an attempt was made on King Humbert of Italy, and the Empress of Austria was assassinated in 1898: Jensen, R., 'The International Anti-Anarchist Conference of 1898 and the Origins of Interpol' (1981) 16 *Journal of Contemporary History* 323 at 324–5.

138 Ibid., 323.

139 The Rome Conference was attended by 54 delegates from 21 European countries: Deflem, M., 'International Police Cooperation – History of', in *Encyclopedia of Criminology*, Wright, R. and Miller, J. (eds) (New York: Routledge, 2005). On matters of practical policing, the Rome protocol included plans to encourage police to keep watch over anarchists, to establish in every participating country a specialised surveillance agency to achieve this goal, and to organise a system of information exchange among these national agencies.

140 Ibid.

countries adopted a Secret Protocol for the International War on Anarchism.[141] It provided for police co-operation and information exchange between the signatory states. Both the Rome and St Petersburg conferences conceived of anarchism as a strictly criminal matter, the enforcement of which was to be handled by police institutions.

There are parallels between the threat posed by violent anarchism and modern terrorism. The fact that the anarchists' targets were often killed in cinemas, restaurants and religious celebrations meant that a 'sense of alarm swept though the bourgeoisie'[142] and created a general sense of fear and anxiety. Secondly, the assassinations were generally carried out by individuals on the fringes of anarchism and there were estimated as being fewer than 5,000 violent anarchists in all of Europe.[143] Thirdly, one of the difficulties experienced by delegates at the 1898 Rome conference was attaining agreement on the definition of anarchism.[144] Finally, it is significant that violent anarchism was considered by the targeted states as being *criminal* in nature. Virtually all of the mechanisms suggested at the Rome conference by Baron de Rolland, which were eventually accepted, resonate with recent attempts to curb terrorism.[145] Success in the 'war on anarchism' was perceived as requiring trans-national co-operation through policing and intelligence exchange.

Terrorism Trends: 1919–1960s

In between World War I and World War II, anarchist violence subsided, due in part to the emergence of governments that advocated more flexible and progressive social policies.[146] Anarchists were still active in Italy, France and particularly Spain during the fight against General Franco in the Spanish Civil War, but their use of violence and terror tactics across the rest of Europe declined. Whilst the overlap between anarchism and terrorism is acknowledged,[147] terrorism, in a more general sense, and piracy were the two dominant sources of violence from non-state

---

141 Ibid.

142 Jensen, supra n. 137 at 324–35.

143 Ibid.

144 Ibid., 327; see also discussion in Chapter 3 on the definition of terrorism.

145 Baron de Rolland advocated the prohibition and punishment of the possession of explosives for illegitimate reasons, membership in anarchist associations, provocation to or support of anarchist acts, spreading anarchist propaganda, publicising anarchist trials and rendering assistance to anarchists (such as providing lodgings and instruments of crime): ibid., 327–38.

146 See Jensen, supra n. 137 at 340.

147 A simple example of the interconnectedness of these two concepts arises out of events that occurred in 1964, when the anarchist, Stuart Christie, attempted to kill General Franco; he later wrote a book entitled *General Franco Made Me a Terrorist.* See also Bookchin, M., *The Spanish Anarchists – The Heroic Years 1868–1936* (New York: Free Life Editions, 1977) especially at 114: '... The identification of Anarchism with terrorism

actors during the inter-war period. Following World War I, there was an upsurge in international activity which sought to control the recent increase in terrorist activity. Under the auspices of the International Conference for the Unification of Penal Law, a number of meetings were held in the late 1920s and early 1930s which focused attention on the problem of terrorism. The assassination on 9 October 1934 of King Alexander of Yugoslavia and Louis Barthou, the French Foreign Minister, led to a request to the Council of the League of Nations for an enquiry. The Council passed a resolution stating that:[148] '[T]he rules of international law concerning the repression of terrorist activity are not at present sufficiently precise to guarantee efficiently international co-operation in this matter.'

The Council decided to establish a committee of experts to consider the question, with a view to drawing up a preliminary draft of an international convention. The culmination of the League's efforts was the 1937 Convention for the Prevention and Punishment of Terrorism.[149] This Convention, which was only ever ratified by one state (India), never entered into force.[150] The 1937 Convention was concerned with 'acts of terrorism' which it defined as criminal acts directed against a state intended or calculated to create a state of terror in the minds of particular persons, or a group of persons, or the general public.[151] The Convention criminalised certain acts and sought to ensure that the individuals who committed those acts were dealt with appropriately, namely, via procedures of extradition and prosecution.

If a terrorist act ('a criminal act directed against a state')[152] was committed, the Convention set out the procedure for dealing with the alleged criminals and the method by which they ought to be brought to justice. Even if the states involved disagreed over the way that the processes were being employed, they were not permitted to resort to force. In the wake of a terrorist attack, states would have been compelled to use all methods of peaceful dispute settlement including the option of bringing the matter before the Council of the League of Nations, if all else failed.[153] Thus, there were a number of peaceful dispute resolution mechanisms open to the dissatisfied party, but employing force was not an option.

Although the threat of terrorism had become significant enough to warrant an international conference and the drafting of a convention, it was not seen as a specific threat to aircraft.[154] That fact is evidenced by the adoption of the

was the result not merely of earlier bombings but of a new emphasis in libertarian circles on "propaganda by the deed."'

148 Proceedings of the International Conference on the Repression of Terrorism, League of Nations Doc C.94.M.47.1938.V (1938.V3) at 49–50.

149 Convention for the Prevention and Punishment of Terrorism, 19 *LNOJ* 23 (1938), League of Nations Doc. 546(I).M.383(I).1937.V (1938) (16 November 1937).

150 See Chapter 3.

151 Article 1(2).

152 Ibid.

153 Article 20(3).

154 See Chapter 5 on the numerous conventions that were later adopted.

International Air Transportation Convention and Additional Protocol, concluded in 1929, which addressed a number of issues regarding the safety of air transport, but which did not mention terrorist acts in any of its articles.[155]

Terrorism Trends: 1960s–1980s

From the late 1960s until the late 1980s, international terrorism was primarily motivated by nationalism, separatism, political ideology, racism, nihilism and economic inequality.[156] The late 1980s and early 1990s saw the demise of many leftist groups, due in part to an increase in domestic efforts by some terrorism-prone nations (such as France, Germany, Italy, Spain and the UK) to capture and bring to justice members of such groups. There was also a reduction in state-sponsorship by East European and Middle Eastern countries, coupled with a general decline in the popularity of Marxism following the collapse of many communist regimes.[157] These three factors were bolstered by collective initiatives by the European Union (EU) to foster co-operation among EU states over extradition, shared intelligence and accreditation of foreign diplomats.[158]

Terrorism Trends: 1980s–2001

Since the 1980s, more data regarding terrorist activity has become available with an increasing emphasis in the research community on tracking terrorism trends. The US Department of State's figures show that from 1981 to 2001, the total number of international terrorist attacks peaked in 1987, with 665 attacks that year. Thereafter, there was a steady decline in the number of attacks, but with slightly higher than normal figures in 1991, 1995 and 2000.[159] By comparison, 2001 experienced a relatively low total (348 international terrorist attacks, including the attacks that occurred on 11 September 2001). That figure was the lowest since 1998.[160]

---

155 International Air Transportation Convention and Additional Protocol, concluded at Warsaw on 12 October 1929, 49 Stat. 3000 TS 876, reprinted in Alexander, Y. (ed.), *International Terrorism: Political and Legal Documents* (Dordeecht/Boston: Martinus Nijhoff, 1992) 5.

156 Terrorist groups that were prominent in this period included the Red Brigade, the Red Army Faction, Fighting Communist Cells, Direct Action, Popular Forces 25 April, the Revolutionary Cells, the First of October Anti-Fascists Resistance Group (GRAPO), Revolutionary Organisation 17 November and Dev Sol: Wilkinson, P., *Terrorism and the Liberal State* (London: Macmillan, 1986).

157 Enders and Sandler, supra n. 135 at 310.

158 Wilkinson, P., 'The European Response to Terrorism: Retrospect and Prospect' (1992) 3 *Defence Economics* 298–304.

159 With those years experiencing 565, 440 and 426 attacks, respectively.

160 US Department of State, *Patterns of Global Terrorism 2002* at 157, available at: <http://www.state.gov/s/ct/rls/pgtrpt/> at 16 October 2008.

The US statistics show that from 1996 to 2001, Latin America was by far the worst affected region. In 2001, there were 194 terrorist attacks in the Latin American region, a figure that was not surpassed in any other region in any other year. The second-highest number of total attacks in any one year also occurred in Latin America, with 192 attacks in 2000. The third-highest number of attacks in any one year was again in Latin America, in 1997, with 128 attacks recorded that year. Interestingly, Latin America was the only region in which the number of terrorist attacks peaked in 2001; for all of the other regions, 2001 was a relatively peaceful year.

The next most terrorism-afflicted region for the 1996–2001 period was Western Europe, where international terrorist incidents peaked with 121 incidents in 1996 and thereafter declined to a low of 17 attacks in 2001. The third most affected region was Asia, where terrorist incidents peaked in 2000 with 98 attacks. Africa was the next most affected region: the number of attacks peaked in 2000 after a steady increase from 1996. The fifth-most terrorist prone region for that period was the Middle East, in which attacks peaked in 1996 with 45 international terrorist attacks recorded. In 2001, it experienced only 29. Following the Middle East was Eurasia. The region that was least affected by terrorist attacks was North America which experienced no terrorist attacks in 1996, 1998 and 2000. In the intervening years, it experienced its worst years in 1997 (with 13 attacks), 1999 (two attacks) and 2001 (four attacks).[161]

These statistics show that although the attacks that occurred on 11 September 2001 attracted a great deal of attention, they occurred in a region that otherwise experienced very few international terrorist attacks in the five-year period from 1996 to 2001.

Terrorism Trends: 2001–2007

The US Department of State initially claimed that between 2001 and 2003, there was a 45 per cent decrease in the number of international terrorist attacks.[162] The 190 attacks which occurred in 2003 were claimed to represent the lowest figure since 1969. However, that analysis was challenged and a new report was issued.[163] The challenge, which was not altogether addressed in the re-released report, was that the US Department of State's figures were based on a *total* number of terrorist attacks, taking into account both 'significant' and 'non-significant' attacks.[164] If only 'significant' attacks had been counted, then the claim of a 45 per cent decrease

161 Ibid., 172, Appendix 1.

162 US Department of State, *Patterns of Global Terrorism 2003*.

163 Krueger, A. and Laitin, D., 'Faulty Terror Report Card', *Washington Post* 17 May 2004.

164 'Significant' meant attacks which involved loss of life, serious injury or major property damage of more than US$10,000. 'Non-significant' attacks were neither defined nor listed in the initial 2003 report.

would have been erroneous – there was in fact a *36 per cent increase in verifiable significant international terrorist attacks*.[165] The US Department of State's claims regarding a decrease between 2001 and 2003 could only be sustained when non-verifiable, non-significant terrorist events were also included in the overall figures.[166]

Krueger and Laitin produced figures which suggested that from 1982 to 2003, significant terrorist attacks increased more than eightfold.[167] Krueger asserted that the US Department of State's figures actually showed that in 2003, significant terrorist attacks reached a 20-year peak.[168] Another study, which compared the number of terrorist events and terrorist-related deaths in seven six-month segments prior and subsequent to 11 September 2001, showed an initial sharp increase in the number of terrorist attacks shortly after 11 September 2001.[169] But this short, sharp increase was explained almost entirely by the adoption of a highly specialised tactic of warfare by militants in five locations, and when those instances of domestic terrorism were removed, the trends showed approximately a doubling of terrorist activity in the post-9/11 period, to about three events per year.[170] There was thus 'scant evidence of a global terrorist conspiracy in the post 9/11 world that would constitute a threat to global peace and security'.[171]

It must be acknowledged that recent US government statistics are of limited assistance in determining an overall trend for the 2001–2007 period. As of April 2005, terrorism statistics are now kept by the National Counterterrorism Centre (NCTC), which states in its 2005 report (released in April 2006) that its figures are not directly comparable with pre-2005 figures because a different definition of terrorism has been adopted by the NCTC since 2005.[172] One of the main differences is that the NCTC uses a definition of 'terrorism' rather than 'international terrorism'. Furthermore, the NCTC states that it does not believe that 'a simple comparison of the total number of incidents from year to year provides meaningful analysis'.[173] Perhaps an example of how bare statistics could be misleading is demonstrated by the NCTC's data regarding the significant rise in terrorist attacks between 2003 and 2005; the rise was mainly due to attacks which occurred in Iraq alone.[174]

---

165 Supra n. 163.

166 'Non-verifiable' because the US Department of State initially listed only the significant events, which could be verified, but not the non-significant events.

167 Mack, supra n. 37 at 43, Figure 1.13.

168 Krueger, A., 'Errors on Terror', Op-ed, *New York Times* 25 June 2004, A23.

169 Marshall and Gurr, supra n. 78 at 73, Figure 9.2.

170 Ibid.

171 Ibid.

172 National Counterterrorism Center (NCTC), 'Report on Incidents of Terrorism in 2005', 11 April 2006, at ii: <http://wits.nctc.gov/reports/crot2005nctcannexfinal.pdf> at 3 June 2008.

173 Ibid. The reasons put forward by the NTSC are outlined in its report at iii–iv.

174 In 2003, total attacks were estimated to be 175; in 2004 there were 651; and in 2005 there were 11,111. In 2005, an increase in terrorist incidents in Iraq accounted for

The NCTC provides a Worldwide Incidents Tracking System (WITS) which is available to the public via its website.[175] The WITS is the NCTC's database of terrorist incidents upon which it bases its annual reports. For any researcher interested in terrorism statistics, familiarity with the methodology adopted by the NCTC in compiling the WITS is essential.[176] The NCTC advises that 'Determination of what constitutes a terrorist act ... can be more art than science' and that 'The very definition of terrorism relative to all other forms of political violence is open to debate'.[177] The NCTC openly acknowledges the limitations on the accuracy of its statistics and on the statistics' usefulness in either tracking terrorist attacks over time or in assessing the effectiveness of the international community in preventing attacks.

Taking those factors into account, however, recent US statistics do provide some interesting insights into the number and type of attacks which have occurred during the past few years. The NCTC data shows that in 2005, more than half of all terrorist attacks resulted in no deaths (and only 2 per cent of terrorist attacks resulted in ten or more deaths).[178] In terms of the location of lethal terrorist attacks, the Near East, followed by South Asia, suffered the most attacks as well as the highest deaths in those attacks.[179] When comparing the top 15 countries by fatalities, Iraq suffered the highest number, followed at a considerable distance by India, Colombia and Afghanistan. No Western country was in the top 15.[180] One of the most interesting statistics in the NCTC report is that in 2005, a total of 56 US citizens were killed in terrorist attacks, which equates to 0.4 per cent of the global fatalities from terrorism in 2005.[181] Thus, 99.6 per cent (or 14,546) of terrorist

---

approximately one third of all incidents that year and more than half of all deaths from terrorism: see US Department of State, 'Fact Sheet on Country Reports on Terrorism 2005' [28 April 2006]: <http://www.state.gov/r/pa/prs/ps/2006/65422.htm> at 3 June 2008.

175 See the Worldwide Incidents Tracking System (WITS) at <http://wits.nctc.gov/Main.do> at 3 June 2008.

176 See the WITS website, then click on the link to 'Methodology'.

177 See WITS, 'Criteria' [22 November 2005] at <http://wits.nctc.giv/Methodology.do> at 3 June 2008.

178 Supra n. 172, at xxvi, Chart 13. There were 11,111 attacks in 2005. Of those, 5,980 attacks (53.8 per cent) resulted in no fatalities; 2,884 attacks (25.9 per cent) resulted in one fatality; 1,617 attacks (14.5 per cent) resulted in two to four fatalities; 404 (3.6 per cent) attacks resulted in five to nine fatalities; and 226 attacks (2.03 per cent) resulted in ten or more fatalities.

179 Ibid., xiv, Chart 1.

180 Ibid., xix, Chart 6. For the top 15 countries by hostages, the worst-hit country was Nepal, followed by Colombia and Iraq; no Western country was in the 'top' 15: ibid., xxii, Chart 9.

181 83 per cent of the US fatalities (47 from a total of 56) in 2005 were in Iraq: ibid., xx, Chart 7.

fatalities were non-Americans.[182] That figure was down on the previous year in which 1 per cent of terrorist fatalities were American.[183]

The NCTC data for 2004 and 2005 shows that the number of terrorist attacks apparently rose sharply during those two years (from 651 attacks in 2004 to 11,111 in 2005), as did the number of fatalities (from 9,321 in 2004 to 14,546 in 2005), but the NCTC notes that, due to changes in the way that it defines terrorism, the figures produced for 2005 cannot be compared with pre-2005 data. The 2006 report (released by the NCTC on 30 April 2007) shows that the number of terrorist attacks increased by approximately 3,000 (25 per cent) in 2006 as compared with the previous year, and that the number of fatalities increased by approximately 5,800 (40 per cent).[184] Of the approximately 14,000 terrorist attacks in 2006, 45 per cent occurred in Iraq, and of the approximately 20,000 deaths resulting from terrorist attacks, 65 per cent were in Iraq.[185] One of the many interesting details noted by the NCTC was that, as in 2005, 'Muslims bore a substantial share of being the victims of terrorist attacks in 2006',[186] with well over 50 per cent of the total victims of terrorist attacks being victims of attacks in Iraq.[187]

The latest report from the NCTC, the '2007 Report on Terrorism' (issued on 30 April 2008), is prefaced by even greater warnings that its data may not be entirely accurate and that many factors contribute to its reliability.[188] It also reiterates that 'NCTC does not believe that a simple comparison of the total number of attacks from year to year provides a meaningful measure'.[189] That aside, the NCTC report released in 2008 shows that approximately 14,000 terrorist attacks occurred in 2007 resulting in over 22,000 deaths.[190] Thus, the number of attacks remained much the same as in 2006 but the number of deaths from those attacks increased by 1,800, or nine per cent.[191]

---

182 Ibid., xxi, Chart 8.

183 NCTC, 'A Chronology of Significant International Terrorism for 2004', 27 April 2005, at 87. There were 103 US victims in 2004, or 1 per cent of the total number of victims, being 9,321.

184 NCTC, 'Reports on Terrorist Incidents – 2006' [30 April 2007], available at: <http://wits.nctc.gov/reports/crot2006nctcannexfinal.pdf> at 3 June 2008.

185 Ibid.

186 Ibid., 3

187 Ibid.

188 The NCTC cites, *inter alia*, the lack of reliable open source data, the difficulty in differentiating between terrorism and other forms of violence including crime and sectarian violence, the difficulty in distinguishing between terrorism and insurgency especially in Iraq and Afghanistan, and the counting of 'non-combatants' versus 'combatants' as victims: see NCTC '2007 Report on Terrorism' [30 April 2008], available at: <http://wits.nctc.gov/reports/crot2007nctcannexfinal.pdf> at 10 June 2008.

189 Ibid., 3.

190 Ibid., 9.

191 Ibid.

As in 2005 and 2006, by far the greatest number of reported attacks and deaths occurred in Near East and South Asia, with those two regions accounting for around 87 per cent of the total casualty attacks that killed ten or more people.[192] In terms of fatalities, the five worst affected countries were Iraq (13,606), Afghanistan (1,966), Pakistan (1,335), India (1,093) and Thailand (859).[193]

Once again, Iraq loomed large in the statistics: 43 per cent of the total number of attacks, and 60 per cent of the total fatalities, occurred there.[194] However, due to an improvement in the security situation during the last five months of 2007, the overall number of attacks declined by 67 per cent between May and December.[195] Attacks in Pakistan rose by 137 per cent over the number of 2006 attacks.[196] Attacks in Africa (especially in or near Somalia, Kenya and Niger) rose by 96 per cent, totalling 835 attacks in 2007 as compared with 425 attacks the previous year.[197] There was also an increase in the number of attacks in Afghanistan, with 16 per cent more attacks than the previous year, as well as a doubling in the number of kidnappings.[198] On a more positive note, there was a 42 per cent decrease in attacks in the Western hemisphere, in Europe and Eurasia (8 per cent) and in South Asia (nearly 7 per cent).[199]

As for victims of terrorist attacks, the NCTC data shows a total of 22,666 non-US fatalities and 19 US fatalities,[200] which means that 0.08 per cent of deaths in 2007 were American citizens, a percentage so small that it is virtually impossible to accurately represent in diagrammatic form. Moreover, of those 19 US fatalities, 17 died in Iraq and two in Afghanistan.[201] As in 2006, a substantial number of victims of attacks were Muslims: approximately 67,000 individuals worldwide were killed or injured by terrorist attacks in 2007; around 50 per cent of them were Muslims, and most were in Iraq.[202]

Although the NCTC data is certainly interesting and informative, and has been carefully prepared, the statistics released in the NCTC's annual reports are probably insufficient to deduce the presence of an overall trend – such as whether terrorist attacks are becoming more or less prevalent – firstly because the data covers a short period of time, secondly, because the post-2005 data cannot be compared with earlier years when a different definition of terrorism was used, and thirdly, because there are so many variables in terms of the reliability of data and the

192 Ibid., see charts at 22 and 26.

193 Ibid., 26.

194 Ibid.

195 Ibid., 13–16.

196 Ibid., 17–18.

197 Ibid.

198 Ibid., 19.

199 Ibid.; also see statistical charts and graphs at 21–2.

200 Ibid., 28.

201 Ibid., 27.

202 Ibid., 11.

inclusion of incidents.[203] When Iraq is taken out of the calculations, the rate of both incidents and deaths between 2005 and 2007 shows a gradual increase between each of those three years, which tends to suggest that there is currently a gradual global increase in both the number and the severity of terrorist incidents.[204]

Conclusion

It is difficult to state with certainty whether there are clear trends in the incidence of international terrorist attacks. That uncertainty is driven by many factors including unreliable data, definitional irregularities and a lack of consistency and accuracy in both data collection and analysis. Most research suggests a general downward trend in terrorist incidents of all types since the early 1980s.[205] But it is unclear whether terrorism incidents have risen rapidly in the past few years, as some data suggests,[206] or whether, once Iraq is excluded, there has been a more gradual increase.

What is clear is that international terrorism looms large in the media and in the psyche of individuals as a threat to their security. Research has shown that globally, 15 per cent of people fear terrorism as a threat to their personal security compared with 8 per cent who fear war; yet as this chapter has shown, war is responsible for a far greater numbers of deaths per annum.[207] Very few examples of terrorism result in more than 100 deaths; the above data shows that in 2005, only 2 per cent of terrorist attacks resulted in more than ten deaths (and more than half of the attacks in 2005 resulted in no deaths). The NCTC itself acknowledges that approximately half of the attacks in the NCTC database involve no loss of life.[208]

To put the threat of terrorism in perspective, it may be observed that in the 1990s, there was an average of *3,000 terrorism-related deaths* per year, but an average of *300,000 war-related deaths*.[209] People fear terrorism more than they ought to, and whilst international terrorism may be a threat to global peace and

---

203 NCTC, supra n. 172 at ii.

204 See NCTC, supra n. 188 at 26, Chart 16.

205 US Department of State, *Patterns of Global Terrorism*; see the International Terrorism: Attributes of Terrorist Events (ITERATE) database, and see the MEPV data, cited above.

206 Krueger and Laitin in Mack, supra n. 37 at 43; see Marshall and Gurr, supra n. 78.

207 The Human Security Centre commissioned Ipsos-Reid to conduct a global survey of people's fears and experiences of political and criminal violence in 11 countries. The greatest single cause of fear was criminal violence: see Mack, supra n. 37 at 50–51.

208 NCTC, supra n. 188 at 3.

209 Marshall and Gurr, supra n. 78 at 65.

security, it is not as substantial a threat as either armed conflict, or other types of violence, such as genocide.[210]

Thus, there is a gap between what the public and the policymakers *perceive* as the greatest threats to international peace and security, and reality. It is clear that we live in a world that is generally safer, more so, perhaps, than ever before. There are fewer new conflicts being initiated; when new conflicts do occur they are generally on a smaller scale with a relatively lower cost in both human and material measures, and in the past five years there has been an increase in the number of existing conflicts being resolved. Terrorism is a phenomenon which largely affects states outside North America. When one considers both the states and the individuals most affected by terrorism, it is somewhat ironic that American citizens are some of the least affected, yet, as subsequent chapters will show, the US's Bush Administration has been at the forefront of attempting to enforce an interpretation of self-defence that would allow the use of force in a much broader range of situations than ever before to counter the supposedly increasing threat of international terrorism.

---

210 Mack, supra n. 37 at 40–42. Genocide is not discussed in this chapter but the numbers killed in recent genocides, such as in Cambodia (estimates range from 1.7 to 2.4 million), Bangladesh (between 1.56 and 3.12 million), Rwanda (approximately 800,000), Srebrenica (approximately 7,000) and Darfur (estimated at between 70,000 and 340,000), illustrate that annual terrorism fatalities are far less significant by comparison.

Chapter 3
A Definition of 'Terrorism'

> The term 'terrorism' is unsatisfactory. It is emotive, highly loaded politically and lacking a universally, or even generally, accepted definition ... the labelling of a particular act as terroristic tells less about that act than it does about the labeller's political perspective, ... it is more of a formulation of a social judgment than a description of a set of phenomena.[1]

Introduction

Terrorism, and the 'war on terrorism', has possibly become the most important security theme of the twenty-first century.[2] This chapter examines how 'terrorism' has been defined, politically and legally. There are three reasons why understanding the meaning of terrorism is important in the present context. First, terrorism is one form of violence that is a part of the overall changing nature of conflict, as described in Chapter 2. Secondly, the UN Security Council regarded the attacks that occurred on 11 September 2001, like all acts of international terrorism, as a threat to international peace and security.[3] Thirdly, since the US and the UK justified their use of force against Afghanistan, *inter alia*, on the grounds of preventing or deterring future *terror* attacks, it is crucial to grasp what this term means in international law.[4]

Chapter 2 described the changing nature of conflict, of which terrorism may be regarded as a subset, a kind of surrogate, asymmetric form of warfare.[5] The term 'terrorism' is so frequently referred to by scholars, the media, states and international organisations that one might conclude that there exists a consensus as to what 'terrorism' means. The material canvassed in this chapter suggests otherwise. The analysis is divided into three parts: in the first part the historical

---

1 Lambert, J., *Terrorism and Hostages in International Law* (Cambridge: Grotius Publications, 1990) at 13.

2 Marshall, M., 'Global Terrorism: An Overview and Analysis', in Marshall, M. and Gurr, T. (eds), *Peace and Conflict 2005 – A Global Survey of Armed Conflicts, Self-Determination Movements and Democracy* (College Park, Maryland: Center for International Development and Conflict Management (CIDCM), 2005): <http://www.systemicpeace.org/PC2005.pdf> (2005) at 62.

3 S/Res/1368, 12 September 2001 and S/Res/1373, 28 September 2001; see discussion in Chapter 6 regarding these resolutions.

4 The legality of the use of force against Afghanistan in 2001 is discussed in Chapter 6.

5 Motley, J., 'Target America: The Undeclared War', in Livingstone, N. and Arnold, T. (eds), *Fighting Back – Winning the War against Terrorism* (Lexington, Mass.: Lexington Books, 1986) at 59–83.

roots of terrorism and its original meaning are briefly discussed; in the second part political scientists' attempts to define terrorism are examined; and in the third part of the chapter the focus shifts to the efforts that have been made to define terrorism in international law.

The Difficulty of Defining Terrorism

'Terrorism' is a term that is notoriously difficult to define. One view is that 'it is imprecise, ambiguous and above all it serves no operative purpose'.[6] Scholars in the fields of political science, law, history, psychology, theology and criminology have tried to define it, but it seems that there is no single definition.[7] A conundrum, acknowledged by Mallison and Mallison, is created by the fact that since political scientists cannot agree on the physical reality of what 'terrorism' is, international lawyers do not have a factual definition upon which they can base a legal definition.[8] Yet it is essential to define a concept that is considered a threat to international peace and security. It is also logically necessary to define 'terrorism' before analysing the lawful responses to it. There may never be one universally acceptable definition of the term 'terrorism'. Nevertheless, entering into the 'definitional quagmire'[9] will at least provide an awareness of the difficulties which preclude consensus and will provide clarity on the main points of disagreement. An international legal definition will only be possible once those points of disagreement have been acknowledged, and, as far as possible, addressed.

6 Baxter, R., 'A Sceptical Look at the Concept of Terrorism', (1974) 7 *Akron Law Review* 380.

7 'There is no consensus on the bounds of terrorism: some observers define as terrorism nearly every act of disruptive violence and ignore violence by established regimes; some scholars want psychopaths and criminals to be examined and others do not; and there are those who, defending a cherished cause, deny that their patriots are terrorists ... No one has a definition of terrorism.': Bower Bell, J., 'Trends in Terror: The Analysis of Political Violence' (1977) 29 (3) *World Politics* 447 at 481.

8 '"Terror" and "terrorism" are not words which refer to a well-defined and clearly identified set of factual events. Neither do the words have any widely accepted meaning in legal doctrine. "Terror" and "terrorism" consequently, do not refer to a unitary concept in either fact or law.': Mallison, W. and Mallison, S., 'The Concept of Public Purpose Terror in International Law: Doctrines and Sanctions to Reduce the Destruction of Human and Material Values' (1973) 18 *Howard Law Journal* 12.

9 Murphy, J., *State Support of International Terrorism – Legal, Political and Economic Dimensions* (1989) 3–30: Chapter 1 is titled 'International Terrorism: The Definitional Quagmire'.

Dictionary Definitions

The Shorter Oxford English Dictionary defines terrorism as follows:[10]

> **Terrorism** (te~rõriz'm). 1795. [- Fr. terrorisme, f. L. terror; see -ism.] A system of terror. **1**. Government by intimidation; the system of the 'Terror' (1793–4); ... **2**. gen. A policy intended to strike with terror those against whom it is adopted; the fact of terrorizing or condition of being terrorized 1798.

The *Webster's New Twentieth Century Dictionary* provides a similar definition:[11]

> **ter'ror~ism**, n. **1**. a terrorizing; use of terror and violence to intimidate, subjugate, etc., especially as a political weapon or policy. **2**. intimidation and subjugation so produced.

On the basis of the above definitions, five observations are made regarding the ordinary meaning of terrorism. Both definitions above give only a basic idea about the common understanding of the term. They do not include all the potential elements encompassed by the complicated formulae that have been compiled by scholars, governments, public and private institutions.

Secondly, the definitions suggest that the term 'terrorism' originated from the French word *terrorisme*, which was used to describe a period during the French Revolution known as the 'Reign of Terror' from approximately September 1793 to July 1794. However, when the term 'terrorism' is used today, it refers to a more recent phenomenon, not to that particular historical period.

Thirdly, the *Shorter Oxford* definition states that terrorism can be used as intimidation by a government. Whilst many scholars agree that acts of terrorism can be committed by governments,[12] there are also arguments made by international organisations, governments, private institutions and scholars who regard terrorism as being restricted to acts carried out exclusively by non-state actors.[13] Historically, terrorism was a type of behaviour perpetrated by *governments* against their *citizens*,

---

10 Little, W., Fowler, H., Coulson, J. and Onions, C. (rev. and ed.), *The Shorter Oxford English Dictionary – on historical principles*, 3rd edn (1973) at 2268.

11 Webster, N., McKechnie, J. (rev.), *Webster's New Twentieth Century Dictionary of the English Language Unabridged*, 2nd edn (1975) at 1884.

12 Chomsky, N., *September 11* (New South Wales: Allen and Unwin, 2001) 23 and 43–54 where he describes the US as a 'leading terrorist state'; see Laquer, W., *The Age of Terrorism* (Boston and Toronto: Little, Brown and Company, 1987); George, A. (ed.), *Western State Terrorism* (Cambridge: Polity Press, 1991); and Zinn, H., *Terrorism and War* (New York: Seven Stories Press, 2002).

13 Report of the Secretary-General's High Level Panel on Threats, Challenges and Change, 'A More Secure World: Our Shared Responsibility', (2004) at 51–2, <http://www.un.org/secureworld/report3.pdf> at 12 June 2008.

whereas now it is more often perceived as a strategy directed against governments via the targeting of civilians.

Fourthly, only the *Webster's* definition notes that acts of terrorism have political objectives; the *Shorter Oxford* does not mention this element, although its definition of a 'terrorist' provides greater clarity on this point.[14] The political dimension of terrorism has been described by some as the 'key characteristic' of terrorism and that its recognition is critical to distinguishing it from other forms of violence.[15] 'Terrorism' is generally understood to be intimidation with a political or ideological purpose: the terror is meant to cause others to do things that they would otherwise not do. This characteristic is what distinguishes terrorists from other non-state actors, such as pirates, who are motivated by purely private, material gain rather than achieving wider political or ideological objectives.

Finally, neither of these dictionary definitions mentions that 'terrorism' requires the targeting of civilians or non-combatants. As will be noted in the analysis below, many political and legal scholars consider that a terrorist act must necessarily be directed against a civilian target. It may be concluded that the ordinary definition of 'terrorism', as represented by these dictionaries, does not adequately describe the modern usage of the term.

Terrorism in Historical Perspective

Despite differences of opinion as to how 'terrorism' should be defined, there is general agreement that this is not a new phenomenon. Terrorism is often said to be as old as history itself.[16] One of the earliest-known examples of a terrorist-type movement was the *sicarii*,[17] a highly organised religious sect consisting of men of lower orders active in the Jewish Zealot struggle in Palestine in around

---

14 'Terrorist ... 1. As a political term: a. Applied to the Jacobins and their agents and partisans in the French Revolution. b. Any one who attempts to further his views by a system of coercive intimidation; spec. applied to members of one of the extreme revolutionary societies in Russia 1866. 2. An alarmist, a scaremonger 1803' (punctuation as it appears in original): *The Shorter Oxford English Dictionary*, supra n. 10 at 2268.

15 '... [T]he terrorist does not strike blindly and pointlessly, left and right, but rather plans his actions carefully, weighing his options and trying for the course of action that will best promote his objective at the lowest cost to himself': Primoratz, I., 'What is Terrorism?' (1990) 7 (2) *Journal of Applied Philosophy* (1990) 129–30, in Gearty, C. (ed.), *Terrorism* (Aldershot: Ashgate Dartmouth Publishing, 1996) at 17–18; see also Hoffman, B., *Inside Terrorism* (New York: Colombia University Press, 1998) at 14.

16 Alexander, Y. (ed). *International Terrorism: Political and Legal Documents* (Dordrecht/Boston: Martinus Nijhoff, 1992) at ix; Erickson, R.J., *Legitimate Use of Military Force Against State-Sponsored International Terrorism* (Maxwell Air Force Base, Alabama: Air University Press, 1989) at 34; see also Marshall and Gurr, supra n. 2 at 62: '[T]errorism is as old as humanity.'

17 Latin plural of the word 'sicarius' meaning dagger and, later, contract-killer.

66–73 AD.[18] The *sicarii* used unorthodox tactics such as attacking their enemies by daylight, preferably on holidays when crowds congregated in Jerusalem. Their favourite weapon was a short sword, a *sica,* which was kept hidden under their coats. They were an extremist, nationalist, anti-Roman party and their victims were the moderates, the Jewish peace party and Roman sympathisers.[19] Some characteristics of the *sicarii* resonate with the acts of modern terrorists. For example, there was debate over whether the *sicarii* were robbers, out for personal gain and manipulated by outside forces, or whether they were a social protest movement, intent on inciting the poor to rise against the rich, inviting parallels with the modern 'terrorism/freedom fighter' distinction. There was an inclination among the *sicarii* to regard martyrdom as something joyful. They believed that after the fall of Jerusalem, the sinful regime would no longer be in authority and God would reveal Himself to His people and deliver them[20] – evincing a parallel with the political/religious motivations of many modern terrorists. What mattered most to the *sicarii* was not the action itself but the wider purpose behind it.[21]

The Assassins[22] appeared in the eleventh century and were suppressed by the Mongols in the thirteenth century.[23] They were a Shi'ite sect originally based in Persia who later spread to Syria and who were opposed to the Sunni establishment. They killed political and religious leaders, including prefects, governors and caliphs. The vast majority of the Assassins' victims were Sunni Muslims. The first leader of the sect, Hassan Bin Sabbah,[24] realised that his group was too small to confront the enemy in open battle and thus he calculated that a planned, systematic, long-term campaign of terror carried out by a small, disciplined force could be a most effective political weapon.[25] Their *modus operandi* is described by Laquer: "The Assassins always used the dagger, never poison or missiles, and not just because the dagger was considered the safer weapon: murder was a sacramental act ... they courted death and martyrdom ..."[26]

The Assassins' asymmetric method of warfare was characterised by their utilisation of the surprise attack, their blending in and targeting of non-combatants and their religious/political motivations. Similarities between the medieval

18 Laquer, supra n. 12 at 12.

19 Ibid.

20 Ibid., citing Josephus Flavius.

21 Ibid., 335, n. 7.

22 The term 'assassin' is said to be derived from the Arabic word 'hashashin' (those who smoke hashish). It referred to the followers of this sect who apparently conducted their assassinations under the influence of hashish: ibid., 10–12.

23 Lewis, B., *The Assassins: A Radical Sect in Islam* (London: Weidenfeld and Nicholson, 1967; republished London: Phoenix, 2003).

24 Born in 1007 AD.

25 See Laquer, supra n. 12 at 13; see also Han, H., *Terrorism and Political Violence: Limits and Possibilities of Legal Control* (New York: Oceana Publications Inc, 1993) at 15; see also Erickson, supra n. 16 at 34.

26 Laquer, supra n. 12 at 13.

assassins and their modern counterparts have been noted elsewhere.[27] The use of the suicide attack is one that has recently struck a chord.[28] But there are also points of distinction: the Assassins attacked only the 'great and powerful, and never harmed ordinary people going about their vocations'.[29] Their goal was realised with the elimination of the individual concerned, whereas modern terrorism has a broader objective: the main target is usually *not* the particular individuals who are killed, rather, it is the intended demonstrative effect of the killing on the wider social and political environment, including the foreign policy of the victims' government.[30]

Scholars provide conflicting answers as to whether the Assassins were the first terrorists. Lewis opposes the Assassins being labelled the 'first terrorists in history',[31] yet he acknowledges that Hassan Bin Sabbah may well have invented a method of attack which latterly became known as 'terrorism'.[32] The Assassins were not the first group in history to employ the tactics of murder and tyrannicide, but they may well have been the first group to use these tactics in an *organised, systematic and sustained programme*, that had as its goal the defeat of the Seljuk state.

To complete this brief summary of the historical origins of the term 'terrorism', a few observations are made regarding the 'Reign of Terror'. Both *The Shorter Oxford English Dictionary* and *Webster's New Twentieth Century Dictionary* refer to France in the late 1700s.[33] The 'Reign of Terror' which occurred during the French Revolution is the period from which the term 'terrorism' is etymologically

27 Lewis, supra n. 23 at viii: '... [T]he Syrian-Iranian connection, the calculated use of terror, the total dedication of the assassin emissary to the point of self-immolation, in the service of his cause and in the expectation of heavenly recompense.'

28 The Assassins' strategy of stabbing political opponents at close range with a short dagger, virtually ensuring their own deaths, was noted as a parallel with modern Islamic terrorists' use of people as weapons: see 'The Terror Industry Fields Its Own Weapons', *The New York Times*, Week in Review, 24 August 2003.

29 Lewis, supra n. 23 at ix.

30 For a discussion of the interaction between the terms 'terrorism' and 'assassination', see Schmid, A., *Political Terrorism: A Research Guide to Concepts, Theories, Data Bases and Literature* (New Brunswick: Transaction Books, 1983) at 57–63.

31 In the preface to the latest publication of his book, *The Assassins – A Radical Sect in Islam*, Lewis notes that an Italian translator of his book retained his subtitle and added 'The First Terrorists in History' to the title. Lewis commented that this was 'not, by the way, a correct statement': Lewis, supra n. 23 at viii.

32 'Hasan [Bin Sabbah] found a new way, by which a small force, disciplined and devoted, could strike effectively against an overwhelmingly superior enemy. "Terrorism" ... is carried on by a narrowly limited organization and is inspired by a sustained program of large-scale objectives in the name of which terror is practised. This was the method that Hasan chose – the method, it may well be, that he invented.': ibid., 130.

33 Supra n. 10 and n. 11 respectively.

derived.[34] The system of terror or *régime de la terreur* of 1793–94 had a positive connotation at that time and was of a domestic nature. Revolutionary France was threatened by the upper class emigrants, who were thought to have been conspiring with foreign rulers to invade the country. Treason at home, in support of this reactionary movement, was a clear and present danger. Therefore, the National Convent, led by the Jacobins, declared terror to be the solution, thereby giving legal sanction to a number of emergency measures.[35]

The regime of terror was designed to consolidate the new government's power by intimidating counter-revolutionaries, subversives and all other dissidents whom the new regime regarded as 'enemies of the people'.[36] Approximately 300,000 people were arrested during the Reign of Terror, and between 17,000 and 40,000 were officially executed while many died in prison or without a trial.[37] The purpose was to send a clear message to all who might oppose the revolution or grow nostalgic for the old regime. In this sense, the campaign of terrorism that was carried out by Robespierre and the Jacobin government is an accurate reference point for the *Webster's* definition, which defines 'terrorism' as the use of terror 'especially as a political weapon or policy'.

The etymology of 'terrorism' gives rise to two observations. First, the meaning of 'terrorism' has undergone a transformation. During the Reign of Terror, a regime or system of terrorism was used as an instrument of governance, wielded by a recently established revolutionary *state* against the enemies of the people. Now the term 'terrorism' is commonly used to describe terrorist acts committed by *non-state or sub-national entities* against a state. From around 1848, terrorism in Europe and Russia was conceived by its exponents as comprising a kind of action against tyrannical rulers. A German radical democrat, Karl Heinzen, wrote an essay in which he set out the philosophical underpinnings of a policy of terrorism directed at tyrannical leaders.[38] He argued that while murder was forbidden in principle, this prohibition did not apply to politics, and the murder of political leaders might well be a 'physical necessity'. Heinzen was perhaps the first person to provide a fully fledged doctrine of modern terrorism.[39] Thus, terrorism has undergone a transformation in *meaning* and *perception*. When the Jacobins used the word 'terror' to describe their regime, it had positive connotations, whereas

34 Loomis, S., *Paris in the Terror: June 1793–July 1794* (London: Jonathan Cape, 1965); and Cobb, R., *The People's Armies – The armées révolutionnaires: Instrument of the Terror in the Departments April 1793 to Floréal Year II* (Elliott, M. trans.) (New Haven and London: Yale University Press, 1987).

35 'It is necessary that the terror caused by the guillotine spreads in all of France and brings to justice all the traitors. There is no other means to inspire this necessary terror which will consolidate the Revolution ...': Schmid, supra n. 30 at 66.

36 Hoffman, supra n. 15 at 15.

37 Ibid., 16; also Schmid, supra n. 30 at 66.

38 Laquer, supra n. 12 at 27–9.

39 Ibid., at 28.

modern commentators agree[40] that the word 'terrorism' is now perceived as an inherently negative, pejorative, term.[41]

The second observation regarding the etymology of 'terrorism' is that since its inception, the term has been linked with virtuous ideals such as justice, liberty and morality. In 1794, Robespierre linked the goals of the Jacobin system of terror with the objectives of the revolution.[42] This idealism continued to be attached to 'terrorism' into the mid-1800s, even though a transition had occurred in the meaning of the term.[43] The connection between terrorism and its idealistic objectives continues today. Many organisations, officially considered as 'terrorist organisations', have chosen for themselves names which suggest that they are also idealistic.[44] Self-perception often differs from outsiders' perceptions of their *raison d'être*.[45]

The gulf that exists between the way that 'terrorists' see themselves and the way that others, particularly target governments, see them, is often explained by the well-worn dictum that 'one man's terrorist is another man's freedom fighter'.[46] This cliché inevitably appears whenever the issue of defining terrorism is addressed. It represents the idea that terrorism is a *political* term, that it is often used by opponents of the terrorists' motivating cause in an attempt to attach a stigma to the

40 See Crenshaw, M., *Terrorism and International Co-operation*, Occassional Paper Series No. 11 (New York: Institute for East-West Security Studies, 1989) at 5; Jenkins, B., *The Study of Terrorism: Definitional Problems* (Santa Monica: Rand Corporation, 1980) at 10; Sick, G., 'The Political Underpinnings of Terrorism', in Kegley Jr, C. (ed.), *International Terrorism: Characteristics, Causes, Controls* (New York: St Martin's Press, 1990) at 52; Wilkinson, P., 'Terrorism', in Foley, M. (ed.), *Ideas that Shape Politics* (Manchester: Manchester University Press, 1994) at 189.

41 Barker, J., *The No-Nonsense Guide to Terrorism* (London: Verso, 2002) at 21–3.

42 Hoffman, supra n. 15 at 16.

43 Stepniak-Kravchiski in 1884: 'The terrorist is noble, terrible, irresistibly fascinating, for he combines in himself the two sublimities [sic] of human grandeur: the martyr and the hero': Teichmann, J., 'How to Define Terrorism' (1989) 64 *Philosophy* 508.

44 For example, the National Liberation Front, the National Liberation Army, the Palestine Liberation Front, the Basque Fatherland and Liberty, the Popular Liberation Army, the Lashkar-e-Tayyiba (Army of the Righteous), the Liberation Tigers of Tamil Eelam, the Shining Path and the Irish Republican Army. All of these groups have been categorised by the US Department of State as Foreign Terrorist Organisations (FTOs): US Department of State, *Patterns of Global Terrorism 2001* (US: US Department of State, 2002): <http://www.state.gov/s/ct/rls/crt/2001/pdf/index.htm>, Appendix B. Their inclusion here should not be taken as an acknowledgement that these groups necessarily deserve to be categorised as FTOs.

45 'We don't see ourselves as terrorists because we don't believe in terrorism. We don't see resisting the occupier as a terrorist action. We see ourselves as mujhadeen [holy warriors] who fight a Holy War for the people': Sheikh Muhammad Hussein Fadlallah, the spiritual leader of the Lebanese group Hezbollah, which is categorised by the US Department of State as an FTO: ibid., Appendix B.

46 Sometimes also phrased as 'one man's terrorist is another man's patriot'.

'terrorist', and it represents the idea that the meaning of 'terrorism' in a particular situation is *fluid*, in so far as a group or person might be labelled a terrorist at one point in time, but at another, they might be a legitimate representative of their people.[47] Schmid has warned against this corruption of the concept, caused by subjecting 'terrorism' to a double standard, based on definition power and an in-group/out-group distinction.[48]

It may be noted that the political, ideological or religious objective, which has been an integral aspect of terrorism since its inception (whether that be seen as having occurred with the Assassins in the Middle East or with the Jacobins in France) is what differentiates it from mere criminal violence which has no greater goal in mind and which is carried out for instant gratification.[49] Although it is important to be aware of the political element, it is also vital to note that the UN Security Council and General Assembly frequently condemn acts of terrorism, regardless of their justifications and irrespective of their motives.[50]

Political Scholars' Attempts to Define 'Terrorism'

The field of political science has produced many definitions of 'terrorism'. A scientific approach was adopted by Schmid who produced a comprehensive analysis of the term. When he asked scholars to submit their definitions, he found that no single author's definition was universally acceptable to his or her colleagues. The highest response from the scholars was in the category that 'there is no adequate definition'.[51] The most popular definition was favoured by only four of the 45 respondents.[52] Since no single author's definition was acceptable to all, or even a majority, of respondents, Schmid identified a number of elements in each definition in order to determine whether there was some consensus. He

47 During World War II, members of the French resistance were regarded as criminals; during the Algerian War, the French government called the resistance 'terrorists'; Nelson Mandela was once famously labelled a 'terrorist'; and Yasser Arafat, who was once branded in the US as a 'terrorist', was later received in the White House as a respectable Head of State: see Elagab, O., *International Documents Relating to Terrorism* (London: Cavendish Publishing Limited, 1995) at iii; and see Chomsky, N. in Sterba, J. (ed.), *International Justice and Terrorism* (Oxford; New York: Oxford University Press, 2003).

48 Schmid, supra n. 30 at 112.

49 A fact that distinguishes piracy from terrorism.

50 For example, see S/Res/1269 (1999); S/Res/1456 (2003) Appendix 2H; and see UNGA Res 49/60 (1994), Appendix 2I.

51 See Schmid, supra n. 30 at 73, Table IV where ten of the 45 respondents to Schmid's questionnaire replied that there was no adequate definition. This was closely followed by the number of respondents who felt that their own definition of terrorism was the most adequate (nine out of 45 respondents).

52 That was E.V. Walter's definition, published in 1964, Schmid's paraphrasing of which ran to 29 lines: ibid., 121–2.

discovered that there were 22 distinct elements within 109 definitions, which had been constructed over a 45-year span.[53] He then tried to reduce the 22 elements into one universally acceptable definition.[54] In an attempt to incorporate most of the elements, Schmid created a comprehensive but unwieldy definition.[55] Although this definition would be too cumbersome to be incorporated into a dictionary, statute or convention, Schmid at least demonstrated that this is a term that is extremely difficult to define.

Other political scholars have put forward more concise definitions which emphasise the elements they consider essential. Laquer notes that terrorism aims to induce a state of fear, that it does not conform to humanitarian norms[56] and that it depends on publicity for its success.[57] Ganor emphasises that the essence of the activity is violence (or the threat of violence), that it deliberately targets civilians and that it does so for political ends.[58] Theoretically, this definition would apply

53 From 1936–81, ibid., 73–8, Table V.

54 'Terrorism is a method of combat in which random or symbolic victims serve as instrumental *target[s] of violence.* These instrumental victims share group or class characteristics which form the basis for their selection for victimization. Through previous use of violence or the credible threat of violence other members of that group or class are put in a *state of chronic fear (terror)*. This group or class, whose members' sense of security is purposively undermined, is the *target of terror*. The victimization of the target of violence is considered extra-normal by most observers from the witnessing audience on the basis of its atrocity; the time (e.g. peacetime) or place (not a battlefield) of victimization or the disregard for rules of combat accepted in conventional warfare. The norm violation creates an attentive audience beyond the target of terror; sectors of this audience might in turn form the main object of manipulation. The purpose of this indirect method of combat is either to immobilize the target of terror in order to produce disorientation and/or compliance, or to mobilize secondary *targets of demands* (e.g. a government) or *targets of attention* (e.g. public opinion) to changes of attitude or behaviour favouring the short or long-term interests of the users of this method of combat.' (Emphasis as in the original): ibid., 111.

55 Schmid described it as 'a rather long definition'. It includes 13 of the 22 elements that were identified but it also contains some new elements. It excludes violence against inanimate things and it demands the existence of a target of terror: ibid., 111–13.

56 Terrorism (which Laquer says 'does not conform to humanitarian norms') must involve attacks against civilians/non-combatants. Presumably, 'terrorism' is limited to *only* these targets. Laquer did not clarify his position on this point in the article from which the definition was quoted.

57 'Most experts agree that terrorism is the use or threat of violence, a method of combat or a strategy to achieve certain goals, that its aim is to induce a state of fear in the victim, that it is ruthless and does not conform to humanitarian norms, and that publicity is an essential factor in terrorist strategy': Laquer, W., 'Reflections on Terrorism' (1986) 64 *Foreign Affairs* 88.

58 'Terrorism is the intentional use of, or threat to use violence against civilians or against civilian targets, in order to attain political aims.': Ganor, B., 'Defining Terrorism: Is One Man's Terrorist Another Man's Freedom Fighter?,' The International Policy Institute for Counter-Terrorism: <http://www.ict.org.il> at 12 June 2008.

to governments (and their agencies and proxies) as well as to non-governmental groups and individuals. It excludes non-violent political actions such as protests, strikes, demonstrations and civil disobedience, and it excludes violent actions against military and police forces. Therefore, acts of guerrilla warfare and urban insurrection would not be acts of terrorism, in so far as they are usually directed against military forces.

Erickson formulated his definition by reviewing three 'authoritative' versions, from the Vice President's Task Force on Combating Terrorism, the US Department of State and the US Department of Defense. He found that all three of the definitions provided by those agencies were flawed and he constructed his definition by combining what he regarded as the most accurate elements from each.[59] Erickson's definition does not confine itself to civilians or non-combatants, but it does emphasise the element of generating fear with wider political, social or ideological objectives.[60] His definition also explicitly requires the target of a terrorist attack to be a person, excluding attacks against property: since property is inanimate, it cannot be subjected to feelings of terror. Ultimately, property put at risk must threaten a human being if it is to generate fear or terror – an essential element of terrorism.

Hoffman's definition incorporates what he regards as the five key elements of terrorism: it is political in its aims and motives; it uses or threatens to use violence; it is designed to have far-reaching psychological repercussions; it is conducted by an organisation with an identifiable chain of command or conspiratorial cell structure (whose members wear no uniform or identifying insignia); and it is perpetrated by a sub-national group or non-state entity.[61] The last two elements are contentious because they presume that acts of terrorism can *only* be carried out by non-state actors.

---

59 'Terrorism is the unlawful use or threatened use of force or violence against individuals to generate fear with the intent of coercing or intimidating governments, societies, or individuals for political, social, or ideological purposes': Erickson, supra n. 16 at 28.

60 It is unclear whether the reference to 'unlawful' in Erickson's definition refers to domestic or international law, or both.

61 '... [T]errorism [is] the deliberate creation and exploitation of fear through violence or the threat of violence in the pursuit of political change. All terrorist acts involve violence or the threat of violence. Terrorism is specifically designed to have far-reaching psychological effects beyond the immediate victim(s) or object of the terrorist attack. It is meant to instil fear within, and thereby intimidate, a wider "target audience" that might include a rival or ethnic or religious group, an entire country, a national government or political party, or public opinion in general. Terrorism is designed to create power where there is none or to consolidate power where there is very little. Through the publicity generated by their violence, terrorists seek to obtain the leverage, influence and power they otherwise lack to effect political change on either a local or an international scale': Hoffman, supra n. 15 at 43–4.

In contrast, Wardlaw does not exclude state actors.[62] He defines terrorism according to the act itself, regardless of where it originates. Nor does he emphasise the civilian/non-combatant aspect; he focuses on the use of fear to achieve political ends. Wardlaw considers that terrorism may be used by both insurgents and incumbent regimes and, rather than being mindless, senseless or wanton, acts of terrorism are a means to an end: terrorists have firm goals in mind, however perverse these may seem to the terrorist's adversaries.[63]

Schmid, Laquer, Ganor, Erickson, Hoffman and Wardlaw have arrived at different definitions, each based on their individual understanding of the concept of 'terrorism'. These six definitions could be added to, virtually *ad infinitum*, since every scholar who writes on the subject seems to offer their own description.[64] Schmid has already demonstrated that there are more than a hundred to choose from. The main points to note are, first, that modern terrorism has very little in common with its etymological origins and its historical antecedents.[65] Second, it is difficult to define terrorism in any meaningful way because of its inherent political dimensions.[66] Terrorism is purportedly easier to describe than to define.[67] Third, despite the controversies over its definition, there do seem to be some elements of terrorism which are beyond, or almost beyond, controversy, such as its use of extreme fear in carrying out violent attacks which seek to achieve political, ideological or religious objectives. But there is disagreement over other elements, especially as to whether terrorism can be carried out by the state, or only by non-state actors such as sub-national groups or clandestine agents, and whether it is limited to the deliberate targeting of civilians/non-combatants or whether acts of terrorism can also be carried out against military targets.

62 '[T]he use, or threat of use, of violence by an individual or a group, whether acting for or in opposition to established authority, when such action is designed to create extreme anxiety and/or fear-inducing effects in a target group larger than the immediate victims with the purpose of coercing that group into acceding to the political demands of the perpetrators': Wardlaw, G., *Political Terrorism: Theory, Tactics and Counter-Measures* (Cambridge: Cambridge University Press, 1982).

63 Ibid., 19.

64 For more definitions, see Schmid, supra n. 30 at 119–52; see also Shafritz, J., Gibbons, E. and Scott, G., *Almanac of Modern Terrorism* (1991) at part IV.

65 There is little if anything in common between the 'Russian terrorists of the nineteenth century and Abu Nidal': Laquer, supra n. 57 at 88.

66 'There is no such thing as terrorism pure and unadulterated, specific and unchanging, comparable to a chemical element; rather there are a great many terrorisms. Historians and sociologists are not in full agreement on what socialism or fascism was. It would be unrealistic to expect unanimity on a topic so close to us in time': ibid.

67 The US Vice President's Task Force on Combating Terrorism concluded in 1986 that terrorism is 'a phenomenon that is easier to describe than define'. Others have drawn parallels between terrorism and pornography, referencing Associate Justice Potter Stewart of the US Supreme Court, who asserted (in relation to pornography) that he could not define it, but he knew it when he saw it.

International Legal Definitions of 'Terrorism'

There are currently 13 international and nine regional conventions or protocols regarding terrorism. The latest addition was the International Convention for the Suppression of Acts of Nuclear Terrorism which entered into force in July 2007. Despite the proliferation of instruments condemning terrorism, there has never been a universal definition of terrorism in international law.

Pre-World War II Efforts to Define 'Terrorism'

The first international attempt to address the legal definition of 'terrorism' occurred in the late 1920s and early 1930s, in response to an increase in terrorist activity following World War I. A series of meetings was held under the auspices of the International Conference for the Unification of Penal Law in various European capitals. The meetings were attended by delegations representing states, intergovernmental and private international organisations.[68] The term 'terrorism' was expressly used for the first time in an international penal instrument at the Third (Brussels) International Conference for the Unification of Penal Law in 1930.[69]

Moves to prohibit terrorism intensified with the assassination of King Alexander of Yugoslavia and Mr Louis Barthou, the Foreign Minister of the French Republic, at Marseilles on 6 October 1934. Following the assassination, the French government submitted to the Council of the League of Nations a memorandum on bases for an agreement with a view to the suppression of terrorism. A committee of experts set up under a Council resolution met in April–May 1935 and in January 1936 and prepared a draft convention.[70] In addition, the Sixth Conference in the Unification of Penal Law series, held in Copenhagen in 1935, adopted a model penal provision on terrorism. The key articles covered a series of acts including wilful acts directed against the life, physical integrity, health and freedom of various officials, wilful destruction of public buildings, wilful use of explosives

68 The first conference was held in Warsaw (1–5 November 1927); the second in Rome (21–25 May 1928); the third in Brussels (26–30 June 1930); the fourth in Paris (27–31 December 1931); the fifth in Madrid (14–20 October 1934) and the sixth in Copenhagen (31 August–3 September 1935): see Franck, T. and Lockwood Jr, B., 'Preliminary Thoughts Towards an International Convention on Terrorism' (1978) 68 *AJIL* 69.

69 Held from 26–30 June 1930, study prepared by the Secretariat for the Sixth Committee, 'Measures to Prevent International Terrorism Which Endangers or Takes Innocent Human Lives or Jeopardises Fundamental Freedoms, And Study of the Underlying Causes Of Those Forms of Terrorism And Acts Of Terrorism And Acts of Violence Which Lie In Misery, Frustration, Grievances and Despair And Which Cause Some People to Sacrifice Human Lives, Including Their Own, In an Attempt to Effect Radical Changes', UN Doc. A/C.6/418 (1972) at 11–12.

70 See 'Proceedings of the International Conference on the Repression of Terrorism', League of Nations Doc. C.94.M.47.1938.V (1938.V.3) at 49–50.

in a public place, or any other wilful act which endangered human lives and the community, where any of those acts 'has endangered the community or created a state of terror calculated to cause a change in or impediment to the operation of the public authorities or to disturb international relations'.[71]

Pre-war efforts to define and prohibit terrorism culminated in Geneva on 16 November 1937 when the League of Nations Convention for the Prevention and Punishment of Terrorism was opened for signature.[72] Article 1(2) states: 'In the present Convention, the expression "acts of terrorism" means criminal acts directed against a State and intended or calculated to create a state of terror in the minds of particular persons, or a group of persons of the general public.' The 'criminal acts' referred to in Article 1(2) were listed in Article 2. Conspiracy, incitement, or assistance to commit the criminal acts were also prohibited, by virtue of Article 3. Thus, 'acts of terrorism' included any wilful act causing death or grievous bodily harm to heads of state, their wives or husbands, and persons holding public positions when the act was directed against them in their public capacity.[73] As for prosecution, the Committee of Experts also drafted a Convention for the Creation of an International Criminal Court.[74] The proposed Court was to have been given jurisdiction to prosecute persons accused of offences under the Convention for the Prevention and Punishment of Terrorism.[75] Contracting Parties would have been given the choice of either prosecuting alleged terrorists in their own courts or committing the accused for trial to the International Court.[76]

Although the Convention was signed by 24 states,[77] it was only ratified by India[78] and acceded to by Mexico. The breadth of the definition of 'terrorism'

71 Sixth International Conference for the Unification of Penal Law, Copenhagen, 31 August–3 September 1935.

72 Convention for the Prevention and Punishment of Terrorism, 19 League of Nations OJ 23 (1938); League of Nations Doc. C.546(I).M383(I).1937.V. (1938) (16 November 1937). The Convention is reproduced in Hudson, M., *International Legislation – A Collection of the Texts of Multipartite International Instruments of General Interest*, vol VII, 1935–37 (New York: Oceana Publications Inc, 1972) at 862–78.

73 Ibid., Article 2(1).

74 Convention for the Creation of an International Criminal Court, 19 League of Nations OJ 23 (1938); League of Nations Doc. C.546(I).M.383(I).1937.V (1938) (16 November 1937), opened for signature at Geneva on 16 November 1937, reproduced in Hudson, supra n. 72 at 878–93.

75 See Article 1 of the Convention for the Creation of an International Criminal Court, ibid.

76 Ibid., see Article 2.

77 Albania, Argentine Republic, Belgium, Bulgaria, Cuba, Czechoslovakia, Dominican Republic, Ecuador, Egypt, Estonia, France, Greece, Haiti, India, Monaco, the Netherlands, Norway, Peru, Romania, Spain, Turkey, Union of Soviet Socialist Republics, Venezuela and Yugoslavia.

78 On 1 January 1941.

may have contributed to its ultimate failure.[79] The UK apparently declined to ratify it 'due to an anticipation of the difficulty of framing the relevant domestic legislation'.[80] The Convention never entered into force.

Conventions Related to Air Hijacking – 1960s and early 1970s

The international community's attention to the problem of suppressing terrorism was reactivated in the 1960s when a spate of airline hijackings prompted both the UN and the International Civil Aviation Organisation (ICAO) to act. Incidents involving the forcible seizure of aircraft had occurred in isolated instances in the 1940s and 1950s, but modern hijacking, on a large scale, began in 1961.[81] The first reaction to this type of terrorist activity was the signing of the Convention of Offences and Certain Other Acts Committed Onboard Aircraft.[82] This Convention prohibited the unlawful seizure of aircraft.[83] It did not mention the word 'terrorism' or any similar term.

During the late 1960s there was a significant increase in the number of air hijackings.[84] This prompted the ICAO to draft an updated agreement, which resulted in the Convention for the Suppression of the Unlawful Seizure of Aircraft.[85] It rendered air hijackings a distinct, separate crime and also provided that the state in which the alleged offender was found had to either extradite or prosecute.[86] A further convention regarding aircraft was concluded in 1971.[87] As with the previous two conventions, 'terrorism' was not specifically mentioned and the enforcement mechanisms for extradition and prosecution of offenders were weak. Therefore, the ICAO convened a meeting in Washington DC in September

79 Dugard, J., 'Toward the Definition of International Terrorism', Proceedings of the American Society of International Law (1973) 67 *AJIL* 94.

80 Franck and Lockwood, supra n. 68 at 70.

81 On 1 May 1961, a Cuban, Antulio Ramirez Ortiz, diverted a National Airlines plane and forced the pilot to land in Havana. This incident probably marked the beginning of an era in the 1960s and 1970s plagued by this phenomenon: see von Glahn, G., *Law Among Nations – An Introduction to Public International Law*, 6th edn (New York: Macmillan, 1992) at 332; see also Horlick, G., 'The Developing Law of Air Hijacking' (1971) 12 *Harvard International Law Journal* 33, n. 1.

82 Convention on Offences and Certain Other Acts Committed on Board Aircraft, Tokyo, 14 September 1963.

83 Article 11 provides: '1. When a person onboard has unlawfully committed by force or threat thereof an act of interference, seizure, or other wrongful exercise of control of an aircraft in flight or when such an act is about to be committed ...'

84 There were 30 instances in 1968 and 81 in 1969: von Glahn, supra n. 81 at 333.

85 Convention for the Suppression of the Unlawful Seizure of Aircraft, 16 December 1970.

86 Article 7.

87 Convention for the Suppression of Unlawful Acts Against the Safety of Civil Aviation, 23 September 1971.

1972 with the aim of considering a convention which would provide penalties for countries which did not comply with the rules in the existing conventions. However, the proposals were all voted down when the ICAO assembly met in Rome in August–September 1973.[88] The strengthening of the three air-hijacking conventions did not take place until 1988, when the Protocol for the Suppression of Unlawful Acts of Violence at Airports Serving International Civil Aviation was concluded in Montreal.[89]

There were also a number of bilateral and regional agreements complementing those international instruments[90] but all of those documents were only concerned with one particular type of terrorist activity, air hijacking. A definition of 'terrorism' was not specifically addressed in any of them.

Regional and Multilateral Conventions Related to Terrorism – 1970s

Attempts to suppress terrorism continued throughout the 1970s in a piecemeal fashion. The UN issued its Declaration on Principles of International Law Concerning Friendly Relations and Cooperation Between States in 1970 which provided, *inter alia*, that each state had the duty to refrain from encouraging the organisation of armed bands, irregular forces and mercenaries from incursion into the territory of another state, and that each state had a 'duty to refrain from organizing, instigating, assisting or participating in acts of civil strife or terrorist acts in another State or acquiescing in organized activities within its territory directed towards the commission of such acts'.[91]

The Organisation of American States (OAS) adopted the Convention to Prevent and Punish the Acts of Terrorism Taking the Form of Crimes Against Persons and Related Extortion that are of International Significance.[92] That instrument was aimed mainly at the kidnapping of diplomats. Although the word 'terrorism' was used in the Convention, it was not defined.[93] With similar objectives, the UN General

88 See von Glahn, supra n. 81 at 333–4.

89 Protocol for the Suppression of Unlawful Acts of Violence at Airports Serving International Civil Aviation, supplementary to the Convention for the Suppression of Unlawful Acts against the Safety of Civil Aviation, done at Montreal on 23 September 1971; done at Montreal on 24 February 1988, in force on 6 August 1989; 27 ILM 627 (1988).

90 See von Glahn, supra n. 81 at 334–41.

91 UN Declaration on Principles of International Law Concerning Friendly Relations and Cooperation Between States in Accordance with the Charter of the United Nations, GA Res. 2625 (XXV) of 24 October 1970, UN GAOR, 25th Sess., Supp. 28, p121, UN Doc. A/8028 (1971).

92 OAS Convention to Prevent and Punish the Acts of Terrorism Taking the Form of Crimes Against Persons and Related Extortion that are of International Significance.

93 The preamble stated that the OAS General Assembly 'strongly condemned acts of terrorism, especially the kidnapping of persons and extortion in connection with that crime'.

Assembly adopted the Convention on the Prevention and Punishment of Crimes Against Internationally Protected Persons, including Diplomatic Agents.[94] That Convention listed five offences against 'internationally protected persons' which each State Party was obliged to make a crime under its internal law. 'Terrorism' was not mentioned in that document. Another instrument was the International Convention against the Taking of Hostages, which continued the UN's piecemeal approach to the problem of legislating against terrorist-like activities.[95] It referred to the crime of hostage-taking as a 'manifestation of international terrorism',[96] but it was concerned with making this *particular* activity unlawful, rather than tackling terrorism generally.

One further document of note was the Council of Europe's Convention on the Suppression of Terrorism.[97] Its adoption was prompted by a desire to 'take effective measures'[98] against the increase in acts of terrorism and to prosecute and punish perpetrators of such acts. This Convention was mainly concerned with facilitating the extradition of persons who had committed terrorist-like crimes. It did not define 'terrorism' but it implied that all five of the categories of acts referred to in Articles 1 and 2 were *acts* of terrorism.[99] Thus, one commentator has observed that the European Convention 'represents a legal "definition" of terrorism as an enumerated series of specific criminal acts'[100] even though there was no linkage of the acts via common characteristics or elements such as intent or motive, identity of the act or identity of the victim.

---

94 UN Convention on the Prevention and Punishment of Crimes Against Internationally Protected Persons, including Diplomatic Agents, adopted on 14 December 1973; entered into force on 20 February 1977; UNTS vol. 1035, no. 15410.

95 UN International Convention against the Taking of Hostages, adopted on 17 December 1979; entered into force on 3 June 1983; UNTS vol. 1316, no. 21931.

96 See paragraph 5 of the preamble, which stated that it was necessary to develop international co-operation in devising and adopting effective measures for the 'prevention, prosecution and punishment of all acts of taking of hostages as manifestations of international terrorism'.

97 European Convention on the Suppression of Terrorism, done at Strasbourg on 27 January 1977; entered into force on 4 August 1978; UNTS vol. 1137, no. 17828.

98 Ibid., paragraphs 3 and 4 of the preamble.

99 Ibid., Article 1, which listed any offence within the scope of the Hague or Montreal Conventions as offences, as well as offences that involved kidnapping, the taking of hostages, offences involving bombs, grenades and rockets.

100 Levitt, G., 'Is Terrorism Worth Defining?' (1986) 13 *Ohio Northern University Law Review* 97 at 103.

Early Efforts Towards an International Convention on Terrorism[101]

The international instruments referred to above were evidence of the international community's desire to address the increasingly prevalent problem of terrorism. However, the regional and multilateral documents adopted during the 1970s represented a piecemeal approach. Although many of the instruments used the word 'terrorism' (usually only in the title and/or the preamble) they did not attempt to *define* it, instead opting to criminalise a range of acts, on a convention-by-convention basis. On 18 December 1972, the UN General Assembly, on the recommendation of the Sixth Committee, decided to establish an Ad Hoc Committee on Terrorism.[102] The Ad Hoc Committee's objectives were to define international terrorism, to study the underlying causes of terrorism and to agree on recommendations for an international document aimed at the prevention of terrorism.[103] Differences of opinion emerged between various factions within the Ad Hoc Committee, particularly over the need to preserve the right of self-determination and the issue of whether states and their military forces could be held responsible for acts of terrorism. The Non-Aligned Group proposed a definition of international terrorism which would have specifically preserved the 'inalienable right to self-determination and independence of all peoples under colonial and racist regimes',[104] implying that the use of force, which might otherwise be considered terrorism, could be justified in some instances.

On 25 September 1972, the US introduced a Draft Convention for the Prevention and Punishment of Certain Acts of International Terrorism in the Sixth Committee of the General Assembly.[105] The word 'terrorism' did not appear anywhere in the operative text; instead, the neutral phrase 'offense of international significance' was employed. It virtually defined international terrorism as an act that met four conditions: the act had to be committed or take effect outside the territory of a state of which the alleged offender was a national; the act had to be committed or take effect outside the state against which the act was directed; the act could not

---

101 For a more detailed account of the Ad Hoc Committee process and the 1972 Draft Convention, see, *inter alia*, Lambert, supra n. 1 at 29–39; also Murphy, J., *State Support of International Terrorism – Legal, Political and Economic Dimensions* (San Francisco: Westview Press, 1989; London: Mansell Publishing Ltd, 1989) 5–8.

102 See UN Doc. A/8969 (1972) regarding the Sixth Committee's recommendations to establish an Ad Hoc Committee on Terrorism; see GA Res. 3034, 27 UN GAOR Supp. (No 30) at 119, UN Doc. A/Res/3034 (1972), paragraphs 9 and 10 regarding the establishment and objectives of the Ad Hoc Committee.

103 For a detailed account of the Ad Hoc Committee's study of international terrorism, see Franck and Lockwood, supra n. 68.

104 See 28 UN GAOR Supp. (1973). The 'Non-Aligned Group' included the Arab states, China and a block of African states: see discussion in Murphy, supra n. 101 at 5.

105 Draft Convention for the Prevention and Punishment of Certain Acts of International Terrorism (Draft Convention to Prevent the Spread of Terrorist Violence), UN Doc. A/C.6/L.850 (1972).

be committed by or against a member of the armed forces of a state in the course of military hostilities; and the act had to be intended to damage the interests of or obtain concessions from a state or an international organisation.[106] The US – in contrast to the Non-Aligned states – did not consider that a state's armed forces could commit acts of terrorism. The Libyan representative described the US's initiative as 'a ploy ... against the legitimate struggle of the people under the yoke of colonialism and alien domination'.[107] The disagreement over the meaning of 'terrorism' reflected much deeper ideological differences between Western states and developing states on the permissible use of violence, especially with regard to national liberation. Due to the failure of the international community to agree on a definition of 'terrorism', a comprehensive convention was unattainable. Therefore, the UN and regional organisations again resorted to a piecemeal approach which resulted in a set of international laws that covered acts of terrorism, without having to address what the term 'terrorism' meant.

Regional and Multilateral Instruments – 1980s

During the 1980s, the UN's methodology of criminalising particular acts of terrorism continued to prevail. Two UN conventions,[108] two UN protocols[109] and one regional convention were adopted.[110] These instruments created criminal, extraditable offences in respect of terrorist-like activities.[111] The term 'terrorism' was used sparingly in these instruments and none of them offered a definition of

---

106 Ibid.

107 See Murphy, 'United Nations Proposals on the Control and Repression of Terrorism', in Bassiouni, M. (ed.), *International Terrorism and Political Crimes* (Springfield, Illinois: Charles C. Thomas Pub. Ltd, 1975) at 493–9.

108 The Convention for the Suppression of Unlawful Acts against the Safety of Maritime Navigation, Rome on 10 March 1988, entered into force on 1 March 1992; IMO Doc. Sua/Conf/15; 27 ILM 668; and the Convention on the Physical Protection of Nuclear Material, IAEA Doc. C/225; 1456 UNTS 101; 18 ILM 1419 (3 March 1980).

109 Protocol for the Suppression of Unlawful Acts of Violence at Airports Serving Civil Aviation (discussed above) and the Protocol for the Suppression of Unlawful Acts against the Safety of Fixed Platforms Located on the Continental Shelf, Rome on 10 March 1988, entered into force on 1 March 1992; IMO Doc. Sua/Conf/16/Rev.1; 27 ILM 685.

110 The States of the South Asian Association for Regional Cooperation (SAARC) adopted the Regional Convention on Suppression of Terrorism in Kathmandu on 4 November 1987, entered into force on 22 August 1988, reprinted in UN Doc. A/51/136.

111 For example, Article 7(e)(i) of the Convention on the Physical Protection of Nuclear Material created the offence of threatening 'to use nuclear material to cause death or serious injury to any person or substantial property damage ... in order to compel a natural or legal person, international organization or State to do or to refrain from doing any act'.

it.[112] Although these conventions can loosely be described as 'anti-terrorist', the acts they covered were criminalised regardless of whether the actors involved had a wider *political, religious or ideological objective* in carrying out the prohibited acts.[113]

In addition to the above-mentioned conventions and protocols, several UN General Assembly Resolutions were passed condemning terrorism.[114] General Assembly Resolution 40/61 was adopted by consensus on 9 December 1985 in the immediate aftermath of the *Achille Lauro* hijacking.[115] The General Assembly 'unequivocally condemn[ed], as criminal acts, all methods and practices of terrorism wherever and by whomever committed'.[116] The resolution hinted at a possible definition of 'terrorism' when it referred to acts that 'endanger or take innocent human lives, jeopardize fundamental freedoms and seriously impair the dignity of human beings'.[117]

A notable shift occurred in the General Assembly's attitude towards terrorism between 1972 and 1985. In 1972, the focus was on the need to study the underlying causes of terrorism, rather than condemning it outright.[118] By contrast, in 1985 the General Assembly may have 'reaffirmed the inalienable right to self-determination' but it specifically limited that right by demanding that the struggle of national liberation movements be 'in accordance with the purposes and principles of the Charter and of the Declaration on Principles of International Law Concerning Friendly Relations and Co-operation among States'.[119] The latter document, discussed above, explicitly prohibits recourse to terrorism.

In 1987, the General Assembly adopted Resolution 42/159. It was another significant development because the draft resolution had called for the convening of an international conference which would define the difference between terrorism and the legitimate right of oppressed peoples to fight for freedom. The draft resolution was not adopted. Instead, the resolution that was adopted called

---

112 'Terrorism' appears in the preamble of the Convention for the Suppression of Unlawful Acts against the Safety of Maritime Navigation but not in the body of the Convention (see paragraphs 4 and 8–10 of the preamble) and it does not appear at all in the Protocol for the Suppression of Unlawful Acts against the Safety of Fixed Platforms Located on the Continental Shelf.

113 Murphy, supra n. 101 at 8.

114 For compilations of terrorism instruments, see Bassiouni, M., *International Terrorism: Multilateral Conventions (1937–2001)* (New York: Transnational Publishers Inc, 2001); Elagab, supra n. 47; and UN, *International Instruments related to the Prevention and Suppression of International Terrorism* (New York: United Nations, 2001).

115 GA Res 40/61, 40 UN GAOR Supp. (No 53) at 301, UN Doc. A/40/53 (1985) also in 25 ILM 239 (1986).

116 GA Res 40/61 (1985), Article 1.

117 Ibid., para 4 of the preamble.

118 GA Res 3034 (XXVIII) of 18 December 1972, UN GAOR, 27th Sess., Supp. 30, UN Doc A/9730 (1973).

119 See paragraphs 7–8 of GA Res 40/61 (1985).

upon the Secretary-General to seek the members' views on international terrorism in all its aspects and on ways to combat it. In addition, the resolution contained another unequivocal condemnation of terrorism, without referring to terrorism by colonial, racist or alien regimes, as it had done in the 1970s.

Regional and Multilateral Instruments – 1990s

Multilateral instruments During the 1990s, four relevant UN conventions were adopted: the Convention on the Making of Plastic Explosives for the Purpose of Detection;[120] the Convention on the Safety of United Nations and Associated Personnel;[121] the International Convention for the Suppression of Terrorist Bombings;[122] and the International Convention for the Suppression of the Financing of Terrorism.[123]

The first of those conventions was aimed at ensuring plastic explosives were appropriately marked for ease of identification, in order to improve detection and prevent plastic explosives from being employed in terrorism.[124] Although concern was expressed in the preamble about the use of plastic explosives in terrorist acts, the word 'terrorism' and 'terrorist acts' were not defined. The second convention aimed at improving the protection of UN and associated personnel. Although the term 'terrorism' was not used, it was apparent that acts of terrorism were the focus. This Convention criminalised certain acts and provided for the trial or extradition of offenders.[125] However, there was no legislative requirement that the criminal acts be carried out in pursuance of a political or ideological objective. The third convention was prompted by the realisation that terrorist attacks by means of explosives and similar devices were becoming increasingly prevalent and that the existing multilateral legal provisions did not adequately address the problem.[126] The Terrorist Bombings Convention sought to provide effective and practical

120 Convention on the Making of Plastic Explosives for the Purpose of Detection, signed on 1 March 1991, entered into force on 21 June 1998; UN Doc S/22393/Corr. 1; also 30 ILM 721.

121 Convention on the Safety of United Nations and Associated Personnel, adopted on 9 December 1994, entered into force on 15 January 1999; UN Doc A/Res/49/59, Annex.

122 International Convention for the Suppression of Terrorist Bombings, UNGA Doc A/RES/52/164; adopted by the General Assembly on 15 December 1997 at New York; entered into force on 23 May 2001, UN Doc A/Res/52/164.

123 International Convention for the Suppression of the Financing of Terrorism, adopted on 9 December 1999, entered into force on 10 April 2002; UNGA Doc A/54/109.

124 See the preamble to the Convention on the Prohibition of the Development, Production, Stockpiling and Use of Chemical Weapons and on their Destruction, especially paragraphs 2–4.

125 Prohibited acts are set out in Article 9 and include murder, kidnapping and violent attacks.

126 International Convention for the Suppression of Terrorist Bombings, supra n. 122, preamble.

measures for the prevention of acts of terrorism, as well as for the prosecution and punishment of perpetrators. A list of definitions was provided in Article 1, including the definition of the 'military forces of a state', but the Convention did not define 'terrorism' or a 'terrorist bombing'. This conspicuous omission suggests that '*terrorist bombing*' is just as difficult to define as '*terrorism*', since a definition was provided for the 'bombing' aspect of this phrase (an 'explosive or other lethal device' is defined in Article 1(3)). It is indicative of the UN's difficulties in defining 'terrorism' that this Convention was called the International Convention for the Suppression of Terrorist Bombings, but the term 'terrorist bombing' is nowhere to be found in the text itself. Significantly, the Terrorist Bombings Convention does not apply to the activities of military forces of states during an armed conflict, which are governed by other rules of international law.[127] That exclusion prompted several declarations from states.[128]

The fourth convention was the Terrorism Financing Convention.[129] Unlike the others, this instrument contains what could be interpreted as a definition of an act of terrorism in Article 2(1)(b). This Convention defines an act of terrorism as *either* an offence against one of the existing 'anti-terrorism' conventions (Article 2(1)(a)), *or* any other act which aims to kill or injure a civilian or non-combatant with the purpose of intimidating a population or compelling a government or international organisation to act (Article 2(1)(b)). The definition excludes attacks on military personnel, but theoretically includes both state and non-state actors as persons who can potentially commit an offence. It is interesting to note that there must be an intention to cause death or bodily harm – damage to property alone is insufficient. There is no requirement that the act be committed in furtherance of a political or ideological cause.

Although the UN General Assembly adopted the Terrorist Bombings Convention in 1997 and the Terrorism Financing Convention in 1999, both of which are now in force,[130] gaps in the international anti-terrorism legislation remained. Neither of those instruments provided a comprehensive definition of the term 'terrorism', and difficulties arose over the extent to which states and their military forces should be excluded from their provisions. The depth of division

127 See the last paragraph to the preamble of the International Convention for the Suppression of Terrorist Bombings, supra n. 122; see Article 1(4) and Article 19.

128 See the declaration made by Cuba that this Convention applies to the armed forces of one state against another state; see also the declarations of Germany (that 'military forces' also means 'police forces'), Israel (that military, police and security forces are all excluded, but civilians who direct military forces are not) and the US regarding the meaning of 'military forces of a State'.

129 International Convention for the Suppression of the Financing of Terrorism, supra n. 123.

130 The Terrorist Bombings Convention came into force on 23 May 2001; the Terrorism Financing Convention came into force on 10 April 2002, supra n. 122 and n. 123 respectively.

is evident from the declaration made by Pakistan when it acceded to the Terrorist Bombings Convention.[131]

The Terrorist Bombing Convention has attracted widespread support from states. Pakistan was the only state to lodge a declaration preserving the right of oppressed peoples to use armed struggle in resisting foreign occupation or domination; significantly, Pakistan's declaration prompted objections from 18 states.[132] However, the four regional conventions, discussed below, suggest that many African and Arab states hold similar views to that expressed by Pakistan, and it may be implied that many states still hold the view that 'terrorism' by definition does not include acts of armed struggle by oppressed peoples.

Regional instruments – 1990s Four anti-terrorism instruments were adopted by regional organisations in the 1990s. The Arab Convention on the Suppression of Terrorism (the 'Arab Convention') was the first comprehensive attempt by Arab states to legislate collectively against terrorism.[133] The Arab Convention set out a definition of 'terrorism' in Article 1.[134] The definition is immediately followed by an article that expressly excludes acts that are undertaken as part of a struggle against foreign occupation.[135] That exclusion is underlined in the preamble, which affirms the rights of peoples to combat foreign occupation and aggression by any means, including armed struggle, in order to liberate their territories and secure their right to self-determination and independence. However, that right must be exercised in accordance with the purposes and principles of the Charter of the UN and with the UN's resolutions.[136] These references to the right to armed struggle

131 'The Government of the Islamic Republic of Pakistan declares that nothing in this Convention shall be applicable to struggles, including armed struggle, for the realization of right of self-determination launched against any alien or foreign occupation or domination, in accordance with the rules of international law': Pakistan acceded to the Terrorist Bombing Convention on 13 August 2002.

132 Australia, Austria, Canada, Denmark, Finland, France, Germany, India, Israel, Italy, Japan, the Netherlands, New Zealand, Norway, Spain, Sweden, the United Kingdom and the United States.

133 The Arab Convention on the Suppression of Terrorism, signed at Cairo on 22 April 1998, entered into force on 7 May 1999.

134 '2. Terrorism. Any act or threat of violence, whatever its motives or purposes, that occurs for the advancement of an individual or collective criminal agenda, causing terror among people, causing fear by harming them, or placing their lives, liberty or security in danger, or aiming to cause damage to the environment or to public or private installations or property or to occupy or seize them, or aiming to jeopardize a national resource': Article 1(2) of the Arab Convention. This translation from the Arabic original was provided by the United Nations Secretariat, as reprinted in UN, *International Instruments* (2001) at 152.

135 See Article 2(a) of the Arab Convention.

136 See preamble to the Arab Convention, especially para 5.

against oppression suggest where some of the difficulties may lie in achieving a universal definition of 'terrorism'.

The Commonwealth of Independent States (CIS) signed a Treaty on Cooperation among the States Members of the Commonwealth of Independent States in Combating Terrorism in 1999.[137] A definition of 'terrorism' was set out in Article 1, followed by a separate definition of 'technological terrorism'. Unlike the Arab Convention (above) and the OAU Convention (below), there was no mention of the right of peoples to engage in armed struggle against oppression and aggression. This omission would suggest that the CIS's definition of terrorism is more akin to the Western states' view of 'terrorism'.

The Convention of the Organisation of the Islamic Conference (OIC) on Combating International Terrorism (referred to here as the Islamic Conference Convention), was adopted in July 1999.[138] The preamble confirms the 'legitimacy of the right of peoples to struggle against foreign occupation and colonialist and racist regimes by all means, including armed struggle'.[139] 'Terrorism' is defined in Article 1(2).[140] The Islamic Conference Convention provides a separate definition of a 'terrorist crime' and also stipulates that crimes against UN terrorism-related conventions are considered to be 'terrorist crimes'.[141] Struggle, including armed struggle, by peoples against foreign occupation, aggression, colonialism and hegemony, aimed at liberation and self-determination in accordance with the principles of international law, is not to be considered a terrorist crime.[142]

The fourth and final regional convention of the 1990s was the Organization of African Unity Convention on the Prevention and Combating of Terrorism (OAU Convention).[143] It marked the 'first major comprehensive legislative approach to

137 Treaty on Cooperation among the States Members of the Commonwealth of Independent States in Combating Terrorism in 1999, done at Minsk on 4 June 1999. The state signatories to the Treaty are Armenia, Azerbaijan, Georgia, Kazakhstan, Kyrgyzstan, the Republic of Moldova, the Russian Federation and Tajikstan.

138 Convention of the Organisation of the Islamic Conference (OIC) on Combating International Terrorism, adopted at Ouagadougou on 1 July 1999.

139 See preamble to the OIC Convention, para 9.

140 '"Terrorism" means any act of violence or threat thereof notwithstanding its motives or intentions perpetrated to carry out an individual or collective criminal plan with the aim of terrorizing people or threatening to harm them or imperiling (sic) their lives, honour, freedoms, security or rights or exposing the environment or any facility or public or private property to hazards or occupying or seizing them, or endangering a national resource, or international facilities, or threatening the stability, territorial integrity, political unity or sovereignty of independent States': ibid., Article 1(2).

141 Ibid., Article 1(3) and (4).

142 Ibid., Article 2(a).

143 Organization of African Unity (OAU) Convention on the Prevention and Combating of Terrorism, adopted at Algiers on 14 July 1999; not yet in force.

addressing the scourge of terrorism in Africa'.[144] As in the Arab Convention and the Islamic Conference Convention, the OAU Convention reaffirms the 'legitimate right of peoples for self-determination and independence pursuant to the principles of international law'.[145] A 'terrorist act' is defined in Article 1(3). The struggle of peoples for liberation or self-determination, including armed struggle, against colonialism, occupation, aggression and domination by foreign forces, is expressly excluded from the definition of a 'terrorist act' by virtue of Article 3. That exclusion is limited by the immediately following provision which states that 'political, ideological, racial, ethnic, religious or other motives shall *not* be a justifiable defence against a terrorist act'.[146] The Convention is described by the African Union as offering an 'African definition and concept of terrorism'.[147] The African Union also asserts that this Convention '... clearly delineat[es] the legitimate struggle of peoples under colonial rule or foreign occupation for freedom from crimes of terrorism'.[148]

Reflections on the 1990s The 1990s was a decade in which some in-roads were made into the enduring problem of reaching an internationally acceptable legal definition of 'terrorism'. However, the progress was mainly made by regional organisations drafting their own multilateral instruments, with their own specific interpretations of what the term means. The UN adopted a piecemeal, subject-driven approach, criminalising particular acts as the need arose via separate conventions, without defining 'terrorism' itself. Contradictions emerged between some regional approaches to terrorism, which reserved the right to armed struggle for oppressed peoples,[149] and the statements from the wider international community, including the UN General Assembly, which condemned terrorism outright, regardless of its objectives.[150] There was only one example of a definition of 'terrorism' being incorporated into a UN convention, in the 1999 International Convention for the Suppression of the Financing of Terrorism, but even there, the definition was necessary for the creation of a crime of financing terrorism, rather than prohibiting terrorism per se. Although terrorism was universally

---

144 This comment was made by the OAU in its submission to the Secretary-General of the UN, published in the Report of the Secretary-General on measures to eliminate international terrorism in July 2003: see *Report of the Secretary-General, Measures to Eliminate International Terrorism*, UNGA (58th Sess.) UNGA Doc A/58/116 at p14.

145 OAU Convention, preamble, supra n. 143.

146 OAU Convention, Article 3(2), supra n. 143.

147 *Report of the Secretary-General on Measures to Eliminate International Terrorism*, supra n. 144 at 14.

148 Ibid.

149 See discussion above regarding the Arab Convention, the OAU Convention and the OIC Convention.

150 See, for example, A/Res/51/210, adopted on 16 January 1997, 51st Sess., Agenda Item 151, at paras 1 and 2; and see also A/Res/49/60 adopted on 17 February 1995, 49th Sess., Agenda Item 142, Annex 'Declaration on Measures to Eliminate International Terrorism'.

condemned by states and regional organisations, disagreement remained as to exactly what was being condemned.

Recent International Developments

Since 2000, there has been a surge in international efforts to use legal instruments to suppress terrorism. On numerous occasions the Security Council has unequivocally condemned terrorism, in all its forms and manifestations, whenever and by whomsoever committed, regardless of motivation.[151] The most recently adopted multilateral international instrument, the International Convention for the Suppression of Acts of Nuclear Terrorism, which was adopted by the General Assembly on 13 April 2005 and which came into force in July 2007, seeks to suppress acts of nuclear terrorism carried out by individuals.[152] Although it does not expressly define 'terrorism' or 'nuclear terrorism', there are elements of a definition in Article 2. It does not apply to offences which are committed within a single state where the alleged offender and the victims are nationals of that state and no other state has the right to exercise jurisdiction.[153] This Convention is a further example of the UN's overall approach to legislating against particular acts which are seemingly terroristic in nature, in this case creating particular offences regarding the possession or use of radioactive or nuclear material or devices.[154] It is important to note that 'the activities of armed forces during an armed conflict' and 'the activities undertaken by military forces of a State in the exercise of their official duties', which are governed by international humanitarian law, are both expressly excluded from the Nuclear Terrorism Convention.[155] That provision has so far been the subject of declarations by two states.[156]

---

151 S/Res/1377 (2001) adopted by the Security Council on 12 November 2001 at its 4413th Meeting; and S/Res/1456 (2003) adopted by the Security Council on 20 January 2003 at its 4688th Meeting; and S/Res/1566 (2004) adopted by the Security Council on 8 October 2004 at its 5053rd meeting. More recently, the current UN Secretary-General, Ban Ki-Moon, condemned the terrorist attack at Glasgow Airport on 2 July 2007 and the attempted attacks in London: see SG/SM/11068, UN Department of Public Information, 'Secretary-General Deplores Terrorist Incidents in Great Britain', 2 July 2007, available at: <http://www.un.org/News/Press/docs/2007/sgsm11068.doc.htm> at 12 June 2008. The Secretary-General reiterated that 'no cause or belief can justify such acts of terrorism'.

152 For general information about this Convention, see the UN Treaty Collection: <http://untreaty.un.org/English/Terrorism/summary.pdf> at 12 June 2008.

153 Nuclear Terrorism Convention, Article 3.

154 Ibid., Article 2.

155 Ibid., Article 4(2). The same definition of the 'military forces of a State' was adopted in the Terrorist Bombings Convention, and the same exclusion for the activities of the armed forces is used in this Convention.

156 See declarations by Egypt and Turkey regarding the exclusion of activities by the armed forces of a state. Egypt's declaration seems to suggest that it considers that actions

At the regional level, two new documents have been adopted since 2000. On 3 June 2002, the Organization of American States (OAS) adopted the Inter-American Convention Against Terrorism.[157] On 15 May 2003, the Council of Europe adopted a Protocol Amending the European Convention on the Suppression of Terrorism.[158] Neither of these regional instruments offers a definition of 'terrorism'. A number of existing UN instruments have been amended or have had protocols adopted in relation to them: the Amendment to the Convention on the Physical Protection of Nuclear Material,[159] the Protocol of 2005 to the Convention for the Suppression of Unlawful Acts Against the Safety of Marine Navigation,[160] and the Protocol of 2005 to the Protocol for the Suppression of Unlawful Acts Against the Safety of Fixed Platforms Located on the Continental Shelf.[161] Many of the existing pre-2001 conventions and protocols have received further ratifications from states that were previously not parties.[162]

UN Draft Comprehensive Convention

The main source of progress in obtaining a definition of 'terrorism' in a universal, international legal instrument has been made via the UN Draft Comprehensive Convention on International Terrorism (referred to here as the Draft Comprehensive

---

of the armed forces of a state should be included and that states can theoretically commit acts of terrorism.

157 Inter-American Convention Against Terrorism, adopted by the General Assembly of the OAS in Bridgetown, Barbados on 3 June 2002, entered into force on 10 July 2003. General information on the treaty is available from the Office of International Law, Organization of America States, Washington DC: <http://www.oas.org/juridico/english/sigs/a-66.html> at 12 June 2008. This Convention seeks to, *inter alia*, prevent the financing of terrorist activities, strengthen border controls and increase law enforcement co-operation. It refers to terrorism as 'a serious threat to democratic values and to international peace and security'. However, it does not define 'terrorism' or a 'terrorist act'.

158 See Council of Europe, 'Protocol Amending the European Convention on the Suppression of Terrorism', ETS No.190, available at: <http://www.conventions.coe.int/Treaty/en/Summaries/Html/190.htm> at 12 June 2008.

159 Adopted on 8 July 2005 by the Conference to Consider Proposed Amendments to the Convention on the Physical Protection of Nuclear Material: see A/Res/60/43, 6 January 2006, 60th Sess., Agenda Item 108.

160 Adopted on 14 October 2005 by the Diplomatic Conference on the Revision of the SUA Treaties (LEG/CONF.15/21): see A/Res/60/43, 6 January 2006, 60th Sess., Agenda Item 108.

161 Ibid.

162 For a list of the total number of parties to each of the 12 UN instruments, as of 15 March 2005, see UN Office on Drugs and Crime, 'Delivering Counter-Terrorism Assistance' (April 2005) Annex I: <http://www.unodc.org/pdf/crime/terrorism/Brochure_GPT_April2005.pdf> at 12 June 2008.

Convention).[163] The Draft Comprehensive Convention was submitted by India on 28 August 2000 and is a revised draft of the version that was submitted by India in 1996. One of the key objectives of this convention is to provide a definition of terrorism.

The Draft Comprehensive Convention has been repeatedly discussed and revised under the guidance of the Ad Hoc Committee established by General Assembly resolution 51/210 of 17 December 1996 (referred to here as the Ad Hoc Committee).[164] The Ad Hoc Committee has experienced considerable difficulty in obtaining agreement on the text of the Draft Comprehensive Convention. While preliminary agreement has been reached on the majority of the 27 articles, three issues remain outstanding: the legal definition of terrorism, the relationship between terrorism and anti-colonialism and national liberation movements and whether the activities of the armed forces of a state, during armed conflict or during the official exercise of their duties, should be excluded.[165] These are the same three issues that the above analysis has shown to have long posed a problem in relation to both UN and regional instruments on terrorism.

A definition of terrorism *per se* is not included in the Draft Comprehensive Convention. Instead, Article 2 defines the offence of committing a terrorist act.[166] The definition in Article 2 also makes it an offence to *attempt* to commit one of the above offences, or to act as an accomplice.[167] A person would also commit an offence if they organised, directed or instigated others to commit an offence;[168] as well as if they aided, abetted, facilitated or counselled the commission of one of the offences in Article 2(1)(a).[169] Somewhat controversially, it would also be an

163 Draft Comprehensive Convention on International Terrorism, UN Doc A/C.6/55/1 (28 August 2000).

164 The official name of this committee is the 'Ad Hoc Committee established by General Assembly resolution 51/210 of 17 December 1996'. It was created by the General Assembly resolution from whence it takes its name: see UN General Assembly, 'Measures to Eliminate International Terrorism', UN Doc A/Res/51/210 (16 January 1997), 88th plenary meeting on 17 December 1996. The decision to establish the Ad Hoc Committee is found in Articles 9–13.

165 See UN Press Release L/2993, 1 February 2002, 'Finalizing Treaty Requires Agreement on "Armed Forces", "Foreign Occupation", Anti-Terrorism Committee Told': <http://www.un.org/News/Press/docs/2002/L2993.doc.htm> at 12 June 2008. For a year-by-year account of progress made on the Draft Comprehensive Convention, see 'Draft Convention on International Terrorism' Centre for Non-Proliferation Studies (as of 11 August 2006): <http://cns.miis.edu/pubs/inven/pdfs/intlterr.pdf#search=%22UN%20Draft%20Convention%20on%20Terrorism%22> at 12 June 2008.

166 Draft Comprehensive Convention, supra n. 163, Article 2(2).

167 Ibid.

168 Ibid., Article 2(3)(a).

169 Ibid., Article 2(3)(b).

offence to contribute 'in any other way'[170] to the commission of one or more of the proscribed offences.

Article 18 would exclude certain activities of armed/military forces. Article 18, and especially the second paragraph, has attracted as much attention from states as has Article 2.[171] The proposed exclusion of the activities of the military forces of a state repeats the exclusions in the Terrorist Bombings and the Nuclear Terrorism Conventions. This is indicative of the UN's recent stance on defining terrorism: it apparently does not consider that acts committed by the armed/military forces of the state should be covered by terrorism instruments.

A Definition of 'Terrorism' – The Way Forward

The term 'terrorism' has not been defined in the Draft Comprehensive Convention, despite the efforts of some states to have it included. The OIC considered that a definition of terrorism was a 'necessary condition for the usefulness and applicability of the convention'.[172] Malaysia, on behalf of the OIC states, proposed that the definition of 'terrorism' and 'terrorist crime' which are contained in the Islamic Conference Convention be imported into Article 1 of the Draft Comprehensive Convention.[173] Lebanon and the Syrian Arab Republic made the same proposal.[174] Côte d'Ivoire also proposed that a definition of 'terrorism' be included in Article 2.[175]

So far, those suggestions have been rejected. The prevailing attitude is that there is no need to define 'terrorism' because Article 2 provides an 'operational definition' of a terrorist act, especially with the use of the phrase 'within the meaning of this Convention'.[176] However, it has also been suggested that in order to take into account the OIC's concerns, Article 2 may be redrafted so as to indicate more clearly that the phrase 'within the meaning of this Convention' referred to terrorist acts.[177] That suggestion has not, as yet, been implemented.

---

170 Ibid., Article 2(3)(c). Human Rights Watch and Amnesty International have both objected to the use of this wide-ranging phrase.

171 Ibid., Article 18.

172 For the views of Malaysia on behalf of the OIC, see its proposals submitted to the Working Group of the Sixth Committee at the 55th session of the General Assembly in connection with the elaboration of a draft comprehensive convention on international terrorism, UN Doc A/C.6/55/WG.1/CRP.30.

173 *Measures to Eliminate International Terrorism, Report of the Working Group*, 55th Sess., Sixth Committee, 19 October 2000; Un Doc A/C.6/55/L.2; Annex III, paragraph 30.

174 Ibid.

175 Ibid, para 26.

176 Draft International Convention, supra n. 163, Article 2.

177 See *Report of the Ad Hoc Committee Established by General Assembly Resolution 51/210 of 17 December 1996*, 5th Sess., General Assembly Official Records, 56th Sess., Supplement No. 37, UN Doc A/56/37. This report, along with all of the other reports of

The tenth session of the Ad Hoc Committee convened in New York from 27 February to 3 March 2006. No consensus was reached on the three key points of disagreement (the definition of terrorism, exclusion of military forces and struggles for self-determination). The eleventh session of the Ad Hoc Committee met in New York on 5, 6 and 15 February 2007. Once again, no consensus was reached although several new amendments were proposed.[178] The most recent session was held on 25 and 26 February and 6 March 2008. The report suggests that progress has stalled: whilst the delegations continue to unequivocally condemn international terrorism in all its forms and manifestation, and continue to stress the need to finalise the Draft Convention, the reality is that there is still considerable distance between them on key issues.[179] Most of the disagreement concerns Draft Article 18 and two issues remain unresolved: the expressed desire to have a clear delineation between those activities governed by international humanitarian law and those covered by the Draft Convention, and the question of the possible impunity of military forces during peacetime.[180] The apparent frustration of the Coordinator of the Draft Convention is apparent in her expression of concern that there may be a 'certain reluctance to seize the moment and move ahead towards the completion of the draft convention'.[181] Although there is supposedly a 'continued interest in completing the draft convention', some delegations took the opportunity to reconfirm that their proposals remained on the table.[182]

Although the process of negotiation has not been completed at the time of writing,[183] it would appear that three significant trends are evident. First, the UN and its Member States have adopted a position of unequivocal condemnation of terrorist tactics, 'even for the most defensible of causes'[184] and, despite the protracted nature of the negotiating process, there seems to be a continuing willingness amongst delegations to reach consensus on a comprehensive terrorism convention.[185] Secondly, the Ad Hoc Committee, which is responsible for steering the negotiations towards a conclusion, maintains that the activities of the

---

the Ad Hoc Committee, can be downloaded from its website, available at: <http://www.un.org/law/terrorism> at 12 June 2008.

178 See *Report of the Ad Hoc Committee Established by General Assembly Resolution 51/210 of 17 December 1996*, 11th Sess., General Assembly Official Records, 62nd Sess., Supplement No. 37 (A/62/37).

179 See *Report of the Ad Hoc Committee Established by General Assembly Resolution 51/210 of 17 December 1996*, 12th Sess., General Assembly Official Records, 63rd Sess., Supplement No. 37 (A/63/37).

180 Ibid., Annex II.

181 Ibid., para A.7 per Maria Telalian (Greece).

182 Ibid., para B.8–10.

183 June 2008.

184 Report of the Secretary-General's High Level Panel on Threats, Challenges and Change, supra n. 13 at 51, para 157.

185 Report of the Ad Hoc Committee Established by General Assembly Resolution 51/210 of 17 December 1996, 12th Sess., supra n. 179.

armed forces of a state should be excluded from the Draft Convention because those forces are already governed by other rules of international law, namely international humanitarian law. The intention to proceed with those exclusions in the Draft Convention has already been signalled in two existing UN conventions on terrorism.[186] That is also the view favoured in the Report of the Secretary-General's High Level Panel on Threats, Challenges and Change[187] and appears to be the solution preferred by the Draft Convention's Coordinator.[188] However, the Coordinator has yet to convince all delegations that Draft Article 18, and especially the new 'without prejudice' clause in paragraph 5, serve only to provide a demarcation between what is covered in the Draft Convention and what is covered by international humanitarian law. Some delegations remain convinced that Article 18 will provide impunity to the military forces of a state and that the Draft Convention will prevent the members of the military forces of a state from being held accountable for committing what would otherwise be terrorist acts.[189] The third and final point is that the Draft Convention is regarded as a criminal law enforcement mechanism and if it comes into force, it will clarify the way in which acts of terrorism should be regarded. It will be argued in Chapter 6 of this text that any act of terrorism is by definition a criminal act, not an act of war, and the Draft Convention would confirm that acts of international terrorism ought to be dealt with by the utilisation of international criminal law tools such as extradition and prosecution. Whilst it is impossible to predict when, or if, agreement will be reached on the Draft Convention, reaching consensus on the text is only the first hurdle: states that disagree with the final text may simply choose not to sign or ratify it and its effectiveness may ultimately rest as much upon the wording of the key articles as upon the particular states that opt to be bound by it.[190]

---

186 The Terrorist Bombings Convention, Article 19 and the Nuclear Terrorism Convention, Article 4.

187 Report of the Secretary-General's High Level Panel on Threats, Challenges and Change, supra n. 13 at 51–2, paras 160–64.

188 Report of the Ad Hoc Committee Established by General Assembly Resolution 51/210 of 17 December 1996, 12th Sess., supra n. 179, Annex II.

189 The Coordinator refutes that by arguing that paragraphs 3 and 4 of Draft Article 18 are merely intended to close any gap in relation to the military forces of a state; they do not make lawful otherwise unlawful acts, but they recognise that other laws apply in such circumstances: ibid., Annex II.

190 A parallel might be drawn with the Convention on Cluster Munitions (CCM) which was adopted in Dublin by 107 states on 30 May 2008. During the signing conference in Oslo, Norway on 3–4 December 2008, 94 states signed the Convention, four of which also ratified it (see the Convention on Cluster Munitions website for signatories and ratifications, available at: <http://www.clusterconvention.org/pages/pages_i/i_statessigning.html> at 8 January 2009). It is significant that although there was unanimous agreement between the delegates at the May conference on the text of the Convention, and thus it was adopted, the US, China, Russia, Israel, India and Pakistan (all major producers and stockpilers of cluster bombs) were absent from the talks and, furthermore, none of those states have become

The evolution of international law pertaining to terrorism suggests that defining 'terrorism' is immensely difficult and is influenced by both legal and political considerations. International lawyers have had much more success in criminalising specific acts, which are considered as manifestations of terrorism, rather than describing and outlawing terrorism *per se*. Even though virtually all acts of terrorism are prohibited in one of the UN instruments, the development of a normative framework against terrorism is still deemed an important, yet thus far elusive, goal. Developments in 2008 and beyond are likely to focus on the adoption of the Draft Convention on International Terrorism and the success of this endeavour will depend on whether the existing disagreements, especially concerning Articles 2 and 18 (relating to the meaning of terrorism, the exclusion of states' armed forces and the right to use force against colonial oppressors or foreign occupying forces) can be overcome. The definitions of 'terrorism' which have been put forward by the Security Council and by the Secretary-General's High Level Panel are likely to form the basis of the definition of terrorism in the comprehensive convention.

Conclusion

This chapter has established the following points. First, terrorism is a tactic, a method of asymmetrical warfare, which has been utilised for millennia. The historical analysis in the first part of the chapter showed that the *sicarii* and the Assassins were probably the first groups to discover that force could be used to greater effect by small groups against the majority and/or ruling group, to achieve the objectives of the former against the latter, when that force was directed against civilians or non-combatants; when it was used at close range such as through the use of hidden daggers in crowded marketplaces; and when the physical act was combined with the wider objective of creating fear within the minds of individuals within the target society.

Secondly, the meaning of 'terrorism' has evolved over time and its current usage is rather different from its etymological origins, which were in the French Reign of Terror. Whereas 'terrorism' was once a term used to describe violence by the state, which carried positive connotations, the above analysis has shown that, despite the above-mentioned dictionary definitions' continued references to those origins,[191] the term in modern usage usually refers to violence by non-state entities, and it is universally regarded as carrying negative connotations.

---

signatories to the CCM. The CCM is currently open for signature and will come into effect after 30 nations have signed and ratified it. The point is that if militarily significant states also choose to ignore the proposed Terrorism Convention, its ultimate usefulness as a criminal enforcement mechanism, and as a benchmark for defining a terrorist act, will be compromised.

191 See discussion above at 39–45.

Thirdly, it has been demonstrated that the term 'terrorism' is full of political meaning and its usage is fluid. Individuals who have been labelled 'terrorists' at one point in time have, at another point, become respected leaders and statesmen. Affixing the label of 'terrorist' on a person or group may sometimes be indicative of nothing more than the labeller's political stance towards that particular person or group. It is also apparent that so-called 'terrorist organisations' perceive themselves very differently to the way in which others perceive them, and determining who is deserving of the label 'terrorist' changes from time-to-time. Its attribution should not be considered an objective and timeless characterisation.

Fourthly, it has been demonstrated that experts in the study of terrorism cannot agree on a definition. Even if analysis is limited to just a few scholars' interpretations, the differences remain significant.[192] This chapter has highlighted some of those differences without even turning to the disparities which exist between different states in their respective legislative definitions, or between government departments and states even within a single jurisdiction, a discussion of which is beyond the scope of this work. Suffice to say that the wider the research net is cast, the more disparities that are unearthed.

This leads into the fifth point, which is that in order to legislate against terrorism, the most successful approach has not been to define 'terrorism' but to define criminal *acts* that target civilians, which are aimed at intimidating a population or influencing a government and that have a wider political or ideological objective than the immediate target.

There may never be universal agreement on the meaning of 'terrorism'. To quote the US's National Counterterrorism Center (NCTC), whose statistics were analysed in the preceding chapter of this book, 'The very definition of terrorism relative to all other forms of political violence is open to debate'; they are convinced that 'there will never be a "bright red line"'.[193] The contentious issue of whether the military forces of a state should be included within the international convention on terrorism is an especially difficult one to resolve, because excluding them would amount to making a judgement that they, by definition, are incapable of committing acts of terrorism (although they may be caught by other provisions of international law). It is suggested that this is a step that many states will find difficult to take. If the military actions of state actors *are* excluded from the international convention on terrorism, that may present some difficulties for states such as New Zealand which have legislation which seemingly allows for the prosecution of terrorist acts in armed conflict.[194]

---

192 See discussion above at 45–48 regarding the definitions favoured by Laquer, Ganor, Erickson, Hoffman and Wardlaw.

193 NCTC, World Incidents Tracking System (WITS), 'Criteria', available at: <http://wits.nctc.gov> at 12 June 2008.

194 For example, New Zealand: see the Terrorism Suppression Act 2002 (NZ) ss 4(1), 5(1)(c) and s 5(4) and compare with the UN's position, discussed above, that only non-state actors ought to be covered by the Draft Comprehensive Convention.

The sixth and final point made in this chapter is that the search for an internationally acceptable definition continues and that defining 'terrorism' is still an important goal for the international community. The Secretary-General's High Level Panel has recommended that a definition of terrorism be reached in order for the UN to be able to exert its moral authority and to 'send an unequivocal message that terrorism is never an acceptable tactic, even for the most defensible of causes'.[195] That may be a highly admirable and inherently sensible objective, but, perhaps more than anything else, this chapter has shown the degree of inconsistency and disagreement that currently exists between scholars and states regarding the meaning of terrorism. One implication that could be drawn from this analysis is that it is bound to be difficult to accurately assess the legality of states' *responses* to terrorism if states and scholars cannot first agree on what terrorism *is*.

195 See Report of the Secretary-General's High Level Panel on Threats, Challenges and Change, supra n. 13 at 51, para 157.

Chapter 4

Evolution of Limitations on the Use of Force: From the League of Nations to the United Nations – 1919–1944

Introduction

This chapter traverses the developments that occurred in relation to the *ius ad bellum* in the inter-war period, from the formation of the League of Nations in 1919 until 1944, immediately prior to the formation of the United Nations. A brief summary of the political climate which formed the backdrop to this period is provided below, followed by a five-part analysis which traces the developments in the use of force generally, the use of force specifically in self-defence, pre-emptive self-defence, forcible measures short of war and non-state actors. The emphasis here is on the primary documents that evidenced developments in those five areas. The objective is to demonstrate the source of the UN Charter prohibitions on the use of force which are discussed in the following chapter and to provide a broader picture of how the limitations on the use of force in self-defence, which were ultimately to find expression in Article 51, were understood prior to the adoption of the Charter. The rationale for undertaking this historical approach stems from the phrase 'inherent right of self-defence' in Article 51, which prompts an inquiry which must necessarily pre-date the Charter.

Of course, development of the *ius ad bellum* had begun long before the inter-war period that is the focus of this chapter. Any comprehensive study of the development of the law in this area would have to take into account the contributions of numerous scholars, from the Greek and Roman scholars of antiquity, such as Plato, Aristotle and Cicero, through to the Christian scholars of the Middle Ages, such as St Ambrose, St Augustine and St Thomas Aquinas, through to the natural law theorists and the positivists of the seventeenth to the nineteenth centuries, a number of whom expressed important opinions on various matters concerning the use of force.[1] A survey of all the relevant contributors to the development of the *ius ad bellum* is beyond the scope of the present work. The focus here is confined to

1 A comprehensive historical analysis is beyond the scope of this work. Some of the works cited herein are useful in providing more historical background; see also Sorabji, R. and Rodin, D. (eds), *The Ethics of War – Shared Problems in Different Traditions* (Aldershot: Ashgate, 2006); Robinson, P., *Just War in Comparative Perspective* (Aldershot; Burlington, VT: Ashgate, 2003).

the inter-war period when the laws which currently constrain states' resort to force began to evolve into a form that is recognisable, and immediately relevant to the questions that will be addressed in Chapters 6 and 7.

There were two quite different normative orientations towards the use of force during the inter-war period. From 1919–28 war was not outlawed: it was permitted but it was regulated via procedural limitations. From 1928–45 war was expressly prohibited except in certain circumstances, that is, in the case of self-defence or with authorisation from the League. That progression from prevention to prohibition becomes evident during the course of the inter-war period.

The Transition from the Nineteenth to the Twentieth century

The eighteenth and nineteenth centuries witnessed the degradation of the concept that war should be restricted by notions of a 'just war' (*bellum iustum*) and the evolution of an unrestricted right of war.[2] That trend continued into the early twentieth century when 'the majority of writers ... following the positivist school, rejected the distinction between just and unjust wars'[3] and 'considered war as an act entirely within the uncontrolled sovereignty of the individual State'.[4] However, the right of war was increasingly confronted by a peace movement which focused on the use of arbitral settlement of disputes.[5] Hague Conferences were held in 1899 and 1907 which highlighted the emergence of a trend towards limiting the right of war. The Hague Conferences resulted in the 1899[6] and 1907[7] Conventions for the Pacific Settlement of International Disputes. The right of war was also seriously challenged by the establishment of the Permanent Court of Arbitration in 1899 and the Central American Court of Justice in 1907. The establishment of these bodies, and a number of other bilateral arbitration conventions and agreements, such as the Bryan treaties, emphasised that war was increasingly being perceived as a last resort, once all other options had been exhausted. That newly evolving

---

2 See Grewe, W., *Epochs of International Law* (1984) (Byers, M. trans. and rev., Berlin; New York: Walter de Gruyter, 2000) 530–34; Alexandrov, S., *Self-Defense Against the Use of Force in International Law* (The Hague: Kluwer Law International, 1996) 9–11.

3 Alexandrov, ibid., 10.

4 Ibid.

5 See Grewe, supra n. 2 at 524–34.

6 International Convention for the Pacific Settlement of International Disputes (Hague I), signed at The Hague on 29 July 1899, entered into force 4 September 1900, UKTS 9 (1901), Cd.798; P. (1902) CXXX, 517; 91 BSP 970; 23 HCT 509; 1907 AJIL Supp 107; 26 Martens (IV) 920; 1 Bevans, 230; 187 CTS, 410.

7 International Convention for the Pacific Settlement of International Disputes (Hague No. I), signed at The Hague on 18 October 1907, entered into force 26 January 1910, UKTS 6 (1971), Cd 4, 575; P (1970–71) XXVIII, 643; 100 BSP, 298; 1908 AJIL Supp, 43; 1 Bevans, 577; 205 CTS, 233.

attitude towards war was expressed in the 1907 Hague Convention for the Pacific Settlement of International Disputes, which did not forbid states from using force but did attempt to limit recourse to force.[8]

Both the 1899 and 1907 Hague Conventions encouraged states to have recourse, as far as circumstances allowed, to the good offices or mediation of one or more friendly powers. Arbitration had its limitations, the most significant of which was the fact that it was not used for settling *armed* disputes between states. The great political conflicts of the nineteenth century were excluded from arbitral settlement and the idea that arbitration could be used for political disputes of this nature did not arise until after 1919.[9] Furthermore, Germany was one state that was suspicious of the British–American-led arbitration movement. Some German scholars and statesmen regarded compulsory arbitration as being incompatible with sovereignty.[10] In any case, after Germany's defeat in World War I, it no longer posed an obstacle to the development of peaceful means of dispute settlement.

In the early 1900s, even before the Hague Conferences, limitations on the use of force by states to recover debt were evolving. The Venezuelan Arbitrations of 1903 laid the foundations for history's first conventional expression of a restriction on the right of states to resort to force.[11] The Venezuelan Arbitrations became the basis of the Porter–Drago Convention, formally known as the Convention Respecting the Limitation of the Employment of Force for the Recovery of Contract Debts (Hague II), signed in 1907.[12] Although states retained the right to resort to war if the debtor-state failed to reply or submit to a request for arbitration, or perform a settlement, and thus the limitations were rather modest, nevertheless, these developments were important in qualifying an absolute right to war.[13]

---

8 'With a view to obviating as far as possible recourse to force in the relations between States, the Contracting Powers agree to use their best efforts to ensure the pacific settlement of international differences': Part I, Article I, the Hague Convention of 1907 for the Pacific Settlement of International Disputes, ibid.

9 The problems associated with the unification of Germany and Italy, the question of the Balkans, and the political decisions that led to the Crimean War, the Spanish–American War, the Boer War and the Russian–Japanese War could not be removed from the world stage by way of arbitration: see Grewe, supra n. 2 at 523.

10 Koskenniemi, M., *The Gentle Civilizer of Nations – The Rise and Fall of International Law 1870–1960* (Cambridge: Cambridge University Press, 2002) 211–12.

11 Rossi, C., 'Jus ad Bellum in the Shadow of the 20th Century' (1994) 15 *New York Law School Journal of International and Comparative Law* 49 at 51.

12 Convention Respecting the Limitation of the Employment of Force for the Recovery of Contract Debts (Hague II), signed at The Hague on 18 October 1907, 36 Stat. 2241, Treaty Series 537, text available online at: <http://www.yale.edu/lawweb/avalon/lawofwar/hague072.htm> at 12 June 2008; also reprinted in Scott, J. (ed.), *The Reports to the Hague Conferences of 1899 and 1907* (Oxford: Clarendon Press, 1917): <http://www.worldcat.org/oclc/216411080&ht=edition> at 489.

13 Rossi, supra n. 11 at 60.

The Resort to Force

Covenant of the League of Nations

The delegates at the Paris Peace Conference of 1919 were determined to implement measures that would prevent a war of such magnitude as the First World War from occurring again.[14] Thus, the main objective for which the League of Nations was created was the *prevention of war*.[15] As expressed in the Covenant of the League of Nations, that objective was to be achieved via a tripartite approach: limiting the resort to war in principle, making any act or threat of war a matter of concern to the League and establishing a set of procedures for dealing with such threats. Those three aspects of the Covenant are discussed below.

As for the first element, the Covenant was not an attempt to *prohibit war*, but to provide *safeguards against war*.[16] The Covenant stated that the contracting parties, 'in order to promote international co-operation and to achieve international peace and security' would 'accept obligations not to resort to war'.[17] Whether war was 'legal' or 'illegal' therefore depended on whether the elaborate set of procedures for pacific settlement had been followed. The key articles regarding the recourse to force were Articles 10–16. There was no general prohibition on the resort to force and states were permitted to take such action as they considered necessary once the procedures in the Covenant designed to achieve a peaceful settlement had first been applied (Article 15).

The second feature of the Covenant which aimed to prevent war was the Article 11 provision, which made *war, or the threat of war, a matter of concern to the entire League*.[18] The League had to 'take any action that may be deemed wise

14 Drummond, E., *Ten Years of World Co-Operation* (Geneva: Secretariat of the League of Nations, 1930): <http://www.worldcat.org/oclc/492220> 19.

15 For a general history of the League of Nations, see Walters, F., *A History of the League of Nations* (London: Oxford University Press, 1952); Dexter, B., *The Years of Opportunity: The League of Nations 1920–1926* (New York: Viking Press, 1967); and Nussbaum, A., *A Concise History of the Law of Nations* (New York: Macmillan, 1947) 251–61. For a list of general studies of the Covenant, see Brownlie, I., *International Law and the Use of Force by States* (Oxford: Clarendon Press, 1963) 473. For a record of the work done by the League during its first ten years of existence, see *Ten Years of World Co-Operation*, supra n. 14.

16 'The Members of the League did not believe that they could totally prevent war. They only wished to apply the principle "no one can administer justice to himself"': Statement of Mr Rolin (Belgium), Records of the Second Assembly (1921), Meetings of Committees, Minutes of the First Committee, cited in Alexandrov, supra n. 2 at 30.

17 Covenant of the League of Nations, as part of the Treaty of Peace with Germany (Treaty of Versailles); signed 29 June 1919, entered into force 10 January 1920; 2 Bevans 48, 225 CTS 189. This objective is set out in the preamble to the Covenant.

18 Covenant of the League of Nations, Article 11. It was a significant change because war was no longer 'to have the aspect of a private duel', rather a breach of the peace was

and effectual to safeguard the peace of nations'.[19] This was a significant change because war was no longer 'to have the aspect of a private duel' between states.[20] A breach of the peace was thereafter perceived to affect the whole community of nations.

The *third* significant element was the Covenant's creation of a *system for the peaceful settlement of disputes*. If any dispute arose which was 'likely to lead to a rupture'[21] amongst the Members of the League, they would either submit the matter to arbitration or to inquiry by the League's Council. The Members also agreed to a 'cooling-off' period and to hold back from resorting to war for three months.[22] Although the concept of a cooling-off period was not new,[23] the overall procedure for seeking peaceful settlement of disputes was novel in its comprehensiveness.

Article 13 specified which disputes were 'generally suitable' for arbitration or judicial settlement. The Members agreed to carry out an award or judgement in good faith, and not to resort to war against a Member that complied with the award or decision. If disputes were not referred to arbitration or judicial settlement, they had to be referred to the Council, whose task it was 'to endeavour to effect a settlement of the dispute.'[24] If the Council's report was carried unanimously, Members agreed not to go to war with any party to the dispute that complied with its recommendations. However, if the Council failed to reach a unanimous report, excluding the parties to the dispute, Members had the right to take any action that they considered necessary for the maintenance of right and justice.[25]

In summary, the Covenant was a significant development in the use of international law to restrict states' resort to force. The League's first Secretary-General observed in 1929 that 'the mere creation of the League and its continued existence ... is one of those great facts which invariably stand out as landmarks in the history of the world'.[26] By the time the League collapsed, more than 60 international disputes had been brought before it. During its first ten years, 30 disputes were brought before the League and of those, only eight disputants

seen to affect the whole community: Brownlie, supra n. 15 at 57.

19 Covenant of the League of Nations, Article 11; see also Alexandrov, supra n. 2 at 30–31.

20 'Any act or threat of war, whether immediately affecting any of the Members of the League or not, is hereby declared a matter of concern to the whole League ...': Covenant of the League of Nations, Article 11.

21 Article 12.

22 Ibid.

23 The Treaties for the Advancement of Peace, concluded by the United States in 1913 and 1914 (generally known as the 'Bryan Treaties') provided for a cooling-off period of 12 months during which time an investigation of and a report on a dispute would occur. The parties agreed not to declare war or begin hostilities during the investigation and report.

24 Covenant of the League of Nations, Article 15.

25 Ibid., para 7.

26 Drummond, E., 'Foreword', in *Ten Years of World Co-Operation*, supra n. 14 at vi.

resorted to hostilities or war.[27] However, the Covenant ultimately failed to achieve its objective of preventing large-scale warfare. The failure may have been partly due to defects in its framing, such as its theoretical allowance for states to resort to war after the prescribed interval had been observed[28] or if the Council was unable to reach a unanimous decision,[29] or the fact that the Covenant did not apply to non-Members unless they agreed to be bound.[30] Despite the presence of those 'gaps' or 'loopholes', in practice they did not have serious consequences and the major reason for the Covenant's failure was more likely due to political factors.[31] The major hostilities of the period[32] occurred not because Members took advantage of the loopholes, but because the Members ignored the obligations in the Covenant altogether. Members had legal powers at their disposal which they opted not to employ, thus it has been observed that: 'States did not exploit the loopholes, instead they simply knocked down the structure of the League.'[33]

Draft Treaty of Mutual Assistance

Following the League of Nations' Covenant, a number of treaties were drafted which attempted to increase security by further restricting the resort to force. Regardless of whether they eventually came into force or not, each treaty made its own attempt to close the loopholes that existed in the Covenant. The Draft Treaty of Mutual Assistance of 1923 declared, *inter alia*, that aggressive war was an international crime and imposed on the parties an obligation not to commit such a crime. Although the Treaty did not define an act of aggression, it was forwarded to the governments with a commentary which stated that although there was no definite technical criterion of aggression, that it might be advisable for the Council to fix a neutral zone which the parties would be forbidden to cross, a refusal to obey being considered a factor in deciding which was the aggressor.[34] The difficulty of determining which party was the aggressor was acknowledged by the League of Nations' Third Committee:[35] 'Under the conditions of modern warfare, it would seem impossible to decide even in theory what constitutes an act of aggression.'

---

27 United Nations Office at Geneva, Library/Archives, available at: <http://www.unog.ch/80256EE60057D930/(httpPages)/C3CC141ADEC42C68C1256F32002E983B?OpenDocument> at 12 June 2008.

28 Covenant of the League of Nations, Article 15, para 7.

29 Ibid., Article 15(6).

30 Ibid., Article 17.

31 Brownlie, supra n. 15 at 60.

32 Such as the Japanese conquest of Manchuria in 1931–32, the Italian conquest of Abyssinia in 1935–36 and perhaps also the Spanish Civil War from 1936–39.

33 McCoubrey, H. and White, N., *International Law and Armed Conflict* (Brookfield, VT: Dartmouth Publishing, 1992) 21.

34 *Ten Years of World Co-Operation*, supra n. 14 at 63.

35 *Commentary on the Definition of a Case of Aggression*, Records of the Fourth Assembly (1923), Meetings of Committees, Minutes of the Third Committee, 16–23 April

Ultimately, discretion was left to the Council to decide whether a specific act amounted to aggression. This approach was later adopted in the UN Charter.[36] The Draft Treaty of Mutual Assistance met with opposition from both within and outside the League. The US and the Soviet Union, both non-Member States, submitted replies pointing out their reasons for opposing it, whilst Great Britain, a Member State, also opposed it.[37] Other states pointed out that the determination of an aggressor was uncertain, both on account of the Council's unanimity rule and because of the absence of sufficient criteria.[38]

Geneva Protocol

In the wake of the failure of the Draft Treaty, there was increasing support in the Assembly for the notion that a refusal to submit to arbitration could be the criterion for defining aggression. The 1924 Protocol for the Pacific Settlement of International Disputes, also known as the Geneva Protocol, represented the interconnectedness of the concepts of security, disarmament and arbitration.[39] Its main goal was to close the gaps left by Article 15(7) of the Covenant which, in the case of a non-unanimous report by the Council, allowed the Members to resort to force after an interval of three months.

The Protocol came close to arriving at a *general prohibition on aggressive war* in the preamble:[40] 'Recognising the solidarity of the members of the international community: Asserting that a war of aggression constitutes a violation of this solidarity and an international crime.'

Article 8 declared that the signatory states would undertake to 'abstain from any act which might constitute a threat of aggression against another State'.[41] Arbitration was the cornerstone of the system set forth in the Protocol; it provided for the compulsory arbitration of all disputes.[42] Article 10 defined the aggressor as a state that was unwilling to submit its case to arbitration.[43] There was a presumption

---

1923, Annex 4.

36 See discussion in Alexandrov, supra n. 2 at 42. For analysis of attempts to define aggression in international law after World War I, see Wright, W., 'The Concept of Aggression in International Law' (1935) *AJIL* 373.

37 *Ten Years of World Co-Operation*, supra n. 14 at 65.

38 Ibid., 64–5.

39 Ibid., 67–8.

40 Protocol for the Pacific Settlement of International Disputes, 1924, Preamble, available at: <http://www.worldcourts.com/pcij/eng/documents/1924.10.02_protocol.htm> at 12 June 2008.

41 Ibid., Article 8.

42 Ibid., Article 4.

43 Ibid., Article 10. This method of defining aggression was viewed by the drafters as the solution to the earlier difficulties that had been encountered in the Draft Treaty of Mutual Assistance.

of aggression which would remain in place until evidence to the contrary was brought before the Council.[44]

Although the Geneva Protocol was adopted by the Assembly of the League on 2 October 1924, it never came into force. It was signed by 19 nations and ratified by one.[45] However, Great Britain, among others, opposed its provisions for compulsory arbitration[46] and instead expressed a preference for the text of the Covenant as it stood, supplemented by 'special arrangements in order to meet special needs'.[47]

Although neither the Treaty for Mutual Assistance nor the Protocol came into force, they are noteworthy for the spirit which they represented, to strengthen the Covenant and further restrict states' resort to war. The debate that the Protocol provoked resulted in further negotiations between states which were concerned with concluding arbitration conventions and treaties of mutual security 'in the spirit of the Covenant of the League of Nations and in harmony with the principles of the Protocol'.[48] The Locarno agreements were a direct result of that discussion.

Locarno Treaty

Limitations on the resort to force by the major European powers were taken a step further in the Locarno Agreements, signed in October 1925, which were ratified and entered into force in 1926.[49] Although they were negotiated outside of the League, they were a direct result of the ideas which had evolved during the previous years by the organs of the League. The parties to the Treaty of Mutual Guarantee (Germany, Belgium, France, Great Britain and Italy), usually referred to as the Locarno Treaty, were anxious to 'satisfy the desire for security and protection which animates people upon whom fell the scourge of the war of 1914–1918'.[50] The Locarno Treaty did not just refer to 'war' or 'aggression'; it went further to

44 Geneva Protocol, Article 10.

45 The Protocol was signed by Albania, Belgium, Brazil, Bulgaria, Chile, Czechoslovakia, Estonia, Finland, France, Greece, Haiti, Kingdom of the Serbs, Croats and Slovenes (Yugoslavia), Latvia, Liberia, Paraguay, Poland, Portugal, Spain and Uruguay; it was ratified by Czechoslovakia: League of Nations, Secratariat Section, *Illustrated Album of the League of Nations* (Geneva: Atar, 1926) 41.

46 Foreign and Commonwealth Office, Official Documents, *Historical and Research Papers: History of the FCO.*

47 *Illustrated Album of the League of Nations*, supra n. 45 at 42.

48 This phrase is from the speech of the Spanish delegate, Mr Quiñones de León, in the Sixth Assembly: reproduced in *Ten Years of World Co-Operation* supra n14 at 76–7.

49 A number of agreements were signed at Locarno, the principal one of interest here is the Treaty of Mutual Guaranty (sic) Between Germany, Belgium, France, Great Britain and Italy, initialled at Locarno on 16 October 1925, signed at London on 1 December 1925; deposited with the Secretariat of the League of Nations on 14 December 1925; entered into force 14 December 1926: 54 LNTS 289.

50 Ibid., preamble.

include, at least between some of the parties, 'attack' and 'invasion':[51] 'Germany and Belgium, and also Germany and France, mutually undertake that they will in no case attack or invade each other or resort to war against each other.'

That prohibition broadened the existing restrictions on war but it was subject to exceptions: legitimate self-defence, action authorised by the League or if the League failed to reach a unanimous decision to settle the conflict.[52] The Locarno Treaty, and the various arbitration agreements that were entered into at the Locarno Conference, were evidence of a general desire to prevent states, as far as possible, from using force against one another to settle their disputes and to encourage states to use arbitral and judicial tribunals to settle their differences.

Pact of Paris

The failure of the Draft Treaty of Mutual Assistance and the Geneva Protocol to gain widespread support prompted some states to pursue a new, multilateral agreement. France was particularly interested in pursuing an agreement with the US and the negotiations between them eventually resulted in the signing of the General Pact for the Renunciation of War. The agreement, also known as the Kellogg–Briand Pact or the Pact of Paris, was initially signed by 11 states.[53] The major flaw in the Covenant of the League of Nations, namely, its failure to prohibit war as a means of solving inter-state disputes, was remedied in the Pact of Paris.[54]

The Pact of Paris consisted of only three operative articles, the third being of a technical nature. In Article 1 the parties renounced war as a method of solving international controversies and renounced it as an instrument of national policy in their relations with one another.[55] This was a significant development because it was the first time that a treaty had come into force that contained a general prohibition on the recourse to war.[56] By virtue of this article, the Pact of Paris was 'an instrument of outstanding importance … [because it declared] in the most categorical terms the absolute illegality of war in pursuit of national policies'.[57]

51 Ibid., Article 2.

52 Ibid., Article 2(1), 2(2) and 2(3) respectively.

53 General Treaty Providing for the Renunciation of War as an Instrument of National Policy (Pact of Paris), signed 27 August 1928; entered into force on 24 July 1929; 94 LNTS 57. Eleven states initially signed: Australia, Canada, Czechoslovakia, Germany, India, the Irish Free State, Italy, New Zealand, South Africa, the United Kingdom and the United States. Four states added their support before it was proclaimed: Belgium, France, Japan and Poland. Sixty-two nations eventually signed the pact.

54 Ibid.

55 Ibid., Article 1.

56 The Geneva Protocol of 1924 also contained such a provision but it never gained enough ratifications to enter into force.

57 Brierly, J., *The Law of Nations* (Waldock, C. rev.) 6th edn (London: Oxford University Press, 1963) 408–9.

In Article 2 the parties agreed to submit all their disputes or conflicts to peaceful settlement.[58] This was not a novel concept, but it underlined the parties' desire, as expressed in several earlier agreements, to resolve their disputes by peaceful means. The Pact of Paris thereby closed some of the procedural loopholes in the Covenant, by forbidding outright the use of war as a tool of national policy, not just until the parties had complied with the Covenant's framework.

Although the Pact of Paris was regarded at the time of its signing as a major milestone, it did not achieve its aim of preventing war. One of the signatories noted that 'its moral value is greater than its practical significance'.[59] One of its major defects was that it provided no means of enforcement against parties that violated its provisions. In addition, it did not address the use of force in self-defence. The need to determine precisely what type of war was outlawed by the Pact of Paris became apparent at the trials of alleged war criminals subsequent to the conclusion of World War II. The Principles of the Nuremberg Tribunal stated that 'crimes against the peace' were punishable under international law, and that 'crimes against the peace' included the preparation, planning and initiation of wars of aggression.[60] The Nuremberg Tribunal adopted the view that the Pact of Paris had outlawed *aggressive* war.[61] It found that wars of aggression were not only *illegal*, but by virtue of the Pact of Paris and other supporting treaties and declarations, they were also *criminal*. It found that 'certain of the defendants planned and waged aggressive wars against 12 nations, and were therefore guilty of war crimes'.[62] The Nuremberg Judgment confirmed that by the time that World War II broke out, waging an aggressive war was illegal and criminal in international law.

Post-Pact of Paris Developments: 1929–44

Subsequent to the Pact of Paris, a number of treaties were concluded which reaffirmed the obligation to refrain from aggressive war.[63] The Pact was often referred to in state practice and states made an effort to show that their use of

---

58 Pact of Paris, Article 2.

59 Dr Gustav Stresemann, Germany's Minister of Foreign Affairs, quoted in Bendiner, E., *A Time for Angels – The Tragicomic History of the League of Nations* (New York: Alfred A. Knopf, 1975) 228.

60 Principles of the Nuremberg Tribunal, 1950, Principle VI (a).

61 Judgment of the International Military Tribunal for the Trial of German Major War Criminals, Nuremberg, 30 September and 1 October 1946, 'The Charter Provisions', available at The Avalon Project at Yale Law School: <http://www.yale.edu/lawweb/avalon/imt/proc/judlawch.htm> at 12 June 2008.

62 Ibid.

63 For example, treaties of non-aggression were signed between Estonia and the USSR (4 May 1932); Poland and the USSR (25 July 1932); Germany, France, Great Britain and Italy (15 July 1933); Romania and Turkey (17 October 1933); Yugoslavia and Turkey (27 November 1933); Greece, Romania, Turkey and Yugoslavia (9 February 1934): see Brownlie, supra n. 15 at 76, n. 1 for a comprehensive list.

force was permissible self-defence, rather than a violation of the Pact.[64] Statesmen considered the Pact as a source of legal obligations in their communications with one another.[65]

In the post-Pact of Paris period, legal developments regarding the *ius ad bellum* moved in three directions. First, there was an attempt to extend the prohibition in the Pact beyond 'war' to include *armed force in general*. States were aware that not only resort to war needed to be controlled, but also resort to forcible measures short of war, such as reprisals.[66] Second, there was an attempt to include in the prohibition *threats* to resort to force. These two developments were incorporated into the Budapest Articles of Interpretation of the Pact of Paris.[67] Whether those Articles had any effect on the legal limitations on the recourse to force is open to debate.[68] It was not until the UN Charter that the term 'war' was abandoned, but the Budapest Articles evinced an increasing awareness that there were still significant gaps that required urgent attention.

Thirdly, developments occurred during the latter years of this epoch regarding the *definition of aggression*. There is a close relationship between defining aggression and self-defence. Kellogg described the search for a definition of aggression in relation to a definition of self-defence as the 'identical question approached from the other side'.[69] In 1933, Conventions for the Definition of Aggression were signed which defined the aggressor as the first state to commit any

64 For example, following hostilities between China and the USSR, the latter claimed that its forces were acting in self-defence and not in violation of the Pact. The same argument was made by Japan in relation to China in 1931. It was cited in the dispute between Peru and Colombia over the presence of Peruvian forces in Colombian territory in 1933. During the Italian–Ethiopian conflict, the obligations of the parties to the Pact were referred to in a report adopted by the Council of the League in 1935.

65 For an account of the role that the Pact played in state practice from 1938 to 1942, see Brownlie, supra n. 15 at 105.

66 See discussion below at 92–94 under the heading 'Forcible Measures Short of War'.

67 Budapest Articles of Interpretation, approved by the International Law Association, 8 September 1934, Report of the 38th Conference (Budapest, 6–10 September 1934) at 66–70; see also Hudson, M., 'The Budapest Resolutions of 1934 on the Briand–Kellogg Pact of Paris' (1935) 29 *AJIL* 92.

68 Lauterpacht doubts that they had any legal effect on the interpretation of the Pact because the parties to the Pact were aware of the limitations of the term 'war', and opted for it anyway: Lauterpacht, E., 'The Pact of Paris and the Budapest Articles of Interpretation' (1935) 20 *Transactions of the Grotius Society* 178 at 197–201. Viscount Sankey, in debate in the House of Lords on 20 February 1925, described the International Law Association as a 'purely private and unofficial conference' and denied that its views had any legal effect: see Bowett, D., *Self-Defence in International Law* (New York: Praeger, 1958) 136.

69 'Express recognition by treaty of this inalienable right, however, gives rise to the same difficulty encountered in any effort to define aggression. It is the identical question approached from the other side': see 'The Secretary of State to the Ambassador in France (Herrick), 23 April 1928' in US Department of State, *Foreign Relations of the United States,*

of the following acts: (i) declaration of war; (ii) armed invasion, with or without a declaration of war; (iii) attack on another state's territory, navy or airforce; (iv) naval blockade; (v) aid to armed bands formed on its own territory and invading another state or refusal, despite demands, to take all possible measures to deprive the armed bands of aid and protection.[70] This definition of aggression was also accepted in the Protocol-Annex of the Balkan Entente[71] and a similar definition was adopted in the Saadabad Pact of 1937.[72] Although the Conventions for the Definition of Aggression did not expressly reserve the right of self-defence, the right presumably arose whenever one of the above acts of aggression occurred.

These instruments sought to encompass a much wider range of aggressive activity than the Covenant or the Pact, which only condemned the recourse to 'war'. Although some of the above-mentioned conventions were multilateral, they lacked the coverage that the Covenant and Pact had attracted.[73] Nevertheless, they indicated the direction in which the UN Charter would later move, towards expanding the prohibition of war, beyond declared war, to all uses of force.

Self-defence

Covenant of the League of Nations

The Covenant did not mention the right of states to use force in self-defence. As to why the Covenant failed to expressly reserve a right of self-defence, Bowett suggests that it was possibly because it was deemed unnecessary:[74] '[P]ursuant to the Covenant … defensive war is never prohibited … the military defence of a country is not only a right but even a duty for a member state of the League.'

General, 1928 Volume I at 36–7, at: <http://images.library.wisc.edu/FRUS/EFacs/1928v01/reference/frus.frus1928v01.i0006.pdf>.

70 Convention for the Definition of Aggression, signed at London on 3, 4 and 5 July 1933; signed at London on 2 July 1933, ratified by Afghanistan, Estonia, Latvia, Persia, Poland, Romania, Soviet Union and Turkey, acceded to by Finland, 147 LNTS 67; 148 LNTS 79 and 148 LNTS 211, see Article 2; text available online at: <http://www.letton.ch/lvx_33da.htm> at 12 June 2008. See also the discussion in Brownlie, supra n. 15 at 247–8; and Alexandrov, supra n. 2 at 72–3.

71 Signed at Athens on 9 February 1934; 153 LNTS 156; Brownlie, supra n. 15 at 248.

72 Signed at Tehran, 8 July 1937, 190 LNTS 21. The Saadabad Pact did not include support for armed bands and naval blockades in its definition of aggression, but it did include aid and assistance to an aggressor.

73 The Conventions for the Definition of Aggression entered into force in 1933 and 1934 between Afghanistan, Estonia, Finland, Latvia, Persia, Poland, Romania, Turkey and the USSR.

74 See Bowett, supra n. 68 at 124.

Brownlie also supports the conclusion that members did not consider it necessary to explicitly reserve a right of self-defence: 'it was universally agreed that the "right of legitimate defence" was *impliedly reserved* by members.'[75] Some states regarded the right to self-defence as inherent and thus unaffected by the Covenant,[76] whilst others, such as the US, were probably of the view that the use of force in self-defence was a purely political judgement, for individual states to make, and that positive law could not restrict it. That interpretation can be drawn from the position adopted by the US in relation to the Pact of Paris.[77]

Draft Treaty of Mutual Assistance

The 1923 Draft Treaty of Mutual Assistance was the first treaty of this era to seriously address the aggressive/defensive war distinction. As noted already, the Draft Treaty attempted to limit resort to force by declaring aggressive war an international crime. The issue then arose as to how 'aggressive war' should be defined. Although the Draft Treaty did not contain a definition of 'aggression', it was forwarded to governments with a commentary on this issue.[78] The old test of aggression, such as a military mobilisation or a violation of a frontier, had lost its value; instead, it was thought that the test ought to cover 'all measures that give evidence to an *intention* to go to war … securing decisive advantages to the aggressor unless action be taken'.[79]

Geneva Protocol

The Draft Treaty was followed by the Geneva Protocol which almost provided a self-defence exception to the general prohibition on aggression:[80]

> [The signatory states] agree in *no case to resort to war with one another* or against a state which, if the occasion arises, accepts all the obligations hereinafter set out,

75 Report to the Assembly by the First Commission, 1931, *LNOJ*, Spec. Supp. No 94; A. 1931 C.I. Annex 18, point 5 of the report; also see Brownlie, supra n. 15 at 61.

76 In 1920, the delegate of the Serb-Croat-Slovene State opposed a proposal that certain territory should be demilitarised, referring to the right of self-defence under the Covenant of the League: *Documents on British Foreign Policy, 1919–1939*, First Series, vol. II, no. 67 at 821; also see comments in Alexandrov, supra n. 2 at 37.

77 The US Secretary of State Kellogg wrote (with regard to the Kellogg–Briand Treaty) that every nation was free at all times and regardless of any treaty provisions to defend its territory from attack or invasion, and it alone was competent to decide whether circumstances required recourse to war in self-defence: see Note of 23 June 1928, as quoted in Bowett, supra n. 68 at 133.

78 *Commentary on the Definition of a Case of Aggression*, Records of the Fourth Assembly (1923), Meetings of Committees, Minutes of the Third Committee at 206–8.

79 Ibid.

80 Geneva Protocol, Article 2.

> *except in case of resistance to acts of aggression* or when acting in agreement with the Council or the Assembly of the League of Nations in accordance with the provisions of the Covenant and of the present Protocol. (Emphasis added)

Whilst the above provision reserved the right to use force in case of 'resistance to acts of aggression',[81] it did not explicitly mention the right to use force in self-defence because the drafters did not think it was necessary to expressly include it. In a preliminary report, two of the national representatives to the League of Nations, Mr Politis from Greece and Mr Benes from Czechoslovakia, stated:[82]

> The prohibition affects only aggressive war. It does not, of course, extend to defensive war. The right of legitimate self-defence continues, as it must, to be respected. The State attacked retains complete liberty to resist by all means in its power any acts of aggression of which it may be the victim. Without waiting for the assistance which it is entitled to receive from the international community, it may and should at once defend itself with its own force.

That was a clear endorsement that the right to use force in self-defence continued, unaffected by its lack of specific protection in the Protocol. It also emphasized that the right to self-defence was triggered by 'acts of aggression', the meaning of which was alluded to in Article 10 of the Protocol. An 'aggressor' was defined there as a state which resorted to war in violation of the Covenant or the Protocol.[83] In the event of hostilities breaking out, any state would be presumed the aggressor until the Council had made a unanimous decision to the contrary.[84] Any state that was a victim of an act of aggression could expect to receive the support of all other Member States in a system of collective security.[85] Thus, Article 2 of the Geneva Protocol came close to recognising the concept of legitimate self-defence in positive international law, and its formula foreshadowed the regime of the UN Charter, allowing the use of force only in self-defence or under the authority of an international organ.[86]

---

81 Ibid.

82 Records of the Fifth Assembly (1924), Plenary Meetings, at 483; see also Alexandrov, supra n. 2 at 43–4.

83 Geneva Protocol, Article 10: 'Every State which resorts to war in violation of the undertakings contained in the Covenant or in the present Protocol is an aggressor.'

84 Ibid.

85 Ibid., Article 11.

86 Similar observations are made by Alexandrov, supra n. 2 at 43; Brownlie, supra n. 15 at 70; and see Bowett, supra n. 68 at 126.

Locarno Treaty

The following year, the Locarno Treaty went a step further than the Geneva Protocol and expressly reserved the right of self-defence. The mutual undertaking by Germany, France, Great Britain, Belgium and Italy that they would not attack or invade each other or resort to war against each other was subject to the proviso that it would not apply in the case of the exercise of legitimate self-defence.[87] The assembling of forces in the demilitarised zone would constitute an unprovoked act of aggression, which would also trigger the right to use force in legitimate self-defence.[88]

Pact of Paris

The 1928 Pact of Paris, possibly the most important treaty of the inter-war period, condemned the recourse to war for the settling of international controversies, but it did not mention the right of states to use force in self-defence. However, formal notes were exchanged between the signatories prior to the conclusion of the Pact, which indicated the respective states' positions on this issue.[89] Briand wanted to specifically reserve the right to use force in self-defence[90] but the US position was that it was unnecessary to make an express reservation:[91]

> There is nothing in the American draft of an anti-war treaty which restricts or impairs in any way the right of self-defense. *That right is inherent in every sovereign state and is implicit in every treaty. Every nation is free at all times and regardless of treaty provisions to defend its territory from attack or invasion* and it alone is competent to decide whether circumstances require recourse to war in self-defense. (Emphasis added)

The comments of Germany, Great Britain and Japan revealed their agreement with the US position.[92] Ultimately, the American version was the one adopted and the French concerns to have the right of self-defence incorporated in the text were

---

87 Locarno Treaty, Article 2(1).

88 Ibid.

89 On the negotiating history, see Shotwell, J., *War as an Instrument of Public Policy* (Paris: A. Pedone, 1928); Bowett, supra n. 68 at 132ff; Brownlie, supra n. 15 at 74ff; and Alexandrov, supra n. 2 at 52ff.

90 Article 1 of the revised French draft contained several reservations to the renunciation of war: legitimate self-defence, action under the Locarno Treaties and under the Covenant: French Draft, 20 April 1928 in *Foreign Relations of the United States, 1928-I* at 33; Alexandrov, supra n. 2 at 54, n. 14.

91 Note of 23 June 1928 supra n. 69; see also Brownlie, supra n. 15 at 80–92; and Alexandrov, supra n. 2 at 54.

92 For example, see Miller, H., *The Peace Pact of Paris: A Study of the Kellogg–Briand Treaty* (New York: G.P. Putnam's Sons, 1928); also Bowett, supra n. 68 at 133.

ignored. Even though there was no express reservation of the right of self-defence, the parties agreed that it remained and was not restricted by the Pact. Secretary of State Kellogg's explanation regarding the existence of the right of self-defence, as set out in the Note of 23 June 1928, was circulated to 14 governments.[93] The recipients notified acceptance of the US's text and expressly accepted the US's interpretation of it.[94] Thus, the reservations, if not the text, of the Pact of Paris, reserved the right to resort to war in self-defence.[95]

Meaning of Self-defence in the Pact of Paris: Les Travaux Préparatoires

To determine the meaning of the right of self-defence that the signatories reserved for themselves, recourse must be had to *les travaux préparatoires*. There was extensive diplomatic correspondence prior to the signing of the Pact that provides insights into the meaning of self-defence as it existed in international law at that time.[96] Although the notes received from various governments were unilateral statements, lacking the force of formal reservations, they are generally considered to be 'an authentic and binding commentary on and interpretation of the text of the Treaty'.[97] However, it is difficult to determine what the term 'right of legitimate self-defence' meant, because each state gave different accounts of what 'right' they considered they were reserving.[98] That difficulty was noted by a US Senator at the time as a weakness in the treaty itself.[99]

---

93 Australia, Belgium, Canada, Czechoslovakia, France, Germany, Great Britain, India, the Irish Free State, Italy, Japan, New Zealand, Poland and South Africa.

94 For example, see the Czechoslovak Note of 20 July 1928, which noted the reservations and stated that the right of self-defence is in no way weakened or restricted by the proposed treaty and that 'each power is entirely free to defend itself according to its will and its necessities against attack and foreign invasion.': see Brownlie, supra n. 15 at 237.

95 Brownlie claims the parties' decision to keep the exception out of the text 'was to deceive public opinion': ibid., 90.

96 Reference to the *travaux préparatoires* is essential to understand why the Pact does not refer to the right of self-defence. It would appear that the signatories did not believe that the prohibition on war applied to self-defence, therefore, no formal reservation of self-defence was necessary: see Report of the Senate Committee on Foreign Relations, *Congressional Record*, 70th Congress, 2nd Session, 15 January 1929 at 1730, as cited in Alexandrov, supra n. 2 at 58.

97 Miller, supra n. 92 at 111; see also Wright, Q., 'The Interpretation of Multilateral Treaties' (1929) 23 *AJIL* 94 at 104 and 106.

98 Contrast the statement of Czechoslovakia, supra n. 94, with that of the Irish Free State: 'the pact does not affect in any way the right of legitimate defense inherent in each State'; Japan, which simply reserved the 'right of self-defence' and South Africa, which reserved the obligations of the Covenant and the 'natural right of legitimate self-defence': Brownlie, supra n. 15 at 236–7; Alexandrov, supra n. 2 at 52–62.

99 Senator Borah, Chairman of the US Senate Committee on Foreign Relations: '[W]e must admit that the fact that every nation had a right to determine for itself what constitutes self-defense, and how it should apply, is a weakness upon the part of the treaty.'

The signatories agreed that the right of self-defence was an 'inherent' or 'inalienable' or 'natural right'[100] that remained untouched and unimpaired by the Pact,[101] and they agreed that the right to use force in self-defence could be exercised when a state was *attacked by another country* or *when it was subject to invasion.*[102] Although the right to self-defence was not expressly mentioned in the Pact, and therefore it was not defined, there was apparently some degree of consensus among states as to what the right meant and when it could legitimately be used to justify recourse to war.

The diplomatic correspondence that preceded the signing of the Pact of Paris suggests that the right to wage war in self-defence was *only available when the state was under attack or invasion from another country*. This interpretation was confirmed by Secretary of State Kellogg in a speech that post-dated the above-mentioned notes[103] from individual states:[104]

> The question was raised as to whether this treaty [the Pact of Paris] prevented a country from defending itself *in the event of attack.* It seemed to me incomprehensible that any nation should believe that a country should be deprived of its legitimate right of self-defense. No nation would sign a treaty

---

Congressional Record, 70th Congress, 2nd Session, 3 January 1929, at 1070, as cited in Alexandrov, supra n. 2 at 60, n. 46.

100 See discussion in Chapters 4, 5 and 6 regarding the natural law origins of the right of self-defence.

101 See the United States' position as set out in Kellogg's Note of 23 June 1928, supra n. 69, in which he stated that 'the right [of self-defence] is *inherent* in every sovereign state and is implicit in every treaty'; see also the reservation from South Africa which stated that the treaty was not intended to 'deprive any party … of any of its *natural right* of legitimate self-defense': Note of South Africa, 15 June 1928, in *Foreign Relations of the United States 1928-I* at 67, cited in Alexandrov, supra n. 2 at 55, n. 18. The British position was that the right of self-defence was 'inalienable': British Note, 19 May 1928 in *Foreign Relations of the United States 1928-I* at 67. Poland's position was that the Pact did not affect in any way the right of legitimate defence which was 'inherent in each State': Note of Poland, 17 July 1928, *Foreign Relations of the United States 1928-I* at 119. Similar statements were made in the reservations of Australia, Belgium, Germany and the Irish Free State.

102 The US noted that every state was 'free to defend its territory from attack or invasion': Note of the United States supra n. 69; France pointed out that each nation would always remain free to 'defend its territory against attack or invasion'. Czechoslovakia noted 'each power is entirely free to defend itself according to its will and its necessities against attack and foreign invasion': Note of Czechoslovakia, supra n. 94.

103 This statement was made in November 1929; the previously quoted excerpts from the Notes of France and Czechoslovakia were made in July 1928. Thus, Kellogg was reiterating that this was the 'correct' interpretation of the right of self-defence.

104 Speech of Secretary of State Kellogg of 11 November 1928, quoted in *Congressional Record,* 70th Congress, 2nd Session, 3 January 1929 at 1063, as cited in Alexandrov, supra n. 2 at 59–60 and n. 44.

> expressly or clearly implying an obligation denying it the right to defend itself *if attacked by another country.* (Emphasis added)

Obviously, states were concerned that signing the Pact of Paris would impair their inherent right of self-defence. However, even at that time, international law had restricted the right to cases where there was a need to take defensive action occasioned by an attack or invasion from another country. It was *this* right that was deemed by states as being 'inherent'.[105]

The relevance of these points to the arguments that are advanced in Chapters 6 and 7 of this book is based on the close relationship between the Pact of Paris and the UN Charter. The Pact and the Charter stand together as the two major sources of the customary norm limiting resort to force by states. The Pact of Paris has been described as being:[106] '… [P]arallel to and a complement of the Charter. It reinforces the obligations of the latter although in some ways the Charter improves on the Pact by being more explicit in references to "threat or use of force" and self-defence.'

That close relationship is troublesome in the sense that the UN Charter preserves an 'inherent right of self-defence' but that right was not even mentioned in the Pact of Paris, let alone defined. By failing to specifically refer to the right of self-defence, its definition remained open to speculation and interpretation.

Pre-emptive Self-defence

The phrase 'pre-emptive self-defence' was not used in any of the inter-war treaties but developments occurred during this epoch which may suggest that states were becoming increasingly concerned that they should be able to act before they became the victim of an act of war or aggression. In 1837, the *Caroline* case provided guidelines as to when force could be used in self-defence.[107] Although

---

105 A number of US Senators admitted to voting for the ratification of the Pact even though they were of the view that it was a 'worthless but perfectly harmless peace treaty' and that it would in no way restrict the US's freedom of action: *Congressional Record*, 70th Congress, 2nd Session, 10 January 1929 at 1467, and 15 January 1929 at 1728. See also the statements from other US Senators expressing similar sentiments, as cited in Alexandrov, supra n. 2 at 60–61. Edwin Borchard argued that as no modern nation had ever gone to war for any motive other than legitimate self-defence, the Pact could hardly ever be legally violated: Borchard, E., 'The Multilateral Treaty for the Renunciation of War' (1929) 23 *AJIL* 116 at 117.

106 Brownlie, supra n. 15 at 91.

107 Jennings, R., *The Caroline and McLeod Cases* (1938) 32 *AJIL* 82. An incident between the US and the UK occurred on 28 December 1837 when British subjects, led by Captain Alexander McLeod, seized a vessel (the *Caroline*) in an American port, then set the steamer on fire and set it adrift towards eventual destruction over the Niagara Falls. Two US citizens were killed in the process. The British troops had taken such action because

US Secretary of State Webster's formula, that there must be a 'necessity of self-defence ... instant, overwhelming, leaving no choice of means and no moment for deliberation',[108] was issued in the context of an incident that occurred prior to the period presently under discussion, it was cited during this period by states that employed force in self-defence.[109] The *Caroline* case highlighted the fact that states would sometimes be justified in using force prior to an actual act of aggression, based on preparations that were being undertaken.

Covenant of the League of Nations

The 1919 League of Nations Covenant recognised that action could and should be taken against a state even if war had not yet broken out. A dispute could be referred to the League's Council if there was actual aggression or 'in case of any threat or danger of such aggression'.[110] Article 11 provided that any war or threat of war, whether immediately affecting the members of the League or not, was a matter of concern to the whole League[111] and 'any circumstance whatever, affecting international relations which threatens to disturb international peace'[112] could be brought to the attention of the Assembly or the Council. This implies that the Council would be able to take action in relation to the actions of a state, even though there had not yet been any actual use of aggression by that state.

---

the *Caroline* was allegedly being used to supply groups of American insurgents with reinforcements of men and arms. The US objected to the actions of the British forces in destroying the *Caroline* and in killing the US citizens, on the grounds that the British had violated American sovereignty. Great Britain considered that it had acted in legitimate self-defence. The correspondence between US Secretary of State Webster and Lord Ashburton contains the classic statement of the proper limits for the plea of self-defence. Secretary of State Webster called upon Britain to show the existence of a 'necessity of self-defence, instant, overwhelming, leaving no choice of means, and no moment for deliberation ...' Webster then went on to state that it was for Great Britain: '... [T]o show, also, that the local authorities of Canada ... did nothing unreasonable or excessive, since the act, justified by the necessity of self-defence, must be limited by that necessity and kept clearly within it.' In these few sentences, Secretary of State Webster formulated the customary law principles that have, ever since, been applied to the resort to force in self-defence.

108 Jennings, ibid.; see also Parliamentary Papers (1843), vol. LXI; British and Foreign State Papers, vol. 30, 193.

109 In relation to the hostilities arising out of Japanese forces in Manchuria in 1931, Japan described its action as 'justifiable measures of self-protection on the standard principle laid down in the *Caroline* case': see Brownlie, supra n. 15 at 242.

110 League of Nations Covenant, Article 10.

111 Ibid., Article 11.

112 Ibid.

Draft Treaty of Mutual Assistance

The concern amongst nations to reserve for themselves the power to act before they became a victim of aggression was also expressed in the 1923 Draft Treaty of Mutual Assistance. It was noted above that the Draft Treaty declared aggressive war to be an international crime which led states to wrestle with the meaning of 'aggression'. The commentary which was distributed to governments with the Draft Treaty stated that the test of aggression should cover 'all measures that give evidence to an intention to go to war',[113] thereby expanding upon the traditional understanding of aggression which was hitherto limited to *actual* mobilisation of forces or the violation of a frontier.

Geneva Protocol

By virtue of Article 8, the signatories to the Geneva Protocol undertook to:[114]

> [A]bstain from any act which might constitute a threat of aggression against another State. If one of the signatory States is of opinion that another State is *making preparations for war*, it shall have the right to bring the matter to the notice of the Council. The Council, if it ascertains that the facts are as alleged, shall proceed as provided in paragraphs 2, 4 and 5 of Article 7. (Emphasis added)

Had it been ratified and entered into force, this Protocol would have given the League the power to investigate *threats* of aggression and impose a variety of measures on potential aggressors, including sanctions. The fact that a state could be brought before the Council for making *preparations for war* implies that collective action of a pre-emptive nature conceivably could have been taken against a state before it had committed an actual act of aggression. But the power to take such action was reserved for the Council, not for individual states.[115]

Locarno Treaty

The 1925 Locarno Treaty also supports the conclusion that states wanted to be able to take action against neighbours who were preparing for war. Assembly of armed forces in the demilitarised zones between Germany and Belgium, and Germany and France, would have given rise to a right to seek assistance from the Council, and for the victim state to call for help from the other Contracting Party, even though an attack, invasion or declaration of war had not yet occurred. However,

---

113 *Commentary on the Definition of a Case of Aggression*, Records of the Fourth Assembly (1923), Meetings of Committees, Minutes of the Third Committee, at 206–8.

114 Geneva Protocol, Article 8.

115 See discussion in Chapters 5 and 6 on pre-emptive self-defence.

the victim state's options were limited by the requirement that it had to 'bring the question at once before the Council of the League of Nations'[116] which suggests that the concerned state could not use pre-emptive force without the Council's permission. Thus, the Council's involvement presumably would have prevented the resort to self-help, even in cases of armed attack and frontier incidents.[117]

Pact of Paris

The 1928 Pact of Paris did not address the issue of self-defence nor pre-emptive self-defence. As discussed above, reference to *les travaux préparatoires* suggests that states nevertheless considered that they retained the right to use force in self-defence. The nature of that right, as defined by the various states, suggests they perceived they would only be entitled to use force to repel an *actual* armed attack, not the *threat* of an attack or the *preparations for a future attack*. The statements referred to above from France, the US and Czechoslovakia suggest that states would only invoke the right to use force in self-defence once they had come under actual attack or were subject to an invasion.[118] It may be surmised that during the inter-war period, although military mobilisation, violation of demilitarised zones and frontier incidents were regarded as serious and worthy of the League's attention, states did not consider that such incidents would give rise to the right to use force in pre-emptive self-defence. Statesmen were concerned that states should not take matters into their own hands, except in the most flagrant of cases:[119]

> It was essential that such ideas should not take root in the minds of nations which were Members of the League, and become a kind of jurisprudence, for it would be extremely dangerous. Under the pretext of legitimate defence, disputes might arise which, though limited in extent, were extremely unfortunate owing to the damage they entailed. These disputes, once they had broken out, might assume such proportions that the Government, which started them under a feeling of legitimate defence, would no longer be able to control them.

Briand was commenting in the context of the Greek–Bulgarian conflict which broke out on 19 October 1925. Greece's invasion and occupation of Bulgarian territory, in response to the shooting of a Greek officer on the border, was found to be a violation of the Covenant. Briand, on behalf of the League, adopted the position that states ought to resort to the Council rather than using force as a measure of self-help. There was a prevailing sense amongst many statesmen that they ought

116 Geneva Protocol, Article 4.

117 Ibid. Alexandrov also interprets the provisions in this way; see Alexandrov, supra n. 2 at 46.

118 Ibid.

119 Statement of Mr Briand, President of the League Council, Minutes of the 36th (Extraordinary) Session of the Council, Meeting of 28 October 1925, *LNOJ* (1925) 1709.

to use all means available to prevent states from using force as a measure of self-help, and to interpret 'self-defence' restrictively. If force was ever to be used pre-emptively, that right was almost certainly reserved for the Council.

Forcible Measures Short of War

Many of the treaties discussed above referred only to 'war' or 'aggression', which meant that other uses of force short of war, such as reprisals, were excluded by the agreements and seemed to remain lawful.

Covenant of the League of Nations

A number of defects or loopholes were identified above that limited the effectiveness of the League of Nations' Covenant. Perhaps the Covenant's most significant defect was not the loopholes that left war open as an option to states, but the fact that the Covenant only applied to 'war' in the legal sense. The phrase 'resort to war' in Articles 12 to 16 meant that any uses of force short of declared war went 'under the radar' of the Covenant, and none of its elaborate provisions even applied. This was evident, for example, in relation to the conflict that occurred between China and Japan between 1937 and 1941 where the victim, the aggressor and all other interested states 'actively connived in maintaining the fiction that war did not exist'.[120]

As to why the drafters of the Covenant opted for the word 'war', rather than, say, 'recourse to force', no clear reason is discernible. Apparently, the phrase 'recourse to armed force' was used in previous drafts.[121] Some scholars suggest that the Covenant was modelled on the earlier Bryan Treaties and adopted the same restrictive use of the word 'war'.[122] On a literal reading of the Covenant's reference to 'resort to war', it would seem that reprisals were excluded. The lack of clarity concerning uses of force short of war was amply illustrated in the 1923 incident between Greece and Italy over Corfu.[123] Italy bombarded and occupied Corfu as a

120 See Brownlie, supra n. 15 at 60.

121 Miller, D., *The Drafting of the Covenant Vols I and II* (New York; London: G.P. Putnam's Sons, 1928) at 68, 213, 222 (vol. 1) and at 14, 74, 82, 100, 101, 143, 267, 306, 311 (vol. II), as cited in Brownlie, supra n. 15 at 60, and in Alexandrov, supra n. 2 at 34, n. 33.

122 See Brownlie, supra n. 15 at 56–60; see also Bowett, supra n. 68 at 124; McCoubrey and White, supra n. 33 at 22; and Alexandrov, supra n. 2 at 34–5.

123 The incident arose out of the murder in Greece of General Tellini, the Italian chairman of the Greek–Albanian boundary commission. Italy addressed an ultimatum to Greece, but Greece refused to pay compensation. In response, Italy bombarded and then occupied the Greek island of Corfu, killing a number of Greeks in the process: see Brierly, supra n. 57 at 411–12; Bowett, supra n. 68 at 124; and Alexandrov, supra n. 2 at 35.

measure of reprisal, without a declaration of war.[124] A Commission of Jurists was appointed by the Council to determine whether coercive measures, lacking the character of war, were inconsistent with the Covenant. The Commission's rather unhelpful finding was that:[125] '[C]oercive measures which are not intended to constitute acts of war *may or may not be consistent* with the provisions of Articles 12 to 15 of the Covenant …' (emphasis added).

Although the Covenant did not expressly prohibit the use of armed reprisals, the general consensus amongst the Members of the League was that forcible reprisals and armed interventions were not permitted under the Covenant unless the peaceful settlement procedures had been exhausted.[126]

Draft Treaty of Mutual Assistance, Geneva Protocol and the Locarno Treaty

By the 1930s, states had become accustomed to using force without a formal declaration of war, under the guise of either 'self-defence' or 'reprisal'. The barriers erected by the Covenant, and later by the Pact of Paris, were undermined by the lack of formal declarations of war, and the concept of reprisal 'was thus deprived of its legal precision and became a caricature which contributed to the undermining of international law's authority'.[127] The agreements that were drafted between the Covenant and the Pact of Paris, such as the Draft Treaty of Mutual Assistance, the Geneva Protocol and the Locarno Treaty, all attempted to limit the resort to force; but none of them defined 'war' or 'aggression' or mentioned the use of forcible measures short of war, such as reprisals. Thus, they did not assist in clarifying the legal position on the use of reprisals.[128]

---

124 Italy claimed that since it had no intention of declaring war on Greece, the Council of the League of Nations had no right to deal with the question. Italy viewed its actions not as an act of war but as a temporary measure intended to maintain Italian prestige and to show Italy's resolve to enforce due reparation: for a full account of the incident, see Alexandrov, supra n. 2 at 35.

125 Minutes of the Twenty-Eighth Session of the Council, Sixth Meeting, 13 March 1924, *LNOJ* (1924) 523–7.

126 Brierly, J., 'International Law and Resort to Armed Force' (1932) *Cambridge Law Journal* 308; see also Brierly, supra n. 57 at 412 where he noted that: 'the general opinion of jurists was that such armed reprisals taken without prior recourse to pacific settlement were a violation of the Covenant; for, even if not regarded as a recourse to "war", they were quite inconsistent with the observance in good faith of the express obligations in the Covenant and the Pact [of Paris] to have recourse to pacific means for settling disputes likely to lead to a rupture.' He also remarked that: 'The Corfu incident and the reply of the jurists at least served as a warning to the draftsmen of the [United Nations] Charter …': see also discussion in Alexandrov, supra n. 2 at 36–7.

127 Grewe, supra n. 2 at 622.

128 But note that the *Naulilaa* arbitration, concluded in 1928, provided guidelines on the use of reprisals: see Case XXVIIa: Responsabilité de l'Allemagne à raison des

Pact of Paris

The Pact of Paris provided a prohibition on 'war' rather than on the 'recourse to force'. The limitation of the Pact to the renunciation of 'war' led to the 'disturbing implication'[129] that the use of force short of war was left to the discretion of each state. The ultimate failure of the Pact of Paris to prevent the use of force by states against one another was amply illustrated in 1931 with the Japanese invasion of Manchuria; in 1935 with the Italian invasion of Ethiopia; and in 1938 when Germany invaded and occupied Austria. In summary, whenever states chose to use force in undeclared wars, the various agreements that were in place to prevent war were inapplicable.[130]

Convention for the Definition of Aggression

The Convention for the Definition of Aggression[131] represented an important development in limiting resort to forcible measures short of war. It defined the 'aggressor' as the first state to invade or attack 'with or without a declaration of war',[132] thereby preventing states from claiming the right to use force on the basis that they were not technically at war. It also declared that a 'naval blockade of the coasts or port of another state'[133] would constitute an act of aggression. Further, it declared that no act of aggression could be justified on the grounds of the internal condition of a state[134] or the international conduct of a state.[135] Although it was only ratified by a few states, this document was a genuine attempt to prevent states from using force that fell short of the technical definition of war.[136]

---

dommages causes dans les colonies Portugaises du Sud de l'Afrique (1928) 2 *RIAA* 1012 (the *Naulilaa* arbitration).

129 See Dinstein, Y., *War, Aggression and Self-Defence* (3rd edn) (Cambridge; New York: Cambridge University Press, 2001) 80; also Waldock, C., 'The Regulation of the Use of Force by Individual States in International Law' (1952) 81 *Rec. des Cours* 455, at 471–4.

130 Fourteen years after the signing of the Pact of Paris which supposedly outlawed 'war', all of the signatories were belligerents in World War II.

131 Supra n. 70.

132 Ibid., Article 2(2) and (3).

133 Ibid., Article 2(5).

134 For example, its political, economic or social structure, alleged defects in its administration, or disturbances due to strikes, revolutions, counter-revolutions: ibid., Annex to Article III.

135 For example, the violation of the material or moral rights or interests of a foreign state: ibid.

136 A number of other non-aggression treaties were entered into in the inter-war period, including the Anti-War Treaty of Non-Aggression and Conciliation (Saavedra lamas Treaty) signed on 10 October 1933 between the US and several South American states,

Non-state Actors

During the inter-war period, states generally regarded war and aggression as threats that were posed by other *states*. Conversely, the right to use force in self-defence was a right conferred on states to repel force from other *states*.[137] But states were also concerned with non-state actors and they were acutely aware that individuals' use of force was an issue that international law had to grapple with. Incidentally, the 1933 Convention for the Definition of Aggression would have applied to a state which provided aid to armed bands formed on its own territory which invaded another state, as well as refusal, despite demands, to take all possible measures to deprive the armed bands of aid and protection.[138]

In terms of specific types of threats from non-state actors, anarchism, terrorism and piracy were probably the three most significant. Some key developments in relation to anarchism and terrorism during the inter-war period were discussed in Chapter 2 in the context of analysing the changing nature of conflict.[139] A number of developments also occurred in relation to piracy, the most significant of which was the Draft Convention on Piracy with Comments, referred to here as the Harvard Draft Convention.[140] The Harvard Draft Convention was important because the Harvard researchers discussed every possible aspect of sea and air piracy which conceivably could have been raised in 1932, and because the laws on piracy that were eventually incorporated into the International Law Commission's draft articles and ultimately adopted in the 1958 Convention on the High Seas were based on the Harvard Draft Convention. The Harvard Group provided detailed analysis of issues such as the definition of piracy, the meaning and justification inherent in the views expressed by various scholars and in domestic laws that piracy was a crime against the law of nations and whether universal jurisdiction existed in relation to acts of piracy.[141]

As for the definition of piracy, the Harvard Group concluded that piracy was not a crime under international law, but that it was merely the basis of some extraordinary jurisdiction in every state to seize, prosecute and to punish persons.[142] How far that extraordinary jurisdiction was used would depend upon the municipal

---

which condemned wars of aggression and which underlined the parties' commitments to settle territorial questions by methods other than 'violence'.

137 Kellogg: 'No nation would sign a treaty expressly or clearly implying an obligation denying it the right to defend itself *if attacked by another country*.': quoted supra n. 104.

138 See Convention for the Definition of Aggression, Article 2.

139 See Chapter 2 at 25–28.

140 Harvard Research in International Law, *Draft Convention on Piracy with Comments* (1932) 26 *AJIL* 749.

141 See Hubner, B., *The Law of International Sea Piracy* (The Hague: Martinus Nijhoff, 1980) 37–102.

142 For comments on the Harvard researchers' findings, see Rubin, A., *The Law of Piracy*, 2nd edn (New York: Transnational Publishers, 1998) 335–48.

law of the state, not on *the law of nations*.[143] Piracy was defined in Article 3 by describing a series of acts.[144] The Harvard Group concluded that a pirate act was 'any act of violence or depredation …'[145] that was carried out 'for *private* ends without bona fide purpose',[146] thereby excluding acts which were carried out for *political* ends. Notably, the Harvard Draft Convention omitted any reference to the resort to war, aggression, arbitration or sanctions. There was no suggestion in the Draft Convention on Piracy that states would resort to force against one another as a result of piratical acts, nor was there a suggestion that states would have to solve any disputes that might arise by arbitration, reference to the League Council or through any of the other mechanisms that were used at that time to resolve *inter-state* disputes. Acts of piracy were clearly regarded as criminal acts, carried out for private ends, on the high seas, and in response to which states could seize, prosecute and punish in accordance with their respective domestic laws.

Conclusion

This chapter has traced the developments pertaining to the resort to force, the use of force in self-defence, pre-emptive self-defence, reprisals and the use of force by non-state actors in the inter-war period from 1919 to 1944. This period witnessed a gradual progression from attempts at *preventing* war to *prohibiting* war outright, via binding, multilateral treaties as well as bilateral, arbitration and non-aggression agreements.

The League of Nations Covenant was a major development in the limitation of the resort to war by states. It had many flaws, but it also represented a genuine desire by members to avoid the use of war to solve disputes. It was a major turning point in the development of international law relating to the recourse to force because, by virtue of its procedures for the pacific settlement of disputes, it created a clear legal distinction between 'legal' and 'illegal' wars. 'Legal' wars were those that were waged once the rules in the Covenant had been complied with. 'Illegal' wars were those that had been waged without proper resort to the peaceful means of dispute resolution. However, the Covenant did not prohibit war, nor did it prohibit the recourse to force short of war. Armed reprisals and interventions were still permitted. Although the term 'self-defence' was not used in the Covenant, Members generally considered that the right continued to exist.[147]

---

143 Harvard Draft Convention, supra n. 140, 760.

144 For the full text of the Harvard Draft Convention, see Rubin, supra n. 142, Appendix III.A.

145 Harvard Draft Convention, Article 3(1).

146 Ibid.

147 In a statement of the First Committee in its report to the Assembly in 1931, it was stated that: 'One point appears beyond dispute – namely, that … in the Covenant of the League in its present form … the prohibition of recourse to war [does not] exclude the right

The foregoing analysis has referred to a number of treaties concluded in the early 1920s that attempted to refine the *ius ad bellum*. The most notable among them were the 1923 Draft Treaty on Mutual Assistance, the 1924 Geneva Protocol for the Pacific Settlement of Disputes and the 1925 Locarno Treaties. Each of these represented a step in the development of legal norms restricting the use of force. The culmination of these efforts was the 1928 General Treaty for the Renunciation of War/Kellogg–Briand Pact/Pact of Paris, which condemned the use of *war* for the settlement of international controversies and supposedly prohibited the use of force as an instrument of national policy.

When treaties such as these are read in conjunction with resolutions of the League Assembly[148] they suggest that there was an evolving international consensus in favour of a broad prohibition on the resort to war as a means of resolving disputes between states, whilst simultaneously preserving the right of states to use force in legitimate self-defence (even though the latter right was implicitly, rather than explicitly, preserved). States assumed that the right to self-defence remained unaffected by the treaties that they entered into, and states remained free to determine the exact content of that right, leading to a situation where there was an absence of consensus as to exactly what the right of self-defence meant. Nevertheless, there was general agreement that international law allowed force to be used in self-defence if a state was the subject of attack or invasion by *another state*.

Regarding pre-emptive self-defence, it was observed that the Council of the League of Nations theoretically could take action *before* a threat had materialised into aggressive action, but the parameters of when force could be used in pre-emptive self-defence were not defined. If the right existed, it was only to be exercised in response to an actual armed attack, not the threat of attack, and it vested in the Council, not in individual states.

The use of reprisals was also analysed here and it was noted that the use of the terms 'war' and 'aggression' employed by the drafters of treaties allowed states to employ force that was not technically prohibited. Reprisals, which are essentially punitive in nature, and which have been employed throughout the history of international law, continued to be used in this particular period, not as a means of protection (thereby distinguishing it from self-defence) but as an apparently lawful means of exacting revenge for harm done to a state.

The fifth and final theme that was highlighted here was the evolution of the threat posed by non-state actors. As the threat from anarchism receded, the threat

---

of legitimate self-defence': Report to the Assembly by the First Committee, *Records of the Twelfth Assembly* (1931), Meetings of Committees, Minutes of the First Committee, Annex 18, point 5 at 146; see also Alexandrov, supra n. 2 at 37.

148 For example, the Sixth Assembly adopted a resolution on 25 September 1925 which stated that a 'war of aggression' constituted 'an international crime': Resolutions of the Sixth Assembly, *Records of the Committees of the League of Nations Assembly*, p21, A. 1925, as discussed in Brownlie, supra n. 15 at 71–2.

from piracy remained, and terrorism in a more general sense became a source of considerable concern. States looked increasingly to international law to provide protection from the criminal actions of individuals. Important treaties were drafted in this period in relation to both terrorism and piracy. Even though the 1937 Convention for the Prevention and Punishment of Terrorism, discussed in Chapter 2, did not enter into force, both this and the Harvard Draft Convention on Piracy amounted to recognition by states that they were increasingly concerned with the threat posed to their security by non-state actors.

This chapter has summarised the law regarding the resort to force by states, as it stood immediately prior to the adoption of the UN Charter. In Chapter 5 it will be observed that since Article 51 of the Charter reserves the '*inherent* right of self-defence', there must have been a right that existed *prior* to the Charter. This chapter has sought to demonstrate that a right to self-defence certainly *did* exist; the right was recognised in reservations by the state signatories to the Pact of Paris as already having been in existence in 1928, but it must be acknowledged that it was a vague concept and there was no consensus amongst states on its precise content.

Chapter 5
Evolution of Limitations on the Use of Force: From the United Nations Charter to the Present – 1945–2008

Introduction

This chapter continues to trace the development of legal limitations on the use of force. Whilst Chapter 4 focused on the pre-Charter period, this chapter focuses on the developments that occurred from the negotiations phase that ultimately resulted in the signing of the UN Charter until the present. As in Chapter 4, the structure is again based upon a five-part analysis: limitations on the resort to force generally, the use of force specifically in self-defence, pre-emptive self-defence, forcible measures short of war and, finally, the use of force by non-state actors. The analysis here draws primarily on international treaties, judgements of the International Court of Justice and resolutions of the General Assembly and the Security Council, with an acknowledgement of the importance of the *opinio juris* of states, and an analysis of the contributions made by academics. The main objective of this chapter is to provide a comprehensive overview of the law which existed at the time that force was used against Afghanistan in October 2001. Thus, this chapter is a precursor to the discussion in Chapter 6 regarding the legality of the use of force in a particular instance.

Limiting the Resort to Force

Dumbarton Oaks

The signing of the UN Charter on 26 June 1945 was the most important development in this period regarding limitations on the resort to force.[1] The Charter was based on the Dumbarton Oaks Proposals for a General International Organisation. The main purpose of the new organisation was to 'maintain international peace and

1 The UN Charter, signed on 26 June 1945, following final approval by the UN Conference on International Organization the previous day: see UNCIO, *Verbatim Minutes of the Ninth Plenary Session*, Doc 1210, 20.

security'[2] and to 'take effective collective measures for the prevention and removal of threats to the peace'.[3] The Dumbarton Oaks Proposals encapsulated a desire to limit the opportunities for states to employ the use of force by moving beyond the earlier treaties' restrictive references to 'war' or 'aggression' and include 'threats to the peace' or 'other breaches of the peace'. The primary responsibility for determining when such a threat to, or breach of, the peace had occurred was to be given to the Security Council[4] which would have the power to '[D]etermine the existence of any threat to the peace, breach of the peace or act of aggression'.[5] The Security Council was then supposed to make recommendations or decide upon the measures to be taken to maintain or restore peace and security.

The Committee which had been assigned to make recommendations on this article realised that a definition of 'aggression' or 'threat to the peace' was required in order for the Security Council to effectively carry out its duties.[6] The various suggestions by states regarding whether a definition was needed and what form it ought to take were indicative of the divide that existed.[7] The four main powers responsible for drafting the original proposals (the US, the UK, the Soviet Union and China) did not support the call for a definition but they suggested an amendment which would have given the Security Council the power to call upon

---

2 Dumbarton Oaks Proposal for a General International Organisation, Chapter 1, Article 1, reproduced in Ferencz, B., *Defining International Aggression: The Search For World Peace – A Documentary History and Analysis*, vol. 1 (Dobbs Ferry, New York: Oceana Publications Inc, 1975) 285–306.

3 Ibid.

4 Ibid., Chapter 2, Section B, Article 1, as reproduced in Ferencz, ibid., at 291–2.

5 Ibid., Article 2, as reproduced in Ferencz, ibid., at 297–8. This wording is very similar to that adopted in Article 1 of the UN Charter.

6 See Committee 3 of Commission III; see Russell, R., *A History of the UN Charter – the Role of the United States 1940–1945* (Washington DC: Brookings Institution, 1958).

7 Czechoslovakia did not favour a specific definition because 'past experience has proved sufficiently that rigidity and over-elaborate definitions may not always produce the desired results': UNCIO Doc 2 (English) G/14(b), 1 May 1945, reproduced in Ferencz, supra n. 2 at 307–12. Bolivia considered that 'a previous definition of typically aggressive acts is absolutely essential'; the Philippines also proposed that a definition of 'aggression' be written into the Charter. Iran and Egypt agreed that the Charter should include a clear and exact definition of the term 'aggressor' without offering a specific definition. Mexico considered that the General Assembly ought to have a say in determining which state was the aggressor. New Zealand wanted concurrence by majority vote of the Assembly before sanctions could be applied. Greece suggested that if the Security Council could not decide on which party was the aggressor, it could take a decision by a majority of seven: UNCIO *Amendments to Dumbarton Oaks Proposals Supplemented by the Texts Adopted at Yalta, Submitted by the Greek Delegation, 3 May 1945*, Doc 2 (English) G/14 (i), 4 May 1945, Chapter VI Section C, Chapter VIII Section A, reproduced in Ferencz, supra n. 2 at 328–30.

parties to comply with provisional measures and would have directed the Security Council to take due account of any state's failure to comply.[8]

The definition of aggression was the subject of much discussion in the Ninth and Tenth Meetings of the Third Committee in May 1945. A number of states[9] were in favour of including a specific definition in the Charter on the grounds that it should be known beforehand what acts would constitute aggression and, consequently, what acts would be subject to sanctions, but the majority, led by the US and the UK,[10] opposed the inclusion of a definition on the grounds that 'it would be impossible to enumerate all the acts that constitute aggression'.[11] They were also concerned that including a list of acts which would attract *automatic* Council action might bring about a 'premature application of enforcement measures'.[12] The Rapporteur, Mr Paul-Boncour, confirmed that the majority of states did not support the amendment of the Dumbarton Oaks Proposals to include a definition of aggression.[13] Those states were clearly in favour of leaving the Security Council with the *absolute discretion* to decide when an act of aggression had occurred.[14] The course of the debate suggests that in June 1945 there was a complete lack of consensus amongst states as to what acts would constitute 'aggression' and a lack of desire amongst the majority of states to attempt to define the term.[15]

---

8 UNCIO *Amendments Proposed by the Governments of the United States, the United Kingdom, the Soviet Union and China*, Doc 2 (English) G/29, 5 May 1945, Chapter VII Section B, reproduced in Ferencz, ibid., 331–7.

9 The delegates from Bolivia, Colombia, Egypt, Ethiopia, Guatemala, Honduras, Iran, Mexico, New Zealand and Uruguay felt that, 'the Council's work would be facilitated if a definite list were written into the Charter': UNCIO *Summary Report of Ninth Meetings of Committee III/3, 18 May 1945*, Restricted Doc. 442 (English) III/3/20, 19 May 1945, reproduced in Ferencz, ibid., 345–6.

10 Supported by Czechoslovakia, the Netherlands, Norway, Paraguay and the Union of South Africa.

11 UNCIO *Summary Report of Ninth Meetings of Committee III/3, 18 May 1945*, Restricted Doc. 442 (English) III/3/20, 19 May 1945.

12 UNCIO *Report of Mr Paul-Boncour, Rapporteur, on Chapter VIII, Section B*, Restricted Doc. 881 (English) III/3/46, 10 June 1945, reproduced in Ferencz, supra n. 2 at 352.

13 'Although this proposition [the Bolivian proposition for a definition of aggression] evoked considerable support, it nevertheless became clear to a majority of the Committee that a preliminary definition of aggression went well beyond the possibilities of this Conference and the purpose of the Charter. The progress of the technique of modern warfare renders very difficult the definition of all cases of aggression … the list of such cases being necessarily incomplete …': ibid.

14 'The Committee therefore decided to adhere to the text drawn up at Dumbarton Oaks and to leave to the Council the entire decision as to what constitutes a threat to peace, a breach of the peace, or an act of aggression': ibid.

15 The discussion on the subject of including criteria for an act of 'aggression' continued into the Tenth Meeting of the Third Committee, held on 21 May 1945: see

As the records show, there seemed to be a considerable amount of self-interest involved in so far as the major powers (the proposed Permanent Members of the Security Council) wanted a document that would promote the ideals of peace and security, but they also wanted the discretion to judge when an act of aggression had occurred, without being hampered by a list of actions that would attract automatic Security Council action. It was argued that any act of aggression, even an 'invasion by armed force of a foreign territory',[16] could, in some circumstances, be justified as 'legitimate self-defence'. Therefore, the UN Charter represented not so much an advance on the *status quo*, as a confirmation of it, whereby states would retain the power to use force if it was deemed to be in legitimate self-defence and not an act of aggression. However, exactly what would constitute an act of aggression remained unclear because the majority of states were absolutely opposed to defining the crucial term.

The UN Charter

The text ultimately adopted in Article 2(4), which created a general prohibition on the use of force, was similar to that of the Dumbarton Oaks Proposals.[17] This provision not only proscribed the use of force, but the *threat* of force and its reference to *force* instead of 'war' or 'aggression' encompassed a much broader range of action.[18] The Charter provided four possible exceptions to the general prohibition, only two of which are currently relevant: the use of force in individual or collective self-defence under Article 51 and enforcement actions authorised by the Security Council under Chapter VII.[19] The general prohibition on the recourse to force in Article 2(4) was further strengthened by the requirement in Article 2(3)

UNCIO *Summary Report of Tenth Meeting of Committee III/3, May 21 1945*, Restricted Doc. 502 (English) III/3/22, 23 May 1945, reproduced in Ferencz, supra n. 2 at 347–8.

16 'There was no one kind of act, defined as an act of aggression, which in conceivable circumstances, might not be a legitimate act of self-defense': UNCIO *Summary Report of Ninth Meetings of Committee III/3, 18 May 1945*, Restricted Doc. 442 (English) III/3/20, 19 May 1945, reproduced in Ferencz, supra n. 2 at 346.

17 Article 2(4) was based on Chapter II, Article 4 of the Dumbarton Oaks Proposals and the wording is the same except for the Charter's addition of the phrase 'against the territorial integrity or political independence of any state'.

18 Including forcible measures short of war.

19 The other two theoretical exceptions (collective use of force before the Security Council is functional, pursuant to Article 106, and force against 'enemy' states pursuant to Articles 107 and 53) are now considered to be largely irrelevant and unlikely to be relied upon by Member States: see Arend, A. and Beck, R., *International Law and the Use of Force* (USA and Canada: Routledge, 1993) 32–3; also Akehurst, M., *A Modern Introduction to International Law*, 5th edn (New York; London: Routledge, 1984) 225. Although the Charter originally provided for four explicit exceptions, only two are now considered extant (self-defence pursuant to Article 51 and action authorised by the Security Council pursuant to Chapter VII). Some scholars would argue that there are currently three

that members settle their differences by peaceful means, reaffirming a requirement that had been included in virtually all peace and non-aggression treaties discussed in the preceding chapter.[20]

Since its incorporation in Article 2(4), the prohibition on the recourse to force has been reaffirmed by the Security Council, the General Assembly and the ICJ. When adopting resolutions pertaining to actual or potential armed conflict, the Security Council has often referred, explicitly or implicitly, to the Article 2(4) principles.[21] For instance, the General Assembly adopted the Declaration on the Inadmissibility of Intervention in the Domestic Affairs of States and the Protection of their Independence and Sovereignty in 1965[22] and then the Declaration of Principles of International Law Concerning Friendly Relations and Co-operation among States in Accordance with the Charter of the United Nations, in 1970.[23] Both Declarations included articles that were virtually identical to Article 2(4).[24] The ICJ (and states that have made submissions to it) has also reaffirmed that the prohibition on the use of force is not only treaty law, but it also represents customary law.[25]

Other Legal Instruments Regarding Limitations on the Use of Force

At the same time that the victorious states were meeting in San Francisco to discuss the Charter, the war crimes tribunals were faced with the practical problem of defining 'aggression' in order to facilitate prosecutions of alleged war criminals. The issue of whether 'aggression' should be defined and, if so, how, was just as contentious in the discussions prior to the adoption of the Charter for the International Military Tribunals (IMT Charter) as it had been prior to the adoption of the UN Charter. The American delegation took the view that a detailed and precise definition, such as that used in the 1933 Convention on Aggression,[26]

exceptions to the prohibition on the resort to force, by dividing self-defence into individual and collective self-defence.

20 Article 2(3) employs the same wording used in the Dumbarton Oaks Proposals except for the Charter's addition of the phrase 'and justice'.

21 In relation to the 1980 Iran–Iraq conflict, explicit reference to Article 2(4) was made in SC Resolution 479 (1980); regarding the Ethiopia–Eritrea conflict, implicit reference to Article 2(4) was made in SC Resolution 1177 (1998).

22 UNGA Resolution 2131 Declaration on the Inadmissibility of Intervention in the Domestic Affairs of States and the Protection of their Independence and Sovereignty, 1408th plenary meeting, 21 December 1965.

23 UNGA 2625 (XXV) Declaration of Principles of International Law Concerning Friendly Relations and Co-operation among States in Accordance with the Charter of the United Nations, 1883rd plenary meeting, 24 October 1970.

24 See the 1965 Non-Intervention Declaration, supra n. 22, second paragraph, and the 1970 Declaration Concerning Friendly Relations, supra n. 23, the first principle.

25 *Case Concerning Military and Paramilitary Activities In and Against Nicaragua (Nicaragua v United States)* (Merits) [1986] ICJ Reports 14, para 188.

26 The so-called 'Litvinoff' definition of aggression.

ought to be adopted, but that proposal was ultimately defeated.[27] Although the parties to the IMT Charter were deeply divided over what 'aggression' meant, it did not prevent them from finding that the alleged war criminals were responsible for initiating aggressive wars.

In essence, the international community was unable and unwilling to define a 'war of aggression'. The absence of such a definition has implications for the meaning of self-defence since wars of aggression and wars of self-defence are opposite sides of the same coin. The international community continued to conclude treaties and conduct its relations on the basis of an assumption of the illegality of aggressive war, as evidenced by the Pact of the Arab League,[28] the Inter-American Treaty of Reciprocal Assistance,[29] the Charter of the Organisation of American States[30] and the 'Five Principles of Peaceful Co-Existence'.[31] Since the early years of the post-World War II period, the general illegality of the use of force as a means of self-help has been accepted by states. An international consensus has emerged that deems aggressive war illegal, regardless of motive. Treaties, state practice and international bodies such as the General Assembly, the Security Council and the ICJ have continued to reiterate that basic norm. However, the difficulty of defining what amounts to aggressive war has not been overcome. As with the difficulties in defining 'terrorism',[32] states prefer to be left to decide

---

27 *Revision of Definition of 'Crimes', Submitted by American Delegation, July 31 1945.* Note that the International Military Tribunal for the Far East was modelled on the Nuremberg Tribunals and, as such, virtually the same terminology was adopted. The Tribunal did not have a definition of 'aggressive war' but it assumed that in its present context it meant 'unprovoked attacks, prompted by the desire to seize the possessions of these nations': *International Military Tribunal for the Far East, Judgment, Conclusions.*

28 The Pact of the Arab League stated that 'recourse to force for the settlement of disputes …' was prohibited: Article 5, Pact of the Arab League, signed 22 March 1945, translation in (1945) 39 *AJIL* Suppl., p266; 70 UNTS No 241. The original parties were Egypt, Iraq, Lebanon, Saudi Arabia, Syria, Transjordan and Yemen.

29 The parties reaffirmed that they condemned war and they undertook 'not to resort to the threat or use of force in any manner inconsistent with the provisions of the Charter of the UN or this Treaty': Inter-American Treaty of Reciprocal Assistance, Rio de Janeiro, 2 September 1947, came into force 3 December 1948, 21 UNTS no 334, Article 1.

30 Also known as the Bogotá Charter, it stated that the American states 'condemn wars of aggression' and they bound themselves 'not to have recourse to the use of force' except in the case of self-defence: The Charter of the Organisation of American States of 1948, 30 UNTS no 449.

31 They were originally contained within a treaty between India and China and became widely accepted by states as expressing principles similar to those of the Charter. The *Pancha Shila*, or Five Principles, have been affirmed in a vast number of documents. Between 1954 and 1962, Brownlie lists 81 documents, including treaties, declarations and communiqués that mentioned the Five Principles: see Brownlie, I., *Principles of International Law*, 6th edn (Oxford: Oxford University Press, 2003) Appendix I.

32 See Chapter 3.

matters on a case-by-case basis without being beholden to the limitations of an entrenched definition.

Self-defence

Article 51 of the Charter provides an exception to the general prohibition on the use of force. An analysis of this Article can be broken down into various individual elements, all of which must be satisfied if the use of force is to be considered lawful. The five main elements of Article 51 are discussed in turn below, in the order in which they appear in Article 51.

Nothing ... shall impair the inherent right of individual or collective self-defence ... Article 51's reference to an *inherent* right of self-defence has been the subject of considerable debate. One interpretation is that Article 51 supplements a customary law right of self-defence that existed prior to the Charter and which continues to exist. This interpretation would not require a state to prove that it had suffered a prior 'armed attack' before resorting to force in self-defence (the so-called 'broad interpretation' of Article 51). The other possible interpretation is that the combined effect of Articles 2(3), 2(4) and 51 of the UN Charter extinguishes any other right to resort to force, otherwise than in accordance with the strict letter of the Charter (the so-called 'restrictive interpretation'). This interpretation suggests that any customary law right is subservient to the wording of Article 51. Both interpretations are supported by a body of scholarly opinion.[33]

Proponents of the restrictive interpretation include Brownlie,[34] Henkin[35] and Kelsen[36] who consider that Article 51 contains the *only* right of self-defence permitted under the Charter.[37] More recently, other scholars who have reached

33 For a summary of each, see McCormack, T., *Self-Defense in International Law: The Israeli Raid on the Iraqi Nuclear Reactor* (New York: St Martin's Press, 1996) 122–48; Ross, A., 'The Military Response to Terrorism: Self-Defence and Reprisals in International Law', unpublished Honours thesis, University of Auckland (1989) Section III; and Dinstein, Y., *War, Aggression and Self-Defence*, 3rd edn) (Cambridge; New York: Cambridge University Press, 2001) Part III.

34 Brownlie, supra n. 31 at 273.

35 Henkin, L., *How Nations Behave* (New York: Columbia University Press, 1968) 262.

36 Kelsen, H., *The Law of the United Nations* (London: Stevens, 1951) 792.

37 Brownlie cited authorities dating back to 1948 such as Goodrich and Hambro, Kunz, Briggs, Jessup, Bebr, Nguyen Quoc Dinh, Wehberg, Sloan, Zourek, Nasim Hassan Shah, Skubiszewski, Schwarzenberger, Al Chalabi, Jiménez de Aréchaga, and see also the reports of the Sixth Committee's meetings cited in Brownlie, supra n. 31 at 271, n. 5.

the same conclusion include Kathryn Elliott,[38] Stanimir Alexandrov[39] and Alex Conte.[40] Support for the restrictive interpretation of Article 51 is based in part on the Charter's *travaux préparatoires.* The Dumbarton Oaks Proposals did not originally refer to self-defence but, as with the League of Nations' Covenant and the Pact of Paris (neither of which mentioned the right of self-defence), that was not interpreted as precluding the right to use force in self-defence. States such as China and the US raised the issue of whether a specific right of self-defence should be mentioned, but states chose not to specifically include a 'right of self-defence' on the basis that the issue would probably be raised at the Conference. At the San Francisco Conference, the view of Committee I/1 was that the 'use of arms in legitimate self-defense remains admitted and unimpaired'.[41] In considering the prohibition on force in Article 2(4), some states thought it would be useful to include a provision justifying the use of force in self-defence in response to an attack by another state, but no amendment was adopted.[42]

The provision on self-defence only made its way into the UN Charter because of a disagreement over regional security arrangements.[43] The Dumbarton Oaks Proposals would have allowed the Security Council to veto any action proposed by a regional organisation – a prospect which was deemed unacceptable, particularly for the Latin American states.[44] The various amendments that were put forward emphasised that self-defence action had to be preserved in case the Security Council was unsuccessful in preventing aggression or in the event that the Security Council

38 Elliott, K., 'The New World Order and the Right to Self-Defense in the United Nations Charter' (1991) 15 *Hastings Int'l & Comp. L. Rev* 67.

39 Alexandrov, S., *Self-Defence Against the Use of Force in International Law* (The Hague: Kluwer Law International, 1996) 93. '… the question has been asked whether *apart from the right of self-defense in Article 51, there was some other "inherent" right of self-defense, "unimpaired" by Article 2(4), which was not affected by the Charter*. The answer is clearly in the negative.' (Emphasis in original).

40 Conte, A., *Security in the 21st Century* (Aldershot: Ashgate, 2005) 102.

41 Report of the Rapporteur of Committee I/1 to Commission I, *UNCIO Documents*, vol. 6, at 459.

42 See Turkey's statement, *UNCIO Documents*, vol. 4 at 675.

43 See Chapter VIII, Section C 'Regional Arrangements' in the Dumbarton Oaks Proposals for the Establishment of a General International Organization, reproduced in Russell, supra n. 6 at Appendix 1. The problematic provision was paragraph 2 which stated that no enforcement action should be taken under regional arrangements or by regional agencies without the authorisation of the Security Council.

44 The Latin American countries had concluded a regional arrangement, the Act of Chapultepec, and were concerned that if the Proposals were not amended, actions in self-defence under regional agreements such as this would be subject to the Security Council veto. They argued that to give European and Asian powers a veto over action within the Western Hemisphere would be a violation of the Monroe Doctrine: see Alexandrov, supra n. 39 at 81–5; Russell, ibid., chapter XXVII. Arab states were also concerned with this issue after the formation of the League of Arab States on 22 March 1945.

failed to take the necessary measures to maintain or restore international security. Although states were willing to accept that the Security Council retained control over all uses of force, there had to be a mechanism to allow states to repel an attack by another state, if the Council was *unable* or *unwilling* to act. Eventually, the Russian delegation's suggestion of a phrase that started with the words, 'nothing in this Charter impairs the inherent right of self-defence ...' was adopted.[45]

The use of the word 'inherent' was not meant to preserve a wide-ranging right of action; it was inserted to recognise that states could still act in self-defence but that the Security Council was ultimately responsible for overseeing the use of force.[46] The fact that states were determined to restrict the right to use force unilaterally is evident from the decision to insert into Article 51 the well-known provisos, 'if an armed attack occurs' and 'until the Security Council has taken the necessary measures'.[47] As Brownlie has noted, the whole purpose of the Charter was to render unilateral use of force, even in self-defence, subject to the control of the UN. But even if the Charter *had* preserved a right of customary self-defence, the customary right would probably only have entitled states to use force in response to an armed attack from another state, since that was the extent of the customary law right of self-defence at the time that the UN Charter was adopted.[48]

Despite the arguments in favour of a restrictive interpretation of Article 51, a number of scholars support a broader interpretation. Among others, Bowett,[49] Waldock[50] and Moore[51] hold the view that a customary law right of self-defence existed prior to the UN Charter and it remains in existence. In the *Case Concerning Military and Paramilitary Activities In and Against Nicaragua (Merits)*, the US argued that the rules of customary international law had been 'subsumed' and

45 Note that the US's proposal used the phrase, 'Nothing in this Charter should invalidate the right of self-defense against armed attack': *Foreign Relations of the United States 1945* (1967) vol. 1 at 691–8. The Russian delegation suggested, 'Nothing in this Charter impairs the inherent right of self-defense ...' which was adopted, but the wording of the proviso, that self-defence measures could be taken 'up to the time the necessary measures by the Security Council [were] being taken', was not adopted.

46 The US Acting Secretary of State, Mr Grew, stated on 21 May 1945 that the new provision (Article 51) recognised the inherent right of self-defence but that it left unaffected the ultimate authority of the Security Council: ibid., 306.

47 Goodrich, L. and Hambro, E., *Charter of the United Nations: Commentary and Documents* (Boston: World Peace Foundation, 1946) 178.

48 See Brownlie, supra n. 31 at 274. Many statements were made when the Pact of Paris was concluded in 1928 that confirmed the understanding that states considered they retained the right to use force to repel an attack or invasion from *another state*.

49 Bowett, D., *Self-Defence in International Law* (New York: Praeger, 1958) 185.

50 Waldock, C., 'The Regulation of the Use of Force by Individual States in International Law' (1952) 81 *Rec. des Cours* 451 at 496–7.

51 Moore, J., *Law and the Indo-China War* (Princeton: Princeton University Press, 1972) 363.

'supervened' by those of treaty law, and especially those of the UN Charter.[52] The ICJ attempted to clarify the issue when it held that in relation to the use of force by states, customary law and treaty law 'do not exactly overlap' and that:[53]

> ... Article 51 of the Charter is only meaningful on the basis that there is a 'natural' or 'inherent' right of self-defence, and it is hard to see how this can be other than of a customary nature, even if its present content has been confirmed and influenced by the Charter.

Although this may seem like an endorsement of the broad interpretation, the ICJ's references to customary law were confined to the context of defining the meaning of 'armed attack' and the requirement of 'proportionality'. The ICJ did not suggest that there was an entirely *different* customary law right of self-defence; it acknowledged that as Article 51 did not define important elements of the right, recourse must be had to customary law. In its 1996 Advisory Opinion on the *Legality of the Threat or Use of Nuclear Weapons*, the ICJ appeared to endorse a restrictive interpretation, that the Charter alone contains the right to use force in self-defence, when it stated that:[54] '... [T]he Court cannot lose sight of the fundamental right of every State to survival, and thus its right to resort to self-defence, in accordance with Article 51 of the Charter, when its survival is at stake.' The inference that may be drawn from the foregoing analysis is that the right to use force in self-defence is a natural or inherent right of states which, in the post-Charter era, must be exercised in accordance with the express limitations placed on that right by the Charter. In determining the extent of the right, but only in so far as Article 51 is silent, resort may be had to customary international law.

... if an armed attack occurs against a Member of the UN Article 51 provides that a state may act in individual or collective self-defence 'if an armed attack occurs'. This phrase requires consideration of the meaning of 'armed attack' and whether this proviso means *if and only if* an armed attack occurs. The term 'armed attack' was not defined, perhaps because it was regarded as being sufficiently clear and self-evident,[55] but evidence suggests that the insertion of the 'armed attack' element was a deliberate attempt to limit the instances in which a state could resort

52 *Nicaragua* case, supra n. 25 at 93. This is somewhat ironic given that the US has recently been at the forefront of advocating a right of pre-emptive self-defence, which, if it exists, would have to be based in customary international law.

53 *Nicaragua* case, supra n. 25 at 94.

54 *Legality of the Threat or Use of Nuclear Weapons* Advisory Opinion [1996] ICJ Reports 226 at 263, para 96.

55 Brownlie, supra n. 31 at 278; Goodrich and Hambro, supra n. 47 at 178.

to force. Alternatives, such as 'direct attack', and even omitting a reference to an attack, were both rejected.[56]

Significantly, 'armed attack' was also used in the North Atlantic Treaty (NATO Treaty).[57] Article 5 of the NATO Treaty states that if an armed attack occurs against any of the parties in Europe or North America, it will be considered as an armed attack against them all. As with the UN Charter, no definition of 'armed attack' was included. In 1949, the Foreign Relations Committee of the US Senate commented on the meaning of 'armed attack' in Article 5 of the NATO Treaty:[58]

> Experience has shown that armed attack is ordinarily self-evident; there is rarely, if ever, any doubt as to whether it has occurred or by whom it was launched. In this connexion, *it should be pointed out the words 'armed attack' clearly do not mean an incident created by irresponsible groups or individuals, but rather an attack by one state upon another.* (Emphasis added)

Since Article 5 of the NATO Treaty uses exactly the same phrase as Article 51 of the UN Charter, and the NATO Treaty expressly purports to be based on Article 51, statements such as this are important in understanding and interpreting the Charter signatories' understanding of 'armed attack'. The US understood that it involved an *actual* attack, which had *already occurred*, conducted by one *state* against *another state*. That interpretation was also favoured by the UK.[59]

In 1986, the ICJ commented on the meaning of 'armed attack':[60]

> ... [I]t may be considered to be agreed that an armed attack must be understood as including not merely action by regular armed forces across an international border, but also 'the sending by or on behalf of a State of armed bands, irregulars or mercenaries, which carry out acts of armed force against another State of such gravity as to amount to' (inter alia) an actual armed attack conducted by regular forces, or its substantial involvement therein.

56 Alexandrov, supra n. 39 at 97–8.

57 The NATO Treaty came into force on 24 August 1949. For an analysis of the relationship between the NATO Treaty and the Charter, see Beckett, W., *The North Atlantic Treaty, the Brussels Treaty and the Charter of the United Nations* (London: Stevens & Sons Ltd, 1950).

58 US Senate, *Report of the Committee on Foreign Relations on the North Atlantic Treaty June 6, 1949*, Executive Report no 8, 13.

59 Beckett, supra n. 57 at 13 and 27–9. As Sir Eric Beckett was the Legal Advisor to the British Foreign Office, it may be implied that his interpretation of the phrase 'armed attack' in the Charter and the NATO Treaty was also that of the British government.

60 *Nicaragua* case, supra n. 25 at 103.

The ICJ held that this interpretation of 'armed attack' reflected customary international law,[61] which prohibited the sending by a state of armed bands to the territory of another state, if such an operation, because of its scale and effects, would have been classified as an armed attack had it been carried out by regular armed forces.[62] However, merely providing logistical support would not suffice:[63] '... [T]he Court does not believe that the concept of 'armed attack' includes not only acts by armed bands where such acts occur on a significant scale but also assistance to rebels in the form of the provision of weapons or logistical or other support.' Such assistance may be regarded as a 'threat or use of force, or amount to intervention in the internal or external affairs of other States'[64] but it would not be an 'armed attack'.[65] Two important points may be made in relation to the ICJ's statements. First, a *threat* of force is not sufficient to satisfy the requirement in Article 51; self-defence may be resorted to by a state *if and only if* an armed attack *has occurred.* Secondly, attacks made by armed bands, irregulars or mercenaries can only be attributed to the state if the state sent them or had sufficient involvement therein; providing weapons or logistical support is insufficient.

The requirement that an 'armed attack' must originate from a *state* has subsequently been reaffirmed by the ICJ in its 2004 Advisory Opinion on the *Legal Consequences of the Construction of a Wall in the Occupied Palestinian Territory.*[66] Although this Advisory Opinion post-dates the events of 11 September 2001, it confirms the prevailing interpretation of 'armed attack' by the pre-eminent international judicial body. Adopting a somewhat cursory approach to the examination of Article 51, the ICJ held that:[67] 'Article 51 of the Charter thus recognizes the existence of *an inherent right of self-defence in the case of armed attack by one State against another State.* However, Israel does not claim that the attacks against it are imputable to a foreign state ...' (emphasis added). Article 51 was found to have no relevance in that particular instance because the attacks in question were not alleged to have come from a state. The Court's sparse reasoning that Article 51 only applies to armed attacks by *states* has been criticised,[68] but it is indisputable that in 2004 the ICJ pronounced that Article 51 only applies when an 'armed attack' has been launched by a state (or by a state's agents).

---

61 Ibid., 93; see the Definition of Aggression annexed to General Assembly Resolution 3314 (XXIX) of 14 December 1974; 29 GAOR, Supp. No. 31, at 42; UN Doc. A/9631 (1974), reprinted in 69 *AJIL* 480 (1975), Article 3(g).

62 *Nicaragua* case, supra n. 25 at 93.

63 Ibid. at 103–4.

64 Ibid.

65 Ibid.

66 *Legal Consequences of the Construction of a Wall in the Occupied Palestinian Territory*, Advisory Opinion, 2004 ICJ Rep.; 43 (5) ILM 1009 (2004).

67 Ibid.

68 Murphy, S., 'Agora: ICJ Advisory Opinion on Construction of a Wall in the Occupied Palestinian Territory: Self-Defense and the Israeli Wall Advisory Opinion: An *Ipse Dixit* from the ICJ?' (2005) 99 *AJIL* 62.

... *until the Security Council has taken the measures necessary to maintain international peace and security* The right of self-defence has been described as provisional because it only exists until the Security Council has taken the measures necessary to maintain international peace and security.[69] A literal reading of Article 51 supports the notion that the exercise of self-defence must stop as soon as the Security Council takes the measures necessary to maintain peace and security.[70] This interpretation is also supported by the drafting history of the Charter.[71] Accordingly, any action by an individual member under Article 51 was envisaged to be a *temporary* measure and in no way a substitute for the collective action of the Organisation.[72]

A difficulty arises in determining *when* the Security Council can be assessed as having 'taken measures necessary to maintain international peace and security'.[73] The fact that the term 'maintain' was used in Article 51, rather than 'restore', may suggest a lower threshold for action.[74] As to who decides when the 'measures' have been taken, the Article itself provides no clear answers and scholars are divided.[75] It is probably for the Security Council to decide what measures it will take and whether those measures are sufficient to maintain international peace and security, since the Charter gives the Security Council (not individual states) the primary responsibility for maintaining international peace and security. This is also consistent with the drafting history of Article 51 whereby the right of self-defence was perceived as an immediate, short-term response to an armed attack should the Security Council be unable or unwilling to act. Waldock asserts that the

---

69 See Bowett, supra n. 49 at 195; see Kelsen, H., 'Collective Security and Collective Self-Defence under the Charter of the United Nations' (1978) 42 *AJIL* 783 at 795. See also Lauterpacht, Tucker, Dinh and Greig, as cited in Alexandrov, supra n. 39 at 104, n. 121. See also Greig, D., 'Self-Defence and the Security Council: What Does Article 51 Require' (1991) 40 *ICLQ* 366 at 389.

70 See Kelsen, supra n. 36 at 792; see Beckett, supra n. 57 at 14.

71 At the San Francisco Conference, the right of self-defence was seen as an interim measure of protection which should cease when the machinery of the centralised system operates as an effective protection of the individual members' rights: Bowett, supra n. 49 at 195.

72 Ibid.; see also Beckett, supra n. 57 at 13: 'Even in the sunny San Francisco days of the summer of 1945, it was realised that there might be some delay in Security Council action, and that a State might be attacked and it must have full liberty to defend itself if it was.'

73 Bowett, supra n. 49 at 195–6; also Greig, supra n. 69 at 398ff.

74 On the 'maintain' versus 'restore' issue, see Greig, ibid., 389, n. 78.

75 Goodrich and Hambro argue that it is for each defending state to decide both when and for how long conditions exist which justify the exercise of the right: supra n. 47 at 300. The same view is expressed by Beckett, supra n. 57 at 29. For the opposite perspective, see Stone, who regards the decision as being exclusively within the competence of the Security Council: see Stone, J., *Legal Controls of International Conflict* (New York: Rineheart and Co, 1954) at 244; and Waldock, supra n. 50 at 496.

right to act in self-defence continues until the Security Council acts to bring any self-defence action to an end.[76] But that interpretation has been criticised as being politically naïve, ignoring the fact that the Security Council may fail to make any pronouncement because of political rivalries, and that there must be circumstances in which the right to act in self-defence comes to an end once the objective has been achieved, whatever the Security Council may or may not have done.[77]

Conte asserts that the right is limited not just 'until the Security Council has taken measures'[78] but also only for as long as the exercise of self-defence is necessary to prevent further attacks against the victim state. Citing the *Nicaragua* case, Conte argues that action taken in reliance on the right of self-defence is no longer legitimate once it is evident that the action is unnecessary to prevent further attacks.[79]

Although disagreement exists as to what role the Security Council ought to play once a self-defence action has been undertaken, it cannot be denied that both Article 51 and the views of scholars support the notion that it is *ultimately* for the Security Council, not individual states, to determine when the Council has taken the necessary measures to 'maintain international peace and security'.[80] The British Commentary on the Charter expresses the same view.[81] Assuming that this is correct, a significant problem arises: the veto (or threat of) could be used to protect a Permanent Member which has illegitimately resorted to force in self-defence, or which has continued to act in self-defence, even though the Security Council may well have 'taken measures to maintain international peace and security'.[82] This is an argument that will be addressed in Chapter 6 regarding the US's use of force against Afghanistan.[83]

Measures taken ... shall be immediately reported to the Security Council Article 51 requires states which have taken measures in the exercise of their right to

76 '... Thus, action in self-defence under Article 51 cannot be barred by the veto and cannot be terminated except by the unanimous decision of the Permanent Members': Waldock, supra n. 50 at 496.

77 Greig, supra n. 69 at 391, n. 85.

78 Conte, supra n. 40 at 65; see also *Nicaragua* case, supra n. 25 at 122–3: '... [T]he reaction of the United States in the context of what it regarded as self-defence was continued long after the period in which any presumed attacks by Nicaragua [on El Salvador] could reasonably be contemplated.'

79 Conte, supra n. 40 at 65.

80 Article 51 of the UN Charter.

81 See Bowett, supra n. 49 at 196.

82 Waldock has observed that this is a 'very serious drawback' because acts of aggression are very commonly represented to be acts of self-defence: supra n. 50 at 496; also Alexandrov, supra n. 39 at 105.

83 It will be argued that SC Resolution 1373 (2001) included 'measures to maintain international peace and security', thereby ending the period within which the US could have employed force in self-defence: see Chapter 6.

self-defence to immediately report them to the Security Council. Bowett[84] and Dinstein[85] consider that it is a mandatory, legal obligation for states to report to the Security Council, whilst others argue that the reporting requirement is merely directory[86] or that it is only a procedural requirement.[87] In *Nicaragua*, the ICJ found that non-reporting is an aspect of the conduct of a state which the Court is entitled to take into account as indicative of the state's view of its own actions.[88] However, reporting in conformity with Article 51 is not proof *per se* that the state's actions are legitimate acts of self-defence.[89] Self-defence has often been pleaded by states whose actions are unlawful reprisals.[90] Many examples are cited below where force has been used purportedly in self-defence, and reporting in accordance with Article 51 has occurred, but the Security Council has rejected the claims.[91] States have shown a tendency to report their actions in purported self-defence to the Security Council, often in an attempt to lend legitimacy to their actions, but reporting, in and of itself, is no proof that the use of force was lawful. The Security Council's members, the General Assembly and individual states have all expressed on occasion their rejection of formal claims of self-defence, despite strict adherence by states to the reporting requirement.[92]

... and shall not in any way affect the authority and responsibility of the Security Council under the present Charter to take at any time such action as it deems

---

84 Bowett, supra n. 49 at 197.

85 Dinstein, supra n. 33 at 190.

86 Greig, supra n. 69 at 384.

87 See Judge Schwebel in his Dissenting Opinion in the *Nicaragua* case, supra n. 25 at 376: 'the term in question [the reporting requirement] is a procedural term; of itself it does not, and by the terms of Article 51, cannot, impair the substantive, inherent right of self-defence, individual or collective.'

88 In that case, the failure of the US to report its actions to the Security Council was criticised because it did not conform with the US's claim that it believed it was acting in self-defence: *Nicaragua* case, supra n. 25 at 121. The US had previously stated that a state's failure to report its self-defence actions to the Security Council contradicts its claim to be acting on the basis of self-defence: UN Doc S/PV.2187 as cited in *Nicaragua*, supra n. 25 at 122.

89 'The dispatch of a report to the Security Council is only one of many factors bearing upon the legitimacy of a State's claim to self-defence. The instantaneous transmittal of a report is no guarantee that the Council will accept that claim': Dinstein, supra n. 33 at 191.

90 See discussion later in this chapter under the heading 'Forcible Measures Short of War'.

91 Examples include the British attacks on Yemen in 1964, the actions of Portugal against Senegal in 1969, the use of force by Israel against Lebanon, Syria and Jordan in the 1960s and 1970s, including the Litani operation in 1978, as well as the use of force by Israel in 1985 against Tunis and the US raids on Libya in 1986: see discussion below.

92 The statesmen who drafted the Charter were well aware that states often made spurious claims to be acting in self-defence. Goodrich and Hambro observed in 1946 that states commonly justify the resort to the use of armed force on the ground of self-defence: supra n. 47 at 178.

necessary in order to maintain or restore international peace and security The fifth and final element of Article 51 reiterates the fact that the Security Council possesses the primary responsibility for maintaining international peace and security, and that even if a state takes measures in self-defence, that does not detract from the authority and responsibility of the Council. Some scholars see this phrase as being 'superfluous and without legal effect'[93] and argue that it does nothing more than illustrate the intended provisional nature of individual or collective action in self-defence. Others, such as Conte, have read something deeper into this phrase, claiming that it points to the existence of an obligation, even a *duty*, on the Security Council to monitor the conduct of self-defence actions.[94]

The final phrase in Article 51 adds little to the power and responsibility already vested in the Security Council by Articles 24(1) and 39, which categorically state that the Security Council has the primary responsibility for the maintenance of international peace and security. Any arguments which can be constructed, based on Article 51, in favour of a 'duty to monitor' seem to be overshadowed by the importance of Articles 24(1) and 39; the Article 51 phrase probably only restates the existing position – rather than creating any new obligation or duty on the Council.[95] In the context of the current inquiry, this aspect of Article 51 confirms that the Security Council's authority remains paramount, regardless of action taken by individual states in self-defence.

The Nature of the Right of Self-defence

If a state can satisfy Article 51, it has the right to use force in self-defence, at which point resort must be had to customary international law to determine the scope and limits of that right.[96] In *Nicaragua*, both parties agreed that whether a response to an armed attack is lawful depends on the observance of the criteria of *necessity* and *proportionality* regarding the measures taken in self-defence.[97] In that instance, the Court held that the US's actions did not meet either criterion.[98]

---

93 Bowett, supra n. 49 at 198.

94 Conte, supra n. 40 at 66–9 for the 'duty to monitor' argument.

95 Although Conte argues that there exists a 'duty to monitor' actions taken in self-defence, it seems more plausible that a 'duty to act' exists because of the words 'until the Security Council has taken measures necessary to maintain international peace and security'. The phrasing adopted in Article 51 underlines the fact that any action in self-defence is provisional, available only until the Security Council acts, which implies that it *will* act to maintain international peace and security. Thus, there is arguably no 'duty to monitor' since it is subsumed within the 'duty to act' as implied in Article 51.

96 *Nicaragua*, supra n. 25 at 94.

97 Ibid., 103.

98 Regarding necessity, the US's actions against Nicaragua occurred a considerable time after the armed opposition against the government of El Salvador had been completely repulsed so that 'it was possible to eliminate the main danger to the Salvadorian Government without the United States embarking on activities in and against Nicaragua'. Regarding

The Court also made a finding on *immediacy*, without referring to it as a separate element, when it stated that the US's activities 'continued long after the period in which any presumed armed attack by Nicaragua could reasonably be contemplated'.[99] In his Dissenting Opinion, Judge Schwebel agreed that necessity and proportionality were customary law principles that had to be applied to self-defence actions under the Charter, but came to different conclusions based on different findings of fact.[100]

Although the findings on necessity and proportionality were not strictly necessary in the *Nicaragua* case (the Court having already found that there was no 'armed attack'), the ICJ's findings show that the *Caroline* principles of necessity and proportionality[101] are still relevant in the post-Charter era. The *Caroline* formulation confined acts of self-defence to situations where the necessity of that self-defence is instant, overwhelming, leaving no choice of means and no moment for deliberation. Furthermore, actions taken in self-defence must not be unreasonable or excessive, 'since the act, justified by the necessity of self-defence, must be limited by that necessity, and kept clearly within it'.[102] Although a literal interpretation of Article 51 does not require a state to adhere to the principles of necessity, proportionality and immediacy, the ICJ has ruled that these principles must be applied.[103]

The element of *necessity* requires the state to show that it had no choice other than to resort to force in self-defence. Judge Ago has declared that in order to satisfy this element:[104]

> … [T]he State attacked … must not, in the particular circumstances, have had any means of halting the attack other than recourse to armed force. In other words, had it been able to achieve the same result by measures not involving the use of armed force, it would have no justification for adopting conduct which contravened the general prohibition on the use of armed force.

---

proportionality, the US's actions in mining the Nicaraguan harbours and attacking oil and port installations were not proportional to the scale of aid received from the Salvadorian armed opposition from Nicaragua: ibid., 122.

99 Ibid., 123.

100 See Dissenting Opinion of Judge Schwebel, especially at 362ff.

101 See discussion of the *Caroline* case in Chapter 5.

102 Jennings, R., 'The Caroline and McLeod Cases' (1938) 32 *AJIL* at 82.

103 In addition to the *Nicaragua* case, the ICJ also stated in its Advisory Opinion on the *Legality of the Threat or Use of Nuclear Weapons* that '[t]he submission of the exercise of the right of self-defence to the conditions of necessity and proportionality is a rule of customary international law', but this 'dual condition applies equally to Article 51 of the Charter, whatever the means of force employed': supra n. 54 at 245.

104 Judge Ago's Addendum to the Eighth Report on State Responsibility, *Yrbk. ILC* 1980, Vol II, Part 1, 69.

This statement was cited with approval by Judge Schwebel in his Dissenting Opinion in the *Nicaragua* case and similar sentiments have been expressed by numerous scholars.[105]

The element of *proportionality* has been described as 'of the essence of self-defence'.[106] In *Nicaragua*, the ICJ held that it was 'a rule well established in customary international law'[107] that self-defence measures must be proportional to the armed attack. Acts done in self-defence must not exceed in manner or aim the necessity provoking them.[108] A state that is subjected to isolated frontier attacks or naval incidents generally limits itself to force proportionate to the attack: 'it does not bomb cities or launch an invasion'.[109] In many instances in which the Security Council has declared the use of force to be an illegal reprisal rather than legitimate self-defence, the Council has noted the disproportionate number of casualties resulting from the defence action when compared with the earlier attack.[110] However, there has also been an interpretation of 'proportionality' which does not compare the conduct constituting the armed attack with the opposing conduct, but rather the action taken in self-defence and the purpose of halting the attack.[111]

The element of *immediacy* means that self-defence action must occur in a timely fashion and there must not be a significant delay after the events which promoted the state to act.[112] In the *Caroline* case, it was agreed that 'the necessity of that self-defence is instant, overwhelming, and leaving no choice of means, and no moment for deliberation'.[113] Secretary of State Webster also said that, 'it must

105 See Dissenting Opinion of Judge Schwebel in *Nicaragua*, supra n. 25 at 363; see Schachter, O., 'The Right of States to Use Armed Force' (1984) 82 *Mich Law Rev* 1620 at 1635: 'force should not be considered necessary until peaceful measures have been found wanting or when they clearly would be futile'; also Rostow, E., 'Nicaragua and the Law of Self-Defence Revisited' 11 (1985–86) *Yale J. Int'l L.* 437 at 455; see also Dinstein, supra n. 33 at 183–4.

106 Brownlie, supra n. 31 at 279, n. 2.

107 *Nicaragua*, supra n. 25 at 14, 94.

108 Schachter, supra n. 105 at 1637.

109 Ibid.

110 Ibid.; also Security Council resolutions regarding the Qibya incident in 1953; Lake Tiberias in 1955; Jordan incident in 1966; As-Samu incident in 1966; Karameh incident, Es-Salt raid and Beirut raid in 1968; and the invasion of Lebanon in 1970. In all of these instances, the Security Council *inter alia* condemned the *disproportionate* nature of Israel's response.

111 '[T]he action needed to halt and repulse the attack may well have to assume dimensions disproportionate to those of the attack suffered.' Judge Ago's Addendum, supra n. 104 at 69.

112 Immediacy is not always discussed as a separate principle. Schachter, supra n. 105, only discusses the principles of proportionality and necessity; the ICJ in *Nicaragua*, supra n. 25, seemed to blend the notion of immediacy into the principle of proportionality.

113 Jennings, supra n. 102 at 85.

be shown that day-light could not be waited for' and that 'there was a necessity, present and inevitable'.[114] There must not be an undue time-lag between the armed attack and the exercise of self-defence.[115] The requirement of immediacy conflicts in some respects with that of necessity in so far as a state may not use force in self-defence unless it is the last resort and peaceful means of settling the dispute have been exhausted. It takes time to explore peaceful alternatives; thus, in satisfying the element of necessity, a state may theoretically fall foul of the principle of immediacy.[116] Immediacy is a vital element of the customary law notion of self-defence: if the use of force purportedly required in self-defence is indeed legitimate, it must be in a situation where no other response would do because of the time constraints involved in responding to the 'armed attack'. If there is time to negotiate at length, to enter into a 'tedious process of diplomatic negotiations' to use Dinstein's phrase, and explore other options to resolving the crisis, then that would suggest that a forcible response in self-defence is unnecessary.[117] By definition, force in self-defence ought to be used almost without delay, on the basis that there are no other options available.

In summary, the Security Council, the ICJ and the international community of states and scholars have come to accept that the right of self-defence was both preserved and restricted by Article 51, but its precise content, in so far as when and how the right is exercised, can only be understood by reference to customary principles of necessity, proportionality and immediacy, all of which must be considered when assessing whether a state has acted lawfully in self-defence. The use of force in self-defence must be tightly constrained simply because it is a rare exception to the general prohibition on the use of force in Article 2(4). The fact that it is so tightly constrained suggests that the right is supposed to be exercised sparingly, when it is absolutely necessary and when no other option is viable.

Pre-emptive Self-defence

The question of whether a state may use force to pre-empt, anticipate or deter an attack has drawn considerably more attention in the post-World War II era than in the past.[118] The controversy is derived from Article 51 and particularly the phrase 'armed attack'. It was noted earlier that some scholars have interpreted Article 51 to mean that force may be used in self-defence *if and only if* an armed attack has occurred (restrictive interpretation), whilst others consider that an

114 Ibid.

115 Dinstein, supra n. 33 at 184.

116 Ibid.

117 Ibid.

118 'Pre-emptive' and 'anticipatory' self-defence are used interchangeably here and represent the concept of using force in self-defence before an actual armed attack has occurred, and/or to prevent an attack from taking place.

armed attack is only *one* instance which will justify the use of force in self-defence (broad interpretation).[119] Proponents of the latter school argue that a state retains an inherent right to use force in self-defence to *anticipate* or *prevent* an act of aggression.

The *Caroline* case demonstrated that pre-emptive force may only be used if the necessity is 'instant, overwhelming, leaving no choice of means, and no moment for deliberation'.[120] The *Caroline* case's continuing relevance in this period was confirmed by the Nuremberg Tribunal when it considered Germany's plea of self-defence regarding the latter's invasion of Norway,[121] but judicial comment on pre-emptive self-defence has generally been sparse. In *Nicaragua*, the ICJ held that states do not have a right of collective 'armed response' to acts that do not constitute an 'armed attack',[122] but it was not required to rule directly on the question of pre-emptive self-defence and did not express a view on that issue.[123] In his Dissenting Opinion, Judge Schwebel expressed his clear support in principle for anticipatory self-defence[124] and expressed the view that he would not want Article 51 to be interpreted as meaning 'if and only if an armed attack occurs'.[125]

In 1949–50 the US and the UK perceived Article 51 as preserving a right of self-defence but not a right of *pre-emptive* self-defence.[126] Many incidents have occurred since the signing of the Charter which confirm that the international community generally interprets Article 51 literally, as requiring an 'armed attack'

---

119 Ibid. For a comprehensive analysis of the various scholars' positions in respect of each 'school' on this issue, see McCormack supra n. 33 at Part III; Ross, supra n. 33; see Erickson, R., *Legitimate Use of Military Force Against State Sponsored International Terrorism* (Maxwell Air Force Base, Alabama: Air University Press, 1989), chapter 4; Arend and Beck, supra n. 19 at chapter 5.

120 Jennings, supra n. 102 at 85.

121 The Tribunal held that Germany had not acted in self-defence, when that concept was taken to mean that there is a threat in the *Caroline* sense, because Germany's plans to attack Norway were drawn up to prevent an Allied occupation at some future date, not for forestalling an imminent Allied landing: *International Military Tribunal (Nuremberg), Judgments and Sentences* (1947) 41 *AJIL* 172, at 205–7.

122 *Nicaragua*, supra n. 25 at 103 and 110.

123 Ibid., 103.

124 See Dissenting Opinion of Judge Schwebel, *Nicaragua*, supra n. 25 at 347: '… I do not agree that the terms or intent of Article 51 eliminate the right of self-defence under customary international law, or confine its entire scope to the express terms of Article 51.'

125 Ibid. He noted that his comments on anticipatory self-defence were offered *ex abundanti cautela*.

126 See statements from the US Senate Foreign Relations Committee and the Legal Advisor to the British Foreign Office, in Beckett, supra n. 57 and accompanying text.

to have *actually occurred*. The 1956 Suez crisis,[127] the 1962 Cuban missile crisis,[128] the 1967 Arab–Israeli war[129] and the 1981 Israeli strike on the Iraqi nuclear reactor[130] are all instances in which the international community roundly rejected

---

127 The majority of states rejected the self-defence arguments advanced by Israel, France and the UK. The use of force by Israel was considered unwarranted since there had been no armed attack and the use of force by the UK and France was regarded as a violation of the Charter and the Pact of Paris, since they were using force as an instrument of national policy. Although the Security Council was unable to pass any resolutions due to the veto, the General Assembly voiced the concerns of the international community in producing a large majority vote in favour of a resolution which called for Israel, the UK and France to withdraw their forces: GA Res 997 (ES-I), 2 November 1956; GAOR ES-I, Supp Bo 1 at 2; UN Doc A/3354. For commentary on this incident, see Wright, Q., 'Intervention, 1956' (1957) 51 *AJIL* 257 at 272–3; also Alexandrov, supra n. 39 at 151–2. The General Assembly resolution, which called for a ceasefire and the withdrawal of Israeli, British and French forces, was voted for by 64 states, with five against (UK, Israel, France, Australia and New Zealand) and six abstentions. The US rejected the more permissive interpretation of Article 51 that was favoured by its traditional allies.

128 The US did not attempt to justify its naval 'quarantine' of Cuba on the grounds of Article 51, instead relying on Article 52 and the collective security provisions of the Rio Treaty (which covered a situation where there was a threat to the political integrity of an American state, but the aggression was *not* an armed attack). The US implicitly accepted that since no armed attack had occurred, it had to find other ways to justify its actions: see Wright, Q., 'The Cuban Quarantine' (1963) 57 *AJIL* 546 at 560–62; Alexandrov, supra n. 39 at 154–9; and Franck, T., *Recourse to Force: State Action Against Threats and Armed Attacks* (Cambridge; New York: Cambridge University Press, 2002) at 99–101. US officials refused to rely on Article 51 because of concern that it would set a bad precedent and would weaken the requirement that self-defence not be invoked except in cases of 'armed attack': Nydell, M., 'Tensions Between International Law and Strategic Security: Implications of Israel's Preemptive Raid on Iraq's Nuclear Reactor' (1984) 24 *Va. J. Int'l L.* 459 at 485.

129 Israel justified its pre-emptive air strikes on Egypt, Jordan and Syria both on the grounds of actual self-defence (on the basis that the closure of the Straits of Tiran to Israeli vessels was an act of war) and on the basis of anticipatory self-defence. Although the Security Council neither apportioned blame for the outbreak of fighting nor did it condemn the exercise of self-defence by Israel, Alexandrov and Dinstein argue that the anticipatory self-defence claim found little support: see Alexandrov, supra n. 39 at 154; and Dinstein, supra n. 33 at 173; compare with Shaw, M., *International Law*, 5th edn (2003) at 1029; and Franck, supra n. 128 at 104–5.

130 On 7 June 1981, the Israeli Air Force launched an attack against the Iraqi nuclear reactor, 'Osirak' (Tammuz-I) which was under construction. Israel relied *solely* on the grounds of anticipatory self-defence: Israel's Permanent Representative to the UN, Yehuda Blum, claimed that Israel was exercising its inalienable right to self-defence under Article 51 of the Charter and that anticipatory self-defence was permissible under international law: Statement of Mr Blum, UN Doc S/PV 2280 12 June 1981 at 37 and 52–5. All members of the Security Council rejected Israel's interpretation of Article 51. The Security Council unanimously adopted Resolution 487 in which it stated that it 'strongly condemns the military attack by Israel in clear violation of the Charter of the United Nations and the

the use of force in pre-emptive self-defence. The 'Osirak' incident was perhaps the most unambiguous demonstration of the Security Council's rejection of the claim that Article 51 permits the use of force in pre-emptive self-defence.[131] The international community showed there that it required strict adherence to the text of Article 51.

Further examples can be drawn from the later decades of the post-Charter period. In 1985, the Israeli raid on Tunis[132] was condemned by the Security Council.[133] The 1986 US strikes against Libya were condemned by the General Assembly.[134] In 1993 the US attempted to justify its missile strikes against Baghdad as not only being a response to a planned but thwarted terrorist attack but also on the basis that it was acting to *prevent further attacks in the future.*[135] Although no formal condemnation in the Security Council was sought, the states which expressed support for the US accepted that an 'armed attack' had occurred and that the US was reacting to it.[136] No state chose to endorse the US's use of force on the basis of pre-emptive self-defence.

In justifying its missile strikes against Iraq in 2001, the US stated that it was acting to *prevent possible future attacks* on its aircraft when patrolling the 'no-fly' zone. International reaction was almost universally negative: only the US, the UK and Israel accepted the legitimacy of the missile strikes. Three Permanent Members of the Security Council publicly questioned the use of force without Security Council authority.

---

norms of international conduct': SC Resolution 487, 1981. For commentary on the 'Osirak' incident, see *inter alia* Alexandrov, supra n. 39 at 159–65; Franck, supra n. 128 at 105–7; Dinstein, supra n. 33 at 169; D'Amato, A., 'Israel's Air Strike Upon the Iraqi Nuclear Reactor' (1983) 77 *AJIL* 584; Mallison, W. and Mallison, S., 'The Israeli Aerial Attack of June 7 1981, Upon the Iraqi Nuclear Reactor: Aggression or Self-Defence?' (1982) 15 *Vand. J. Transnat'l L.* 417; and Nydell, supra n. 128 at 459. For a comprehensive analysis of the incident, see McCormack, supra n. 33.

131 Spain and Mexico stated that Article 51 did not permit pre-emptive self-defence in any form and that force was only permissible in response to an actual armed attack: see speeches of the representatives of Spain and Mexico, 36 UN SCOR, (2282nd meeting) 7–8, UN Doc S/PV 2282, 15 June 1981 and 36 UN SCOR (2288th meeting) 10–12, UN Doc S/PV 2288, 19 June 1981, respectively. For discussion of the statements made prior to the adoption of the resolution, see McCormack, supra n. 33 at 31–3; and Mallison and Mallison, supra n. 130, 434–40.

132 Israel justified its use of force both as a response to previous attacks and as a means of preventing future terrorist attacks.

133 By a vote of 14-0.

134 By a vote of 79-28. See GA Res 41/38 (1986), and for the US actions in blocking a Security Council resolution, see UN SCOR 41st Session (2682nd meeting) at 43 UN Doc S/PV 2682 (1986).

135 Kritsiotis, D., 'The Legality of the 1993 US Missile Strike on Iraq and the Right of Self-Defence in International Law' (1996) 45 *ICLQ* 162.

136 An attempted assassination of former President George Bush.

Although the majority of states reject the notion of pre-emptive self-defence, the *opinio juris* of some states has evolved over time. For example, the adjustment in the US's stance on pre-emptive self-defence is apparent by comparing its stance in 1981 (when it supported Security Council Resolution 487 against Israel's pre-emptive attack on the Iraqi Osirak reactor) to the position set forth in the 2002 National Security Strategy (2002 NSS).[137] In the 2002 NSS, the Bush administration set out its doctrine of pre-emptive self-defence in response to terrorism:[138]

> While the United States will constantly strive to enlist the support of the international community, we will not hesitate to act alone, if necessary, to exercise our right of self-defense by acting pre-emptively against such terrorists, to prevent them from doing harm against our people and our country ... (Emphasis added)

With regards to weapons of mass destruction, a similar pre-emptive theory was espoused:[139]

> We must be prepared to stop rogue states and their terrorist clients *before they are able to threaten or use weapons of mass destruction* against the United States and our allies and friends ... *we cannot let our enemies strike first* ... (Emphasis added)

The *opinio juris* of the US is that using force in unilateral, pre-emptive self-defence is lawful (for the US). The George W. Bush Administration advanced its view that the concept of 'imminent threat' had to be redefined given the new types of threats facing it, and it claimed that, 'to forestall or prevent hostile acts', the 'US will, if necessary, act pre-emptively'.[140] This is a direct challenge to the traditional, essentially restrictive, interpretation of Article 51 which, at least as recently as 1981, was interpreted by the US and all other members of the Security Council as precluding unilateral, pre-emptive use of force. Not only is this a new interpretation of Article 51, but it goes further than even allowing force to be used to preclude an 'imminent' attack, to allowing force to be used *before* an adversary is even able to pose a threat. It is unclear from the NSS what level of danger would be required to be present before force could theoretically be employed, but the threshold for action in the 2002 NSS certainly falls short of requiring an 'armed attack' to have occurred.

137 National Security Strategy of the United States, September 2002, available at: <http://www.whitehouse.gov/nsc/nss.pdf> at 12 June 2008.

138 Ibid.

139 Ibid.

140 Ibid.

Whilst several European states were 'concerned' about the new doctrine,[141] Australia was quick to endorse it. In June 2002, in a speech to the Australian Defence College, Defence Minister Robert Hill flagged Australia's 'in principle'[142] support for the doctrine of pre-emptive self-defence. Although the interpretation of self-defence adopted by the US and endorsed in principle by Australia appears to contradict Article 51, neither the Bush Administration nor the Howard government considered that their newly adopted doctrine was in violation of international law.[143] Hill stated that 'Australia has a long and proud tradition of contributing to the development of international law' and that 'any actions Australia takes will be consistent with international law'.[144] He called for 'a new and distinct doctrine of pre-emptive action to avert a threat' or a redefining of the meaning of self-defence.[145] The Australian Prime Minister at the time, John Howard, called for the UN Charter to be reviewed on the basis that it was written in a time when global security was threatened by state-versus-state conflicts and that the new threats to global security were from 'random stateless terrorists', which meant that it was

---

141 Frankel, G., 'New US Doctrine Worries Europeans', *Washington Post*, 30 September 2002, A1.

142 'The need to act swiftly and firmly *before threats become attacks* is perhaps the clearest lesson of 11 September, and is one that is clearly driving US policy and strategy. It is a position which we share, in principle' (emphasis added): Minister for Defence, Senator Robert Hill, *Address to Defence and Strategic Studies Course*, 'Beyond the White Paper: Strategic Directions for Defence', Australian Defence College, Canberra, 18 June 2002, available at: <http://www.minister.defence.gov.au/2002/180602.doc> at 12 June 2008; see also Nguyen, M., '"Just Cause" or Just Callous? Australia's Justification for War in Iraq', January 2004, Uniya <http://www.uniya.org/talks/nguyen_iraq_jan04.html> at 12 June 2008.

143 Howard: 'I would always want to see Australia act in accordance with proper international practices. But that proper international practice has always recognised legitimate self-defence … that is really the essence of wanting to address the issue [of pre-emptive self-defence] within a proper legal framework and not go outside the existing legal framework': Australian Broadcasting Corporation, *Lateline*, 'Prime Minister takes cautious line in face of terrorist threat', broadcast 29 November 2002, transcript at: <http://www.abc.net.au/lateline/stories/s738064.htm> at 12 June 2008.

144 Senator Robert Hill, John Bray Memorial Oration, University of Adelaide, 28 November 2002: <http://www.defence.gov.au/minister/HillSpeechtpl.cfm?CurrentId=2121> at 12 June 2008.

145 'Some would argue that it's time for a new and distinct doctrine of pre-emptive action to avert a threat. A better outcome might be for the international community and the international lawyers to seek an agreement on the ambit of the right to self-defence better suited to contemporary realities': ibid.; see also ABC *Lateline*, 'The issue now is how you define self-defence in an environment of unconventional conflict, non-state parties, weapons of mass destruction, global terrorism and whilst anticipatory self-defence has also been permissible, clearly this new environment requires a more liberal definition of self-defence to be meaningful': 'Hill makes case for pre-emptive strikes', broadcast 27 November 2002, transcript at: <http://www.abc.net.au/lateline/stories/s736373.htm> at 12 June 2008.

no longer 'legitimate' to respond to the new threats under rules that were written when that kind of conduct was never contemplated.[146] Howard expressed the view that he wanted 'international law, including the UN Charter, to reflect the new reality'.[147] Problematically, whilst calling for the Charter to be changed to 'reflect the new reality', Howard, Hill and the Bush Administration were simultaneously advancing the view that pre-emptive strikes were already permitted and that they were already prepared to use force in pre-emptive self-defence if necessary.[148]

The proposition that Australia would contemplate using pre-emptive force provoked a negative reaction from, among others, Malaysia, Indonesia, the Philippines and Thailand.[149] Those states' reactions suggested that they did not share the US–Australian interpretation of Article 51.[150] The New Zealand Prime Minister, Helen Clark, also expressed her view that the UN Charter does not permit force to be used in pre-emptive self-defence.[151] The UK Attorney-General, Lord Goldsmith, in legal advice provided in 2003 to then British Prime Minister, Tony Blair, advised that international law does not permit force to be used in pre-emptive self-defence unless the attack which it aims to pre-empt is 'imminent'.[152]

In summary, it is contended that in 2008, the *opinio juris* of the majority of states remains unchanged, that there is no right to use force in pre-emptive self-

---

146 ABC *Lateline*, 'Prime Minister takes cautious line in face of terrorist threat', supra n. 143.

147 Ibid.

148 'But there's nothing illegitimate, illegal, improper, provocative about somebody arguing that current international law has been overtaken by changed circumstances where individually-sponsored aggression and terror and not state-sponsored aggression and terror is now the greatest challenge the world has … if I were given clear evidence that this country were likely to suffer an attack – and I had a capacity, as PM, to do something to prevent that attack occurring – I would be negligent to the people of Australia if I didn't take that action': ibid.

149 The Acting Indonesian Ambassador described Howard's comments as 'unhelpful' and the Malaysian High Commission released a statement saying that Australia could not operate in Malaysia without the Malaysian government's approval: Australian Government, Department of Foreign Affairs and Trade, interview between Minister of Foreign Affairs and Trade, Alexander Downer, and the ABC Radio, 2 December 2002; see also Grattan, M., 'Words are Bullets, Mr Howard', *The Age*, 4 December 2002, available at: <http://www.theage.com.au/articles/2002/12/03/1038712935246.html> at 12 June 2008.

150 Haidon, T., 'The Possibility of Australian Pre-emptive Military Action: Political and Legal Implications', 11 December 2002, *IslamOnline.net*, available at: <http://www.islamonline.net/English/Views/2002/12/article04.shtml> at 12 June 2008.

151 'It's certainly not what is envisaged in the UN Charter … to move to a pre-emptive position is very significant … If the ground is being shifted from self-defence to pre-emption, then that is not what was contemplated when the UN Charter was being written': Campbell, G., 'A Rock and a Hard Place', *New Zealand Listener*, 1–7 March 2003, 18–21.

152 'Full-text: Iraq legal advice', *Guardian Unlimited*, 28 April 2005, available at: <http://www.guardian.co.uk/Iraq/Story/0,,1472450,00.html> at 12 June 2008.

defence under current international law, except perhaps if the threat is imminent and the use of force is inevitable.[153] Only three states (Israel, the US and Australia) have seriously advanced the concept of pre-emptive self-defence as having a basis in international law, and Australia's assertions must be tempered with its simultaneous calls for a review of international law to permit pre-emptive strikes, a review that would logically be unnecessary if such a right already existed. It cannot be concluded that the Bush or Howard doctrines on pre-emption have become entrenched as the dominant interpretation of self-defence at this time.

Forcible Measures Short of War

The legal standing of forcible measures short of war, and in particular reprisals,[154] changed with the adoption of the UN Charter. Reprisals which involve the use or threat[155] of force were rendered unlawful by virtue of Article 2(4). That conclusion is supported by scholars,[156] case law[157] and pronouncements of the Security Council.[158] In the post-Charter era, if there is an 'armed attack', the victim state will have the right to use force in self-defence under Article 51, but if there is no prior 'armed attack', any use of force by a state (without the permission of the Security Council under Chapter VII) is generally considered to be unlawful.[159] The

153 That interpretation of Article 51 is further supported by the general consensus amongst international lawyers that the use of force against Iraq in 2003 (with the apparent objective of removing Iraq's potential ability to acquire and use weapons of mass destruction) was unlawful.

154 Reprisals are acts which are in themselves illegal and have been adopted by one state in retaliation for the commission of an earlier illegal act by another state.

155 The *threat* to use force is unlawful pursuant to Article 2(4), as confirmed by the UNGA in the 1965 Declaration on the Inadmissibility of Intervention in the Domestic Affairs of States, GA Resolution 2131, supra n. 22, Article 1, and by the ICJ in *Legality of the Threat or Use of Nuclear Weapons*, supra n. 54 at para 49; see also White, N. and Cryer, R., 'Unilateral Enforcement of Resolution 687: A Threat Too Far?' (1999) 29 *Cal. W. Int'l L.J.* 243.

156 Brownlie, supra n. 31 at 281 who cites, *inter alia*, Oppenheim, Jessup, Goodrich and Hambro, Bowett, Kotzsche, Brierly and Guggenheim.

157 The US–France Air Services Agreement case 54 ILR 306.

158 SCR 188 (1964), UN Doc S/5650 regarding British strikes on Yemen: 'The Security Council ... condemns reprisals as being incompatible with the purposes and principles of the United Nations.'

159 The difference between unlawful reprisals and lawful self-defence may lie in their objectives, the former being punitive in nature and the latter being protective: 'Self-defence is permissible for the purpose of protecting the security of the state and the essential rights – in particular the rights of territorial integrity and political independence – upon which that security depends', whereas reprisals are '... punitive in character: they seek to impose reparation for the harm done, or to compel a satisfactory settlement of the dispute created by the initial illegal act, or to compel the delinquent state to abide by the law in the

only type of reprisals which are still currently permitted are those which *do not* involve the use of force, usually referred to as 'counter-measures', providing that they meet certain conditions.[160]

The proposition that forcible reprisals were outlawed by Article 2(4) would appear unassailable. Yet, some states have demonstrated that they still consider themselves to possess a right to use forcible reprisals. Israel is one state[161] that has repeatedly attempted to gain acceptance of its position that reprisals are 'an integral element of action constituting self-defence against an ongoing threat'.[162] This has led to the suggestion that there may be a 'credibility gap' between the international law norm and the actual practice of states.[163] By analysing some instances in which reprisals have come to the Security Council's attention, a subtle trend is noticeable, from outright rejection in the early years of the post-Charter period, to conditional acceptance towards the latter years.

Security Council Resolutions: 1950s–1960s

In 1955, in relation to a complaint by Syria regarding an Israeli attack in the area of Lake Tiberias, the Security Council was asked to pass a variety of measures in response to the actions of the Israeli military.[164] In a unanimous resolution, the Security Council acknowledged that there had been interference by the Syrian authorities with Israeli activities on Lake Tiberias as alleged by Israel, but found that such interference in no way justified the Israeli action, even if it was undertaken by way of retaliation.[165] The Security Council condemned the attack by Israel as a 'flagrant violation' of both the General Armistice Agreement and the UN Charter.[166] Some members expressly stated that forcible retaliation and reprisals were unlawful under the UN Charter and had been previously condemned by the

future. But, coming after the event and when the harm has already been inflicted, reprisals cannot be characterised as a means of protection': Bowett, supra n. 49 at 3.

160 Such as, they must be in response to a prior wrongful act, and taken in light of a refusal to remedy it: see *Gabčikovo-Nagymaros Project* case (Hungary/Slovakia) (Judgment) ICJ Reports, 1997, 7 at 55–7; see also the ILC Draft Article Responsibility of States for Internationally Wrongful Acts, ILC, available at: <http://untreaty.un.org/ilc/texts/instruments/english/draft%20articles/9_6_2001.pdf> at 12 June 2008, Articles 49–53, especially Article 50(1)(a).

161 Bowett examined 23 cases of reprisals considered by the Security Council between 1953 and 1970, of which 20 involved Israel: Bowett, D., 'Reprisals Involving Recourse to Armed Force' (1972) 66 *AJIL* 1.

162 This comment is from O'Brien's analysis, updating Bowett's research: O'Brien, W., 'Reprisals, Deterrence and Self-Defense in Counterterror Operations' (1990) 30 *Va. J. Intn'l L.* 421.

163 Bowett, supra n. 161.

164 S/3505, Official Records, *10th Year, Suppl for Oct–Dec 1955*, 21.

165 S/3538 Official Records, *11th Year, Suppl for Jan–Mar, 1956*, 6–7.

166 Ibid.

Security Council.[167] The following year, the British government's Foreign Office issued a statement condemning a reprisal carried out by Israel against Jordanian positions, declaring that the British government deplores *all* reprisals; that the Security Council had repeatedly condemned reprisal raids and that such raids did not come within the limits of legitimate self-defence.[168]

In 1964, the UK attempted to justify its air attacks on Yemen on the basis that it was acting in self-defence, in response to a series of attacks and ongoing hostility. The UK acknowledged the distinction between unlawful reprisals and lawful self-defence, and argued that its actions fell within the latter. However, the Security Council rejected the British argument and condemned the actions as unlawful reprisals.[169] A justification based upon an 'accumulation of events' was employed by the US in relation to the Gulf of Tonkin incident in 1964. The US claimed its missile strikes against North Vietnamese weapons and facilities were a legitimate response to a series of past attacks on US vessels and that they were a 'limited and measured response fitted precisely to the attack that produced it'.[170] Although no resolution was adopted condemning the US's response, the Soviet and Czechoslovak representatives rejected the US's plea of self-defence, as did the Democratic Republic of Vietnam.[171] During the course of the debate it was noted that 'recognition of the right of self-defence in Article 51 of the Charter *ipso jure* precluded the right of retaliation'.[172] Given the evidence which recently came to light concerning the Gulf of Tonkin incident, it appears likely that the international community was correct in refusing to condone the US's use of force.[173] The use of

---

167 Previous condemnations: 692nd Meeting, paras 8, 9; 695th Meeting, para 11.

168 Brownlie, supra n. 31 at 282.

169 UN Doc S/5649, adopted at the 1111th Meeting, 8 April 1964; SCR 188 (1964), UN Doc S/5650. The resolution was adopted by nine votes to zero with two abstentions (the UK and the US); see also the discussion in Bowett, supra n. 161 at 8; and Alexandrov, supra n. 39 at 170–71.

170 United Nations, 'Chapter VII: Action with Respect to Threats to the Peace', at 266, extract available at: <http://untreaty.un.org/cod/repertory/art51/english/rep_supp3_vol2-art51_e.pdf> at 12 June 2008.

171 UNSCOR, 1140th Meeting, at 9, and 1141st Meeting, at 15; 1141st Meeting at 4 respectively; Letter from the USSR to the Secretary General, transmitting the views of the DRV, UN Doc S/5888, UNSCOR Suppl. for July, August and September 1964, 170; see also the discussion in Bowett, supra n. 161 at 8.

172 Security Council 1140th Meeting: UK, para 78, US, paras 33–42 and 44–6; 1141st Meeting, Czechoslovakia, paras 27–32; USSR, paras 81–4; United States, paras 49 and 52: United Nations Security Council, *Chapter XI, Consideration of the Provisions of Chapter VII of the Charter*, 195, available online at: <http://www.un.org/Depts/dpa/repertoire/64-65_11.pdf> at 9 January 2009.

173 In October 2005, the *New York Times* reported that the NSA had deliberately distorted intelligence reports regarding the second of two alleged attacks on US destroyers by the North Vietnamese. It would appear that the incident which the US alleged occurred on 4 August 1964, which led to the approval of the Gulf of Tonkin Resolution by the US Congress,

reprisals in response to a series of prior attacks was again rejected by the Security Council in 1969 when it condemned Portugal for its use of force against the village of Samine in Senegal.[174]

Throughout the 1960s, the Security Council remained steadfast in its refusal to legitimise acts of reprisal, even when they were in response to alleged acts of terrorism. For example, with regards to the As-Samu incident,[175] the Karameh incident,[176] the Es-Salt Raid[177] and the Beirut Reid,[178] the Security Council

---

never actually occurred: Shane, S., 'Vietnam Study, Casting Doubts, Remains Secret', 31 October 2005, *New York Times*, available at: <http://www.nytimes.com/2005/10/31/politics/31war.html?ex=1162443600&en=8849d65750c7410c&ei=5070> at 12 June 2008. There has been substantial discussion on the parallels between the 'lie' which led to the Vietnam War and the intelligence distortions which led to the Iraq War in 2003.

174 Portugal attempted to justify the attacks on the grounds of self-defence based upon the allegation that there had been a whole serious of past incursions into Portuguese territory by armed bands from Senegal. The Security Council reminded Portugal of its obligations to respect the territorial integrity and political independence of Senegal, condemned the Portuguese attacks and called on Portugal to desist immediately: SCR 273 (1969), 9 December 1969, adopted at the 1520th Meeting, by 13 votes to none, with two abstentions (the US and Spain).

175 On 13 November 1966, Israel used jets and heavy artillery to attack villages south of Hebron, causing heavy civilian casualties. Israel claimed it had suffered an increase in terrorist and sabotage raids from Jordan and that villagers in As-Samu were harbouring terrorists from Syria. Israel's use of force was unanimously condemned: SC Resolution 228 (1966).

176 On 18 March 1968, an Israeli bus carrying schoolchildren on a trip from Tel Aviv to the Negev Desert was blown up when it hit a mine. Two adults were killed and 28 children injured. In retaliation, the Israeli military launched a large-scale attack using helicopters, tanks and aircraft on the village of Karameh, resulting in the deaths of 150 guerrillas. Israel claimed that Karameh was harbouring Fatah 'terrorists' who it held responsible for the mine incident. The Security Council unanimously 'condemned the military action launched by Israel in violation of the United Nations Charter and the cease-fire resolutions'. It expressly referred to the Israeli action as a 'military reprisal' and declared that such actions could not be tolerated: SCR 248 (1968), 24 March 1968.

177 In 1968, the Israeli military attacked a village in Jordan which it alleged was a base for terrorist activities. It claimed its actions were lawful on the grounds of self-defence. The Security Council found that the 'massive air attacks by Israel on Jordanian territory were of a large-scale and carefully planned nature in violation of resolution 248 of 1968'. The Security Council unanimously condemned Israel for its premeditated and repeated military attacks: SCR 256 (1968) 16 August 1968.

178 In 1968 an Israeli El Al Boeing 707 was attacked at Athens airport (resulting in the death of one passenger) by two Arabs who were allegedly members of the Popular Front for the Liberation of Palestine and who had flown to Athens from Beirut, but who had otherwise no connection with Lebanon. Israel launched an attack on the Beirut Airport, destroying all 13 Arab-registered aircraft that were either on the runway or in hangers. It justified its actions on the grounds that Lebanon was 'assisting and abetting acts of warfare, violence and terror by irregular forces and organizations': UN Doc S/8946, Letter dated 29

consistently rejected Israel's justifications for its use of force and reiterated that forcible reprisals were unlawful.

The Security Council's justifications varied somewhat with references to the reprisals' 'punitive', 'disproportionate' and 'premeditated' nature.[179] Nevertheless, the Council consistently agreed that reprisals were illegal and in violation of Article 2(4), whether or not they were in response to an isolated attack, a series of attacks or an attempt to prevent future attacks, and regardless of whether the attacks originated from another state or from non-state actors. Some reprisals escaped condemnation, perhaps because the Security Council lacked evidence of the details of the incident or because it felt that the reprisal was somehow 'reasonable' or 'proportionate'.[180] Those are certainly factors which some scholars argue were taken into account by the Security Council when pronouncing on a particular reprisal.[181] In any case, the evidence shows that even though reprisals were repeatedly condemned as being unlawful, and despite sometimes strong threats from the Council to take further steps if its resolutions were not adhered to, the practice of carrying out forcible reprisals continued.

Security Council Resolutions: 1970s

Throughout the early 1970s, Israel, in particular, continued to use military reprisals in a fashion which suggested that it considered them to be lawful. Although the Security Council as a whole generally maintained the position that reprisals were unlawful, there was a distinct softening of its attitude, most notably in the position adopted by the US. In relation to the Israeli invasion of Lebanese territory on 12 May 1970, when Israel attacked villages which it claimed were terrorist bases, the Security Council (with four abstentions) condemned Israel but chose not to call the attacks 'reprisals'. Later that year, in relation to further Israeli attacks on

---

December 1968 from Israel to the President of the Security Council. The Security Council unanimously (15 to zero) 'condemned Israel for its premeditated military action in violation of its obligations under the Charter and the cease-fire resolutions'. The Security Council was unconvinced that Lebanese responsibility had been established for the incident involving the El Al plane: UN Doc S/PV 1460, 28–30. For commentary on this incident, see Falk, R., 'The Beirut Raid and the International Law of Retaliation' (1969) 63 *AJIL* 415.

179 See discussion in Bowett, supra n. 161 at 7.

180 For example, in relation to the Eilat incident in 1967, in which Egyptian aircraft fired upon and sunk an Israeli destroyer, in response to which Israel bombarded Suez oil refineries, the Security Council passed a neutral resolution condemning the 'violation of the ceasefire'.

181 Bowett argues that the Security Council accepts 'reasonable' reprisals, taking into account factors such as: the proportionality of the reaction to the injury, the types of targets attacked, the degree of responsibility of states for irregulars operating within their jurisdiction and the putative legitimacy of the target state: see Bowett, supra n. 161 at 10–19; see also Falk's 12-point framework, supra n. 178.

Lebanese villages, the Security Council only called for Israel's withdrawal of its armed forces, rather than condemning the attacks outright.[182]

In February 1972, Israel reminded the Lebanese government of its obligations to prevent its territory from being used as a base for armed attacks against Israel and that failure to do so would necessitate Israeli attacks.[183] From 25–28 February 1972, Israeli forces attacked PLO bases in a number of south Lebanese villages, and claimed that they had destroyed many houses that were used by terrorist infiltrators and their supporters.[184] The Security Council demanded that Israel immediately desist and refrain from any ground or air military action against Lebanon and to forthwith withdraw its military forces from Lebanese territory,[185] but, again, the attacks were not characterised by the Council as 'reprisals'. A few months later, Israel again attacked alleged PLO bases in Lebanon, in response to a continuation of attacks across the Israeli–Lebanese border. The Security Council condemned Israel's repeated attacks on Lebanon in violation of the UN Charter, but, again, it did not refer to them as 'reprisals' (the US abstained from the vote).[186]

Also notable in 1972 was the Israeli response to the murder of eleven Israeli athletes at the Munich Olympic Games. Israel held Lebanon and Syria responsible for providing support and bases for PLO terrorists.[187] On 7 September 1972, Israel launched ground and air attacks against PLO targets in Lebanon and Syria. Israel justified its attacks not only on the grounds that they were a direct response to Munich, but also on the basis that they were 'part of a continuous war'.[188] The US vetoed a Security Council resolution calling for an immediate cessation of military operations by Israel.[189]

182 SCR 285 (1970), 5 September 1970, passed by 14 votes in favour with one abstention (US).

183 'Israel Warns Lebanon After 2 Die in Border Ambush', *New York Times*, 25 February 1972, 3, col. 3.

184 O'Brien, supra n. 162 at 427.

185 SCR 313 (1972), 28 February 1972, adopted unanimously.

186 SCR 316 (1972), 26 June 1972, adopted by 13 votes to none (Panama and US abstained).

187 'Arab Guerrillas Warned by Israel', *New York Times*, 8 September 1972, 1, col. 1.

188 'Top Israeli General Calls Raids Only "Part of a Continuous War"', *New York Times*, 11 September 1972, 12, col. 2, and see discussion in O'Brien, supra n. 162 at 428–9.

189 27 UN SCOR 1662nd Meeting at 7, UN Doc S/PV 1662 (1972), remarks by Ambassador Bush (US).

The gradual softening in the Security Council's attitude towards reprisals continued in 1973[190] and 1974.[191] The underlying premise for Israel's sustained practice of military reprisals against the PLO in Lebanon and Syria was self-defence. It claimed that its 'self-defence measures' were necessitated by the fact that Lebanon and Syria had failed, under the doctrine of state responsibility, to prevent their territory from being used as a base for attacks on another state, and that Lebanon and Syria had also provided support and co-operation to the PLO.[192] The Security Council generally rejected those grounds and usually found that Israel's use of force amounted to reprisals, not self-defence and, therefore, Israel's actions were unlawful.[193] Even if the Security Council resolutions did not always use the term 'unlawful reprisals', the debates that preceded the resolutions often showed that this was indeed how state representatives viewed Israel's actions.[194] The international community accepted that terrorist actions were unlawful, but insisted that this did not legitimise the use of reprisals:[195]

190 In response to Israel's covert raid on Beirut in 1973, in which a number of PLO leaders were killed, the Council condemned Israel's 'repeated military attacks' against Lebanon and its violation of Lebanon's territorial integrity and sovereignty, but did not categorise Israel's actions as 'reprisals': SCR 331 (1973), 20 April 1973; adopted by 11 votes to none (USSR, US, China and Guinea abstained).

191 When the Security Council was asked to respond to a PLO attack on Kiryat Shemona and the Israeli response, it adopted a resolution condemning all acts of violence and Israel's violation of Lebanese territorial integrity and sovereignty: SCR 347 (1974), 24 April 1974, adopted by 13 votes to none (China and Iraq did not participate in the voting).

192 For instance, see UN Doc S/PV 1644 (1972), statement by Doron that Lebanon had become a 'sanctuary for terror'.

193 In the debates in the Security Council, representatives described Israel's military attacks as, *inter alia*, 'intolerable reprisals': see 27 UN SCOR 1643rd Meeting at 12, UN Doc S/PV 1643 (1972), statement by the French representative. Council members generally condemned them on the grounds that they were totally incompatible with the purposes, principles and prescriptions of the UN.

194 For instance, in the debate on SCR 316 (1972), Belgium's representative made a statement that 'The Belgium Government has never ceased to repudiate energetically the military reprisals undertaken by Israel against Lebanon …'; Argentina's representative stated that 'punitive expeditions and preventive war are totally incompatible with the purposes, principles and prescriptions of the United Nations Charter'; and the French representative stated that France disapproved of all acts of violence and it 'condemned all reprisal operations, whatever the reasons for them': 27 UN SCOR 1649th Meeting UN Doc S/PV 1649 (1972) and 27 UN SCOR 1650th Meeting UN Doc S/PV 1650 (1972).

195 27 UN SCOR 1662nd Meeting at 4, UN Doc S/PV 1662 (1972). Similar remarks during the same debate were made by the representative of Argentina who said: 'While we condemn acts of terrorism, we also condemn acts of reprisal, since they flout the Charter and they are contrary to the purposes on which this very Organization rests …'; see also O'Brien, supra n. 162 at 436–7 especially n. 87.

> If we condemn terrorist activities, we must also condemn, and for the same reason, acts of reprisal. To try to justify one by the other must inevitably lead to the most deadly outbidding, to blind destruction of human lives, to constantly increasing dangers to international peace and security.

One further example from the 1970s is directly relevant, due to the parallels in the justifications advanced and the proportionality of force used. The 1978 Litani Operation was the largest and longest counter-terror operation prior to the 1982 war in Lebanon.[196] Israel's justification for the type and scale of its response was that Lebanon had lost control of part of its territory and that Israel had to act in self-defence to prevent future attacks and to clear the border area 'once and for all' of PLO terrorists.[197] The Security Council rejected the claim of self-defence and several members reiterated their condemnation of reprisals.[198] The Security Council called upon Israel to immediately cease its military action against Lebanese territorial integrity and to withdraw its forces from all Lebanese territory.[199] Numerous representatives noted that Israel's actions were premeditated (implying that self-defence measures were, by definition, *not* premeditated).

---

196 On 11 March 1978, 13 PLO members infiltrated Israel between Haifa and Tel Aviv, seized a bus and engaged in battle with security forces near Tel Aviv. Thirty-two civilians were killed in the course of the gun battle with the Israeli security forces. Al-Fatah claimed responsibility. In retaliation, beginning on the night of 14–15 March, Israel invaded Lebanon and attacked PLO camps; Israeli gunboats shelled PLO targets in Tyre and Said, and the Israeli airforce hit PLO targets in those cities, as well as Beirut. The Israeli Defence Force ultimately advanced its occupation to the Litani River before proclaiming a ceasefire on 21 March 1978: O'Brien, supra n. 162 at 445–50.

197 '[T]he prevailing situation in Southern Lebanon has been for several years … one in which the Government of Lebanon has lost control and, I dare say, sovereignty over a significant part of its own territory. In light of this situation … and in light of the PLO's declared intention to repeat atrocities like the one carried out in Israel last Saturday, the Government of Israel was left with no alternative. It acted in accordance with its legitimate national right of self-defense, the inherent right to defend its territory and population to ensure that no more barbaric attacks will be launched in the future … the aim of the Israeli Defence Force's operation was not revenge or retaliation … It was and is to clear the PLO once and for all from the area bordering on Israel, which it used mercilessly for repeated aggression against my country': UN SCOR 2071st Meeting at 6–7, UN Doc S/PV 2071 (1978).

198 Ambassador Husson of France: 'While it is clear France regards terrorist attacks as totally reprehensible, it is also clear that we have the same attitude towards acts of reprisal. Attempts to justify or explain one by the other necessarily lead to an unacceptable situation of constant escalation, causing much loss of human life and challenging and endangering international security': 33 UN SCOR 2072nd Meeting at 5, UN Doc S/PV 2072 (1978); see other states' similar statements in O'Brien, supra n. 162 at 449, n. 133.

199 SCR 425 (1978), 19 March 1978, adopted at the 2074th Meeting, by 12 votes to none (USSR and Czechoslovakia abstained; China did not participate in the voting).

Security Council Resolutions: 1980s

During the 1980s forcible reprisals continued to be employed. Two examples where reprisals were employed in response to acts of terrorism were the Israeli raid on Tunis and the US attack on Libya.[200]

Israeli raid on Tunis – 1985 When members of the PLO were thought to be responsible for the murder of three Israelis in Cyprus,[201] Israel initially responded with a raid on the Lebanese bases of PLO dissident Abu Musa. Then, on 1 October 1985, the Israeli Air Force attacked Yassir Arafat's headquarters in Hammam Plage, Tunis, killing or injuring more than 100 people, including women and children, many of whom were Tunisians.[202] Israeli Defence Minister, Yitzak Rabin, said that the bombing of the PLO headquarters in Tunis was in retaliation for the deaths of the three Israelis in Larnaca and that it was a warning to terrorists that they were not safe anywhere from Israeli punishment.[203] The attack was condemned by Arab governments including Tunisia, Egypt, Jordan and Saudi Arabia, who called Israel's actions 'state terrorism' and 'a criminal act'.[204]

The US initially justified the attack as a 'legitimate response'[205] to terrorist attacks. However, a few days later it adopted a less supportive stance, stating that although 'the Israeli raid was understandable as an expression of self-defence'[206] the bombing could not be condoned. Virtually all other states were unanimous

---

200 It is not implied that there were not other significant terrorist attacks during this decade. Other terrorist attacks, such as the Libyan agents' bombing of Pan Am flight 103 flying from London to New York, which crashed in Lockerbie, Scotland in December 1988, occurred during this decade, but there was no military reprisal in response. President Reagan apparently refrained from a military response because too many civilians would have been at risk. His successor, President Bush, opted for economic sanctions and a domestic judicial approach: see discussion in Reisman, M., 'International Legal Responses to Terrorism' (1999) 22 *Hous. J. Int'l L.* 3 at 35.

201 Rogg, M., '3 Israelis Slain by Palestinians in Cyprus', *New York Times*, 26 September 1985, A3, col. 4. The Palestinians stormed a private yacht moored in the port of Larnaca and killed three Israelis. The Palestinians had demanded the release of 20 Palestinian prisoners whom it said Israel had recently arrested.

202 Prial, F., 'Israeli Planes Attack PLO in Tunis, Killing at Least 30; Raid "Legitimate" U.S. Says', *New York Times*, 2 October 1985 A1, col. 6.

203 'Israel Calls Bombing a Warning to Terrorists', *New York Times*, 2 October 1985, A8, col. 1.

204 Gwertzman, B., 'As U.S. Supports Attacks, Egypt and Jordan Vow to Press for Peace', *New York Times*, 2 October 1985, A1, col. 4.

205 Prial, supra n. 202.

206 Prial, F., 'Tunisia's Leader Bitter at the U.S.', *New York Times*, 3 October 1985, A11, col. 1.

in their condemnation of the attack.[207] Three days after the attack, the Security Council adopted Resolution 573 which 'condemned vigorously the act of armed aggression perpetrated by Israel against Tunisian territory in flagrant violation of the Charter of the United Nations, international law and norms of conduct'.[208] It also demanded that Israel refrain from perpetrating such acts of aggression, urged Member States to dissuade Israel from resorting to such acts and supported Tunisia's right to reparations.[209]

The Israeli raid on Tunis suggests that virtually all states considered forcible reprisals to be unlawful as a violation of the Charter and international law. Israel continued to regard reprisals as a lawful expression of self-defence. The US position was similar to Israel's.[210] Regarding states which harboured terrorists, Israel put forward the same proposition that it had unsuccessfully advanced in the 1970s in relation to Lebanon: it claimed that because Tunisia had permitted its territory to be used as an extraterritorial base for terrorists, it had to accept the consequences of such actions.[211] It also claimed that the raid was in proportion to the damage suffered by Israel by terrorists, and the damage that would be prevented in the future.[212] The arguments advanced by Israel and the US were rejected by virtually all other states, with several condemning Israel for having engaged in 'state terrorism'.[213] The walk-out in the General Assembly and the 14-0 vote in the Security Council were evidence that in 1985, the overwhelming majority of states opposed the Israeli–US doctrine that military reprisals were a legitimate act

207 As the Security Council met to discuss a resolution, the General Assembly heard Israeli Foreign Minister, Yitzak Shamir, attempt to justify the attacks. All members of the 21-member Arab group (except Egypt) walked out of the Assembly, and several other states also withdrew their entire delegations, or left only one junior delegate to hear Shamir's statement. The walk-out by Arab nations was joined by the representatives of Iran, Vietnam, Nicaragua, Afghanistan and some African nations such as Zimbabwe and Burkina Faso. East Germany also withdrew its representatives. All the other members of the Soviet bloc, including the USSR, only left one junior delegate behind: Sciolino, E., 'Security Council Debates Air Raid', *New York Times*, 3 October 1985, A12, col. 1.

208 SCR 573 (1985) adopted by 14 votes to none (the US abstained).

209 Ibid.

210 'We recognize and strongly support the principle that a state subjected to continuing terrorist attacks may respond with appropriate use of force to defend itself against further attacks. This is an aspect of the inherent right of self-defence recognized in the United Nations Charter. We support this principle regardless of attacker, and regardless of victim': US Ambassador Walters, UN SCOR (2615th Meeting) at 111–12, UN Doc S/PV 2615 (1985).

211 Israeli Ambassador Netanyahu, UN SCOR (2615th Meeting) at 86–7, UN Doc S/PV 2615 (1985).

212 Ibid., 87.

213 See remarks made by the representatives of Afghanistan, East Germany, Indonesia, Nicaragua and Saudi Arabia. The Soviet Union did not participate in the debate.

of self-defence in response to past acts of terrorism and as a preventative measure for future acts of terrorism.

US raid on Libya – 1986 During the 1970s and 1980s, tensions between Libya and the US were high. The US Navy had conducted freedom of navigation exercises in the Gulf of Sidra to challenge Colonel Gadhafi's claim to sovereignty[214] and Libya was also blamed by the US for its support of various terrorist groups including the Palestinian Abu-Nidal group. Gadhafi had threatened terrorist attacks against the US on various occasions and it was thought that Libya was responsible for the bombing of two airline offices in Rome and Vienna.[215] On 5 April 1986, a discothèque in West Berlin was bombed,[216] resulting in the deaths of two US soldiers and a Turkish civilian. Gadhafi congratulated the terrorists and warned that the violence against American targets, civilian and non-civilian, throughout the world would escalate.[217]

Having what it believed to be conclusive evidence of Libyan state responsibility, the US retaliated on 15 April 1986 by conducting air and naval attacks on targets in and around Tripoli and Benghazi.[218] Approximately 37 Libyans, including civilians, were killed and 93 were injured in the US raids. The US claimed its attacks were an act of self-defence intended to disrupt and deter a pattern of terrorist threats and aggressions against US nationals and US interests. The US argued that non-military measures aimed at dealing with Gadhafi's terrorist threats had been ineffective and that the raid was a counter-force operation, against targets that were directly related to terrorist operations. The UK supported the US actions, and argued that the US had sufficient evidence to link Gadhafi to the Berlin bombing

---

214 Gadhafi claimed territorial rights in the Gulf of Sidra which most states considered to be international waters and which the US contested by regularly sending elements of the Sixth Fleet through the Gulf. This resulted in several confrontations with Libya. In 1981, a Libyan attack on US jets in the Gulf of Sidra resulted in the shooting down of two Libyan SU-22 fighter planes. Again, in 1986, US forces sunk two Libyan patrol boats and bombed a Soviet-built missile base on shore: see Ross, supra n. 33 at 7–13; also Parks, W., 'Crossing the Line' (1986) 112 *US Naval Institute Proceedings* 40 at 45.

215 In December 1985, two Abu-Nidal members, using Libyan-supplied passports, simultaneously bombed airline offices in Rome and Vienna, which resulted in the deaths of 20 civilians, including five Americans.

216 The level of Libyan state involvement was unclear at the time of the incident and the Libyan government denied it was responsible. However, in 2001, four people, including a Libyan diplomat and a Libyan embassy worker, were convicted in a Berlin court on charges related to the bombing.

217 Parks, supra n. 214 at 45.

218 The US operation, involving 150 aircraft, targeted the Bab al-Azizia army compound (Qadhafi's command centre and residence), the military part of Tripoli International airport, the Benghazi barracks, a commando training facility at the naval port of Sidi Bilal and the airbase for Libya's MiG-23 interceptors at Benina airfield: ibid., at 47–8; also Ross, supra n. 33 at 10–11; and O'Brien, supra n. 162 at 463.

and many other past and projected terrorist actions.[219] The UK agreed that the US attacks on Libya were in self-defence.

The General Assembly considered the issue and declared that 'the aerial and naval military attack perpetrated against the cities of Tripoli and Benghazi'[220] was a 'serious threat to peace and security in the Mediterranean region'.[221] It condemned the US attacks and declared them to be a violation of the Charter of the United Nations and of international law. The General Assembly called upon the US to refrain from the threat or use of force against Libya, and to resolve its disputes with Libya by peaceful means in accordance with the Charter. It also affirmed the right of Libya to receive appropriate compensation for the material and human losses inflicted upon it.

The Security Council took no action in response to the US attacks on Libya. The debate in the Security Council was characterised by a split between 'Third World' and Communist nations, which condemned the US attacks as 'acts of aggression'[222] and the mainly Western nations which tried to justify the attacks on a broader interpretation of self-defence, taking into account past and present actions. A resolution condemning the US was defeated when negative votes were cast by Australia, Denmark, France, the UK and the US; Venezuela abstained.[223] The General Assembly 'noted with concern'[224] that the Security Council had been prevented from discharging its responsibilities owing to the negative votes of certain Permanent Members.

The US attacks on Libya and the international response gives rise to three observations. First, there was a strong feeling in the Security Council that the reprisals were justified on the grounds of self-defence, as evidenced by the fact that five members of the Security Council, including three Permanent Members, vetoed the resolution that would have condemned the US. This was a much broader show of support for reprisals than had existed in the 1950s, 1960s or 1970s. Secondly, although this was another instance of a military reprisal being apparently provoked

219 Statement by Sir John Thompson (UK), 41 UN SCOR (2679th Meeting).

220 GA Resolution A/Res/41/38, 20 November 1986, 78th plenary meeting, 41 UN GAOR Supp. (No 53) at 34, UN Doc A/41/53 (1986); passed by a vote of 79 to 28.

221 Ibid.

222 Algeria, East Germany, Ghana, India, Qatar, the UAE and the USSR took the position that the US attacks could not be considered as lawful self-defence under Article 51 of the Charter because there had been no antecedent 'armed attack' by Libya. Some nations, such as India, also challenged the presumption that the Libyan government had been proven to be responsible for the terrorist attack on the discothéque: see 41 UN SCOR (2673rd Meeting) at 5, UN Doc S/PV 2677 (1986); UN SCOR (2676th Meeting) at 4, UN Doc S/PV 2676 (1986), and 41 UN SCOR (2675th Meeting) at 6–7, UN Doc S/PV 2675 (1986) for the statement of India's representative, arguing that it was doubtful that an armed attack within the meaning of Article 51 had occurred.

223 41 UN SCOR (2682nd Meeting) at 27, UN Doc S/PV 2682 (1986).

224 GA Resolution A/Res/41/38, 20 November 1986, 78th plenary meeting, 41 UN GAOR Supp. (No 53) at 34, UN Doc A/41/53 (1986).

by a series of alleged terrorist attacks, this incident is distinguishable from those discussed above because the connection between the terrorist acts and state involvement, and hence state responsibility, was much clearer here than in any previous instance. The Libyan leader had threatened the US with terrorism prior to the event and he had subsequently virtually claimed responsibility for it. Thirdly, although the traditional Israeli–US position on reprisals and self-defence gained some further supporters, notably the UK, it remained clear that the majority of nations maintained that reprisals were a violation of the Charter and international law, as evidenced by the General Assembly resolution.[225]

Security Council Resolutions: 1990s

In the 1990s there were further acts and attempted acts of terrorism that prompted military reprisals by one sovereign state against another. The two reprisals that are discussed here are the US missile strikes on Iraq in 1993 and the US air strikes on Afghanistan and Libya in 1998.

US strikes on Iraq – 1993 On 26 June 1993, the US launched a cruise-missile attack against the Iraqi Intelligence Service (IIS) headquarters in Baghdad (Operation Southern Watch).[226] The US attack was ordered by then President Clinton in retaliation for an attempted assassination (allegedly instigated by the IIS) of former President Bush.[227] Clinton claimed that the unsuccessful bomb plot was an attack by the Government of Iraq against the US and the missile strike was intended to deter further violence against the American people.[228] The US Permanent Representative to the UN, Ambassador Albright, reported the

225 Ibid.; also Berlin, M., 'Raid on Libya Condemned by UN General Assembly', *Washington Post*, 21 November 1986, A30.

226 Twenty-three Tomahawk guided missiles, each loaded with a thousand pounds of explosives, were fired from American Navy warships in the Persian Gulf and the Red Sea at the headquarters of the Mukhabarat, the ISS, in downtown Baghdad: Hersh, S., 'A Case Not Closed', *The New Yorker*, 1 November 1993.

227 For further details about the investigations that the CIA conducted to ascertain Iraqi liability, see, *inter alia*, History News Network, 'How Do We Know that Iraq Tried to Assassinate President George H W Bush?', available at: <http://hnn.us/articles/1000.html> at 12 June 2008; and see also Hersh, supra n. 226.

228 US Responds to Attack by Iraqi Government, President Bill Clinton Speech, statement by Office of Press Secretary, 5 July 1993, Transcript, available at: <http://www.findarticles.com/p/articles/mi_m1584/is_n27_v4/ai_13238125> at 12 June 2008.

occurrence of the military strike to the UN Security Council.[229] Albright alleged that the assassination plot was:[230]

> [A] direct attack on the United States, an attack that required a direct United States response [and to which we] responded directly, as we are entitled to do under Article 51 of the United Nations Charter, which provides for the exercise of self-defence in such cases.

International reaction to the US missile attack was mixed. Naturally, Iraq condemned it as 'a totally unjustified act of aggression'.[231] Egypt and Turkey opposed the missile attack, whilst Iran and Libya viewed it as an unmistakable act of aggression. The United Arab Emirates, Qatar, Bahrain, Oman and Saudi Arabia remained silent; Kuwait supported the strikes and noted that they were a natural result of Iraq's involvement in terrorist activities.[232] The Arab League issued a statement in which it said that such force should only have been used if authorised by the Security Council and it expressed 'extreme regret'[233] at the attack. The Western nations generally supported the US's missile strikes. The then German Chancellor, Helmut Kohl, called them a 'justified reaction [to a] deplorable attempted act of terrorism',[234] whilst Austria stated that it was interested in all measures that were aimed at guaranteeing the functioning of the system of collective security.[235]

When the Security Council discussed the incident, a diverse group of states, including France, Japan, Brazil, Hungary, New Zealand and Spain, showed a willingness to *understand* and *accept* the US's actions, even if they did not specifically *endorse* the legal justifications put forward by the US.[236] Japan

229 UN Doc S/26003 (26 June 1993). Reporting of self-defence action is required pursuant to Article 51.

230 'Raid on Baghdad: Excerpts from UN Speech: The Case for Clinton's Strike', *New York Times*, 28 June 1993, A7, col., 1.

231 UN Doc S/26004, 27 June 1993, 2.

232 See Kritsiotis, supra n. 135 at 164.

233 Ibid.

234 Whitney, C., 'European Allies Are Giving Strong Backing to US Raid', *New York Times*, 28 June 1993, A5.

235 Ibid.

236 UN Doc S/PV 3245 (1993): (France) 'The French Government fully understands the reaction of the United States and the reasons for the unilateral action …' at 13; (Japan) 'Given such circumstances, my government considers that there existed an unavoidable situation in which the United States Government could not help but take action' at 16; (Brazil) '… [W]e take note of the fact that the United States Government indicates that there is clear and compelling evidence of the involvement of the Government of Iraq in the assassination attempt, a violation of the most basic norms of international behaviour'; (Hungary) 'The action taken by the United States yesterday in Baghdad was justified, according to the information available to us …' at 18; (New Zealand) 'Any nation that seeks

considered that the facts created an 'unavoidable situation'[237] for the US to take the action it did. By contrast, the Netherlands considered that although the US attack was 'understandable',[238] it was not convinced by the American argument that an appeal could be made to the right of self-defence in accordance with Article 51 of the Charter. The Dutch government's position was based upon a restrictive interpretation of Article 51 whereby it found that 'the criterion of self-defence in Article 51 had not been met'.[239] The non-aligned countries urged restraint by all states and the avoidance of force in international relations, consistent with the spirit and letter of Charter law.[240] China's position was more equivocal than the Netherlands', but indicated that it did not approve of the US's actions.[241]

Ultimately, no resolutions were passed in relation to the US missile strike, either in the Security Council or the General Assembly. It is significant that of the eight Security Council members which expressly supported the US attack on the IIS headquarters, only two (the UK and Russia) accepted that the US's actions were justified on the grounds of self-defence.[242]

The fact that the US clothed its justifications in the language of self-defence, and reported its action to the Security Council in accordance with Article 51, was itself insufficient to deem the attack a *lawful act of self-defence* rather than

---

to assassinate the Head of State or a member of the senior political leadership of another State commits an act of aggression …' at 23; (Spain) 'We understand the action the United States felt forced to take in the exceptional circumstances of this case …' at 24. See also Fletcher and MacIntyre, 'UN Accepts Clinton Evidence that Iraq Plotted to Kill Bush', *The Times*, 29 June 1993, 13.

237 UN Doc S/PV 3245 (1993), ibid.

238 UN Doc S/5657 (27 June 1993) (The Netherlands) and see Letter Addressed to Parliament from the Minister of Foreign Affairs, 29 June 1993 available at: <http://www.ulb.ac.be/droit/cdi/fichiers/PEAV9.htm> at 12 June 2008.

239 Ibid. The Dutch government stated that even if an incumbent President had been involved, that would not have made a difference, because the criterion would not have been met.

240 UN Doc S/5657 (27 June 1993). This position was expressed by the representative of Cape Verde, speaking on behalf of Council members belonging to the group of non-aligned countries, namely, Cape Verde, Djibouti, Morocco, Pakistan and Venezuela. The Chinese representative took a similar view.

241 'China has always held that that disputes between or among countries should be settled through peaceful means of dialogue and consultation. We are opposed to any action that can contravene the Charter of the United Nations and norms of international relations': UN Doc S/PV 3245 (27 June 1993) at 21.

242 Ibid., at 22 and 23. The Russian representative stated: '… the actions of the United States are justified since they arise from the right of States to individual and collective self-defence, in accordance with Article 51 of the Charter': ibid., at 22. Prime Minister John Major: 'Under UN Charter Article 51, I think it was entirely right of the United States to act in self-defence and they have my total support in doing so … If we just stand aside and accept that sort of behaviour, what is to stop that happening again, and again, and again?': see Kritsiotis, supra n. 135 at 165.

an *unlawful forcible reprisal*. The actions were clearly taken in retaliation for a past event, they were meant to 'send a message' to the Iraqi government about attempting such acts in the future, and they would appear to be a classic case of an unlawful forcible reprisal.[243] The US's attempt to bring its actions within the framework of self-defence was, if nothing else, evidence that forcible reprisals were still prohibited.

The fact that the US's actions were not condemned by the Security Council (but recall that only two members accepted the self-defence justification)[244] is indicative of a trend towards a more flexible interpretation of 'self-defence' and a willingness to allow reprisals to occur in response to actual, or attempted, terrorist attacks. Scholars have tried to reconcile the wider implications of the US's violation of the Charter prohibition on the use of force with the apparent acceptance by most states that the US had no choice other than to do what it did.[245]

The fact that only the UK and Russia unambiguously accepted the US's legal justification, but that several of the other Council members were nevertheless willing to accept the US's action as 'understandable' is perplexing. It has been suggested that this was 'an unhealthy development for international law generally because the enterprise of self-help – represented as an action in self-defence – reared its ugly head once again'.[246] Kritsiotis observed in 1996 that unless the international community improves the mechanisms for satisfactorily settling disputes, such as the one that arose in this instance, then the right of self-defence 'will continue to be a regular refuge in the practice of States'.[247]

US missile strikes on Sudan and Afghanistan – 1998 On 20 August 1998 the US fired Tomahawk missiles at sites in Afghanistan and Sudan. The strikes targeted the El Shifa Pharmaceutical Industries building in Khartoum (which the US alleged was assisting terrorists in the production of materials for chemical weapons) and

243 'The retaliatory nature of the strike, and the context of the events in which it took place, strongly suggest that it was a de facto forcible reprisal which would ordinarily have no basis in international law. Yet the US neither defined nor justified the strike as such': ibid., 175.

244 UN Doc S/5657 (27 June 1993).

245 '[Does] the failure of the international system, coupled with fundamentally changed circumstances since the time when the relevant texts [such as the UN Charter] were agreed, make preferable unilateral action for the common good even if it is at variance with the norms articulated in the Charter and elsewhere': Higgins, R., *Problems and Prospects: International Law and How We Use It* (Oxford: Oxford University Press, 1994) 252.

246 Kritsiotis, supra n. 135 at 177.

247 Ibid.

alleged terrorist training facilities in Khost, Kabul and Jalalabad in Afghanistan (which the US claimed were under the control of Osama bin Laden).[248]

The US's justifications for the strikes varied from retaliation for the 1998 embassy bombings to the protection of US citizens abroad to the prevention of future terrorist attacks. On the day of the US missile strikes, President Clinton was reported as saying, 'Today we have struck back'.[249] The US President issued a statement setting out four reasons for the missile attack: first, because the US had convincing evidence that the groups targeted in the strikes had played a key role in the embassy bombings; second, because the groups had executed terrorist attacks against Americans in the past; third, because they had compelling information that they were planning additional terrorist attacks against US citizens in the future; and, fourth, because they were seeking to acquire chemical weapons and other dangerous weapons.[250] Although there was no explicit reference in President Clinton's speech to self-defence under Article 51, US Defence Secretary William Cohen referred to the strikes as 'an exercise of self-defence'.[251]

Two observations arise from the US's justifications for the missile attacks. First, the strikes were unmistakably an act of *retaliation* for past terrorist attacks. The first two reasons advanced by President Clinton made it clear that the missile attacks were reprisals, intended as punishment for past events (the 1998 embassy attacks).[252] Second, the objective of preventing future terrorist attacks was based heavily on factual material that was speculative. Much of the 'compelling evidence' was disputed at the time and (especially with regards to the El Shifa pharmaceutical plant) was eventually proven, in some respects, to have been completely inaccurate.[253] As for the connection between bin Laden and the alleged terrorist training camps in Afghanistan, the US attacks were undertaken while the

---

248 The US held bin Laden responsible for the 1998 bombings of US embassies in Nairobi and Dar-es-Salaam.

249 'US Strikes "Terrorist" Targets in Afghanistan. Sudan', *CNN News*, 20 August 1998, available at: <http://www.cnn.com/US/9808/20/clinton.02/> at 12 June 2008.

250 Statement made by President Bill Clinton from Martha's Vineyard, Massachusetts; US Department of Defence, 'US Strikes Against Terrorist Forces', available at: <http://www.defenselink.mil/news/Aug1998/n08201998_9808201.html> at 12 June 2008.

251 *CNN.com*, 'Pentagon: Strikes Sought to Protect US Citizens Overseas', 21 August 1998, available at: <http://www.cnn.com/US/9808/20/pentagon.02/> at 12 June 2008.

252 That point was also made clear in statements by Madeleine Albright: see *CNN.com*, 'US Missiles Pound Targets in Afghanistan, Sudan', 21 August 1998, available at: <http://www.cnn.com/US/9808/20/us.strikes.02/> at 12 June 2008.

253 Lobel, J., 'The Use of Force to Respond to Terrorist Attacks: The Bombing of Sudan and Afghanistan' (1999) 24 *Yale J. Int'l L.* 537 at 543–7. For media reports of the concerns that were raised about the Clinton Administration's justifications for the missile attacks, see Weiner, T. and Myers, S., 'After the Attacks: The Overview, Flaws in the US Account Raise Questions on Strike in Sudan', *New York Times*, 19 August 1998, A2; and Richter, P., 'Sudan Attacks Claim Faulty, US Admits', *Los Angeles Times*, 1 September 1998, A1.

FBI investigation was still in its preliminary stage.[254] The US Attorney-General at that time, Janet Reno, noted that the FBI had come to 'no final conclusions' about who was responsible for the embassy bombings and she had urged the White House to delay the raids until further evidence could be gathered linking bin Laden to the embassy bombings.[255] Reno warned the White House that the evidence tying bin Laden to the embassy bombings did not meet the 'Tripoli standard' (a reference to the 1986 US missile strike on Libya), which is significant, because even though there was no Security Council resolution, the world reaction to the Libyan strikes was one of general condemnation, mainly because of a lack of clear and compelling evidence linking the Libyan government with the Berlin discothéque attack. The fact that the evidence presented in support of the 1998 US missile attacks was recognised by the US Attorney-General as being even weaker than that presented in 1986 is further evidence that the 1998 attacks did not meet the required evidential standards regarding state responsibility, and it is suggested that the US attacks were nothing other than an unlawful forcible reprisal.

The Security Council did not meet publicly to discuss the US raids on Sudan and Afghanistan, as it had after the US raids on Libya in 1986 and Iraq in 1993. The Council adopted a resolution on 13 August 1998 (after the embassy bombings on 7 August but before the US retaliation on 20 August) in which it strongly condemned the terrorist bomb attacks in Nairobi and Dar-es-Salaam and commended the governments of the US, Kenya and Tanzania for their responses to the terrorist attacks.[256] It did not pass any resolution after the US missile strikes. Sudan tried to initiate a Security Council fact-finding mission to investigate the US claim that the El Shifa plant had produced a precursor of the lethal 'VX gas'. The draft resolution was supported by the Arab states and the OAU, but was blocked by the US.[257]

Beyond the Security Council, the international response to the US missile strikes was mixed. The UN Secretary-General, Kofi Annan, was initially 'concerned over the developments'.[258] In September 1998, he criticised 'individual actions'[259] against terrorism. Russian President, Boris Yeltsin, condemned the action; China initially neither condemned nor condoned the strikes but later criticised the US's actions;[260] the British Prime Minister, Tony Blair, said he strongly supported the US's actions and made a direct link between the missile strikes and the

254 'FBI Chief Visits Africa Bomb Sites', *CNN.com*, 20 August 1998, available at: <http://www.cnn.com/WORLD/africa/9808/20/africa.03/> at 12 June 2008.

255 'FBI Director Says Investigation into Bombings is Preliminary', *Baltimore Sun*, 22 August 1998 at 98; Lobel, supra n. 253 at 548.

256 SC Resolution 1189 (1998).

257 Lobel, supra n. 253 at 537–8.

258 'Muslims, Yeltsin Denounce Attack', *CNN.com*, 21 August 1998, available at: <http://www.cnn.com/WORLD/africa/9808/21/strikes.world.reax.02/> at 12 June 2008.

259 'Annan Faults States' "Individual Actions" Against Terrorism', *Agence France Presse*, 21 September 1998.

260 'Muslims, Yeltsin Denounce Attack', *CNN.com*, supra n. 258; Ching, F., 'China Feels Let Down by US', *Far East Economic Review*, 24 September 1998 at 38.

earlier US embassy bombings; Australia supported the US's actions and said the US was entitled to defend itself; and the Israeli Prime Minister, Benjamin Netanyahu, said he 'welcomed the US decision to strike targets of terrorism in Sudan and Afghanistan'.[261] The non-aligned countries condemned the US attack as 'unilateral and unwarranted'.[262] Many predominantly Muslim nations, such as Indonesia, Pakistan and Libya, also condemned the US strikes as acts of aggression.[263] In summary, the US received support from its usual Western allies, and condemnation from the Arab and Muslim world, which was joined by Russia; China was equivocal. As Franck has observed, there was no effort in the UN to argue that such recourse to force was *ipso facto* illegal.[264] The absence of unified international condemnation following the missile strikes could be interpreted as a further weakening of the international community's resolve to prevent forcible reprisals from being employed under the guise of self-defence in the wake of a terrorist attack.

The use of force by the US against Sudan and Afghanistan in 1998, coming as it did after the 1993 missile strikes against Iraq and the use of reprisals in the 1970s and 1980s, added another layer to an increasingly complex picture of the international law pertaining to the use of force and the supposed unlawfulness of forcible reprisals. The questions that were raised over whether the US produced a satisfactory evidentiary basis for its missile strikes proved that evidence of state responsibility remains an important issue in the ongoing debate over the use of reprisals in response to terrorist attacks. The US's refusal to have the factual justifications for its use of force reviewed by the Security Council has been analysed elsewhere.[265] Suffice to note that the 1998 incident indicated that there is an urgent need, not only for a reconsideration and clarification of the legal status of reprisals as a form of self-defence, but also as to the standard and veracity of factual evidence that ought to be presented by a state before it can embark on retaliatory military action, even if it *can* ultimately be justified under the rubric of self-defence.

The main conclusion for the present analysis is that by the end of the 1990s, at least two states (Israel and the US) had exhibited a practice of carrying out forcible reprisals in response to actual or threatened terrorist attacks, both past and future, and that the international community and, increasingly, the Security Council, was prepared to allow such reprisals to occur, or at least acquiesce in their use, without formal censure.

---

261 Ibid.

262 Ibid.

263 See 'Pakistan to Lodge Complaint about US', *USA Today*, 25 August 1998, A4.

264 Franck, supra n. 128 at 96.

265 Lobel, supra n. 253 at 553–4; but see also Wedgwood, R., 'Responding to Terrorism: The Strikes Against bin Laden' (1999) 24 *Yale J. Int'l L.* 559 at 567–8.

Reprisals and the Security Council: 2000–2006

Two instances during the past five years in which reprisals were used were in the context of the enforcement of the Iraqi 'no-fly zones'. A northern 'no-fly zone', which imposed a ban on Iraqi fixed and rotary-wing aircraft above the 36th parallel, was established by the US, the UK and France in April 1991 as an integral part of the US military's 'Operation Provide Comfort'. The initial objectives of the northern 'no-fly zone' were to ensure the safety of Coalition aircraft providing humanitarian relief to Kurdish refugees and, later, to ensure the safety of Coalition ground troops.[266] A southern 'no-fly zone' was proclaimed by the US, the UK and France in August 1992 over the area below the 32nd parallel.[267] Neither of the so-called 'no-fly zones' were expressly authorised by the UN.[268] Justifications for the 'no-fly zones' were offered by the US and the UK on the basis of humanitarian intervention and upon the argument that the 'no-fly zones' were imposed in support of Security Council Resolution 688.[269]

US–British air strikes on Iraq – 2001 On 16 February 2001, the US led an air strike on four targets south, and one north, of Baghdad. The US claimed that the Iraqi radar and command and control installations threatened US jets patrolling Iraqi air space.[270] The US justified its attack as 'essentially a self-defense operation'; that it was 'part of a strategy' and that it was a 'routine strike', the objective of which

---

266 See discussion in Malone, D., *The International Struggle over Iraq: Politics in the UN Security Council 1980–2005* (New York: Oxford University Press, 2006).

267 Note that France pulled out of joint-enforcement in 1996; note also that the southern 'no-fly zone' was originally established from the 32nd parallel but it was extended by the US to the 33rd parallel in 1996.

268 Security Council Resolution 688 (1991) called upon Iraq to end the repression of its civilian population and to allow access to international humanitarian organisations, but it did not authorise the use of force to assist either the Kurds in the north or the Shi'ites in the south.

269 See Marston, G., 'United Kingdom Materials on International Law 1992, Survey', 63 *BYIL* (1992) 825 for Secretary of State Douglas Hurd on the establishment of the southern zone: '… we are on strong legal as well as humanitarian ground in setting up this "No-Fly" zone'. For a discussion on the legality of the northern and southern 'no-fly zones', see Gray, C., *International Law and the Use of Force* (Oxford: Oxford University Press, 2004) especially 34–5; Shaw, M., *International Law*, 5th edn (New York: Cambridge University Press, 2003) at 1046 and 1136–7; Mahajan, R., *Full Spectrum Dominance – U.S. Power in Iraq and Beyond* (New York: Seven Stories Press, 2003) 106–7; Malone, supra n. 266.

270 In 2001, the US alleged that the British and American planes patrolling the southern 'no-fly zone' were at risk from the increasingly sophisticated Iraqi air defence facilities and, therefore, the US led an attack to destroy those facilities.

was to protect the safety of the pilots and aircraft patrolling the no-fly zone.[271] The British government referred to the strikes as a 'targeted and measured response'.[272] The US claimed to have acted legitimately under the guise of self-defence but, as discussed above, self-defence requires an 'armed attack' to have occurred.[273] In this instance, the 'armed attack' was supposedly the potential threat posed to US and British aircraft and pilots flying above Iraqi airspace by missiles fired from the ground. Both the UK and the US adopted the view that they were under 'armed attack' and the missile strikes were launched as acts of self-defence.[274]

The international reaction was generally negative. Concerns were publicly raised not only by, predictably, Iraq but also by the US and UK's allies in NATO and in the Middle East. France stated that it wanted an explanation for the air strike; several members of the German government criticised the US and the UK for the raid; Spain said that it and other European allies had not been informed of the strike; Turkey rebuked the US for failing to inform it before the strike was launched; the Arab League stated that the air strikes had breached international law and public protest was voiced from within Egypt, Jordan and the Palestinian Occupied Territories. Only Israel gave its muted support for the air strikes.[275]

Iraq called on the Security Council and the UN Secretary-General to condemn the military aggression and to take steps to prevent it from happening again. Three Permanent Members of the Security Council (Russia, France and China) made public statements expressing concern at the use of force without Security Council approval, condemning the attacks and implicitly denying the validity of the self-defence argument put forward by the US and the UK.[276] However, the Security Council did not discuss the attacks and no resolution was adopted by it or by the General Assembly. That lack of formal condemnation in the Security Council could be explained by a sense of pragmatism amongst the allies of the US and the UK. There would have been no possibility of securing a Security Council resolution,

---

271 'Allies hit Iraq with "self-defense" strike', *CNN.com*, 16 February 2001, available at: <http://archives.cnn.com/2001/WORLD/meast/02/16/iraq.airstrike.02/index.html> at 12 June 2008.

272 Amanpour, C., 'The British Connection', *CNN.com*, 16 February 2001, available at: <http://archives.cnn.com/2001/WORLD/meast/02/16/amanpour.debrief/index.html> at 12 June 2008. The targets of the missile attack were north of the 33rd parallel and therefore beyond the actual no-fly zone, but the legitimacy or otherwise of the 'no-fly zone' is not at issue here.

273 See discussion above regarding the 'armed attack' requirement of Article 51, and the discussion on pre-emptive self-defence.

274 British Prime Minister Tony Blair: 'Operations such as the one last night would not be needed if Saddam stopped attacking us … But as long as he does, I will continue to take the steps necessary to protect our forces and to prevent Saddam from once again wreaking havoc, suffering and death': Gordon, M., 'New Bush, Old Team, Ponder Saddam', *New York Times*, 18 February 2001.

275 'Iraqis March in Protest Against Western Air Raids', *Reuters*, 18 February 2001.

276 'Russia Leads Criticism of Iraqi Raids', *CNN.com*, 17 February 2006.

given the US and UK's veto power. Lobel argued in 1999 that states must choose their battles over the US's use of unilateral force carefully. Just as the Sudanese missile strike would not have been a very appealing battle to wage, likewise Iraq in 2001 may in fact have been subject to reprisals that were technically unlawful, but no state was willing to argue the point.[277]

The Current Status of Reprisals in International Law

Scholars have observed the continued use by states of reprisals and have debated their status in international law. One school of thought advocates the formal acceptance of reprisals as a type of 'self-defence' measure. Proponents include Bowett,[278] Falk,[279] Blum,[280] O'Brien,[281] Dinstein[282] and Kelly,[283] who have argued for the adoption of various doctrines, such as 'reasonable reprisals'[284] or 'defensive reprisals'[285] in order for states to be able to resort to reprisals in limited circumstances without violating the Charter. They have set out various guidelines, frameworks[286] and formulae that they consider ought to be used by states before launching a reprisal, with the objective of reconciling the resort to reprisals with the general prohibition on force in the Charter. An alternative perspective, advocated by

277 Lobel, supra n. 253 at 557 for the parallels between international reaction to the 1998 missile strikes on Sudan and Afghanistan and the 2001 missile strike on Iraq.

278 Bowett, D., 'Reprisals Involving Recourse to Armed Force' (1972) 66 *AJIL* 1.

279 Falk, R., 'The Beirut Raid and the International Law of Retaliation' (1969) 63 *AJIL* 415.

280 Blum, Y., 'The Beirut Raid and the International Double Standard: A Reply to Professor Richard A Falk' (1970) 64 *AJIL* 73.

281 O'Brien, W., 'Reprisals, Deterrence and Self-Defense in Counterterror Operations' (1990) 30 *Va. J. Int'l L.* 421.

282 Dinstein, Y., *War, Aggression and Self-Defence*, 4th edn (Cambridge; New York: Cambridge University Press, 2005) especially at 228.

283 Kelly, M., 'Time Warp to 1945 – Resurrection of the Reprisal and Anticipatory Self-defense Doctrines in International Law' (2003) 13 *Journal of Transnational Law and Policy* 1.

284 For a framework of 'reasonable reprisals', see Bowett, supra n. 278.

285 For an analysis of 'defensive reprisals', see Dinstein, supra n. 33 where he argues that armed reprisals ought to be assimilated into the right of legitimate self-defence.

286 Falk, supra n. 279, and Blum, supra n. 280.

Waldock,[287] Shaw,[288] Brownlie,[289] Lobel,[290] Ratner[291] and O'Connell[292] maintains that all forcible reprisals undertaken during peacetime are unlawful, unless they fall within the framework of self-defence. The latter argue against broadening the meaning of self-defence.

The divergence of views on the lawfulness of reprisals demonstrates a lack of consensus amongst scholars on the interpretation of key articles of the Charter. As shown in the foregoing analysis, that lack of consensus has also been demonstrated by states taking an inconsistent and sometimes contradictory position on reprisals. The Security Council's lack of consistency is particularly difficult to reconcile with the apparent unlawfulness of forcible reprisals in international law. At the time of writing,[293] it would appear that if one considers 'hard' international law, the prohibition on the use of force in Article 2(4) is still in force and is generally considered to be *jus cogens*. Furthermore, the weight of opinion is that the UN Charter prohibits states from resorting to the unilateral employment of force, including forcible reprisals, unless they are authorised by the Security Council, or they satisfy the elements of the Article 51 right to self-defence (which requires an 'armed attack' to have occurred). This interpretation of the current position is supported by various Security Council resolutions, General Assembly resolutions and declarations, as well as pronouncements of the ICJ.[294] In the *Nicaragua* case, the ICJ cited the adoption of the Declaration on Principles of International Law Concerning Friendly Relations and Co-operation Among States (General Assembly

---

287 'Armed reprisals to obtain satisfaction for an injury or any armed intervention as an instrument of national policy otherwise than for self-defence is illegal under the Charter': Waldock, supra n. 50 at 493.

288 Shaw, supra n. 129 at 786.

289 '[T]he provisions of the Charter relating to the peaceful settlement of disputes and non-resort to the use of force are universally regarded as prohibiting reprisals which involve the use of force': Brownlie, supra n. 31 at 281.

290 '[T]he relaxation of Article 51 is both unnecessary and counterproductive in the fight against terrorism': Lobel, supra n. 253 at 537.

291 Ratner, M. and Lobel, J., 'An Alternative to the Use of US Military Force', 27 September 2001, available at: <http://jurist.law.pitt.edu/forum/forumnew32.htm> at 12 June 2008: 'A country is not permitted to use military force for purposes of retaliation, vengeance or punishment ...'

292 O'Connell, M., 'Lawful Responses to Terrorism', 18 September 2001, available at: <http://jurist.law.pitt.edu/forum/forumnew30.htm> at 12 June 2008: 'Reprisals are not considered measures of self-defence – they do not repel on-going armed attack or seek to dislodge an unlawful occupation ...'

293 February 2009.

294 Wary of a return to self-help and the unilateral enforcement of international law, the ICJ held in the *Corfu Channel* case in 1949 that modern law on the use of force, which impliedly includes self-defence, is not conditioned by the operational defects of the collective security system of the United Nations: see *Corfu Channel Case: United Kingdom v Albania*, ICJ Reports 1949, 4 at 35.

Resolution 2625 XXV) as evidence of *opinio juris*. That Declaration provided that states have a duty to refrain from acts of reprisal involving the use of force.

The fact that some states (notably, the US, the UK and Israel) have employed forcible reprisals and have, on several occasions, done so without attracting condemnation from the Security Council, is problematic from an analytical standpoint. Some would argue that this is evidence of the development of international law and that the apparent acceptance by many states of reprisals, once they have occurred, suggests that state practice has become a more influential indicator of the norms of customary international law than Security Council resolutions.[295] The wider question of how much regard should be given to state practice, and how much weight can be accorded to Security Council resolutions in the interpretation and formation of international law, is complex, with scholars such as Cassese claiming that 'what matters more than scholarly views is the opinion of states'.[296] The importance of looking at the *opinio juris* of states was also emphasised by the ICJ in the 1985 *Libya/Malta Continental Shelf Case*. In that case, the ICJ explained that the substance of customary international law should be sought, in the first instance, in the effective practice and *opinio juris* of states.[297] Article 31 of the Statute of the ICJ emphasises that the Court must take into account international custom, as evidence of a general practice accepted as law.[298]

The issue of how one can determine the *opinio juris* of states is directly relevant to the question that is being examined here, namely, assessing the legal status of reprisals. General Assembly resolutions, such as Resolution 2625 (XXV) are relevant. Traditionally, international lawyers have presumed the existence of *opinio juris* when a state does nothing in the face of another state's clear and concerted effort to change customary international law.[299] Determining whether state *acquiescence* is evidence of state *acceptance* is an issue that has been addressed by scholars such as Stern, who argues that acquiescence on the part of relatively weak states is often a result of the dynamics of power rather than a freely given consent, and that *opinio juris* thus means different things for weak

---

295 For a discussion of how state practice and Security Council resolutions shape international law relating to the use of force in self-defence, see Byers, M., 'The Shifting Foundations of International Law: A Decade of Forceful Measures Against Iraq' (2002) 13 *EJIL* 21.

296 Cassese, A., *International Law in a Divided World* (Oxford: Clarendon, 1986) 232.

297 (1985) ICJ Reports 29–30.

298 Article 38, para (b) of the Statute of the International Court of Justice.

299 Byers, supra n. 295.

and powerful states.[300] Kritsiotis,[301] White and Cryer have pointed out that lack of condemnation by states for a particular action is not indicative of those states' acceptance of that action, or more importantly, the lawfulness of that action. White and Cryer have taken issue with those who ascribe legal significance to the refusal of states to publicly reject the unilateral use of force by the US:[302]

> It is true ... that deficiency of condemnation is an unfortunate fact of international relations in the post-Charter era, but it is over-simplistic to equate this with a change in the law. For a new customary norm to have emerged, absence of condemnation itself is not enough. There must also be an intention for that failure to condemn to amount to an acceptance of the legality of the threat or an alteration of the pre-existing law, in other words, opinio juris. This has been conspicuous by its absence. *Reluctant tolerance does not evidence opinio juris.* (Emphasis added)

Thus, merely because a few states choose to violate international norms by resorting to forcible reprisals, this does not mean that reprisals are thereby rendered lawful. States may not take a stand on the individual instances in which reprisals are employed, due to political, rather than legal, considerations.[303] But lack of formal criticism does not, *per se*, transform unlawful forcible reprisals into lawful acts of self-defence. It seems much more likely that forcible reprisals are still a breach of international law but states, for one reason or another, are sometimes motivated to 'look the other way' when a powerful state, which has veto power, wishes to use them for its own purposes.[304]

Non-state Actors

The last part of this chapter examines the evolution of international law regarding the use of force by non-state actors, and more specifically, by non-state actors who

---

300 Stern, B., 'La coutume au Coeur du droit international', in *Mélanges offerts à Paul Reuter* (1981) (Byers, M. and Denise, A. trans.) 'Custom at the Heart of International Law' (2001) 11 *Duke J. Comp. & Int'l L.* 89.

301 Kritsiotis, D., 'The Legality of the US Missile Strikes Against Iraq and the Right of Self-Defense in International Law' (1996) 45 *ICLQ* 162.

302 White and Cryer, supra n. 155 at 246.

303 See Lobel, supra n. 253 at 557.

304 The fact that at least five states supported the US missile strikes against Iraq in 1993, because they 'understood' the US reaction to the thwarted assassination plan, but they failed to refer to the self-defence justification put forward by the US as the basis for its actions, is perhaps evidence that they did not accept the reprisal as being within the letter of international law.

are engaged in acts of 'international terrorism'.[305] Some general observations will be made on the relationship between 'aggression' and non-state actors, followed by an analysis of how states may respond to the use of force by non-state actors and the way in which state responsibility may be established. During the course of the post-Charter period, it has become apparent that states have exhibited an increasing willingness not only to use force against non-state actors, but to interpret the 'armed attack' requirement in Article 51 in a way which legitimises the use of force against both state and non-state actors.

The Meaning of 'Aggression' and the State versus Non-state Actor Dichotomy

Whether states may use force in response to force employed by non-state actors is an issue that is linked to the debate surrounding the meaning of 'aggression'. Historically, states wished to draw a line between the use of force by one state against another state and the use of 'indirect force' such as when a state was the victim of 'subversive or terroristic acts'[306] by non-state actors. The draft proposals discussed through the UN committees in the late 1960s showed that states wanted to restrict the right of self-defence to instances where there had been an 'invasion or armed attack by the armed forces of *one State*, against the *territory of another State*'.[307] The Definition of Aggression adopted by the General Assembly via Resolution 3314 (XXIX)[308] also emphasised that 'aggression' meant the use of force by one *state* against the sovereignty, territorial integrity or political independence of another *state*.[309] The Definition of Aggression also stated that it would be an

305 The meaning of 'terrorism' and the efforts to construct an international legal framework to combat it were examined in Chapter 3.

306 'Draft Declaration on Aggression' submitted to the 1968 Special Committee on the Question of Defining Aggression, at the 14th Meeting, 25 June 1968, by Algeria, the Congo, Cyprus, Ghana, Guyana, Indonesia, Madagascar, the Sudan, Syria, Uganda, the UAE and Yugoslavia, A/AC. 134/L.3, reproduced in Ferencz, supra n. 2 at Document 14, 285.

307 '[W]hen a State is a victim in its own territory of subversive and/or terrorist acts by irregular, volunteer or armed bands organized by another State, it may take all reasonable and adequate steps to safeguard its existence and its institutions, *without having recourse to the right of individual or collective self-defence against the other State under Article 51 of the Charter*' (emphasis added): Draft Declaration on Aggression submitted to the 1968 Special Committee on the Question of Defining Aggression, at the 20th Meeting, 3 July 1968, by Colombia, the Congo, Cyprus, Ecuador, Ghana, Guyana, Indonesia, Iran, Mexico, Spain, Uganda, Uruguay and Yugoslavia, A/AC.134/L6, reproduced in Ferencz, supra n. 2 at 286.

308 UNGA Resolution 3314 (XXIX), adopted at the 2319th plenary meeting on 14 December 1974.

309 Ibid., Article 1. Seven types of acts, all of which would amount to aggression, are described in Article 3. All of them, except the last two, refer to the 'armed forces of a state'.

act of aggression if one state placed its territory at the disposal of another state, to be used by that state for perpetrating an act of aggression against a third state.[310] Finally, it included the sending, by or on behalf of a state, of armed bands, groups, irregulars or mercenaries, which carry out acts of armed force against another state of such magnitude as to amount to one of the listed acts of aggression, or its substantial involvement therein.[311] The Definition of Aggression adopted by the General Assembly shows that its members intended to restrict 'aggression' to instances where one state attacked another, or was *responsible* for armed bands, groups, irregulars or mercenaries that attacked another state.

The state versus non-state actor distinction is also evident in the law pertaining to piracy, which was the main threat posed by non-state actors prior to World War II.[312] In 1982, piracy was defined in the UN Convention on the Law of the Sea.[313] Piracy consists of illegal acts of violence or detention committed for *private* ends by the crew or passengers of a *private* ship or aircraft.[314] Thus, acts of piracy are criminal acts, carried out by non-state actors; they do not constitute an 'armed attack' and do not trigger the right to use force in self-defence. Acts of piracy attract universal jurisdiction: any state may seize a pirate ship or aircraft, arrest the persons and seize the property, and the courts of that state may decide upon the penalties to be imposed.[315] The parallels between piracy and terrorism are supposedly so close as to prompt one writer to suggest that the problems which the international community has experienced in defining terrorism could be resolved by adopting the same framework as was adopted for piracy: declare terrorists to be *hostis humani generis*, that is, enemies of all mankind, and ensure that they are legally classified as international criminals, subject to universal jurisdiction.[316]

States' Responses to Terrorism: Law Enforcement Versus the Use of Armed Force

Although the dominant interpretation of Article 51 is that 'armed attack' means attacks by states and their representatives, several examples have been referred

310 Ibid., Article 3(f).

311 Ibid., Article 3(g).

312 See discussion in Chapter 4. The parallels between piracy and terrorism have been touched upon in earlier chapters and elsewhere: see Rubin, A., *The Law of Piracy*, 2nd edn (New York: Transnational Publishers, 1998) 377–9; also Bolton, J., 'Maritime Order and the Development of the International Law of Piracy' (1983) 7(5) *International Relations* 2335.

313 The United Nations Convention on the Law of the Sea, Montego Bay, 10 December 1982, UN Doc A/CONF.62/122, 7 October 1982, Article 101.

314 Ibid., Article 101.

315 Ibid., Article 105.

316 Burgess Jr, D., 'The Dread Pirate bin Laden: How Thinking of Terrorists as Pirates can Help Win the War on Terror', *Legal Affairs*, July/Augusr 2005, available at: <http://www.legalaffairs.org/issues/July-August-2005/feature_burgess_julaug05.msp> at 12 June 2008.

to above which illustrate that there are exceptions to this rule.[317] Since the mid-1980s, the US and Israel have adopted the position that attacks by terrorists (state-sponsored or otherwise) may be considered as 'armed attacks' and can therefore trigger the Article 51 right to use force in self-defence.[318] By the end of the 1990s, the predominant view was that terrorist attacks committed by private, non-state actors were a form of criminal activity to be combated through domestic and international criminal justice mechanisms.[319]

The examples referred to above from the 1970s and 1980s indicate the emergence of a conflict over which of two approaches should be used to respond to terrorism: the law enforcement approach or the use of armed force (conflict management) approach.[320] The law enforcement model assumes that terrorist acts are criminal acts and can be addressed by civil/municipal government functions via the international and/or domestic criminal justice system: the police, prosecutors, judges, juries and the corrections system, if necessary. Evidence that states preferred this approach can be gleaned from the approach adopted since the 1937 Convention on Terrorism was drafted and, subsequently, in the raft of conventions that were signed, and resolutions that were adopted, between 1963 and 1991 which made various terrorist acts criminal offences.[321] However, there was a growing voice within states such as Israel and the US which supported an alternative approach. Statements from within the US Administration and the US military suggested that the armed force model was gaining favour there.[322]

---

317 In 1985, Israel bombed Tunis and in 1986 the US attacked Libya, in response to alleged acts of terrorism by non-state actors, but both Israel and the US attempted to justify their actions under the rubric of self-defence: see discussion supra at 132–136. The Reagan Administration justified the use of force against Nicaragua on notions of 'armed attack' and self-defence, although that was rejected by the ICJ. In 1993, the US employed force against Iraq and in 1998 against Sudan and Afghanistan on the basis that it was acting in 'self-defence' in response to (arguably) non-state actors (namely, a thwarted assassination attempt by the IIS and the bombings of two US embassies in Africa, allegedly orchestrated by Osama bin Laden).

318 The international community has not always been sympathetic to that proposition; for example, see the international reaction to the use of force by Israel against Tunis in 1985, by the US against Libya in 1986, by the US in Nicaragua in 1986; by the US against Iraq in 1993, by the US against Sudan and Afghanistan in 1998; and by the US and the UK against Iraq in 2001: see also the examples discussed in Gray, C., *International Law and the Use of Force*, 2nd edn (Oxford: Oxford University Press, 2004) at 108–34.

319 Garwood-Gowers, A., 'Self-Defence Against Terrorism in the Post-9/11 World' (2004) 13 *QUTLJJ* 4; and Travalio, G. and Altenburg, J., 'Terrorism, State Responsibility and the Use of Military Force' (2003) 30 *Chi. J. Int'l L.* 421.

320 Travalio and Altenburg, ibid., at 98–9.

321 See Elagab, O., *International Documents Relating to Terrorism* (London: Cavendish Publishing Limited, 1995) for a comprehensive list and text of these conventions and resolutions. The terrorism conventions have already been discussed in Chapter 3.

322 For instance, see the statement made by Secretary of State George Shultz in 1986 when he asserted that it was 'absurd to argue that international law prohibits us from …

Terrorism and 'Armed Attack'

Whether 'armed attack' in Article 51 includes actions of non-state actors has been a contentious issue during the period discussed in this chapter. In the *Nicaragua* case, the ICJ discussed the point at which attacks by non-state actors may be attributable to the state, thereby entitling the targeted state to take action in self-defence under Article 51.[323] The ICJ stated that military action by armed bands, groups, irregulars or mercenaries could constitute an armed attack *if* they were sent by or on behalf of a state (or the state had 'substantial involvement therein') and *if* they carried out acts of armed force which were of such gravity as to amount to an actual armed attack by the regular forces of a state. But the Court added that 'armed attack' does not include assistance to rebels in the form of the provision of weapons or logistical or other support. The ICJ theoretically drew a line between terrorists who are state-sponsored and those who are not: the actions of the former may meet the standard of 'armed attack', but the actions of the latter probably would not. The ICJ also distinguished between terrorists and those who harbour them and merely provide support to them. The question of whether 'armed attack' can include actions of non-state actors received further attention from the ICJ in 2004 in its Advisory Opinion on the *Legal Consequences of the Construction of a Wall in the Occupied Palestinian Territory*:[324] 'Article 51 of the Charter thus recognizes the existence of an inherent right of self-defence in the case of an *armed attack by one State against another State*.' (Emphasis added.)

The implication of the ICJ's latter statement is that an 'armed attack' in the context of Article 51 can *only* be made by one state against another state.[325] In the *Legal Consequences of the Construction of a Wall in the Occupied Palestinian Territory* case, the ICJ was aware that the types of attacks from which Israel

---

using force against states that support, train and harbour terrorists or guerillas': Shultz, G., 'Low Intensity Warfare: The Challenge of Ambiguity' (1986) 25 ILM 204 at 206; see also Erickson, supra n. 119.

323 '... [I]t may be considered to be agreed that an armed attack must be understood as including not merely action by regular armed forces across an international border, but also "the sending by or on behalf of a State of armed bands, groups, irregulars or mercenaries, which carry out acts of armed force against another State of such gravity as to amount to" (inter alia) an actual armed attack conducted by regular forces, "or its substantial involvement therein"': *Nicaragua*, supra n. 25, para 195, citing an extract from para (g) of the Definition of Aggression (punctuation and emphasis as in the original).

324 *Legal Consequences of the Construction of a Wall in the Occupied Palestinian Territory*, supra n. 66 at para 139.

325 For analysis and comment on this issue, see Murphy, supra n. 68; Wedgwood, R., 'The ICJ Opinion on the Israeli Security Fence and the Limits of Self-Defence' (2005) 99 *AJIL* 57–9; and Orakhelashvili, A., 'Legal Consequences of the Construction of a Wall in the Occupied Palestinian Territory: Opinion and Reaction' (2006) 11(1) *JCSL* 119.

claimed to be defending itself were from non-state terrorist actors, yet it steadfastly maintained that Article 51 was not relevant.[326]

Aside from Article 51, Israel also relied in that instance upon Security Council Resolutions 1368 and 1373 (2001) which were passed after the events of 11 September 2001 and which referred to acts of international terrorism as a 'threat to international peace and security'[327] *without* ascribing those acts to any particular state. Judge Kooijmans argued that this was a 'completely new element'[328] and 'an undeniably new approach to the concept of self-defence'[329] which the Court had regrettably bypassed in referring only to actions of states. He implied that those two resolutions had placed a new interpretation on the meaning of Article 51 which meant that actions of non-state actors could henceforth be regarded as armed attacks, even if they did not come from another state, despite the fact that this had been the 'generally accepted interpretation for more than 50 years'.[330] In essence, Judge Kooijmans was arguing that the Court had overlooked the importance of the Security Council resolutions in interpreting the meaning of 'armed attack' in Article 51. But despite some interesting and well-reasoned opposition, the majority of the ICJ held in 2004 that 'armed attack' in Article 51 meant an attack by one state against another state.[331] Although this opinion was handed down in 2004, it is still relevant in the current context in so far as it reaffirmed the existing interpretation of Article 51. The ICJ seemed to simply be restating the accepted interpretation of the 'armed attack' requirement.

---

326 Three of the judges objected to the narrowing of Article 51's application in that way. Judge Higgins argued that there is nothing in the text of Article 51 to narrow it to actions of the state: Advisory Opinion of 9 July 2004, Separate Opinion of Judge Higgins, para 33. Judge Buergenthal argued that Article 51 does not make its exercise dependent on an armed attack by another state: Advisory Opinion of 9 July 2004, Declaration of Judge Buergenthal, para 6. Judge Kooijmans acknowledged the Court's statement that Article 51 recognises the inherent right of self-defence in the case of an armed attack by one state against another and noted that this was 'undoubtedly correct', but in response to Israel's argument, this was 'beside the point' because Israel was relying on Security Council resolutions 1368 and 1373 (2001): Advisory Opinion, Separate Opinion of Judge Kooijmans, para 35.

327 SC Res 1368 (2001) and SC Res 1373 (2001) both refer to the 11 September 2001 acts of terrorism as threats to international peace and security.

328 *Legal Consequences of the Construction of a Wall in the Occupied Palestinian Territory*, Advisory Opinion, supra n. 66, Separate Opinion of Judge Kooijmans.

329 Ibid.

330 Ibid.

331 The Court consisted of 15 judges: President Shi, Vice-President Ranjeva, Judges Guillaume, Koroma, Vereshchetin, Higgins, Parra-Aranguren, Kooijmans, Rezek, Al-Khasawneh, Buergenthal, Elaraby, Owada, Simma and Tomka. Separate opinions were written by seven judges, namely, Koroma, Higgins, Kooijmans, Al-Khasawneh, Buergenthal, Elaraby and Owada. Out of those, only the opinions of three judges mentioned the Article 51 issue, namely, Higgins, Kooijmans and Buergenthal, as discussed above.

State Responsibility for Non-state Actors

What may be understood from the ICJ's decisions in 1986 and 2004 is that Article 51 is, and always has been, restricted to only allowing force to be used unilaterally in self-defence in response to armed attacks from *states*. The only extension of that rule to non-state actors is if those non-state actors are sent 'by or on behalf of'[332] the state or the state had 'substantial involvement therein'.[333] This raises the question of what level of state responsibility is necessary before the actions of private individuals may be attributed to the state. The test adopted in the *Nicaragua* case was one of 'effective control'. The Court stated that in order for the Contras' conduct to give rise to legal responsibility, 'it would in principle have to be proved that that State had *effective control* of the military or paramilitary operations'.[334] In an aspect of the judgment that was in the US' favour, the Court set a high threshold for state responsibility:[335]

> The Court has taken the view ... that United States participation, *even if preponderant or decisive, in the financing, organizing, training, supplying and equipping* of the contras, the selection of its military or paramilitary targets, *and the planning of the whole of its operation, is still insufficient in itself*, on the basis of the evidence in the possession of the Court, *for the purpose of attributing to the United States the acts committed by the contras* in the course of their military or paramilitary operations in Nicaragua. (Emphasis added)

The effect of the ICJ judgement is that there must be more than a relationship of mere control and dependence involving the provision of logistical support or weapons in order for actions of non-state actors to be attributed to the state: there must be *effective control* by the state over the actions of those non-state actors.

The 'effective control' test also appears in Article 8 of the ILC Draft Articles on Responsibility of States for Internationally Wrongful Acts:[336]

> The conduct of a person or group of persons shall be considered an act of a State under international law if the person or group of persons is in fact acting on the instructions of, or under the direction or control of, that State in carrying out the conduct.

---

332 *Nicaragua*, supra n. 25, para 115.

333 Ibid.

334 Ibid.

335 Ibid.

336 The text of the ILC Draft Articles was adopted by the International Law Commission in 2001 and submitted to the General Assembly as part of the Commission's report.

The general rule in international law is that the only conduct attributable to the state is that of its organs of government, or of others who have acted under the direction, instigation or control of those organs, that is, as agents of the state.[337] As such, the conduct of private persons is not generally attributable to the state. However, even though a state may not have attributed to it the actions of individuals, it may still be responsible if it fails to take all necessary steps to prevent the effects of the conduct of private parties. For example, a state may not be responsible for the actions of private individuals in seizing an embassy, but it will be responsible if it fails to take all necessary steps to protect the embassy from seizure, or to regain control over it.[338]

Article 8 is important in the present context because it provides that a state is not responsible for the actions of private individuals unless they are acting on the instruction of, or under the direction or control of, organs of the state.[339] The Commentary to the ILC Draft Articles states that 'under the direction or control of a State'[340] means that the state directed or controlled the *specific operation* and the conduct complained of was an integral part of that operation. The principle does *not* extend to conduct that was only incidentally or peripherally associated with an operation and that escaped from the state's direction or control.[341] Moreover, a general situation of dependence and support is insufficient to justify attribution to the state.[342]

In *Prosecutor v Tadić*, the Appeals Chamber of the International Criminal Tribunal for the Former Yugoslavia held that: 'The requirement of international law for the attribution to States of acts performed by private individuals is that the state must exercise *control* over the individuals.'[343] The Appeals Chamber distinguished the situation where individuals might be acting on behalf of a State without specific instructions, from the situation where there are individuals making up an organised and hierarchically structured group, such as a military unit or, in case of civil war or civil strife, armed bands of irregulars or rebels. The Appeals Chamber held that for the attribution to a State of acts of the latter groups, 'it is

---

337 Commentary to the ILC Draft Articles, available at: <http://untreaty.un.org/ilc/texts/instruments/english/commentaries/9_6_2001.pdf> at 12 June 2008.

338 See *United States Diplomatic and Consular Staff in Tehran*, ICJ Reports 1980, 3; see Commentary to the ILC Draft Articles, supra n. 337 at 24.

339 The Commentary to the ILC Draft Articles notes that the three terms used in Article 8, 'instructions', 'direction' and 'control' are disjunctive: it is sufficient to establish any one of them: supra n. 337 at 108, para (7).

340 See Commentary to the ILC Draft Articles, supra n. 337, at 104 para (3).

341 Ibid.

342 Ibid., 106, para (4); *Nicaragua*, supra n. 25.

343 *Prosecutor v Tadić*, Appeals Chamber, Case No IT-94-1-A, ICTY (15 July 1999) at 48; excerpted in (1999) 38 ILM 1518. For a detailed account of the *Tadić* case, see Scharf, M., *Balkan Justice – The Story Behind the First International War Crimes Trial Since Nuremburg* (Durham, North Carolina: Carolina Academic Press, 1997); also Sharf, M., 'International Decision: Prosecutor v Tadić Case No. IT-94-1-T', (1997) 91 *AJIL* 718.

sufficient to require that the group as a whole be under the overall control of the State'.[344] Even though the degree of control may vary from case to case, the court held that 'overall control, going beyond the mere financing and equipping of such forces and involving also participation in the planning and supervision of military operations'[345] was required.

In addition to Article 8, Article 11 establishes that a state may be held responsible for acts that otherwise would not have been attributed to it 'if and to the extent that the State acknowledges and adopts the act in question as its own'.[346] If the state approves of the actions of the non-state actors, even though it did not initiate them, that can transform it into an act of the state.[347] The Commentary to the Draft Articles notes that the phrase 'acknowledges and adopts the conduct in question as its own'[348] is intended to distinguish cases of acknowledgement and adoption from cases of mere support or endorsement:[349]

> ... [A]s a general matter, conduct will not be attributable to a State under Article 11 where a State merely acknowledges the factual existence of conduct or expresses its verbal approval of it ... The language of 'adoption' ... carries with it the idea that the conduct is acknowledged by the State as, in effect, its own conduct.

The legal ramifications for a state which has been found responsible for an intentionally wrongful act include a duty to cease and to provide reparations for injuries caused such as restitution, compensation and satisfaction, as per Articles 28–39. Notably, there is no reference to the right of an aggrieved state to resort to *force* in order to punish a transgressor state.

The International Law Commission considers that the Draft Articles represent current international law on state responsibility. In Chapter 6, the question of Afghanistan's responsibility for the actions of the 11 September hijackers will be

---

344 *Prosecutor v Tadić*, supra, n. 343 at 49.

345 Ibid., 55: 'Judging from international case law and State practice, it would seem that for such control to come about, it is not sufficient for the group to be financially or even militarily assisted by a State'; and at 56: 'In order to attribute the acts of a military or paramilitary group to a State, it must be proved that the State wields overall control over the group, not only by equipping and financing the group, but also by co-ordinating or helping in the general planning of its military activity. Only then can the State be held internationally accountable for any misconduct of the group'; also see Commentary to the ILC Draft Articles, supra n. 337 at 106 para (5). On the facts, the Appeals Chamber held that the Bosnian Serbs were under the *overall control* of the Federal Republic of Yugoslavia.

346 Article 11, Draft Articles on Responsibility of States for Intentionally Wrongful Acts.

347 *United States Diplomatic and Consular Staff in Tehran*, supra n. 338; see Commentary to the ILC Draft Articles, supra n. 337.

348 Commentary to the ILC Draft Articles, supra n. 337.

349 Ibid.

assessed in light of this legal framework. The attribution of state responsibility by the US and its allies will be closely analysed to determine if the standard attribution test was met, or if it was effectively ignored, or if a lower threshold is now in place.[350] The ultimate objective will be to determine if the acts of the non-state actors in that incident were properly attributed to the State of Afghanistan so as to justify the use of force in self-defence.

Conclusion

This chapter has traced the developments in international law since 1945 regarding five distinct but inter-related concepts: the use of force generally, self-defence, pre-emptive self-defence, reprisals and the use of force in response to non-state actors. The key points in the above analysis are summarised as follows. First, the adoption of the UN Charter stands out as the single most important event in this period because it established a general prohibition on the use of force in Article 2(4) and it preserved an inherent right of self-defence in Article 51. However, a lack of consensus has prevailed over the meaning of 'aggression', 'armed attack' and 'self-defence'. From Dumbarton Oaks until the present, it has become evident that states disagree as to the circumstances under which they are entitled to resort to force in self-defence.

Secondly, the apparently simple concept of self-defence as preserved in Article 51 has been the subject of significant controversy. State practice has shown that the concept of 'self-defence' has been stretched, especially in the later decades of the post-World War II era, by states which wish to invoke it for any use of force which they hope to legitimise. The use of force in 'self-defence' by the US against Iraq in 1993, in response to a past, thwarted assassination attempt, would perhaps be one of the most poorly argued instances of 'self-defence' in this era, given that there was no 'armed attack'. That incident was indicative of a trend which has seen the boundaries of self-defence in Article 51 being constantly pushed outward.

Thirdly, the doctrine of pre-emptive self-defence has gained ground. In the early years, it was only seriously advanced by Israel but by the latter stages of this period, the Bush Administration in the US, followed 'in principle' by the Howard government in Australia, advocated pre-emptive self-defence as being actual or potential national policy, and both the US and Australia implied that using force in pre-emptive self-defence was consistent with international law. The fact that pre-emptive self-defence has gained support so quickly must be a cause for concern as it cannot be justified by any literal reading of Article 51, which clearly requires

350 See, for example, Garwood-Gowers who argues that the threshold for attribution is now 'significantly lower': supra n. 319 at 10; see also articles by Travalio and Altenburg, supra n. 319; and Stahn, C., 'International Law Under Fire: Terrorist Acts as "Armed Attacks": The Right to Self-Defense, Article 51 (1/2) of the UN Charter and International Terrorism' (2003) 27 *Fletcher F. World Aff.* 35, especially at 42ff.

an 'armed attack' to have occurred before self-defence is an option for any state. Although Israel's pre-emptive strike on the Iraqi nuclear reactor was unanimously condemned by the Security Council in 1981, pre-emptive self-defence is now gaining legitimacy in the US and Australia's foreign/defence policies. It would seem that the defence policies adopted by some states are now firmly out of step with international law.

Fourthly, although the use of forcible reprisals was supposedly prohibited by the UN Charter, a few states have continued to employ them. The Security Council was initially unanimous in its condemnation of this practice (most notably in the 1960s and 1970s) but other states have of late joined Israel in seeking to use reprisals as a means of dealing with the threat of international terrorism. The US demonstrated in the 1980s and 1990s that it will also use reprisals to respond to actual or thwarted acts of international terrorism.

The fifth point relates to the use of force by non-state actors. Although states traditionally interpreted Article 51 as applying to armed attacks by states, there has been a movement towards including actions of non-state actors. A clear divide has emerged between international law – in the form of pronouncements of the ICJ in the *Nicaragua* and *Legal Consequences of the Construction of a Wall in the Occupied Palestinian Territory* cases – and the practice of some states. The fact that the US used force in 1986, 1993 and 1998 in response to past or planned terrorist acts, and that throughout these episodes it attracted a decreasing amount of condemnation for its actions, is indicative of a significant trend throughout the period towards allowing states the option of using force in response to terrorist acts in some circumstances.

The final point made here is that there is an increasingly urgent need to grapple with the issue of the attribution of actions of non-state actors to the state. Although substantial effort has been put into developing international law in this area, particularly via the ILC's Draft Articles on Responsibility of States for Intentionally Wrongful Acts, some states have appeared to employ force regardless of whether state responsibility has been properly established, and regardless of the suggested rules that ought to guide the international community. Even if the international community is able to enshrine the Draft Articles in law, it is doubtful that all states would adhere to them. For instance, the Draft Articles declare that a state is responsible for actions of individuals which it has directed, instructed or which it has control over. This is not easily reconcilable with the position adopted by the US as set forth in the 2002 NSS which states that the US will 'make no distinction between terrorists and those who knowingly harbour or provide aid to them'.[351] The US policy is somewhat at odds with both the pronouncements of the ICJ and the Draft Articles on State Responsibility which require something more than dependence and control; they require *effective control*. Rather than breaching the law, a small group of states seems to be moving in the direction of simply ignoring it.

351 US 2002 National Security Strategy, supra n. 137 and accompanying text.

This chapter has discussed an era of remarkable achievement in limiting the resort to force, yet, especially towards the latter years of the post-World War II era, some states have demonstrated a reluctance to be constrained by the limits of international law. Decisions of the ICJ – when they have been sought – have often been ignored and the Charter itself has been challenged and has been the subject of calls for review. Having broadly established the legal limits of the use of force by states, Chapter 6 will closely examine one recent episode: it aims to determine the lawfulness of the use of force, purportedly in self-defence, against Afghanistan in 2001.

Chapter 6
The Use of Force Against Afghanistan in 2001

Introduction

This chapter examines the lawfulness of employing military force against Afghanistan in October 2001. The primary issue addressed here is whether or not the use of force was a legitimate exercise of the inherent right of self-defence pursuant to Article 51 of the United Nations Charter. The elements of Article 51 that were discussed in the previous chapter are applied to these particular facts to determine whether those elements were satisfied. This chapter's main focus is on the self-defence justification because both the US and the UK stated that they were acting pursuant to Article 51. In addition, the alternative justifications of pre-emptive self-defence (to prevent future attacks from al Qaeda), humanitarian intervention, Security Council authorisation, and intervention by invitation (from the Northern Alliance) are briefly examined towards the end of the chapter. The objective here is to demonstrate that compelling arguments exist which support the proposition that the use of force against Afghanistan in 2001 was unlawful.

The Events of 11 September 2001 and the Initial Response

The facts concerning what occurred on 11 September 2001 are well known and widely documented.[1] The events that triggered the invasion of Afghanistan took place on Tuesday 11 September 2001 when it is alleged that 19 members of an organisation known as 'al Qaeda' took control of four domestic aircraft in the US.[2]

---

1 Numerous sources, including governmental, academic and media accounts, are available in a plethora of texts, articles and internet sites. The most comprehensive source of factual evidence of what occurred on 11 September is probably *The 9/11 Commission Report*, based on the investigations undertaken by the National Commission on Terrorist Attacks Upon the United States: <http://www.9-11commission.gov/report/index.htm> at 17 June 2008. For websites that provide more concise fact files, see the US Department of State: <http://www.state.gov/coalition/cr/fs/12701.htm> at 17 June 2008.

2 The term 'al Qaeda', which means 'the foundation' or 'the base', is spelt differently in various sources. The spelling 'al Qaeda' has been adopted here as it seems to be the most widely recognised transliteration. In quotes from other sources, the spelling used by the original source is maintained.

American Airlines Flight 11, flying from Logan Airport in Boston, Massachusetts to Los Angeles, was hijacked by five passengers.[3] It was flown into the North Tower of the World Trade Centre at 8.46am.[4] United Airlines Flight 175, also leaving from Logan Airport, was also hijacked by five passengers[5] and it was flown into the South Tower of the World Trade Centre at 9.03am.[6] Shortly after 9.30am, American Airlines Flight 77, which had just departed from Washington's Dulles Airport headed for Los Angeles, was also hijacked.[7] It crashed into the Pentagon at 9.38am. The fourth airplane was United Airlines Flight 93 which left Newark bound for San Francisco but was hijacked at approximately 9.28am.[8] It was thought to have been the hijackers' objective to crash the plane into either the Capitol or the White House,[9] but the hijackers' presumed objective was thwarted by the passengers and the plane crashed into a field in Pennsylvania at 10.10am. In total, the US State Department estimated that 2,948 people, from approximately 90 countries,[10] died as a result of the four airplane hijackings on 11 September 2001.[11]

The US's Immediate Reaction to the Hijackings

The initial response to the hijackings focused on the scrambling of military aircraft to prevent further buildings being targeted and included a variety of

3 Allegedly by Mohammad Atta, Abdul Aziz al Omani, Satam al Suqami, Wali al Shehi and Waleed al Shehi: *The 9/11 Commission Report*, supra n. 1 at 1–2.

4 US Department of State, Fact Sheet, supra n. 1; see also Mattox, H., *Chronology of World Terrorism* (North Carolina: McFarland & Company, 2004) at 155–7; Maxwell, B., *Terrorism: A Documentary History* (Washington DC: CQ Press, 2003) at 351–3; and Sterba, J. (ed), *Terrorism and International Justice* (Oxford; New York: Oxford University Press, 2003) at 1–3.

5 Allegedly by Marwan al Shehhi, Fayez Banihammad, Mohand al Shehri, Ahmed al Ghamdi and Hamza al Ghamdi: *The 9/11 Commission Report*, supra n. 1 at 1–2.

6 It is estimated that 2,823 people were killed, including flight passengers, as well as people inside the buildings, and police and fire department rescuers on the ground, when those two planes collided with the World Trade Centre: US Department of State Fact Sheet, supra n. 1.

7 Allegedly by Khalid al Mihdhar, Majed Moqed, Hani Hanjour, Nawaf al Hazmi and Salem al Hazmi: *The 9/11 Commission Report*, supra n. 1 at 2–3.

8 Allegedly by Saeed al Ghamdi, Ahmed al Nami, Ahmad al Haznawi and Ziad Jarrah: ibid., 10–14.

9 Ibid., 14.

10 US Department of State, Fact Sheet, supra n. 1. The UK's estimate in October 2001 was 80 countries: United Kingdom Parliament, International Affairs and Defence Section, House of Commons Library, Research Paper 01/72, 3 October 2001, '11 September 2001: The Response', at 11: <http://www.parliament.uk/commons/lib/research/rp2001/rp01-072.pdf> at 17 June 2008.

11 US Department of State Fact Sheet, supra n. 1. That figure includes all the people on board the four aircraft, plus the people killed in the Pentagon and in the World Trade Centre buildings.

domestic security measures such as the closure of US airspace,[12] the evacuation of government buildings[13] and the relocation of US President, George W Bush, and Vice-President, Dick Cheney, to safe locations.[14] The President was initially advised of the first aircraft's crash at approximately 8.55am and the second aircraft's demise at 9.05am.[15] At 9.45am, he called the Vice President and said: 'Sounds like we have a minor war going on here, I heard about the Pentagon. We're at war … somebody's going to pay.'[16] Air Force One took to the air at about 9.54am and eventually landed at Barksdale Air Force Base where the President recorded a message to the nation and then re-boarded.[17] In the late afternoon, the President ordered Air Force One back to Andrews Air Force Base and addressed the nation that evening at 8.30pm from the White House.[18]

The US's Initial Political Response

The statements that were issued on 11 September and 12 September 2001 suggest that the White House considered the threat of immediate attack to be over by the late afternoon on 11 September, when the President returned from the Offutt Air Force Base to Washington DC.[19] The first substantial political response was made via a statement to the nation by the President on the evening of 11 September in which he, *inter alia*, referred to the hijackings as criminal acts by describing them as 'acts of mass murder'.[20] He also implied that the US would pursue a law enforcement response:[21] 'The search is underway for those who are behind these evil acts. I've directed the full resources of our intelligence and law enforcement communities to find those responsible and bring them to justice.'

---

12 *The 9/11 Commission Report*, supra n. 1 at 20ff.

13 The Pentagon was evacuated at 9.38am, the White House at 9.45am, followed by the World Bank, US State and Justice Departments at 10.22am, and then all federal office buildings in Washington DC.

14 UK Parliament Research Paper 01/72, supra n. 10 at 11.

15 *The 9/11 Commission Report*, supra n. 1 at 38–9.

16 Ibid., 39.

17 Ibid., 325.

18 Ibid., 326.

19 White House press corps: '"… [I]s it fair to assume that once he left Nebraska and head [sic] for Washington, that it was – that you were confident that the threat was over?", Fleischer replied, "To leave Nebraska and head back to Washington? Yes … Following his meeting in Nebraska, the President made the determination to return [to Washington]. And obviously it was safe enough for him to do so."': The White House, Press Briefing by Ari Fleischer, 12 September 2001: <http://www.whitehouse.gov/news/releases/2001/09/20010912-8.html> at 17 June 2008.

20 The White House, Press Release, 11 September 2001, 8.30pm EDT, 'Statement by the President in his Address to the Nation', <http://www.whitehouse.gov/news/releases/2001/09/20010911-16.html> at 17 June 2008.

21 Ibid.

There was initially no suggestion that a military response was imminent. Aside from the comment that 'our military is powerful, and it's prepared',[22] the overall tenor of the President's speech on 11 September was that the terrorist acts were being treated as *criminal* acts and that intelligence and law enforcement mechanisms would deliver justice.[23] However, the private discussions between the President and his advisors provide a different picture[24] and from 12 September onwards there were increasingly conspicuous references to a possible military response. There were references to revenge, retaliation and pre-emption in the President's speeches on 14 September,[25] 15 September[26] and 16 September 2001,[27] but the target was unspecified; the enemy was referred to in general terms as 'terrorism' or 'evil-doers'.

The 'Authorization for the Use of Military Force' Resolution[28]

The first formal use of the term 'self-defence' by the US Administration occurred in the US Congress' Joint Resolution adopted on 14 September 2001, in which Congress stated that the attacks of 11 September rendered it 'both necessary and

---

22 Ibid.

23 Ari Fleischer's press briefings on 12 September 2001 confirm that there was no immediate resolve to engage in a military response: supra n. 19. When Fleischer was asked if the NATO statement indicated that a unified military response was likely, Fleischer responded that a unified response was likely, but refused on that occasion, and throughout the briefing, to suggest that a military response was likely.

24 The President chaired a National Security Council meeting in the evening of 11 September 2001, with a group that he would later refer to as the 'war council', in which he remarked that it was a 'time for self-defence' and that the US would 'punish not just the perpetrators of the attacks, but also those who harboured them'. He and his advisors also discussed which states might be targeted: *The 9/11 Commission Report*, supra n. 1 at 330.

25 For instance, when addressing rescue workers in New York on 14 September, and in response to calls that the audience could not hear, President Bush replied: 'I can hear you. (Applause) The rest of the world can hear you. (Applause) And the people who knocked these buildings down will hear all of us soon. (Applause)': see The White House, 'President Bush Salutes Heroes in New York', 14 September 2001: <http://www.whitehouse.gov/news/releases/2001/09/20010914-9.html> at 17 June 2008.

26 The White House, Radio Address of the President to the Nation, 15 September 2001: <http://www.whitehouse.gov/news/releases/2001/09/20010915.html> at 17 June 2008.

27 'I also have faith in our military. We have got a job to do … we will rid the world of evil-doers …' The White House, Remarks by the President Upon Arrival, 16 September 2001: <http://www.whitehouse.gov/news/releases/2001/09/20010916-2.html> at 17 June 2008.

28 The 'Use of Force' resolution was passed in the Senate by a vote of 98-0 and in the Congress by 420-1. The sole dissenting vote was cast by Democrat Barbara Lee: see 'Rep. Barbara Lee's Speech Opposing the Post-9-11 Use of Force Act', 14 September 2001: <http://www.wagingpeace.org/articles/2001/09/14_lee-speech.htm> at 17 June 2008.

appropriate that the United States exercise its rights to self-defense'.[29] The Use of Force resolution is significant because it authorised the US President to:[30]

> [U]se all necessary and appropriate force against those nations, organizations, or persons he determines planned, authorized, committed, or aided the terrorist attacks that occurred on September 11, 2001, or harbored such organizations or persons, *in order to prevent any future acts of international terrorism against the United States* by such nations, organizations or persons. (Emphasis added)

The objective for authorising force was 'in order to prevent any future attacks', which implies that on 14 September 2001, the US Senate and Congress considered the immediate threat to be over. Any military force used pursuant to this resolution would not be in response to the imminent threat of an armed attack; it would be used to prevent possible *future* acts of international terrorism.[31]

Another notable feature of the Use of Force resolution was the authorisation to use force against 'organizations or persons'. In previous resolutions authorising the use of military force, Congress had referred to unnamed nations in specific regions of the world, but this was apparently the first time that Congress had authorised force to be used against unnamed 'organizations or persons'.[32] Notably, the Use of Force resolution described the hijackings as 'acts of treacherous violence'; it did not refer to them as either acts of war or armed attacks.[33]

Address to a Joint Session of Congress and the American People[34]

The political reaction within the US quickly evolved into overwhelming support for the use of military force.[35] By the time of the President's Address to a Joint

---

29 United States 107th Congress, 1st Session, SJ Res 23, Joint Resolution, passed by the Senate on 14 September 2001. This resolution was signed into law by the President on 18 September 2001. For media commentary, see 'Congress Approves Resolution Authorizing Use of Force', *CNN.com*, 15 September 2001: <http://archives.cnn.com/2001/US/09/14/congress.terrorism/> at 17 June 2008.

30 Ibid.

31 See discussion below under the heading 'Pre-emptive Self-defence'.

32 Grimmett, R., Congressional Research Service Report for Congress, 'Authorization for Use of Military Force in Response to the 9/11 Attacks (P.L 107-40), Legislative History, 4 January 2006': <http://www.fas.org/sgp/crs/natsec/RS22357.pdf> at 17 June 2008.

33 See discussion below at 189–202 regarding the argument that this was not an 'armed attack'.

34 The White House, President George W. Bush, Address to a Joint Session of Congress and the American People, 20 September 2001: <http://www.whitehouse.gov/news/releases/2001/09/20010920-8.html> at 17 June 2008.

35 For dissenting political voices, see, for instance, Barbara Lee and Jesse Jackson who both made statements urging the Bush Administration to consider other options rather than a retaliatory military strike.

Session of Congress and the American People on 20 September, the hijackings were frequently being described as 'acts of war'.[36] The Bush Administration wanted a military response, which, although formally clothed in legal language as an action to prevent future attacks, was plainly accepted as an act of *retaliation.* In President Bush's 20 September address, he admitted as much when he stated: 'Our response involves far more than *instant retaliation* and isolated strikes.'[37] Later in the address, in the context of claiming that 'the civilized world is rallying to America's side', he said the civilized world 'understands that if this terror goes *unpunished*, their own cities, their own citizens may be next'.[38] It is apparent that the US military response to the hijackings of 11 September would be an act of 'retaliation' or 'punishment', even though those terms were not employed in the official justifications for the use of force provided to the UN Security Council.

In the 20 September 2001 address, President Bush made three other crucial sets of remarks. First, he outlined the US's five-point ultimatum to the Taliban:[39]

> And tonight, the United States of America makes the following demands on the Taliban: Deliver to United States authorities all the leaders of al Qaeda who hide in your land. (Applause) Release all foreign nationals, including American citizens, you have unjustly imprisoned. Protect foreign journalists, diplomats and aid workers in your country. Close immediately and permanently every terrorist training camp in Afghanistan, and hand over every terrorist, and every person in their support structure, to appropriate authorities. (Applause) Give the United States full access to terrorist training camps, so we can make sure they are no longer operating.
>
> These demands are not open to negotiation or discussion. (Applause) The Taliban must act, and act immediately. They will hand over the terrorists, or they will share in their fate.

According to the Bush Administration, the ultimatum was non-negotiable.[40] Yet it did not state that compliance by the Taliban would necessarily preclude military action against Afghanistan. Putting aside the question of whether the ultimatum

---

36 'On September the 11th, enemies of freedom committed an *act of war* against our country … Americans are asking: how will we fight and win this *war*? ... this war will not be like the war against Iraq a decade ago … it will not look like the air war above Kosovo …' (emphasis added): Address to a Joint Session of Congress and the American People, supra n. 34.

37 Ibid.

38 Ibid.

39 Ibid.

40 President Bush reportedly said: 'When I said no negotiations, I meant no negotiations. We know he's [bin Laden] guilty, turn him over': Borger, J. and Norton-Taylor, R., 'Pentagon Split over Battle Plan', *Guardian Weekly*, 18–24 October 2001.

itself was a violation of the UN Charter,[41] the actual requirements of the ultimatum were impracticable: even if the Taliban had had complete control over the whole of Afghanistan, it seems unlikely that its leadership could have complied with such wide-ranging demands as 'protecting foreign journalists, diplomats and aid workers' and delivering to the US 'all the leaders of Al Qaeda who hide in your land'.[42] The US State Department did not expect the Taliban to comply with the ultimatum and thus preparations for war were already underway at the time that it was issued.[43] However, despite the US's statements that its ultimatum was non-negotiable, the Taliban were apparently willing to negotiate.[44]

Secondly, President Bush emphasised the way in which the US had redefined its friends and enemies. He referred to his Administration's intention to not only attack those who attack the US, but to attack those who harbour or assist terrorists:[45]

> And we will pursue nations that provide aid or safe haven to terrorism. Every nation, in every region, now has a decision to make. Either you are with us, or you are with the terrorists. (Applause) From this day forward, any nation that continues to harbor or support terrorism will be regarded by the United States as a hostile regime.

Significantly, the President's address, which set out the framework for the US response, did not use the term 'self-defence' nor did it mention international law. The tenor of the 20 September 2001 address was that the US would do whatever it thought necessary, for as long as it thought necessary, against any nation that was not 'with us'.[46] President Bush did not mention how the US's new definition of its friends and enemies fitted within the context of international law and the limits of the right of self-defence.

---

41 Sybille Kapferer makes the point that this ultimatum, accompanied by the threat of military strikes, was 'in itself, in principle … a violation of Article 2(4) of the U.N. Charter, which prohibits the use of force, or threat thereof, in international relations': Kapferer, S., 'Ends and Means in Politics: International Law as Framework for Political Decisionmaking', in Eden, P. and O'Donnell, T. (eds), *September 11, 2001: A Turning Point in International and Domestic Law?* (New York: Transnational Publishers, 2005) at 39, n. 31. The same point is raised by Kenny, K., 'Ireland, the Security Council and Afghanistan: Promoting or Undermining the International Rule of Law?' (2001) *Trócaire Dev. R.* 101 at 106.

42 Gunaratna, R., *Inside Al Qaeda – Global Network of Terror* (London: Hurst & Co, 2002) 61–2.

43 See *The 9/11 Commission Report*, chapter 10, 'Wartime', supra n. 1.

44 See discussion below at 169–171 regarding 'Afghanistan/The Taliban's Initial Response'.

45 Address to a Joint Session of Congress and the American People, supra n. 34.

46 Ibid.

Thirdly, the Bush Administration showed a desire to bring humanitarian issues to the fore. Even though the objective of the 20 September speech was to set out the reasons why the US had to respond militarily, and to outline its planned 'war on terrorism', President Bush referred to the US's concern for human rights and the humanitarian situation within Afghanistan.[47] The overt connection between terrorism and human rights in Afghanistan is significant. Subsequent to the 20 September address, the international media also focused on the broader human rights/humanitarian situation there, in what could be interpreted as an attempt to bolster the Bush Administration's justifications for regime change in Afghanistan by emphasising its human rights record.[48]

The UK's Initial Response

The UK's immediate response was to offer its condolences to the US and, in practical terms, it was limited to taking precautionary security measures.[49] The first considered statement from the Blair government regarding its likely response was made in the House of Commons on 14 September 2001.[50] Prime Minister Tony Blair adopted a position that was subtly but crucially different to that adopted by the US. Blair referred to the events of 11 September as acts of terrorism that had resulted in the *murder* of British citizens, further emphasising the *criminal* nature of the attacks when he said that 'the murder of British people in New York is no different from their murder in the heart of Britain itself'.[51] He also said that 'we must bring to justice those responsible'[52] and he made specific reference to the laws of extradition and prosecution. Blair did not formally categorise the hijackings as an act of war. Although the British government was initially reluctant to provide details as to whether a military response was being planned, by 24 September 2001 it appeared that a military response of some kind was increasingly likely.[53]

As in the US, a pattern emerged whereby governmental statements regarding possible military strikes against Afghanistan were usually presented alongside references to human rights and humanitarian concerns. Prime Minister Blair

47 Ibid. See also the discussion below at 222–225 wherein the relevant excerpts are cited.

48 See analysis below at 221ff.

49 Prime Minister Tony Blair's statement in response to terrorist attacks in the United States, 11 September 2001: <http://www.primeminister.gov.uk/output/Page1596.asp> at 17 June 2008.

50 Prime Minister's statement to the House of Commons following the September 11 attacks, 14 September 2001: <http://www.number10.gov.uk/output/Page1598.asp> at 17 June 2008.

51 Ibid.

52 '… [W]e need to look once more: nationally and internationally at extradition laws, and the mechanisms for international justice …': ibid.

53 UK Parliament, Research Paper 01/72, supra n. 10 at 23.

warned the Taliban that it would face military action unless it gave up Osama bin Laden, but he also asked the British public to:[54]

> Look for a moment at the Taliban regime. It is undemocratic, that goes without saying ... no art or culture is permitted. All other faiths, all other interpretations of Islam are ruthlessly suppressed. Those who practice their faith are imprisoned. Women are treated in a way almost too revolting to be credible ...

This explicit linking of human rights in Afghanistan to the use of force in self-defence mirrored the strategy adopted in the US.[55]

Afghanistan/The Taliban's Initial Response[56]

On 11 September 2001, the Taliban had received diplomatic recognition from only three states: the United Arab Emirates (UAE), Saudi Arabia and Pakistan. On 22 September, the UAE and later Saudi Arabia withdrew their recognition.

Evidence suggests that prior to 11 September 2001, the Taliban had opposed a large-scale attack on the US, on various grounds.[57] After the attacks on 11 September, the initial reaction from the Taliban leadership was to unequivocally condemn the hijackings. On 11 September 2001, the US media reported that Mullah Omar, the Taliban's spiritual leader, condemned the attacks and denied that Osama bin Laden was responsible. Mullah Abdul Salam Zaeef, the Taliban's ambassador to Pakistan, also expressed his sympathy.[58]

---

54 'Blair Warns Taliban of Military Strikes', *Telegraph.co.uk*, 2 October 2001: <http://www.telegraph.co.uk/news/main.jhtml?xml=/news/2001/10/02/ublair.xml> at 17 June 2008.

55 See discussion above at 168, and see below at 222–225 under the heading 'Humanitarian Intervention'.

56 In 1997, the UN Credentials Committee received one set of credentials from the 'Islamic State of Afghanistan' and another set from the 'Islamic Emirate of Afghanistan'. A decision was deferred on which set to accept. The Permanent Representative of the former continued to represent Afghanistan at the UN. Throughout this book, references to the State of Afghanistan refer to the Islamic Emirate of Afghanistan, over which members of the Taliban claimed to preside, because on 11 September 2001, the Taliban regime was believed to have had control of approximately 90 per cent of the territory in Afghanistan.

57 Members of the Taliban were reported to have openly opposed any al Qaeda attack on the US. Mullah Omar objected on ideological grounds, preferring an attack on Jews to Americans. Abu Hafs, the Mauritanian, wrote to bin Laden objecting to strikes on the US, basing his opposition on the Qur'an: *The 9/11 Commission Report*, supra n. 1 at 251.

58 'We want to tell the American children that Afghanistan feels your pain and we hope that the courts find justice': 'Terror Attacks Hit US', *CNN.com*, 11 September 2001: <http://archives.cnn.com/2001/US/09/11/worldtrade.crash/> at 17 June 2008.

The US's five-point ultimatum to the Taliban[59] was communicated to Mullah Omar by the Pakistani Chief of Intelligence, Mahmud Ahmed, on 17 or 18 September 2001.[60] Ahmed's report back to US Deputy Secretary of State, Richard Armitage, was that Omar's response to the ultimatum was 'not negative on all these points'.[61] Nevertheless, according to *The 9/11 Commission Report*, the Bush Administration 'knew that the Taliban was unlikely to turn over bin Laden'.[62]

The issuing of an ultimatum to the Taliban regarding, *inter alia*, the surrender of Osama bin Laden for trial, is an important aspect of the events that followed 9/11. Publicly, President Bush called upon the Taliban to immediately comply with the demands, or face the consequences.[63] There were several reports of offers from the Taliban to comply with various elements of the ultimatum. Mullah Omar announced that the issue of bin Laden's extradition would be decided by a grand Islamic council of around 800 clerics.[64] The council concluded that bin Laden should be asked to leave Afghanistan, a position endorsed by the Taliban leadership.[65] On 4 October 2001, the Taliban covertly offered to turn Osama bin Laden over to Pakistan for trial in an international tribunal that would operate according to Islamic Shari'a law.[66] In addition, the Taliban offered to release the eight foreign aid workers[67] who had been detained since early August.[68] There appears to have been no official statement from President Bush in response to that

59 See discussion at n. 34 and accompanying text.

60 See UK Parliament, Research Paper 01/72, supra n. 10 at 55; *The 9/11 Commission Report*, supra n. 1 at 333.

61 *The 9/11 Commission Report*, chapter 10, 'Wartime', supra n. 1.

62 Ibid.

63 'These demands are not open to negotiation or discussion. (Applause) The Taliban must act, and act immediately. They will hand over the terrorists, or they will share in their fate': Address to a Joint Session of Congress and the American People, supra n. 34.

64 UK Parliament, Research Paper 01/72, supra n. 10 at 55.

65 Ibid.

66 See 'The Smoking Gun', *Justice not Vengeance*, 8 October 2001: <http://www.j-n-v.org/AW_briefings/ARROW_briefing005.htm> at 17 June 2008; also 'Taliban and bin Laden Agreed to Extradition', *Scoop*, 8 October 2001: <http://www.scoop.co.nz/stories/WO0110/S00046.htm> at 17 June 2008.

67 Two Australians, four Germans and two Americans had been arrested, together with 16 Afghan employees of a Christian aid agency, in August 2001 and were accused of trying to convert Afghans to Christianity: 'Red Cross Can Visit Prisoners', *CNN.com*, 23 August 2001: <http://archives.cnn.com/2001/WORLD/asiapcf/central/08/23/afghan.annanplea/index.html> at 17 June 2008.

68 The Taliban's Foreign Minister, Wakil Ahmed Muttawakil, stated that if the US was ready to assure the Afghan people that their action was not against them, then the Taliban was ready to release the aid workers: 'US Rejects Offer to Try bin Laden', *CNN.com*, 7 October 2001: <http://archives.cnn.com/2001/US/10/07/ret.us.taliban/> at 17 June 2008.

offer. An official from the Bush Administration said that the aid workers should be released unconditionally, stressing that 'this was not a negotiation'.[69]

On 7 October 2001, the Taliban offered to detain bin Laden and try him in Afghanistan in an Islamic court, if the US made a formal request and presented the Taliban with evidence of bin Laden's involvement in the terrorist attacks. The Taliban's counter-offer was immediately rejected as insufficient. The US demanded that bin Laden be turned over unconditionally and reiterated that the terms of the US ultimatum were non-negotiable.[70] No counter-offer was made by the US or the UK, even when further negotiations were requested by the Taliban's Deputy Prime Minister.[71]

The 9/11 Commission Report notes that the Bush Administration 'knew'[72] that the Taliban was unlikely to comply with its demands. It also notes that as of 11 September, the Administration adopted the position that the US would respond with force.[73] That decision is difficult to reconcile with the issuing of the ultimatum. According to then Secretary of Defense, Donald Rumsfeld, from 12 September 2001, the understanding between him and the President was that military force would be used and the only question to be determined was the most appropriate targets. The US had apparently rejected the concept of having bin Laden tried in a third country, similar to the way in which the two Libyans accused of the Lockerbie bombing were tried.[74]

Other International Reactions

The international reaction to the events of 11 September 2001 was almost universally sympathetic towards the US.[75] Individual nations' leaders issued statements shortly after the attacks, condemning them, expressing solidarity and offering their support.[76] Many leaders stated that this was an attack not just on the US but on all humanity.[77] Despite the common tone, there were some notable differences: some leaders specifically referred to the hijackings as criminal acts

---

69 Ibid.

70 Ibid.

71 Kenny, supra n. 41 at 106, citing 'Allies Launch Second Week of Bombing Raids', *The Irish Times*, 15 October 2001.

72 *The 9/11 Commission Report*, supra n. 1 at 334, n. 56.

73 Ibid.; see also US Department of Defense, News Transcript, 9 January 2002: <http://www.defenselink.mil/transcripts/2002/t02052002_t0109wp.html> at 17 June 2008.

74 UK Parliament, Research Paper 01/72, supra n. 10 at 55.

75 'Arafat Horrified by Attacks, but Thousands of Palestinians Celebrate; Rest of World Outraged', *Fox News*, 12 September 2001: <http://www.foxnews.com/story/0,2933,34187,00.html> at 17 June 2008.

76 See *September 11 News.com*: <http://www.september11news.com/InternationalReaction.htm> at 17 June 2008.

77 See statements from Ariel Sharon, Tony Blair, Vladimir Putin and Gerhard Schroeder: ibid.

rather than acts of war,[78] whilst others expressed their hopes that the attacks would not result in retaliation or acts of revenge.[79] Divisions emerged between states regarding the type of response they would support.[80]

The European Union's response The EU issued a Declaration on 12 September 2001 in which it expressed its horror at the terrorist attacks, which it referred to as attacks not just on the US but on 'humanity itself'.[81] It also called on Member States to 'spare no efforts to help identify, bring to justice and punish those responsible'.[82] The EU then issued a Joint Declaration on 14 September 2001, in which it again condemned the attacks and expressed solidarity with the American people.[83] The Joint Declaration stressed a *law enforcement* approach. It called upon the EU to promote an international framework of security and prosperity for all countries, to strengthen intelligence efforts and to accelerate the implementation of a European judicial area which would entail the creation of a European warrant for arrest and extradition and the mutual recognition of legal decisions and verdicts.[84]

The law enforcement approach was further emphasised when the European Commission announced on 19 September 2001 that Europe must have common legal instruments to tackle terrorism. The European Commission adopted two significant proposals: one regarding an agreement on the definition of terrorism and the other regarding the creation of a European arrest warrant.[85] The law enforcement

---

78 Mexican President Vicente Fox; ibid.; see also the statement from French President Jacques Chirac who was reluctant to refer to the hijackings as acts of war: UK Parliament, Research Paper 01/72, supra n. 10 at 27.

79 The Malaysian Prime Minister, Mahathir Mohamad, expressed the hope that the terrorist attacks would not result in the use of force in revenge: ibid.

80 See the response of Mahathir Mohamad, ibid., and see also 'Asia Pledges Cooperation in Hunt for Attackers', *CNN.com*, 13 September 2001: <http://archives.cnn.com/2001/WORLD/asiapcf/east/09/12/asia.reaction/index.html> at 17 June 2008. China officially supported the US stance, but there were also comments from within China that the US shared some of the blame for the increase in terrorism: see comments of Qiao Liang, 'Beijing Pledges to Join US to Fight Terrorism', *CNN.com*, 13 September 2001 <http://archives.cnn.com/2001/WORLD/asiapcf/east/09/12/china.reaction/index.html> (accessed 8 November 2006). For a summary of comments by European leaders, see UK Parliament, Research Paper 01/72, supra n. 10 at 25–31.

81 Declaration by the European Union, 'Terrorism in the US', CL01-052EN, 12 September 2001: <http://europa-eu-un.org/articles/en/article_168_en.htm> at 17 June 2008.

82 Ibid.

83 EU Joint Declaration: September 11 attacks in the US, CL01-054EN: <http://europa-eu-un.org/articles/en/article_46_en.htm> at 17 June 2008.

84 Ibid.

85 European Commission, 'Europe Must Have Common Instruments to Tackle Terrorism', IP/01/1284, 19 September 2001: <http://europa.eu/rapid/pressReleasesAction.do?reference=IP/01/1284&format=HTML&aged=1&language=EN&guiLanguage=en> at 17 June 2008.

approach was also emphasised by the President of the EU.[86] Nevertheless, the EU seemed to have considered it likely, and legitimate, that the US would resort to force:[87] 'The European Council considered that, on the basis of SCR 1368, a *riposte* by the US is legitimate. It also decided that the Union will cooperate with the US to bring to justice and punish the perpetrators, sponsors and accomplices of such barbaric acts …' (emphasis added).

The EU thought that a 'riposte' by the US would be legitimate, but it is unclear what was intended by 'riposte' since this is not a term of international law parlance.[88] It may be implied that the EU envisaged a short, sharp act of retaliation such as an isolated strike/strikes on selected targets.[89] De Ruyt also said that 'the actions must be targeted and may also be directed against states abetting, supporting or harbouring terrorists'.[90] That obviously provided a great deal of scope for the US and reiterated the US position. The EU's support for the use of force was further clarified on 7 October 2001.[91]

Council of Europe's response The Council of Europe drafted a declaration on the fight against international terrorism on 12 September 2001.[92] It called upon Member States to ensure that they had signed and ratified the European Convention on the Suppression of Terrorism and a number of other conventions regarding issues such as extradition. A more comprehensive response was provided via a debate in the Parliamentary Assembly of the Council of Europe (PACE) on 25–26 September

---

86 EU Presidency Statement, 15 October 2001, Statement by Mr Paul Rietjens on behalf of the European Union, PRES01/-262EN: <http://www.europa-eu-un.org/articles/en/article_391_en.htm> at 17 June 2008.

87 Ibid.

88 'Riposte' is not a term used in standard international law textbooks. In fencing it means 'a sharp, swift thrust made after parrying an opponent's lunge': Webster, N. (McKechnie, J. rev.), *Webster's New Twentieth Century Dictionary of the English Language*, 2nd edn (Williams Collins and World Publishing Inc, 1975) at 564.

89 Perhaps the EU envisaged a response similar to the limited air strikes that were undertaken by the Clinton Administration in 1998. Yet, even that interpretation is open to doubt, since forcible reprisals are unlawful: see Chapter 5.

90 EU Presidency Statement – September 11 attacks in the US, PRES01-235EN, 25 September 2001: <http://europa-eu-un.org/articles/en/article_68_en.htm> at 17 June 2008.

91 '[A]t this difficult, solemn and dramatic moment, all Europe stands steadfast with the United States and its coalition allies to pursue the fight against terrorism': Statement by European Commission President Romano Prodi on the military actions against terrorism, IP/01/1375, 7 October 2001: <http://europa.eu/rapid/pressReleasesAction.do?reference=IP/01/1375&format=HTML&aged=1&language=EN&guiLanguage=en> at 17 June 2008.

92 PACE Draft Resolution, Doc. 9228 Rev, 24 September 2001, Appendix 1 'Fight Against International Terrorism, Committee of Ministers' Declaration of 12 September 2001': <http://assembly.coe.int//main.asp?link=http://assembly.coe.int/Documents/WorkingDocs/doc01/edoc9228.htm#a5t> at 17 June 2008.

2001.[93] Resolution 1258 condemned the terrorist attacks as 'barbaric'[94] and stated that they were a crime that violated the most fundamental human right, the right to life.[95] It called on the international community to provide the US government with 'all necessary support'[96] in dealing with the consequences of the attacks and 'in bringing the perpetrators to justice in line with existing international anti-terrorist conventions and United Nations Security Council resolutions'.[97]

The Council of Europe regarded the 'new International Criminal Court as the appropriate institution to consider terrorist acts'[98] and its members agreed that terrorism 'is an international problem to which international solutions must be found based on a global political approach'.[99] It simultaneously condemned the acts of the terrorists whilst also calling for a response within the bounds of international law:[100]

> There can be no justification for terrorism. The Assembly considers these terrorist actions to be *crimes rather than acts of war.* Any actions, either by the United States acting alone or as part of a broader international coalition, must be in line with existing United Nations anti-terrorist conventions and Security Council resolutions and must focus on *bringing the perpetrators, organizers and sponsors of these crimes to justice, instead of inflicting a hasty revenge.* (Emphasis added)

The PACE called for an international convention to combat terrorism which would include a comprehensive definition of international terrorism, as well as specific obligations for participating states to prevent acts of terrorism on a national and global scale and to punish their organisers and executors.[101] If the US opted for a military response, 'the international community must clearly define its objectives and should avoid targeting civilians'.[102] It also stated that 'any action should be taken in conformity with international law and with the agreement of the United Nations Security Council'.[103] It welcomed Security Council Resolution 1368 (2001)

---

93 PACE Draft Resolution, Report of the Political Affairs Committee, Rapporteur Mr Davis, 24 September 2001, Doc 9228, and see Opinion of the Committee on Legal Affairs and Human Rights, Rapporteur Mr Jansson, 25 September 2001, Doc 9232: ibid.

94 PACE Resolution 1258 (2001), adopted on 26 September 2001, 28th Sitting: <http://assembly.coe.int//main.asp?link=http://assembly.coe.int/Documents/AdoptedText/TA01/ERES1258.htm> at 17 June 2008.

95 Ibid., paras 2 and 3.

96 Ibid., para 4.

97 Ibid.

98 Ibid., para 7.

99 Ibid.

100 Ibid., para 8.

101 Ibid., para 10.

102 Ibid., para 12.

103 Ibid.

which it interpreted as an expression of the Security Council's readiness to take all necessary steps to respond to the attacks of 11 September 2001 and to combat all forms of terrorism in accordance with its responsibilities under the UN Charter.[104] The PACE resolution called on the Council of Europe's Member States to adopt ten measures, *none* of which suggested the use of force.[105] It also reaffirmed the Security Council as the ultimate authority for approving international military action.[106]

NATO's response[107] On 11 September 2001, NATO's then Secretary-General, Lord Robertson, condemned the attacks in the 'strongest possible terms'.[108] The North Atlantic Council (NAC)[109] issued a similar statement.[110] NATO unanimously condemned the attacks and confirmed that the US could rely on the 18 NATO nations 'for assistance and support'.[111] Initially, the NAC's threat of possible action against the perpetrators was vague.[112] On 12 September, the NAC met again and within six hours took the unprecedented step of invoking Article 5 of the Washington Treaty.[113] The Council stated that:[114]

> … [I]f it is determined that this attack *was directed from abroad* against the United States, it shall be regarded as an action covered by Article 5 of the Washington Treaty which states that *an armed attack against one or more of the Allies in Europe or North America shall be considered an attack against them all.* (Emphasis added)

---

104 Ibid.

105 Ibid., para 17 (i)–(x).

106 Ibid., para 17 (x).

107 For a comprehensive analysis of NATO's response to the events of 11 September 2001, see Lansford, T., *All for One: Terrorism, NATO and the United States* (Aldershot: Ashgate, 2002).

108 Statement by the Secretary-General of NATO Lord Robertson, Press Release PR/CP (2001)121, 11 September 2001: <http://www.nato.int/docu/pr/2001/p01-121e.htm> at 17 June 2008.

109 By virtue of Article 9 of the NATO Treaty, the North Atlantic Council was established as the political body which controls the NATO alliance.

110 Statement by the North Atlantic Council, PR/CP (2001)122, 11 September 2001: <http://www.nato.int/docu/pr/2001/p01-122e.htm> at 17 June 2008.

111 Ibid.

112 'Our message to those who perpetrated these unspeakable crimes is equally clear: you will not get away with it': ibid.

113 The North Atlantic Treaty, also referred to as the Washington Treaty, was signed in Washington DC on 4 April 1949.

114 Statement by the North Atlantic Council, PR (2001)124, 12 September 2001: <http://www.nato.int/docu/pr/2001/p01-124e.htm> at 17 June 2008.

Article 5 of the Washington Treaty uses the term 'armed attack', the same phrase which is used in Article 51 of the UN Charter and, as with the UN Charter, the term 'armed attack' is not defined.[115] The NAC put a definitional gloss on the term when it stated that the terrorist acts of 11 September would be considered an 'armed attack' if they were found to have been 'directed from abroad'.[116] NATO determined, on 2 October 2001, that the hijackings had been 'directed from abroad';[117] the US-led strikes began on 7 October and the NAC expressed its full support for those 'targeted actions'.[118]

The use of the phrase 'directed from abroad'[119] presents an important interpretational issue. At the time that the NATO Treaty was signed in 1949, the US, and most likely the UK, regarded the term 'armed attack' to mean *an attack by one state against another state.*[120] In 1949, the US Senate Foreign Relations Committee explicitly stated that the term 'armed attack' in Article 5 did not refer to 'an incident created by irresponsible groups or individuals but rather an attack by one State upon another'.[121] That interpretation seems to have been (at best) expanded upon or (at worst) completely abandoned by the NAC in its determination to, first, invoke Article 5 on 12 September 2001 in response to a terrorist attack, then to confirm that it was an attack 'directed from abroad' on 2 October, and then lend its support to the US pursuant to that Article, on 8 October 2001. The NAC was satisfied that:[122] '[T]he individuals who carried out these attacks were part of

---

115 See Chapter 5 and the discussion regarding the interpretation of Article 5 and its relation to Article 51 of the UN Charter.

116 See 'What is Article 5?' *NATO Issues*, 20 September 2001: 'Article 5 has thus been invoked, but no determination has yet been made whether the attack against the United States was directed from abroad.' See also Statement by NATO Secretary-General Lord Robertson, PR (2001) 130, 21 September 2001: <http://www.nato.int/docu/pr/2001/p01-130e.htm> at 17 June 2008: 'NATO has declared that if the terrorist attacks on the United States are found to have been launched from abroad, this will be an attack against all Allied Countries under Article 5.'

117 Statement by NATO Secretary-General Lord Robertson, 2 October 2001: <http://www.nato.int/docu/speech/2001/s011002a.htm> at 17 June 2008.

118 Statement by NATO Secretary-General, Lord Robertson, PR (2001) 138, 8 October 2001: <http://www.nato.int/docu/pr/2001/p01-138e.htm> at 17 June 2008.

119 Statement by the North Atlantic Council, PR (2001) 124, 12 September 2001.

120 See discussion in Chapter 5 at 109.

121 US Senate Foreign Relations Committee, Report of the Committee on Foreign Relations on the North Atlantic Treaty June 6, 1949, Executive Report no 8, at 13, as cited in Beckett, W., *The North Atlantic Treaty, the Brussels Treaty and the Charter of the United Nations* (London: Stevens & Sons, 1950) 28. When interpreting Article 51 of the UN Charter, Beckett, who was the Legal Advisor to the UK Foreign Office in 1950, did not go so far as to say that there must be an armed attack by a state, instead noting that the phrase means 'an armed attack by an aggressor' (his emphasis) and that it rules out 'certain other activities which in various other definitions have also been included in aggression'.

122 See Statement by NATO Secretary-General Lord Robertson, 2 October 2001, supra n. 117.

the world-wide terrorist network of al-Qaida, headed by Osama bin Laden and his lieutenants and protected by the Taliban.' That was the extent of the explanation given by the Council for its determination that this was an armed attack, directed from abroad, and therefore warranted the invocation of Article 5.

Questions were immediately raised over the legality of invoking Article 5 of the NATO Treaty.[123] A divide between the US and Europe as to how terrorism should be classified and what type of action ought to be taken in response to it had existed since at least 1999 when NATO formulated the Alliance's Strategic Concept.[124] After the invocation of Article 5 by Lord Robertson, concerns were expressed by European diplomats that the US had given NATO a 'new role', that it had turned NATO into a counter-terrorist organisation and that 'the legal experts were not asked to question the legality of that act'.[125] Other diplomats felt that there had been little opportunity for debate over whether Article 5 should be invoked, claiming that 'political solidarity with the US took precedence over legality'.[126] Some NATO members subsequently expressed concern at the precedent that was thereby established and sought assurances that in the future they would be able to scrutinise interpretations of Article 5.[127] In light of the opposition that existed to the invocation of Article 5, the significance that should be attributed to that decision must be carefully weighed.

---

123 One senior NATO diplomat reportedly commented that the invocation of Article 5 on 12 September 2001 amounted to Article 24 of the Alliance's Strategic Concept being 'slipped into' Article 5. He added: 'The legal experts should have been consulted. But the allies knew such consultations would drag on for days. It was a *fait accompli.* There was no time for legal niceties': Dempsey, J., 'EU Doubts Grow Over "Switch" in NATO Role" *Financial Times*, 19 September 2001, 4.

124 *The Alliance's Strategic Concept*, approved by the Heads of State and Government participating in the Meeting of the North Atlantic Council in Washington DC on 23 and 24 April 1999; 24 April 1999, Press Release NAC-S(99)65: <http://www.nato.int/docu/pr/1999/p99-065e.htm> at 17 June 2008. Article 24: 'Any armed attack on the territory of the Allies, from whatever direction, would be covered by Articles 5 and 6 of the Washington Treaty …' In the negotiations that led up to the adoption of the Strategic Concept, the US had wanted to broaden the definition of Article 5 by giving NATO a counter-terrorism role and had wanted the definition of 'attack' to include terrorism, sabotage and organised crime, regardless of its origins. The European members were unenthusiastic about expanding the scope of Article 5 and argued that the task of counter-terrorism was better performed by civil institutions such as the police and the judiciary: see UK Parliament, Research Paper 01/72, supra n. 10 at 103.

125 Dempsey, supra n. 123 at 4.

126 Lord Robertson initiated the debate over Article 5, and the NATO ambassadors were apparently told to 'rubber-stamp' the proposal because the Europeans could not be seen to be wavering: ibid.

127 The Benelux countries, Germany, Portugal and France have all since realised the implications of the decision to interpret Article 5 as covering acts of terrorism: ibid.

The Security Council's Initial Response

The Security Council's initial response was to adopt Resolution 1368 on 12 September 2001[128] wherein it stated that it was, 'Determined to combat by all means threats to international peace and security caused by terrorist acts'[129] and that it 'Recogniz[ed] the inherent right of individual or collective self-defence in accordance with the Charter'.[130] The Security Council 'unequivocally condemn[ed] in the strongest terms the horrifying terrorist attacks' and stated that it 'regard[ed] such acts, *like any act of international terrorism*, as a threat to international peace and security'.[131] The Council called on all states to 'work together urgently to bring to justice the perpetrators, organizers and sponsors of these terrorist attacks'.[132] It also called on the international community to redouble its efforts to prevent and suppress terrorist acts and specifically mentioned the need for increased co-operation and full implementation of anti-terrorist conventions and Security Council resolutions.[133] It also indicated that it was ready 'to take all necessary steps to respond to the attacks of 11 September 2001, and to combat all forms of terrorism',[134] and it decided to remain seized of the matter.

Three observations are offered regarding the Security Council's initial response.[135] First, the Security Council advocated a law enforcement-type response to the events of 11 September. The use of phrases such as 'bring to justice' and 'hold accountable' supports that observation, as do the explicit references to anti-terrorist conventions and Security Council resolutions. Furthermore, the reference to Resolution 1269 (1999)[136] is important because that resolution previously endorsed a law enforcement-type response to international terrorism.[137] The fact that the events of 11 September 2001 were repeatedly referred to by the Security

128 S/Res/1368 (2001), 12 September 2001.

129 Ibid., preambular paragraphs 2 and 3.

130 Ibid.

131 Ibid., operative paragraph 1 (emphasis added).

132 Ibid., operative paragraph 3.

133 Ibid., operative paragraph 4.

134 Ibid., operative paragraphs 5 and 6.

135 The significance of the reference to 'inherent right of individual or collective self-defence' in Security Council Resolution 1368 (2001) is not discussed here because it is discussed at length below at 191–195 in the context of determining whether or not an 'armed attack' had occurred.

136 Ibid., operative paragraph 4.

137 S/Res/1269 (1999), 19 October 1999, called upon states to co-operate with each other through bilateral and multilateral agreements and arrangements to prevent and suppress terrorist acts; to prevent and suppress the financing of terrorism in each of their territories through all lawful means; *to deny safe haven to those who plan, finance or commit terrorist acts by 'ensuring their apprehension, prosecution or extradition'*; to exchange information in accordance with international and domestic law and to co-operate on administrative and judicial matters in order to prevent the commission of terrorist acts.

Council as 'terrorist attacks' and 'terrorist acts' rather than 'armed attacks' in Resolution 1368 (2001) is also significant.[138]

Secondly, the Security Council's initial response emphasised that this terrorist attack had to be seen in the context of other attacks. The Council unequivocally condemned these terrorist attacks and stated that it regarded such acts, *like any acts of international terrorism*, as a threat to international peace and security.[139] The Security Council may have intended to downplay any inference that this was an entirely different type of event warranting an entirely different type of response. That inference is supported by a later paragraph in Resolution 1368, wherein the Security Council stated that it was ready to respond to the attacks of 11 September, 'and to combat *all* forms of terrorism', in accordance with the Charter.[140]

Thirdly, the Security Council indicated that it intended to take further measures to respond to the terrorist attacks when it stated that it was ready to 'take all necessary steps'[141] and that it would 'remain seized of the matter'.[142] There was no suggestion in Resolution 1368 that this was the complete and full extent of the Council's response; on the contrary, it appears to have been an interim response until the Council's more substantive response was framed.[143]

The Response of the General Assembly, the OAS and the OAU

Before completing this section on the initial responses to the events of 11 September 2001, brief mention is made regarding the response of other multilateral organisations.[144] On 12 September 2001, the UN General Assembly passed a resolution in which it strongly condemned the attacks; referred to them as heinous acts of terrorism; expressed its condolences and solidarity with the people and government of the US; urgently called for international co-operation to bring to justice the perpetrators, organisers and sponsors of the outrages of 11 September 2001; and urgently called for international co-operation to prevent and eradicate acts of terrorism, stressing that those responsible for aiding, supporting or harbouring the perpetrators, organisers and sponsors of such acts

---

138 S/Res/1368 (2001): the phrase 'terrorist attacks' is used in operative paragraphs 1, 3 and 5; the term 'terrorist acts' is used in operative paragraph 4. The term 'armed attack' is not used.

139 Ibid., operative paragraph 1.

140 Ibid., operative paragraph 5.

141 Ibid.

142 Ibid., operative paragraph 6.

143 The more substantive response being S/Res/1373 (2001) adopted on 28 September 2001.

144 For analysis of international responses to 11 September 2001, see Walker, G., 'The Lawfulness of Operation Enduring Freedom's Self-Defense Responses' (2003) 37 *Val. U.L. Rev.* 489 at 493–505.

would be held accountable.[145] That initial response was subsequently followed by a comprehensive special session to discuss ways to eliminate international terrorism,[146] which resulted in the adoption of a resolution on 12 December 2001.[147] The latter resolution confirmed the stance taken on 12 September 2001.[148] The General Assembly regarded the events of 11 September as criminal acts[149] and impliedly supported a law enforcement response.[150] The General Assembly did not refer to the events of 11 September as 'armed attacks' in either resolution, nor did it mention the term 'self-defence'.[151]

The Organization of American States (OAS) adopted a resolution on 21 September 2001 in which the respective Ministers of Foreign Affairs, *inter alia*, recalled the inherent right of individual or collective self-defence and then resolved that the terrorist attacks against the US were attacks against all American states.[152] The measures which the OAS advocated were all related to inter-state co-operation to bring to justice the perpetrators and to prevent further acts of terrorism. The OAS resolution did not advocate the use of force and did not recognise the *terrorist attacks* as being tantamount to *armed attacks*. Despite that, some scholars have drawn the conclusion that the OAS response constituted further evidence that the terrorist attacks *were* tantamount to 'armed attacks'.[153]

---

145 UNGA Resolution 56/1, A/56/PV.1, 56th session, 1st Plenary meeting, 12 September 2001.

146 Held from 1–5 October 2001. For the themes and outcome of the Plenary Meetings on 'Measures to Eliminate International Terrorism', see Statement by General Assembly President H.E. Han-Seung-Soo.

147 UNGA Resolution 56/88, A/56/PV.85, 56th session, 85th Plenary meeting, 12 December 2001.

148 See A/Res/56/88, ibid.

149 '[The General Assembly] 1. Strongly condemns all acts, methods and practices of terrorism as *criminal* and unjustifiable ... 2. Reiterates that *criminal acts* intended or calculated to provoke a state of terror ...': ibid.

150 See UNGA 56/1, supra n. 145, paragraphs 3 and 4; see UNGA 56/88, supra n. 147, especially paragraphs 3–11.

151 Note that A/Res/56/88, supra n. 147, was a comprehensive response from the General Assembly and it was passed on 12 December 2001, *after* the two Security Council resolutions relating to 11 September, which were passed on 12 September (S/Res/1368 (2001)) and 28 September 2001 (S/Res/1373 (2001)), and subsequent to the use of force against Afghanistan on 7 October 2001.

152 'Strengthening Hemispheric Cooperation to Prevent, Combat and Eliminate Terrorism', adopted at the First Plenary session of the Meeting of Consultation of Ministers of Foreign Affairs, OEA/Ser.F/II.24, RC.23/RES.1/01, 21 September 2001, Washington DC: <http://www.oas.org/OASpage/crisis/RC.23e.htm> (accessed 9 November 2006).

153 Maogoto, J., 'Walking an International Law Tightrope: Use of Military Force to Counter Terrorism – Willing the Ends' (2006) 31 *Brooklyn J. Int'l L.* 405 at 450–51: he asserts that 'the Security Council characterized the attacks as "armed attacks"', and that 'This view was expressly affirmed by other international bodies including NATO and the OAS'. The OAS resolution does not mention the phrase 'armed attack'.

The Organization of the African Union (OAU) adopted the Dakar Declaration on Terrorism on 17 October 2001, which strongly condemned the acts of terrorism but, similarly, did not contain any reference to the terrorist acts being 'armed attacks', nor did it endorse the use of force in response to them. On the contrary, it called upon OAU states to take legal, diplomatic, financial and other measures to fight terrorism.[154]

Was the Use of Force an Act of Self-defence?

The US President officially approved military plans to attack Afghanistan in meetings held on 21 September and 2 October 2001.[155] *Operation Enduring Freedom* was to consist of four phases. In Phase One, the US and its allies would move forces into the region and arrange to operate from or over neighbouring countries such as Uzbekistan and Pakistan: 'this occurred in the weeks following 9/11, aided by overwhelming international sympathy for the United States.'[156] In Phase Two, air strikes and Special Operations attacks would hit key al Qaeda and Taliban targets. The Phase Two strikes and raids commenced on 7 October 2001.[157] In Phase Three the US would carry out 'decisive operations' using all elements of national power, including ground troops, 'to topple the Taliban regime and eliminate al Qaeda's sanctuary in Afghanistan'.[158] Phase Four was intended to involve civilian and military operations whose role was the 'indefinite task'[159] of 'security and stability operations'.[160]

---

154 See Annex to the letter dated 24 October 2001 from the Permanent Representative of Senegal to the United Nations addressed to the Secretary-General, 'Dakar Declaration Against Terrorism', 29 October 2001, UN Doc A/53/913 – S/2001/1021, General Assembly 56th Session, Agenda Item 166, Measures to Eliminate International Terrorism.

155 The meetings were held in response to a request from the President to Secretary of Defense Rumsfeld made on 17 September 2001 to draw up a military campaign plan for Afghanistan: see *The 9/11 Commission Report*, supra n. 1 at 337.

156 Ibid.

157 Ibid.

158 Mazar-e-Sharif fell to a coalition assault by Afghan and US forces on 9 November 2001. Four days later the Taliban had fled from Kabul. By early December, all major cities had fallen to the coalition. On 22 December, Harmid Karzai was installed as the chairman of Afghanistan's interim administration: ibid.

159 Ibid., 338.

160 Ibid. On 5 October 2006, NATO-led International Security Assistance Force (ISAF) troops took over command from the US forces in the remaining regions of Afghanistan, thereby completing the handover of authority from US forces in *Operation Enduring Freedom* to NATO-led forces: McKeeby, D., 'NATO Commanding International Security Operations in Afghanistan', *US International Information Programs*, 5 October 2006: <http://usinfo.state.gov/xarchives/display.html?p=washfile-english&y=2006&m=October&x=20061005175423idybeekcm0.4493524> at 17 June 2008.

The Justifications for the Use of Force and its Objectives

On 7 October 2001 President Bush outlined the Operation's targets and objectives:[161]

> On my orders, the United States military has begun strikes against al Qaeda terrorist training camps and military installations of the Taliban regime in Afghanistan. These carefully targeted operations are designed to disrupt the use of Afghanistan as a terrorist base of operations, and to attack the military capability of the Taliban regime.

Bush declared that the use of force was a direct consequence of the Taliban's failure to meet the terms of the US ultimatum.[162] Bush indicated that although the initial attack was on Afghanistan, the battle was broader.[163] He also noted that the US was engaged in a 'just' mission.[164] However, he did not use the phrase 'self-defence', nor did he refer to Article 51 of the UN Charter.

The Bush Administration was obviously aware of the need to justify *Operation Enduring Freedom* in legal terms.[165] In accordance with the requirement in Article 51, the US notified its use of force to the Security Council via a letter dated 7 October 2001 from the Permanent Representative of the US to the President of the Security Council, wherein it put forth the legal justifications for using force against

161 Presidential Address to the Nation, The White House, 7 October 2001: <http://www.whitehouse.gov/news/releases/2001/10/20011007-8.html> at 17 June 2008.

162 'More than two weeks ago I gave Taliban leaders a series of clear and specific demands: Close terrorist training camps; hand over leaders of the al Qaeda network; and return all foreign nationals, including American citizens unjustly detained in your country. None of these demands were met. And now the Taliban will pay a price': ibid.

163 'Today we focus on Afghanistan, but the battle is broader. Every nation has a choice to make. In this conflict there is no neutral ground …': ibid.

164 'To all the men and women in our military … I say this: Your mission is defined; your objectives are clear; your goal is just': ibid.

165 Compare with Kritsiotis, D., 'The Legality of the US Missile Strikes Against Iraq and the Right of Self-Defense in International Law' (1996) 45 *ICLQ* 45, 162 at 166: 'Underneath the strong torrent of legal rhetoric lay a careful legal opinion which made reference to both the customary and conventional principles which regulate the right of self-defence in modern international law.'

Afghanistan.[166] The UK also submitted a letter to the Security Council setting out its grounds for using force.[167] No other state submitted such notifications.[168]

Three points will be discussed in turn below which arise out of the US–UK decision to resort to force: the significance of the US's reporting of its use of force; the expectation that existed prior to 7 October 2001 that a multilateral response was desirable; and the 'armed attack' requirement in Article 51 and whether it was met in this instance.

The Significance of the Notifications to the Security Council

In accordance with Article 51, 'Measures taken by Members in the exercise of this right of self-defence shall be immediately reported to the Security Council'.[169] Merely reporting the use of force to the Security Council is not proof *per se* that the use of force is legitimate self-defence.[170] It could be argued that the mere fact that the Security Council did not condemn the US–UK use of force may suggest that it implicitly agreed that this was a legitimate exercise of self-defence. However, it must be acknowledged that the Security Council, like the rest of the international community, was affected by what *The 9/11 Commission Report* called 'overwhelming international sympathy'[171] which may help to explain why, even if some members of the Security Council had reservations about the legality of the US decision to use force, they would not have publicly voiced them.

A parallel can be drawn between the Security Council's reaction (or lack thereof) in October 2001, and three other prior incidents: the US's reporting of its missile strikes against Libya in 1986; against the Iraqi Intelligence Service headquarters in 1993; and against Sudan and Afghanistan in 1998.[172] In those three

166 S/2001/946, Letter dated 7 October 2001 from the Permanent Representative of the United States of America to the United Nations addressed to the President of the Security Council. The letter is reproduced in Appendix 1.

167 S/2001/947, Letter dated 7 October 2001 from the Chargé d'affaires a.i. of the Permanent Mission of the United Kingdom of Great Britain and Northern Ireland to the United Nations addressed to the President of the Security Council. The letter is reproduced in Appendix 2.

168 Interestingly, the US and UK letters are searchable in the UN Official Document System database by terms such as 'armed incidents' and 'terrorist attacks' – but not 'armed attack'.

169 Article 51 of the UN Charter.

170 See Chapter 5. The use of force in purported self-defence has been reported and rejected on several occasions; for instance, the British attacks on Yemen in 1964, Portugal against Senegal in 1969, Israel against Lebanon, Syria and Jordan in the 1960s and 1970s, Israel against Iraq in 1981 and against Tunisia in 1985; see also Dinstein, Y., *War, Aggression and Self-Defence*, 3rd edn (Cambridge; New York: Cambridge University Press, 2001) 191.

171 *The 9/11 Commission Report*, supra n. 1 at 337.

172 See Chapter 5 at 134–142.

instances, the use of force in purported self-defence was duly reported without attracting Security Council condemnation, but reservations were voiced by some states.[173] As to why the Security Council failed to respond to the US claims of self-defence in 1998, Lobel surmised that:[174]

> [O]ther governments are reluctant to publicly accuse the United States of lying, even if they believe a mistake was made … any direct confrontation between the Security Council and the United States … is certain to fail, as the United States has made it clear that it will veto any resolution calling for an investigation into the attack.

Likewise, in the post-11 September climate, even if states had reservations about the strict legality of the use of military force, none would have dared criticise the US for its actions against Afghanistan. Any such criticism would have been viewed as anti-American rather than pro-international law, and, in light of the US's demarcation between its friends and enemies, it may even have rendered them targets themselves.[175] Within the US, anti-war sentiment was not tolerated,[176]

---

173 In 1986, even though the Security Council could not agree on a resolution, the General Assembly rejected the claim of self-defence; in 1993, one member of the Security Council (the Netherlands) expressly rejected the self-defence justification on the basis that the US had not suffered an armed attack and only the UK and Russia accepted that this act of apparent retaliation was legitimate self-defence; in 1998, the Security Council acquiesced in the missile strikes against Sudan and Afghanistan, even though the evidence was questionable, perhaps because of a 'general distaste for the Sudanese Government coupled with a disinclination to directly confront the US': see Lobel, J., 'The Use of Force to Respond to Terrorist Attacks: The Bombing of Sudan and Afghanistan' (1999) 24 *Yale J. Int'l L.* 537 at 556.

174 Ibid., 557.

175 In light of the US stance that all states were 'either with us or with the terrorists'. Indeed, evidence has recently come to light that Pakistan was threatened with force by the US if it did not comply with US requests for assistance: 'Armitage Denies Threatening Pakistan after 9/11', *MSNBC News*, 22 September 2006: <http://www.msnbc.msn.com/id/14943975/> at 17 June 2008; and 'Musharraf: In the Line of Fire', *CBSNews*, 24 September 2006: <http://www.cbsnews.com/stories/2006/09/21/60minutes/main2030165.shtml> at 17 June 2008.

176 Retribution was meted out to any commentators, journalists, academics or actors who dared question the legitimacy or effectiveness of the impending war against Afghanistan: '… instead of engaging in serious debate concerning the appropriate response to terrorism, the U.S. broadcasting networks engaged in unrelenting focus on the tragedy of the World Trade Centre victims, the evil of the bin Laden network and the need for military retribution. Criticizing the Bush administration was taboo and would continue to be throughout the Afghanistan Terror War.': Kellner, D., *From 9/11 to Terror War – The Dangers of the Bush Legacy* (New York: Rowman and Littlefield Publishers Inc, 2003) 68–9. See also the comments of Bush that all states were either with the US or with the terrorists: supra n. 34.

and that was also the prevailing tone adopted by the US in its relations with the international community. Thus, the US notification to the Security Council that it was acting in self-defence is not proof *per se* of the lawfulness of its actions, and the fact that the Security Council did not respond negatively is not overly significant, given the climate of sympathy that existed and the fact that lack of condemnation, or even acquiescence, by the Council does not equate to an endorsement.

The Expectation of a Multilateral Response Led by the Security Council

The statements that were delivered in the Security Council on 12 September 2001 divulge the type of response that the Council members envisaged.[177] What is particularly notable about the 16 statements[178] is the recurring reference to the terrorist attacks of 11 September 2001 as an attack not just on the US but on *all humanity*, and the repeated calls for an *international, global* or *multilateral response.* A selection of statements made in the Security Council amply demonstrates the commonality of those themes.

The then UN Secretary-General, Kofi Annan, referred to terrorism as an 'international scourge';[179] he said 'a terrorist attack on one country is an attack on humanity as a whole'[180] and 'all nations of the world must work together to identify the perpetrators and bring them to justice'.[181] Mr Greenstock, on behalf of the UK said, 'we all have to understand that this is a global issue, an attack on the whole of modern civilization' and he called for states to respond 'globally'.[182] The statements from the representatives of Mauritius,[183] Ukraine,[184] Singapore,[185]

177 SC Official Records S/PV.4370, 4370th Meeting, 12 September 2001, 'Threats to International Peace and Security Caused by Terrorist Acts'.

178 All 15 members of the Security Council plus the Secretary-General of the UN made statements. The only statement not specifically mentioned here is the very brief speech delivered by Mr Keita of Mali. In his statement he condemned the attacks, offered condolences to the US and to the victims and said that Mali would stand in solidarity with any decision taken by the Security Council: ibid.

179 Ibid., 2.

180 Ibid.

181 Ibid.

182 Ibid., 2–3.

183 Mr Koonjul said Mauritius favoured a 'framework of international cooperation' and he pledged his country's support in finding the perpetrators and bringing them to justice: ibid., 3.

184 Mr Kuchinsky said that this crime was 'a direct challenge not only to the US but to the entire civilized world' and that the efforts of the entire international community would be needed: ibid., 3–4.

185 Mr Mahbubani expressed his hope that the Security Council would come together and deliver a very effective response: ibid., 4.

Tunisia,[186] Ireland,[187] China,[188] Russia,[189] Jamaica,[190] Bangladesh,[191] Norway[192] Colombia[193] and France[194] expressed the same sentiments, as did the statements from non-Council members, which were annexed to the records of the meeting.[195] States repeatedly emphasised the criminality of the attack, its effect on humanity as a whole and the global nature of the anticipated response. The US statement was notably different. Mr Cunningham confirmed the other speakers' sentiments that 'this was an assault not just on the United States, but on all of us who support peace and democracy and the values for which the United Nations stands'.[196] However, he suggested a course of action that had not been endorsed by any of the previous speakers when he called upon 'all those who stand for peace, justice and security in the world to stand together with the United States to win

186 Mr Mejdoub called it an 'unacceptable crime' and said 'if we want to succeed we must act together. We will be stronger if we are all united ...': ibid.

187 Mr Ryan said the attacks were 'an attack on all humanity and the values of humanity', and called for 'the entire international community' to work together to bring to justice those who committed the acts: ibid., 4–5.

188 Mr Wang Yingfan said the attacks were 'an open challenge to the international community as a whole', and said that the Security Council, 'as the organ with the principal responsibility of maintaining international peace and security', should play a leading role in 'bringing terrorist criminals to justice': ibid., 5.

189 Mr Lavrov said that the events were 'a brazen challenge to all of humankind' and that the resolution they were about to adopt demonstrated the Council's resolve to prevent and end terrorism: ibid.

190 Miss Durant said Jamaica believed 'that the most effective response continues to be full cooperation at an international level, as terrorism poses a serious threat to the peace and stability of nations ...': ibid., 5–6.

191 Mr Ahsan called the attacks 'an affront to all humanity' and said that 'we must collectively face this challenge ...': ibid., 6.

192 Mr Kolby said the attacks were not only directed against targets in the US 'but against freedom and democracy itself ... The attacks were therefore directed against us all.' He stressed that the Security Council was established to defend these values and that it must show that it is ready to support efforts to do just that: ibid., 6.

193 Mr Valdivieso said the attacks were not only against the US but against the community of civilised peoples, the values of humanity and the future of peace: ibid., 6–7.

194 Mr Levitte, President of the Security Council, called them 'an attack on all humanity' and said that it was 'a time for unity and resolve'. He also said that the Security Council is the principal organ entrusted with peace and security and that it should work in a spirit of urgency: ibid., 7.

195 S/2001/864, 'Note by the President of the Security Council', 13 September 2001. In accordance with an understanding reached at the 4370th meeting of the Security Council held on 12 September 2001, the statements of the representatives of Australia, Belgium (on behalf of the European Union), Brazil, Cuba, Israel, Japan, New Zealand, Romania, Slovenia and Yugoslavia to the United Nations were reproduced as annexes I–X of the note S/2001/864.

196 S/PV.4370, supra n. 177 at 7, per Mr Cunningham (United States).

the war against terrorism'.[197] The vote was then taken and the Security Council unanimously adopted Resolution 1368 (2001).[198]

What is apparent from the speeches, and from Resolution 1368 itself, is that a discernible gap existed between the US and the other members of the Security Council (as well as several non-members) as to the most appropriate type of response. Whereas virtually every member called for a *global response led by the Security Council*, the US introduced the novel phrase 'war on terrorism' and called all peace-loving states to stand with the US to win that 'war'. The introduction of the term 'war' by the last speaker seemed quite out of context, as did his emphasis on a unilateral response when the statements are taken in context.[199] Several representatives specifically referred to the Security Council as the organ that possessed the responsibility to shape the response.[200] That was also confirmed by the text of the resolution subsequently adopted.[201] The Security Council's response was consistent with the sentiments that all of humanity, not just the US, had been targeted, and since terrorism was a threat to international peace and security, this was an issue squarely within the Security Council's realm of responsibility.

Scholars who share the view put forth here that the Security Council intended (and was expected) to shape the response include Michael Byers, who observed in April 2002 that:[202]

> … [I]n resolution 1368, the UN Security Council strongly condemned the terrorist attacks against the US but stopped short of authorising the use of force. Instead, the Council expressed 'its readiness to take all necessary steps' *thus implicitly encouraging the US to seek authorisation once its military plans were complete.* (Emphasis added)

Frederic Kirgis, writing on 1 October 2001, also took the view that the Security Council had indicated that it intended to remain in charge of any use of force when

197 Ibid. None of the other 15 statements mentioned the word 'war'. When read in context, this reference is jarring and appears to be out of step with the general tone of the other statements.

198 Supra n. 128.

199 Note that the only other state representative to use the term 'war' in the speeches that preceded the adoption of Resolution 1368 (2001) was Israel – not a member of the Security Council – in a speech by its Deputy Permanent Representative that was annexed to the debate the following day: see S/2001/864, 'Note by the President of the Security Council', 13 September 2001, Annex V: Israel, Statement by Aaron Jacob, Deputy Permanent Representative. Mr Jacob said in his statement that the acts were 'no less than an act of war on civilization itself'.

200 S/PV.4370, supra n. 177, see Norway, Singapore, France and China in particular. Uniquely, the US did not refer to a global, multilateral response.

201 S/Res/1368 (2001), especially operative paragraphs 5 and 6.

202 Byers, M., 'Terrorism, the Use of Force and International Law after 11 September' (2002) *ICLQ* 51 at 401.

it expressed its determination to 'take all necessary steps' in the last paragraph of Resolution 1368. He noted that in Resolution 1373, adopted on 28 September 2001, the Council did not authorise *states* to take all necessary steps, 'instead it stands as a warning that the Council itself stands ready to take further steps'.[203]

The Secretary-General underlined the international community's expectation for a multilateral response led by the UN. Although it was already apparent that the US intended to act without a specific mandate from the Security Council,[204] Annan addressed the General Assembly on 24 September 2001 and again emphasised that the attack was not just against the US but against the entire international community.[205] He urged any response to be multilateral in nature and led by the UN:[206]

> On the very day after the onslaught, the Security Council rightly identified it as a threat to international peace and security. Let us therefore respond to it in a way that strengthens international peace and security, by cementing the ties among nations and not subjecting them to new strains. *This Organization is the natural forum in which to build such a universal coalition. It alone can give global legitimacy to the long-term struggle against terrorism.* (Emphasis added)

The Secretary-General's address to the General Assembly was perhaps a reaction to the growing realisation that the US was intending to respond unilaterally and thereby sideline the Security Council.[207] Rather than endorse the prospect of unilateral action, the Secretary-General made a pointed call for a return to

203 Kirgis, F., *American Society of International Law (ASIL) Insights*, 'Addendum: Security Council Adopts Resolution on Combating International Terrorism', 1 October 2001: <http://www.asil.org/insights/insigh77.htm#addendum7> at 17 June 2008.

204 That intention is particularly evident from the adoption of the 'Use of Force' resolution on 14 September 2001, and from President's Bush's speech to the nation on 20 September 2001, discussed supra at n. 34 and accompanying text; see also *The 9/11 Commission Report*, supra n. 1 at 336–7.

205 'In truth, *this was a blow, not against one city or one country, but against all of us.* It was an attack not only against our innocent fellow citizens – over 60 Member States were affected, including, I am sad to say, my own country – but on our shared values. It struck at everything this Organization stands for: peace, freedom tolerance, human rights and the very idea of a united human family. It struck at all our efforts to create a true international society, based on the rule of law': UN GAOR, A/56/PV.7, General Assembly 56th Session, 7th plenary session, 24 September 2001, Secretary-General at 1.

206 Ibid.

207 President Bush approved military plans to attack Afghanistan in meetings held on 21 September and 2 October 2001. Phase One of *Operation Enduring Freedom* – which involved moving forces into the region and arranging to operate from neighbouring countries – was underway 'in the weeks following 9/11': *The 9/11 Commission Report*, supra n. 1 at 337.

multilateralism and virtually invited the US to seek a mandate from the UN for its intended military response.[208]

Was There an 'Armed Attack'?

In the first paragraph of the US's letter to the Security Council, signed by the US Permanent Representative to the UN, John Negroponte, the US stated that it was acting in individual and collective self-defence '*following the armed attacks* that were carried out against the US on 11 September 2001'[209] (emphasis added). The US considered that it had been subjected to 'armed attacks' which, by virtue of Article 51 of the UN Charter, justified its use of force in self-defence. The US did not declare who it considered responsible for carrying out the 'armed attacks', asserting only that 'al Qaeda had a *central role* in the attacks'.[210] The US acknowledged in its letter to the Security Council that 'there is still much we do not know' and that its inquiry was 'in its early stages'.[211]

Numerous arguments can be raised to support the US's claim that it was subjected to an 'armed attack':[212] NATO had already invoked Article 5 of the Washington Treaty; the Security Council expressly referred to the inherent right of individual and collective self-defence;[213] the Security Council did not subsequently condemn the US's use of force; and non-state actors can sometimes be held responsible for carrying out 'armed attacks'.[214] These four arguments are often raised in the literature in support of the US's claim of self-defence and are addressed in turn below.

NATO's invocation of Article 5 It would not be convincing for the US to invoke Article 51, and claim that it had satisfied the 'armed attack' element therein, *purely*

208 As for possible reasons why the US and the UK acted without seeking Security Council authorisation, Penketh suggests it may have been because veto-wielding nations complicated efforts to obtain swift UN authorisation for the 1999 NATO military campaign in Kosovo: Penketh, A., 'War on Terrorism: Annan – UN Must Have Role in Fight Against Terrorism', *The Independent*, 25 September 2001, at 5. Alternatively, the US may have been concerned that other members might seek to impose a time limit on the mandate or only authorise such force as was necessary to capture bin Laden: Byers, supra n. 202 at 401.

209 S/2001/946, reproduced in Appendix 1.

210 'My Government has obtained clear and compelling information that the Al-Qaeda organization, which is supported by the Taliban regime in Afghanistan, had a central role in the attacks. There is still much we do not know': ibid.

211 Ibid.

212 These four arguments, which appear in the literature regarding the legality of the use of force against Afghanistan, are examined in turn over the following pages.

213 S/Res/1368 (2001) and S/Res/1373 (2001).

214 *Case Concerning Military and Paramilitary Activities In and Against Nicaragua (Nicaragua v United States)* (Merits) [1986] ICJ Reports 14 at para 195; see discussion in Chapter 5 at 148–157.

in reliance upon the invocation of Article 5 by NATO, since serious concerns have been identified as to whether NATO ought to have invoked Article 5 of the NATO Treaty.[215] In any case, the fact that NATO invoked Article 5 cannot be interpreted as pan-European support for the proposition that there was an 'armed attack' against the US. Unequivocal statements were made by other European bodies that the hijackings were 'criminal acts not acts of war'.[216] The Parliamentary Assembly of the Council of Europe stated that 'the International Criminal Court was the appropriate institution to consider terrorist acts'.[217] The Council of Europe also stated that if military action was part of the response, the action should be taken in accordance with international law and *with the agreement of the Security Council.*[218] Significantly, neither the Council of Europe nor the European Union referred to the hijackings as 'armed attacks'.[219]

On the day after the attacks, when the NAC gathered to debate its response, the American delegation made it clear that it would seek the invocation of Article 5 if it could be proven that the attacks originated outside the US.[220] NATO's then Secretary-General, Lord Robertson, openly supported the invocation of Article 5. Robertson pointed out that dissension within NATO could lead the US to bypass the Alliance completely, which might result in the permanent marginalising of NATO.[221] Enormous pressure was placed upon the European states which initially opposed the invocation of Article 5 to lend their support to the American-led bloc's moves to invoke Article 5.[222] This *political pressure* – which was driven by a desire to retain NATO's security role, to underline NATO's solidarity with the US and perhaps to 'repay' a perceived historic debt to the US[223] – was the real reason why the NAC invoked Article 5.[224]

---

215 Supra n. 107 and accompanying text.

216 PACE Resolution 1258 (2001), supra n. 94, Article 8: 'The Assembly considers these terrorist actions to be crimes rather than acts of war.'

217 Ibid., Article 5.

218 Ibid., Article 11.

219 See discussion at 172-175.

220 Lansford, supra n. 107 at 73.

221 Ibid., 74.

222 Ibid. Lansford notes that France, Italy, Spain and the UK strongly supported the US, whereas Germany, the Netherlands, Belgium and Norway were initially opposed to the invocation. Germany opposed invoking Article 5 because it was concerned about an American 'overreaction'. The Benelux states and Norway were concerned at the long-term consequences of NATO assuming a counter-terrorism function.

223 NATO's political and military support for the US after 11 September 'demonstrated the broad utility of the Alliance to American security policy and served as partial repayment for America's underwriting of European security in the post-World War II era': ibid., 71.

224 'Throughout the Cold War and beyond, the United States had underwritten European security and now an opportunity had arisen whereby Western Europe could "repay" its transatlantic partner': ibid.

The existence of an apparent 'moral obligation' owed to the US by the European states was pressed home by the US itself, with reports appearing in the international media in the days following 11 September 2001 by former members of the US National Security Council that 'neutrality is not an option'.[225] Even when the unanimity of the NAC was (somewhat reluctantly) secured, there was significant concern regarding the level of proof that would need to be made available before any actual commitments to military support were made. Although the invocation by NATO of Article 5 may, *prima facie*, appear to bolster the US's assertion that it had suffered an 'armed attack', NATO may have been mistaken to invoke it, and in doing so, it may have been motivated by factors other than strict adherence to the terms of the NATO Treaty.[226]

The credibility of the US's assertion that it suffered an 'armed attack' is further affected by the fact that its NATO partner, the UK, did not refer to the hijackings as 'armed attacks' in its letter to the Security Council. On the same day that the US submitted its letter to the Security Council claiming it had suffered an 'armed attack', the UK's letter referred to the hijackings alternately as an 'operation of terror' and 'the terrorist outrage'.[227] In stark contrast to the US letter, the technical term 'armed attack' did not appear in the UK's letter. The difference in terminology, and the absence of any reference to there having been an 'armed attack', must be taken as deliberate, since the documents were submitted almost simultaneously and Article 51 was explicitly relied upon as the justification for the use of force in both letters.[228] As an indication of the *opinio juris* of the UK, the terminology chosen by the UK would suggest that it was not convinced on 7 October 2001 that the terrorist attacks could satisfy the high legal threshold of the term 'armed attack'.

The Security Council's references to the inherent right of self-defence One of the reasons why some commentators assert that the US and the UK acted in lawful self-defence is because the Security Council expressly referred to the inherent

---

225 Blinken, A. and Gordon, P., 'NATO Is Ready to Play a Central Role', *International Herald Tribune*, 18 September 2001. Blinken and Gordon were former members of the Clinton Administration's National Security Council.

226 The benefits in invoking Article 5 were mutual for NATO and the US: 'For the Europeans, the attacks of 11 September provided an opportunity for NATO to demonstrate its utility to the United States and the organization's ability to counter new security threats. For the Americans, NATO participation provided any military operations with an enhanced degree of legitimacy and reaffirmed the transatlantic link in the face of new competition from emerging security structures in Europe such as the ERRF [European Rapid Reaction Force]': Lansford, supra n. 107 at 83.

227 S/2001/947, Letter from the UK to the Security Council: reproduced in Appendix 2.

228 Both letters were submitted on 7 October 2001 and they were allocated sequential numbering in the UN's Official Document system, being S/2001/946 (the US letter) and S/2001/947 (the UK letter).

right of self-defence in two post-9/11 resolutions. On 12 September 2001, the Security Council adopted Resolution 1368 as its immediate response.[229] The Council's more substantive response was in Resolution 1373, adopted on 28 September 2001.[230] There is a preambular paragraph in both resolutions in which the Security Council 'recognised' and 'reaffirmed' the inherent right of individual or collective self-defence: in Resolution 1368 (2001), the reference was made in the third preambular paragraph, and in Resolution 1373 (2001), it appeared in the fourth preambular paragraph. The line between *acknowledging* the existence of the inherent right of self-defence and formally *categorising the terrorist attacks as 'armed attacks'* is one which many scholars have crossed without hesitation.[231] One scholar makes the connection in the following way:[232]

> Passed by the Council the day after the attacks, Resolution 1368 condemned the attacks and recognized the 'inherent right of self-defence in accordance with the Charter'. Resolution 1373, passed seventeen days later, reaffirmed the right of self-defence in the context of the September 11 attacks and went on to reaffirm 'the need to combat by all means, in accordance with the Charter of the United Nations, threats to international peace and security caused by terrorist acts'. *Moreover, the Security Council's subsequent characterization of those acts as 'armed attacks' was echoed by other bodies. Thus, the US enjoyed strong support from the Security Council before it had to articulate the actual case for its actions in Afghanistan ...* (Emphasis added; footnotes in original omitted)

The Security Council's references to self-defence (which were in *preambular* not *operative* paragraphs)[233] are interpreted by some as an endorsement that the acts

229 S/Res/1368 (2001), adopted by the Security Council at its 4370th meeting on 12 September 2001.

230 S/Res/1373 (2001), adopted by the Security Council at its 4385th meeting on 28 September 2001.

231 Rostow, N., 'Before and After: The Changed UN Response to Terrorism Since September 11th' (2001) 35 *Cornell Int'l L.J.* 475 at 481: '... [T]his affirmation was significant: it implied that the attacks triggered the right [of self-defence] even if, at the time of adoption, the UN Security Council knew almost nothing about who or what had launched them.'; also Beard, J., 'Military Action Against Terrorists Under International Law: America's New War on Terror: The Case for Self-Defense Under International Law' (2002) 25 *Harv. J.L. & Pub. Pol'y* 559 at 566: 'The Council's unprecedented willingness to invoke and reaffirm self-defense under Article 51 in response to the September 11 terrorist attacks is an important act, and, for some states, helped legitimize the US military response'; see also Conte, A., *Security in the 21st Century* (Aldershot: Ashgate, 2005) 45; and Maogoto, J., *Battling Terrorism – Legal Perspectives on the Use of Force and the War on Terror* (Aldershot: Ashgate, 2005) 120.

232 Maogoto, ibid., 120.

233 The fact that the references were in preambular paragraphs has been noted by, *inter alia*, Cassese and Stahn: see Cassese, A., 'Terrorism is Also Disrupting Some Crucial

of terrorism were 'armed attacks'.[234] There are some problems with that line of reasoning. First, the Security Council never described the 11 September terrorist acts as 'armed attacks' in either Resolution 1368 or 1373.[235] Secondly, neither the Secretary-General nor *any* of the Security Council members referred to the terrorist attacks as 'armed attacks' in the debate prior to the adoption of Resolution 1368.[236] Thirdly, the UK did not use the term 'armed attack' when it reported its use of force in purported self-defence to the Security Council.[237]

Comparing the text of Resolutions 1368 (2001) and 1373 (2001) with previous Security Council resolutions lends support to the interpretation that is being advanced here.[238] In 1950, in relation to the attack by North Korean forces on the Republic of Korea, the Security Council repeatedly called the actions an 'armed attack'.[239] In a further contrast to Resolutions 1368 (2001) and 1373 (2001), in 1950 the Security Council stated that the 'armed attack' amounted to a 'breach of the peace' which is stronger than the phrase used in 2001 ('a *threat* to international peace and security').[240] In 1950, the Security Council also set out its recommendations for a response to the 'armed attack': in Resolution 83 (1950) the

---

Legal Categories of International Law' (2001) 12 *EJIL* 993; Stahn, C., 'Security Council Resolutions 1368 (2001) and 1373 (2001): What They Say and What They Do Not Say', *EJIL Discussion Forum*, available at: <www.ejil.org/forum_WTC> at 17 June 2008. The significance of the preamble in Security Council resolutions is discussed briefly by Michael Wood who states that: 'The preambles to SCRs may assist in interpretation, by giving evidence as to their object and purpose, but they need to be treated with caution since they tend to be used as a dumping ground for proposals that are not acceptable in the operative paragraphs': Wood, M., 'The Interpretation of Security Council Resolutions' (1998) 2 *Max Planck Yearbook of United Nations Law* 73 at 86–7.

234 See discussion regarding the debate that preceded the adoption of Resolution 1368, and the positions taken by various scholars, at 185–189.

235 This is a point that is made by Stahn, who notes that the Security Council avoided speaking of an 'armed attack' as required by Article 51 of the Charter, using instead the notion of 'terrorist attack', without expressly linking this notion to Article 51 of the Charter: Stahn, supra n. 233. It is also made by Cassese, who notes that in operative paragraph 1 of S/Res/1368 (2001), the Security Council defines the terrorist acts of 11 September as a 'threat to the peace', hence not as an 'armed attack' legitimising self-defence under Article 51 of the UN Charter: Cassese, supra n. 233.

236 SCOR S/PV.4370, supra n. 177. Even the US statement did not refer to them as 'armed attacks': supra n. 177.

237 UK Letter to the Security Council, supra n. 167, reproduced in Appendix 2.

238 See also Orakhelashvili, A., 'Legal Consequences of the Construction of a Wall in the Occupied Palestinian Territory: Opinion and Reaction' (2006) 11(1) *JCSL* 119 at 127.

239 S/Res/82 (1950) adopted on 25 June 1950, S/1501; S/Res/83 (1950) adopted on 27 June 1950, S/1511 in two separate paragraphs of the resolution; S/Res/84 (1950) adopted on 7 July 1950, S/1588 in three paragraphs; and in S/Res/85 (1950) adopted on 31 July 1950 the Council used the term 'unlawful attack'.

240 The latter phrase was used in S/Res/1368 (2001) and S/Res/1373 (2001).

Council noted that 'urgent military measures are necessary to restore international peace and security';[241] and in Resolution 84 (1950) it 'Recommend[ed] that Members of the United Nations furnish such assistance to the Republic of Korea as may be necessary to repel the armed attack and to restore international peace and security in the area'.[242]

Another comparison can be made between language employed by the Security Council in 1990 (regarding Iraq) and 1993 (regarding Bosnia and Herzegovina) and the post-11 September resolutions. On 2 August 1990, the Security Council adopted Resolution 660 in which it responded to the 'invasion of Kuwait … by the military forces of Iraq'.[243] The Council determined that there existed 'a breach of international peace and security'.[244] It explicitly stated that it was acting under Articles 39 and 40 of the UN Charter and it concluded by noting that it would meet again to consider further steps.[245] Then on 6 August 1990, the Security Council passed Resolution 661 which, *inter alia*, imposed sanctions on Iraq. In the sixth preambular paragraph of Resolution 661 (1990), the Council agreed that it was:[246] 'Affirming the inherent right of individual or collective self-defence, *in response to the armed attack by Iraq against Kuwait*, in accordance with Article 51 of the Charter.' (Emphasis added.) When the above paragraphs are compared to the equivalent paragraphs from Resolutions 1368 (2001) and 1373 (2001), some obvious differences are apparent. The equivalent paragraph in Resolution 1368 (2001) was phrased as follows: '*Recognizing* the inherent right of individual or collective self-defence in accordance with the Charter.' Similarly, in Resolution 1373 (2001) the Council stated it was: '*Reaffirming* the inherent right of individual or collective self-defence as recognized by the Charter of the United Nations as reiterated in resolution 1368 (2001).'

In September 2001, the Council did not take the opportunity, which clearly presented itself on two occasions, to refer to the hijackings as 'armed attacks', yet on two previous occasions, in 1950 and in 1990, it had chosen to use the specific term 'armed attacks'. Another important comparison is provided in relation to the use of force in Bosnia-Herzegovina in 1993 where the Security Council specifically mentioned that the right to act in self-defence included the right to use force.[247]

---

241 S/Res/83 (1950).

242 S/Res/84 (1950).

243 S/Res/660 (1990) adopted on 2 August 1990 at the 2932nd Meeting by 14 votes to none; Yemen did not participate in the vote.

244 Ibid.

245 Ibid.

246 S/Res/661 (1990) adopted on 6 August 1990 at the 2933rd Meeting by 13 votes to none, with two abstentions (Cuba and Yemen).

247 '[The Security Council] Authorizes (UNPROFOR) … *acting in self-defence*, to take the necessary measures, *including the use of force*, in reply to bombardments against the safe areas …' (emphasis added): S/Res/836 (1993), adopted on 4 June 1993 at the 3228th Meeting, paragraph 9.

The comparison between the post-11 September resolutions and Resolution 661 (1990) is especially important because in relation to Iraq, the Council had used the term 'armed attack' in the *same paragraph* in which it reaffirmed the inherent right of self-defence. Additionally, in 1990, the Security Council specifically mentioned Article 51, which it did *not* do in the post-11 September resolutions.

One further point of distinction is that in 1950, in Resolutions 83 and 84, the Security Council referred to a '*breach* of international peace and security';[248] likewise, in 1990 in Resolution 660, the Council stated that there had been a '*breach* of international peace and security'.[249] However, in 2001, the Council stated that this act, *like any act* of international terrorism, was a *threat* to international peace and security. The difference is subtle but significant. The overall tenor of the Security Council's resolutions in September 2001 is quite different from those resolutions adopted in 1950 and 1990, and the decision to employ less specific, and considerably weaker, language must be acknowledged. In summary, the Security Council demonstrated in 1950 and 1990 that when it is convinced that an 'armed attack' has occurred, it is prepared to use that specific term, with the ramifications that then exist under international law, and it is willing to call upon states to render military assistance to repel the attack, and to restore international peace and security, if it has been found to have been *breached.* In relation to the events of 11 September, the Security Council did not use the term 'armed attack'; it did not refer to Article 51; it did not find that there was a breach of international peace and security and, therefore, it cannot be presumed that it endorsed the subsequent use of force by the US and the UK.

The Security Council's response to the use of force[250] It was noted above that among the arguments which could be raised to support the legitimacy of the US–UK actions was the Security Council's reaction (or lack thereof) to the use of force.[251] It might be argued that if the Council had regarded the US and UK's use of force against Afghanistan as an act of unlawful aggression, it would have condemned it as such. Thus, it may be argued that the Council's lack of response, and apparent acquiescence, should accordingly be interpreted as implied acceptance by the

---

248 S/Res/83 and S/Res/84 (1950), supra n. 239.

249 S/Res/660 (1990), supra n. 243.

250 The Security Council's initial response to the terrorist attacks of 11 September 2001 has already been briefly touched upon. The analysis here focuses on the Security Council's response to the use of force by the US and the UK.

251 See discussion at 189.

Council that the actions were indeed lawful acts of self-defence. The extract below is representative of a view expressed by a number of scholars:[252]

> The United States has relied on its right of self-defense in using military force to respond to the September 11 attacks. *Other governments have not challenged the right of the United States to do so*, although some questions have been raised about U.S. tactics and targeting. Because customary international law is often developed through a process of official assertions and acquiescences, *the absence of challenge to the US asserted right of self-defense could be taken to indicate acquiescence in an expansion of the right* to include defense against governments that harbor or support organized terrorist groups that commit armed attacks in other countries. (Emphasis added)

Although the Security Council did not react immediately to the US and UK's letters dated 7 October 2001 reporting their resort to force, the Security Council subsequently passed further resolutions regarding the situation in Afghanistan. The Council adopted Resolutions 1377, 1378, 1383 and 1386 on 12 November, 14 November, 6 December and 20 December 2001, respectively. None of these latter resolutions mentioned the inherent right of self-defence, which had been referred to in the two earlier resolutions (1368 and 1373). Nor did any of these later resolutions explicitly endorse the US and UK's use of force. The closest that the Security Council came to retrospectively condoning the use of force was in Resolution 1378, when it expressed its support for 'international efforts to root out terrorism',[253] but even that phrase could not be interpreted as an endorsement of the use of force *per se*.

The first resolution passed after the military campaign had begun simply reaffirmed the Security Council's view that a *global* response to terrorism was needed.[254] Neither that resolution, nor any of the subsequent resolutions which dealt with terrorism as a threat to international peace and security, or Afghanistan in particular, authorised or endorsed the use of force.[255] Therefore, it is not persuasive

---

252 Kirgis, F., 'Israel's Intensified Military Campaign Against Terrorism' (2001) *(ASIL) Insights*: <http://www.asil.org/insights/insigh78.htm> at 17 June 2008; see also Maogoto, supra n. 231 at 122; Miller, J., 'The Legal Implications of the Response to September 11, 2001: A Tribute to Paul Szasz' (2002) 35 *Cornell Int'l L.J.* 605 at 606; Paust, J., 'The Legal Implications of the Response to September 11, 2001: Use of Armed Force Against Terrorists in Afghanistan, Iraq and Beyond' (2002) 35 *Cornell Int'l L.J.* 533 at 535; Beard, supra n. 231 at 569.

253 S/Res/1378 (2001) adopted on 14 November 2001.

254 '[The Security Council] Affirms that a sustained, comprehensive approach involving the active participation and collaboration of all Member States of the United Nations, and in accordance with the Charter of the United Nations and international law, is essential to combat the scourge of international terrorism': S/Res/1377 (2001) adopted on 12 November 2001, UNSCOR, 56th Session, 4413th Meeting, eighth preambular paragraph.

255 Scholars who have made this point include Stahn, C., *ASIL Insights*, 'Addendum: Security Council Resolution 1377 (2001) and 1378 (2001)', 1 December 2001: <http://

to argue that the Security Council impliedly accepted the lawfulness of the US and UK's actions, simply because the Council did not retrospectively condemn the use of force. As mentioned above, even if some members of the Security Council had held doubts about the legitimacy of the US and UK's military response, it is most unlikely that they would have expressed them openly.[256]

Some scholars have criticised the Security Council for its failure to make a clear pronouncement:[257] 'It is difficult to avoid the impression that, by keeping matters deliberately vague, the Security Council has in fact evaded its responsibility under the UN Charter to determine whether the use of force by the US-led coalition was lawful.' Whether the Security Council kept matters *deliberately* vague is open to debate. The climate at that time was one of overwhelming sympathy for the US and underwhelming sympathy for Afghanistan.[258] What is clear is that the Security Council had the primary responsibility for the maintenance of international peace and security.[259] It was the Council's duty to determine if there was a threat to the peace, breach of the peace or act of aggression.[260] On 12 September 2001, it made such a determination when it declared that the hijackings, like all acts of international terrorism, were a threat to international peace and security.[261] It then had the power and responsibility to take measures to maintain and restore international peace and security.[262] If the Security Council considered that the US and the UK were discharging that responsibility on its behalf, the Council could have *retrospectively* endorsed the use of force, as it has done on other occasions.[263]

---

www.asil.org/insights/insigh77.htm#_ednref7c> at 17 June 2008; Kenny, supra n. 41; and Kapferer, supra n. 41 at 42–4.

256 See discussion in Chapter 5 regarding the US's use of force in 1986, 1993 and 1998 and the international reaction; also Lobel, supra n. 173 at 557.

257 Kapferer, supra n. 41 at 41.

258 Supra n. 156 and accompanying text.

259 Article 24(1) of the UN Charter: 'In order to ensure prompt and effective action by the United Nations, its Members confer on the Security Council primary responsibility for the maintenance of international peace and security …'

260 Ibid., Article 39.

261 S/Res/1368 (2001). It reiterated that finding on 28 September in S/Res/1373 (2001).

262 Article 42 of the UN Charter.

263 In 1950, in relation to Korea, the UN Security Council effectively authorised action in its name by the US and other national contingents in what became known as the 'coalition of the willing'. In 1990, the UN again authorised a 'coalition of the willing' to respond to Iraq's invasion of Kuwait. Those authorisations occurred *prior* to the use of force. In 1997 the Security Council *retrospectively* endorsed the use of force by the armed forces of the Economic Community of Western African States (ECOWAS), the Military Observer Group (ECOMOG) in Liberia and Sierra Leone. Regarding Liberia, see S/Res/1116 (1997) adopted on 27 June 1997, UNSCOR 52nd Session, 3793rd Meeting, at 1, UN Doc S/Res/1116 (1997). Regarding Sierra Leone, see S/Res/1162 (1998) adopted on 17 April 1998, UN SCOR 53rd Session, 3872nd Meeting, at 1, UN Doc S/Res/1162 (1998). See also Franck, T., 'When, If Ever, May States Deploy Military Force Without

Subsequent to the use of force by the US and the UK, the Council passed four resolutions regarding the threat posed by international terrorism to peace and security.[264] None of those resolutions retrospectively authorised the use of force; in fact, there was no mention *whatsoever* of the use of military force by the US and the UK against Afghanistan.

When considering the Security Council's overall response to the use of force by two of its Permanent Members, it is significant that the Council did not note the validity of the US–UK actions, nor did it commend them or express appreciation for their efforts.[265] The failure to even acknowledge that the US and the UK were employing force against Afghanistan is difficult to reconcile with the position adopted by some scholars that the international community supposedly endorsed the use of force. In summary, there was no resolution from the Security Council which either explicitly endorsed or condemned the use of force by the US and the UK against Afghanistan. But even if there had been, it would not have been conclusive as to the legality of that use of force because it is ultimately for the ICJ, not the Security Council, to make determinative legal judgements.[266] Thus, no definitive findings can be reached as to the legality of the US–UK use of force based solely upon the Security Council's reaction, or lack thereof.

Prior Security Council Authorisation?' (2001) 5 *Wash. U.J.L. & Pol'y* 51 at 53–7. When retrospectively authorising the use of force by ECOMOG in Sierra Leone, the Security Council stated that it *commended* ECOWAS and ECOMOG on 'the important role they are playing in support of the objectives related to the restoration of peace and security set out in paragraph 1 above'. Given these precedents, presumably the Security Council would have endorsed the use of force by the US and UK if it had considered that those Member States were playing an important role in the restoration of peace and security in Afghanistan.

264 See S/Res/1377 adopted on 12 November 2001; S/Res/1378 adopted on 14 November 2001; S/Res/1383 (2001) adopted on 6 December 2001; and S/Res/1386 (2001) adopted on 20 December 2001.

265 Compare with the wording of the Security Council's endorsement of the ECOMOG forces in Liberia and Sierra Leone, discussed above. Also compare with resolutions adopted in 2006 whereby the Council 'expressed its appreciation' to the Presidents of Liberia and Nigeria for their assistance in facilitating the transfer of Charles Taylor.

266 Article 92 of the UN Charter states that the International Court of Justice is the United Nations' principal judicial organ. See also discussion in McCormack, T., *Self-Defense in International Law: The Israeli Raid on the Iraqi Nuclear Reactor* (New York: St Martin's Press, 1996) at 24: 'The process of determining the legality of a particular action would be simple for international lawyers if a unanimous resolution of the Security Council amounted to a determinative judgment in international law … However, international legal enquiry is not that simple, and unanimous resolutions of the Security Council condemning or supporting particular actions have never been accorded such status in international law … The Security Council is not a judicial body and does not make legal judgments in factual situations. Although the International Court of Justice does not have compulsory jurisdiction it is the UN body with the judicial capacity to establish the relevant facts and apply the appropriate legal principles in order to make a legal judgment.'

Non-state actors and 'armed attack' The fourth and final argument which might support the inference that there was an 'armed attack' relates to the issue of non-state actors. At issue is whether an 'armed attack' must be carried out by a state, or whether it can be carried out by a non-state actor. Neither the US nor the UK asserted that the hijackings were carried out by a state or by state-directed individuals. The US was more prepared than the UK to place responsibility for the hijackings on al Qaeda, but even the US did not go so far as to say that Osama bin Laden, al Qaeda or the Taliban actually carried out the attacks.[267]

The US said that al Qaeda had a *central role* in the attacks. It did not claim that the Taliban regime had a role in the attacks.[268] The UK was even more careful in its choice of language. It focused on preventing further attacks from al Qaeda rather than asserting that al Qaeda was directly responsible for the 11 September attacks. The UK did not state who it considered was responsible for what it termed the 'terrorist outrage'.[269]

In the *Nicaragua* case, the ICJ held that 'armed attacks' can be carried out by non-state actors if they are sent by or on behalf of a state and if they carry out acts of armed force of such gravity as to amount to an actual armed attack conducted by regular forces, or they have substantial involvement therein.[270] Thus, acts of state-sponsored terrorism can amount to 'armed attacks' if they meet a two-part test: the *source* is the state, and the *gravity* is such that it would amount to an armed attack had it been carried out by the regular forces of a state. The ICJ in the *Nicaragua* case also held that assistance to rebels in the form of the provision of weapons or logistical or other support does *not* amount to an 'armed attack'.[271]

These legal pronouncements on the meaning of 'armed attack' are problematic for the US and the UK. There is no doubt that the second part of the *Nicaragua* test, the 'gravity' element, would be satisfied. The only issue is the first part of the *Nicaragua* test, the 'source' of the attacks. Neither the US nor the UK alleged in their letters to the Security Council that the hijackers were 'sent by or on behalf of a state'.[272] Neither the US nor the UK identified the perpetrators, or their nationalities, or the evidence of their connection to the Taliban regime.

---

267 Note that in an interview with Taysir Alluni recorded on 20 October 2001, and broadcast on 31 January 2002, Osama bin Laden praised the attacks and admitted inciting and rousing to action the young men who carried out the attacks, but he stopped short of admitting that he was directly responsible for organising them: Lawrence, B. (ed.) (Howarth, J. trans.), *Messages to the World – The Statements of Osama bin Laden* (London; New York: Verso, 2005) 107–13.

268 The US asserted that the Taliban regime allowed the parts of Afghanistan that it controlled to be used by al Qaeda as a base of operation.

269 The phrase 'terrorist outrage' is in inverted commas because this is the term used by the UK to describe the 9/11 hijackings – it did not refer to them as 'armed attacks'; see the UK's letter to the Security Council, reproduced in Appendix 2.

270 See Chapter 5.

271 Ibid.

272 See the *Nicaragua* case, supra n. 214 at para 115.

The US and the UK claimed that the Taliban regime was 'supporting'[273] al Qaeda. However, applying the first part of the *Nicaragua* test, mere *support* is insufficient to amount to an armed attack. The ICJ held there that even the 'provision of weapons or logistical or other support'[274] is insufficient. Yet in October 2001, the US and the UK claimed only that there was 'support' from the Taliban – without any specific claims of what form that support took, other than alleging that the Taliban allowed al Qaeda to use parts of Afghanistan which it supposedly controlled.[275] It is submitted that the level of 'support' referred to by the US and the UK was insufficient under international law, as it stood in October 2001, to amount to an armed attack on the US by the Taliban regime.[276]

In *Nicaragua*, the ICJ placed considerable emphasis on the fact that the acts of the Contras could have been carried out without the *control* of the US.[277] In the case of Afghanistan, it is apparent that the incidents that occurred on 11 September 2001 could also have occurred without the *control* of the Taliban. It ought to be remembered that *The 9/11 Commission Report* noted that senior members of the Taliban opposed al Qaeda's plans to attack the US, but they were powerless to prevent it. Thus, the US and the UK did not assert, nor could they have established, that the Taliban directed the 11 September hijackings, because the Taliban lacked a sufficient degree of control over al Qaeda.

In conclusion, serious doubts can be raised as to whether the US was subjected to an 'armed attack' on 11 September 2001. It was stated at the beginning of this part of Chapter 6[278] that four arguments are commonly raised to support the claim that there was indeed an 'armed attack' for the purposes of satisfying Article 51. Those four arguments and the usual evidence that is put forward to support them

273 The UK: '... This military action ... is directed against [O]sama Bin Laden's Al Qaeda terrorist organization and the Taliban regime that is supporting it.' The US: '... the Al Qaeda Organization, which is supported by the Taliban regime in Afghanistan, had a central role in the attacks': see documents reproduced in Appendices 2 and 1, respectively.

274 See the *Nicaragua* case, supra n. 214 at para 115.

275 See the US and UK's letters to the Security Council dated 7 October 2001, reproduced at Appendices 1 and 2, respectively.

276 Compare with the *Nicaragua* case where the majority held at paras 115–16: '... United States participation, even if preponderant or decisive, in the financing, organizing, training, supplying and equipping of the *contras*, the selection of its military or paramilitary targets, and the planning of the whole of its operation, *is still insufficient in itself*, on the basis of the evidence in the possession of the Court, *for the purpose of attributing to the United States the acts committed by the* contras *in the course of their military or paramilitary activities in Nicaragua* ... For this conduct to give rise to legal responsibility of the United States it would in principle have to be proved that that State had *effective control* of the military or paramilitary operations in the course of which the alleged [human rights] violations were committed' (emphasis added).

277 See *Nicaragua* case, supra n. 214 at para 115.

278 See above at 189.

have been analysed here. The conclusion that has been reached is that they are not as strong as they seem at first glance.

First, the support gleaned from NATO's invoking of Article 5 is generally overstated given that there was substantial opposition at the time over the legal basis for its invocation. The decision to invoke Article 5 was likely to have been influenced by political rather than legal considerations.

Secondly, the Security Council's references to the 'inherent right of self-defence' in Resolutions 1368 and 1373 (2001) are often attributed more weight than they deserve, given that the Security Council never used the term 'armed attack', nor referred to Article 51 directly, nor found a *breach* of the international peace in any of the post-9/11 resolutions, despite precedents where it has made precisely such findings.

Thirdly, although the Security Council never condemned the use of force by the US and the UK, it never condoned it either, despite precedents where it has retrospectively authorised the use of force. The first resolution passed after 7 October 2001[279] continued to call for a global, multilateral, law enforcement response.

Finally, although the scale and magnitude of the 11 September hijackings would have rendered them an 'armed attack' had they been carried out by regular armed forces, there was no evidence provided to the Security Council – nor was the claim even made – that the hijackers were directed by or acting on behalf of a foreign state. The definition of 'armed attack' provided by the ICJ in the *Nicaragua* case was not satisfied here.[280]

Since there must be an 'armed attack' before a state can use force in self-defence, the conclusion reached here is that the 'armed attack' element of Article 51 was not satisfied in this instance, and that means, *ipso facto*, that the US and the UK did not act in lawful self-defence when they employed military force against Afghanistan on 7 October 2001. On that basis, the argument about the lawfulness of the US and UK's actions might rest.

However, for the sake of argument, if one were to assume that the foregoing analysis is in error, and that the US *did* experience an 'armed attack', further questions would arise. First, the question of how responsibility for the so-called

279 S/Res/1377 (2001).

280 The definition of 'armed attack' as requiring an attack from a *state* was subsequently reaffirmed by the ICJ in the *Legal Consequences of the Construction of a Wall in the Occupied Palestinian Territory* Advisory Opinion. Obviously, that opinion was given after the events of 11 September 2001; however, it provides further proof of the way in which 'armed attack' has always been interpreted by the ICJ. In relation to the ICJ opinion in 2004, Alexander Orakhelashvili observes: 'In view of the consistency of the established legal position and the insufficiency of the evidence to prove any change in that position, the court had no alternative but to hold that the right to self-defence operates under international law *only in relation to the attack originating from foreign states*' (emphasis added), in Orakhelashvili, supra n. 238 at 128.

'armed attack' was attributed to the targets of the military response (al Qaeda and the Taliban/Afghanistan.) Second, the issue would arise as to whether the customary law requirements of immediacy, necessity and proportionality were adhered to. Thirdly, the issue of whether the right to use force in self-defence, presuming it initially existed, had expired by 7 October 2001 would have to be addressed. Those three questions will in turn be the focus of the next three parts of this chapter.

Attribution of Responsibility for the 'Armed Attacks'

Given the US and UK's employment of military force against Afghanistan, one might presume that the US and the UK were thereby asserting that the Islamic Emirate of Afghanistan, governed (at least in part) by the Taliban regime, was ultimately responsible for the so-called armed attacks. However, the letters from the US and the UK to the Security Council did not make such a claim. The letter from the US representative purported to attribute responsibility to the Taliban regime on the basis that:[281] '[T]he attacks of 11 September 2001 and the ongoing threat to the United States ... have been made possible by the decision of the Taliban regime to allow the parts of Afghanistan that it controls to be used by this organization [al Qaeda] as a base of operation.' The UK claimed that its military action had been carefully planned and was directed against '[O]sama Bin Laden's Al-Qaeda terrorist organization and the Taliban regime that is supporting it'.[282] Neither the US nor the UK asserted that the individuals who had carried out the hijackings were directed by or were acting on behalf of Afghanistan. The attribution of responsibility to the Afghan state, or at least that part of it which was under the Taliban's control, was on the basis that the Taliban regime had *allowed parts of Afghanistan to be used by al Qaeda as a base* (US version) or that *the Taliban was supporting al Qaeda* (UK version).

In Chapter 5, and in an earlier part of this chapter, the 'effective control' test from the *Nicaragua* case was discussed. Applying the *Nicaragua* test to the Taliban regime in relation to al Qaeda, it is apparent that the test would not be met by merely *allowing* parts of Afghan territory under its control to be used by al Qaeda (US allegation) or by *providing support* to al Qaeda (UK allegation).

One could counter that even though the *Nicaragua* test for the attribution of responsibility would not be satisfied here, that case was decided in 1986, before international terrorism became the threat that it is now, or alternatively, that it was decided on its own facts.[283] Even if such an attempt to minimise the importance

281 S/2001/946, 7 October 2001, supra n. 166, reproduced in Appendix 1.

282 S/2001/947, 7 October 2001, supra n. 167, reproduced in Appendix 2.

283 Travilio, G. and Altenburg, J., 'State Responsibility for Sponsorship of Terrorist and Insurgent Groups: Terrorism, State Responsibility and the Use of Military Force' (2003) 4 *Chi. J of Int'l L.* 97 at 5–6.

of the *Nicaragua* case were tenable, the credibility of such an objection is overshadowed by the 2001 Draft Articles on State Responsibility for Intentionally Wrongful Acts.[284] In Chapter 5 it was noted that the ILC's Draft Articles adopted a very similar test for the attribution of state responsibility to that adopted by the ICJ in the *Nicaragua* case.[285] Article 8 states that the conduct of a person or group of persons shall be considered an act of a state under international law if the person or group of persons is *acting on the instructions of*, or *under the direction or control of that state in carrying out the conduct.*[286] Neither the US nor the UK alleged that the individuals who carried out the 11 September hijackings were acting on the instructions of, or under the direction or control of, the Taliban regime.

The phrase in Article 8, 'under the direction or control of a state', means that conduct will only be attributed to a state if it directed or controlled the *specific operation.*[287] Neither the Bush nor the Blair Administrations alleged that the Taliban directed the *specific operation* that occurred on 11 September 2001, nor did the Taliban have overall control of al Qaeda's operations.[288] Far from directing this specific operation, the evidence suggests that the Taliban in fact opposed in principle the concept of attacking the US.

The only other possible way in which the US and the UK may have succeeded in attributing responsibility to the Taliban would have been via an acceptance of responsibility from the Taliban after the event.[289] Neither the US nor the UK alleged that the Taliban had accepted responsibility. Furthermore, the Taliban leadership immediately and unequivocally condemned the hijackings.[290] In 1998, and again in early October 2001, the Taliban leadership indicated that they were willing to turn Osama bin Laden over for trial if evidence was provided as to his involvement in acts of terrorism.[291] The Taliban never adopted the events of 11 September as their own conduct, thus, responsibility could not have been attributed to the Taliban

284 Travilio and Altenburg dealt with the Draft Articles perfunctorily by stating that 'international terrorism was not the focus of the Draft Articles' and that the Draft Articles cannot supersede the 'inherent' right of self-defence: ibid., 110–11.

285 See Chapter 5.

286 Article 8; ibid.

287 See Commentary to the Draft Articles, discussed in Chapter 5.

288 In *Prosecutor v Tadić*, the International Criminal Tribunal for the Former Yugoslavia indicated that a state does not have to issue specific instructions for the direction of every individual operation, nor does it have to select concrete targets, but it still has to be subject to the overall control of the state: *Prosecutor v Tadić* Judgment, ICTY Case No IT-94-A, Appeals Chamber 1999, 38 ILM 1518, 1545 (1999); see discussion in Chapter 5.

289 Draft Articles, Article 11; see also the discussion in Chapter 5 regarding the ILC Draft Articles. Article 11 provides that conduct which is not otherwise attributable to a state can nevertheless be considered an act of that state under international law if and to the extent that the state acknowledges and adopts the act in question as its own.

290 Supra n. 56 and accompanying text.

291 Regarding the 1998 arrangement, see Bodansky, Y., *Bin Laden – The Man Who Declared War on America* (US: Prima Publishing, 2001) 301–6.

regime on the basis of Article 11 or the precedent set forth in the *Diplomatic and Consular Staff (Iran Hostages)* case.[292]

In light of the tests in both the *Nicaragua* case and in the ILC Draft Articles, the US and the UK failed to attribute responsibility to the Taliban regime for the acts which occurred on 11 September 2001 and which they claimed entitled them to use force in self-defence. Therefore, it is concluded that the US and the UK acted in violation of international law when they used military force against the Taliban regime on 7 October 2001.[293] Scholarly support for this conclusion emphasises the distinction between targeting al Qaeda and the Taliban.[294] Although the use of force against the Taliban was highly problematic, it has been argued elsewhere that the use of military force would have been permissible, had it been restricted to targeting Osama bin Laden and members of the al Qaeda network.[295] Some scholars claim that if the US and the UK had restricted themselves to solely al Qaeda targets, they would have been well within their rights because al Qaeda members were responsible for, or complicit in, the 11 September attacks and previous armed attacks on US targets.[296]

That proposition is made more tenable given that bin Laden previously issued declarations of war against the US,[297] including *fatwas* to kill Americans wherever they could be found;[298] and there was some proof that although he initially

292 See discussion in Chapter 5.

293 The US was clear in its intention to target the Taliban. In the US's letter to the Security Council it stated that, 'These actions include measures against ... military installations of the Taliban regime in Afghanistan'; see also n. 172; the US stated that its use of force was aimed at attacking the military capability of the Taliban.

294 Paust: '... the US attacks on the Taliban in 2001 and the arrest or detention of members of the Taliban armed forces, as opposed to bin Laden and al Qaeda [are] highly problematic ... [it] raises serious concerns about future use of military force against states that merely harbour or support or have known links with non-state terrorists or other international criminals': Paust, J., 'Use of Armed Force against Terrorists in Afghanistan, Iraq, and Beyond' (2002) 35 *Cornell Int'l L.J.*533 at 542 and 547. Also see Conte, supra n. 231 at 49, who implies that responsibility was apportioned via a number of Security Council resolutions from 1999–2001, rather than through the ILC's Draft Articles.

295 Paust draws a distinction between the state entity (the Taliban) and the non-state organisation (al Qaeda), and argues that strikes against the former were probably unlawful, but against the latter were lawful: ibid.

296 For example, the attacks on the USS Cole and the US embassies in Nairobi and Dar-es-Salaam: ibid.

297 'Declaration of War Against the Americans Occupying the Land of the Two Holy Places: A Message from Usama bin Laden unto his Muslim Brethren All Over the World Generally, and in the Arab Peninsula Specifically', 23 August 1996, reprinted in Alexander, Y. and Swetnam, M., *Usama bin Laden's al-Qaida: Profile of a Terrorist Network* (New York: Transnational Publishers, 2001) at Appendix 1. Although note that this was mainly directed at the US military forces stationed in the Persian Gulf.

298 In February 1998 bin Laden and al-Zawahiri endorsed a *fatwa* (legal ruling) stating that Muslims should kill Americans, including civilians, anywhere in the world

denied responsibility for the attacks,[299] he later acknowledged some degree of involvement.[300] Those factors support the proposition that the non-state group, al Qaeda, was a more appropriate and, arguably, even a lawful target.

Nevertheless, it is still difficult to provide a legal basis for using force to target even al Qaeda in Afghanistan without a Security Council mandate. The UN Charter only permits force to be used in two situations (when authorised by the Security Council or in self-defence), neither of which would apply to the use of force by individual states against al Qaeda targets within Afghanistan. Furthermore, state practice suggests that historically the legitimacy of military reprisals against non-state groups in response to terrorist acts has been largely rejected by the international community. In the previous chapter, examples of forcible reprisals from the 1950s through to the 2000s were discussed. It was demonstrated there that the Security Council has frequently condemned the use of force, such as air strikes on alleged terrorist bases inside a foreign state, even when those air strikes were in response to previous attacks by non-state actors emanating from the territory of that state.[301] The *opinio juris* of the majority of states does not support the use of military force against a sovereign state in retaliation for attacks by non-state actors.[302] In essence, even though it may be claimed that air strikes against targets within Afghanistan would have been legitimate, had they been confined to al Qaeda and excluded the Taliban, such a proposition is open to criticism on the basis that international law does not currently support the use of force in such situations, as is borne out by state practice.

---

where they could be found. It was published in the *Al-Quds al-Arabi* newspaper on 23 February 1998.

299 'Bin Laden Says He Wasn't Behind Attacks', *CNN*, 17 September 2001: <http://archives.cnn.com/2001/US/09/16/inv.binladen.denial/> at 17 June 2008.

300 See discussion above regarding the interview with Alluni on 20 October 2001; see also 'Bin Laden Video Threatens America', *BBC News*, 30 October 2004: <http://news.bbc.co.uk/2/hi/middle_east/3966741.stm> at 17 June 2008.

301 See Chapter 5: the Security Council condemned Portugal for its attacks on Senegal in 1969; it condemned Israel for its use of force against its neighbours in the 1960s in relation to As-Samu, Karameh, As-Salt and the Beirut Airport raid, all of which were justified on the grounds that Israel had suffered attacks from non-state actors in neighbouring states; several members condemned Israel for its invasion of Lebanon in 1982 which was justified on the grounds that Lebanon could not or would not meet its responsibilities to prevent armed attacks being launched from its territory; and the Council condemned Israel for its attack on Tunisia in 1985, even though Israel alleged that Tunisia had allowed its territory to be used as a base for terrorists.

302 But note that there was a trend away from condemnation towards acquiescence.

The Customary Law Elements of the Inherent Right of Self-defence

If the US and/or the UK had suffered an 'armed attack' by virtue of which they acquired the right to use force in self-defence against an entity directed by or acting on behalf of the State of Afghanistan, the question would arise as to whether they exercised that right within the bounds of international law.

As noted in Chapter 5, the 'inherent right of individual or collective self-defence' is not defined in Article 51 and recourse must be had to customary law to define the content of the right.[303] A state using force in self-defence must do so out of *necessity*, it must respond in a way that is *proportionate* and there must be an element of *immediacy*.[304] These three elements of self-defence, distilled from American Secretary of State Daniel Webster's statement in the 1837 *Caroline* incident,[305] whose modern relevance was reaffirmed in the *Nicaragua* case and whose applicability to both customary law and Article 51 was affirmed in the *Legality of the Threat or Use of Nuclear Weapons* case, are discussed in turn below.[306]

Necessity

The US and the UK must have been able to demonstrate the necessity of self-defence; the need to use force must have been instant, overwhelming, leaving no choice of means.[307] In a modern context, it means that force should not have been considered unless and until other peaceful measures had been found wanting or when they would clearly have been futile.[308] If the US and the UK had been able to achieve their objectives by measures not involving the use of force, then they ought not to have contravened the general prohibition on the use of force.[309]

---

303 Chapter 5; also the *Nicaragua* case, supra n. 214 at 94, especially para 176.

304 See Chapter 4 and the discussion of these elements from the *Caroline* case.

305 The US called upon Great Britain to show the existence of a 'necessity of self-defence, instant, overwhelming, leaving no choice of means, and no moment for deliberation … also, that the local authorities of Canada … did nothing unreasonable or excessive, since the act, justified by the necessity of self-defence, must be limited by that necessity and kept clearly within it'.

306 *Legality of the Threat or Use of Nuclear Weapons* Advisory Opinion [1996] ICJ Reports 226 at 245. The ICJ held that the conditions of necessity and proportionality were not only a rule of customary international law but also applied equally to Article 51, whatever the means of force employed.

307 Paraphrasing Secretary of State Webster; see Jennings, R., 'The Caroline and McLeod Cases' (1938) 32 *AJIL* 82.

308 Schacter, O., 'The Right of States to Use Armed Force' (1984) 82 *Mich Law Rev* 1620 at 1635.

309 Paraphrasing Judge Ago, Addendum to the Eighth Report on State Responsibility, *Yrbk. ILC* ICJ Reports [1996] 226; see discussion in Chapter 5.

It is difficult to determine the precise objectives of the use of force against Afghanistan. The US's official objective was to 'prevent and deter further attacks on the United States'.[310] The UK's objective was similar.[311] Those objectives were somewhat inconsistent with statements from the US Department of Defense.[312] For instance, although the search for Osama bin Laden was portrayed in the media as a key justification for the use of force, it was not put forth *formally* as a key objective.[313]

It is apparent from the earlier analysis in this chapter that the threat of immediate attack against the US had subsided by the evening of 11 September 2001. Thus, force in self-defence was not employed to halt or avert an imminent armed attack. Nor was the US under a full-scale and continuing invasion – had it been so, there would be no question that the US would have been entitled to use force to repel the attack. Force was ultimately used in 'self-defence' by the US and the UK to prevent *future* attacks.[314]

Arguably, the US and UK's objectives could have been achieved through other means. As for the purported aim of securing the arrest of bin Laden,[315] there were negotiations prior to 11 September, notably in 1998 and in the early months of 2001, to secure the surrender of bin Laden to Saudi Arabia for trial.[316] Those negotiations were revived by the Taliban's leader, Mullah Omar, after 11 September 2001. There were reports that Afghanistan's Islamic clerics had urged bin Laden to leave the country of his own accord[317] and Mullah Omar had offered

---

310 US Letter to the President of the Security Council, supra n. 166, see Appendix 1.

311 The UK said it was employing its forces 'to avert the continuing threat of attacks from the same source': UK Letter to the President of the Security Council, supra n. 167, see Appendix 2.

312 In statements from the US Secretary of Defense, Donald Rumsfeld and his British counterpart Geoff Hoon, both the US and the UK set out much more specific objectives. The US stated that the objectives of its air campaign were to 'make clear to the Taliban that harbouring terrorists carries a price; to acquire intelligence to facilitate future operations against al Qaeda and the Taliban; to develop useful relationships with groups in Afghanistan that oppose the Taliban …': see United States Department of Defense, 'Statement of the Secretary of Defense' No.560-01 (1 November 2001).

313 The US President stated that the search was underway for those responsible and that they would be brought to justice. The search for bin Laden is not mentioned in the US and UK's letters to the Security Council.

314 See discussion below under the heading 'Pre-emptive Self-defence'.

315 'Purported' because neither the US nor the UK referred to the arrest of bin Laden as a justification for using force when they reported their actions to the Security Council on 7 October 2001.

316 See Bodansky, supra n. 291 at 301–6.

317 'Taliban Won't Turn Over Bin Laden', *CBS News*, 21 September 2001: a two-day meeting of the Ulema, or council of religious leaders, urged bin Laden to leave but set no deadline for his departure.

to turn bin Laden over if certain conditions were met.[318] However, the US said that its ultimatum to the Taliban was not negotiable.[319] Pursuant to the condition of necessity, the US was obliged to, and could have, negotiated on the terms of its ultimatum, including the possibility of bin Laden's extradition.[320] The condition of necessity requires that any efforts to resolve the problem amicably be undertaken in good faith and not only as a matter of *ritual punctilio*.[321] The evidence suggests that the US's ultimatum was not a genuine attempt at negotiating a peaceful solution, since a decision had already been taken within the Bush Administration that force would be used.[322]

Returning to the official pretext for the necessity of using force in self-defence, which was to prevent and deter future attacks, the US and the UK could also arguably have achieved that objective by other means. Domestically, the Bush Administration could have, *inter alia*, strengthened the US's intelligence capabilities to detect future terrorist activity, strengthened its immigration procedures to prevent potential terrorists from entering the US, undertook covert measures to arrest key al Qaeda figures[323] and increased security measures, all of which were identified by the 9/11 Commission as factors which had in some way contributed to the ultimate success of the 9/11 hijackers' objectives, and which needed to be addressed in order to prevent future attacks.[324]

---

318 Such as the provision by the US of evidence that bin Laden was involved in the attacks and assurances that he would be tried under Islamic law.

319 See supra n. 40.

320 See also Kenny, supra n. 41 at 106 on the obligation to negotiate and the US's refusal to do so. The alliance that formed between al Qaeda and the Taliban in 2001 could have been disrupted 'had the US given Pakistan more time to negotiate with the Islamic Emirate of Afghanistan to hand Osama over to Islamabad immediately after 9/11': Gunaratna, supra n. 42 at 227.

321 Rostow, N., 'Nicaragua and the Law of Self-Defence Revisited' (1985–86) 11 *Yale J. Int'l L.* 437 at 455.

322 If bin Laden had been arrested and extradited, he could have been prosecuted in New York under an indictment for the African embassy bombings, to which charges related to 11 September could have been added. Alternatively, a special military commission could have been employed; the Lockerbie model could have been used (for instance, using US judges and applying the law of New York but sitting in a neutral location). The International Criminal Court probably could not have been utilised because on 11 September 2001, the Rome Statue had 42 ratifications, short of the 60 required, so there would have been no prosecutor in place to investigate responsibility for this crime: on this point, see discussion in Robertson, G., 'Fair Trials for International Terrorists', in Thakur, R. and Malcontent, P. (eds), *From Sovereign Impunity to International Accountability – The Search for Justice in a World of States* (Tokyo; New York; Paris: United Nations University Press, 2004) 224–32.

323 For a summary of the covert actions undertaken in relation to al Qaeda pre-2001, see *The 9/11 Commission Report*, supra n. 1 at 12ff.

324 *The 9/11 Commission Report* set out many recommendations, including information sharing within and between agencies; the implementation of a 'layered security

At an international level, the host of measures put forward by the Security Council on 28 September 2001 would also have helped prevent and deter further attacks.[325] The Council of Europe, as discussed above, put forward a ten-point plan (which emphasised law enforcement measures) which it called upon its Member States to implement and which would also have served as a means of preventing future attacks.[326]

The US could also have increased the likelihood of achieving its goal of preventing and deterring future attacks if it had placed greater emphasis on diplomatic efforts to 'drive a wedge'[327] between the Taliban and al Qaeda. The US and Pakistan could have used diplomatic initiatives to support the moderate elements of the Taliban into relinquishing bin Laden in return for other benefits.[328] The US failed to explore this option as a serious alternative to the use of force.[329]

The point here is that it is debatable whether the necessity to use force existed on 7 October 2001 since there was no ongoing or imminent attack. Other options existed which would have helped the US and the UK to prevent and deter future attacks. The fact that the attacks occurred on 11 September, yet *Operation Enduring Freedom* did not commence until 7 October, suggests that the necessity was not 'overwhelming, leaving no choice of means'.[330] Significantly, the US has previously chosen not to respond with force to a large-scale terrorist attack, thus the use of force in this instance ought not to have been a foregone conclusion.[331]

---

system' including increasing the ability of screening checkpoints at airports to detect explosives; and the establishment of a National Counter-Terrorism Centre.

325 S/Res/1373 (2001) which contained a range of increased anti-terrorism measures such as sharing intelligence, closing borders, considering refugee status of terrorists, a multitude of measures relating to the financing of terrorism and the strengthening of extradition measures.

326 See PACE Resolution 1258 (2001), supra n. 94. The Council of Europe regarded the terrorist acts as crimes, not acts of war (para 8) and it recommended, *inter alia*, that a solution to international terrorism had to involve measures such as signing an international convention on terrorism, with a definition of that term (para 10), as well as making efforts towards 'a proper understanding of its social, economic, political and religious roots and of the individuals' capacity for hatred' (para 9). At paragraph 17, a list of ten measures was set out which would have assisted in meeting the objective of preventing future attacks.

327 Gunaratna, supra n. 42 at 227.

328 Such as international recognition of the Islamic Emirate of Afghanistan, its seat at the UN and international aid: Burke, J., *Al Qaeda – The True Story of Radical Islam* (London; New York: I.B. Tauris, 2004) 192–7.

329 'Had the US intelligence community developed an accurate assessment of the numerical strengths of Al Qaeda and the Taliban, and understood the implications of unity between a relatively unpopular Al Qaeda and a relatively popular Taliban, it could have postponed the US strikes': Gunaratna, supra n. 42 at 227.

330 A phrase from Secretary of State Webster in the *Caroline* case; see Jennings, supra n. 307.

331 In response to the bombing of Pan Am flight 103 over Lockerbie, Scotland, resulting in the deaths of 259 passengers, the US pressed for UN sanctions against Libya,

Finally, on the issue of necessity, it must always be remembered that the right of self-defence in Article 51 of the UN Charter was only inserted to safeguard states until the Security Council could act;[332] on this occasion, there was ample opportunity between 11 September and 7 October for other options to have been explored, including seeking the Security Council's authorisation.

Proportionality

According to customary international law, the use of force in self-defence must be proportional to the armed attack which provoked it.[333] Arguably, there must be a standard of *reasonableness* in the response.[334] Reasonableness can be measured by assessing the scale of response and comparing it to the scale of attack[335] or by comparing casualty rates.[336] If US economics professor Mark Herold's figures of 3,767 verifiable civilian deaths between 7 October 2001 and 10 December 2001 are employed, one might argue that there has been a roughly proportionate casualty rate when compared with the 2,948 civilians killed on 11 September 2001.[337] However, this sort of comparison is not satisfactory, for two reasons. First, because there is considerable disagreement over the exact number of civilian fatalities in Afghanistan. The number of civilians killed as a result of the US–UK invasion varies from study to study depending on whether deaths from direct military hostilities are counted, or whether deaths from indirect causes (such as landmines, unexploded ordnances strikes and the long-term effects of warfare) are also included. Variations also occur depending on the length of time over which the count is taken and the sources which are consulted. Studies estimate that the

---

instead of resorting to force. Political and economic pressure eventually resulted in two Libyans being extradited and prosecuted.

332 See discussion in Chapter 5.

333 See Chapter 5 at 114–117.

334 See Dinstein, supra n. 170 at 184.

335 For instance, comparing the use of 3,000 bombs and missiles against 200 pre-planned target areas with four airplane hijackings: UK House of Commons Research Paper 01/81, '*Operation Enduring Freedom* and the Conflict in Afghanistan: An Update', 31 October 2001: <http://www.parliament.uk/commons/lib/research/rp2001/rp01-081.pdf> at 17 June 2008 at 17.

336 The 11 September attacks resulted in the deaths of almost 3,000 individuals, compared with the deaths of between 1,000 and 8,000 Afghan civilians. Depending on the source and the time of the report, various media organisations have provided varying estimates of the civilian casualties: <http://www.tandl.vt.edu/Foundations/mediaproject/mediaprojecthtml/afghan15.html> at 17 June 2008, for links to the sources of some estimates. A US economics professor, Mark Herold, estimated that between 7 October and 10 December 2001, there were 3,767 verifiable civilian deaths: Milne, S., 'The Innocent Dead in a Coward's War', *The Guardian Unlimited*, 20 December 2001: <http://www.guardian.co.uk/afghanistan/story/0,1284,622000,00.html> at 17 June 2008.

337 See discussion supra at n. 10 and accompanying text.

number of Afghan civilian deaths could be between 1,000 and 1,300,[338] or 3,700,[339] or 5,576[340] or anywhere between 8,000 and 18,000.[341] Secondly, since force is still being employed in Afghanistan, the death rate is continuing to rise. Although the civilian casualties may have initially been roughly, arguably, 'proportionate', they become less so as the conflict continues and casualty numbers continue to increase. Due to these factors, drawing a crude comparison of the numbers of 'civilian dead on each side' is a fairly inaccurate and ultimately unhelpful method of assessing the reasonableness of the response.[342]

At another level, 'reasonableness' can be assessed by focusing on the objectives of the response. Although neither the US nor the UK formally advised the Security Council that they aimed to remove the Taliban regime from power, regime change was certainly one of the key objectives.[343] All members of the UN have agreed to refrain from the threat or use of force against the territorial integrity or political independence of any state.[344] The obligation not to use force unless in self-defence or pursuant to authorisation by the Security Council goes to the core of nationhood – the right of survival as a sovereign entity.[345]

The question then is whether regime change was a proportionate response, given the above-mentioned limitations on intervention in sovereign states. In favour of the US and the UK, one could argue that this objective was legitimate

---

338 Shaw, M., 'Risk-Transfer Militarism, Small Massacres and the Historic Legitimacy of War' (2002) 16 (3) *International Relations* 343 at 347. Shaw estimates that 1,000–1,300 civilians were 'killed by the West' as a direct result of the 2001 invasion of Afghanistan.

339 Herold, M., 'Counting the Dead: Attempts to Hide the Number of Afghan Civilians Killed by US Bombs are an Affront to Justice', *The Guardian*, 8 August 2002. Herold based his figures on media reports and internet searches.

340 Benini, A. and Moulton, L., 'Civilian Victims in an Asymmetrical Conflict: Operation Enduring Freedom, Afghanistan (2004) 41 (4) *Journal of Peace Research* 403 at 417. Benini and Moulton based their figures on a survey of 600 affected communities in Afghanistan.

341 The Project on Defense Alternatives has estimated that there were 1,000–1,300 civilian deaths from air strikes and an additional 8,000–18,000 deaths from indirect war effects: Conetta, C., 'Strange Victory: A Critical Appraisal of Operation Enduring Freedom and the Afghanistan War', Project on Defense Alternatives Research Monogragh 6, 30 January 2002, available from Commonwealth Institute: <http://www.comw.org/pda/0201strangevic.pdf> at 17 June 2008.

342 See also Dinstein, supra n. 170 at 210–12.

343 On 16 October 2001, British Foreign Secretary Jack Straw released a document which outlined a set of objectives: *Defeating International Terrorism: Campaign Objectives*, Dep 01/1460, 16 October 2001. See also Geoffrey Hoon, 'Operation Veritas', Speech to the House of Commons, London (1 November 2001) where that objective was reiterated.

344 Article 2(4) of the UN Charter.

345 In the words of Louis Henkin, this obligation is the 'principal norm of contemporary international law': Henkin, cited in Glennon, M., *Limits of Law, Prerogatives of Power: Intervention After Kosovo* (New York: Palgrave, 2001) 3.

because the removal of the Taliban regime was an integral part of the US's right to *restore the security* of the US after the 'armed attack'.[346] Against the US and the UK is the fact that self-defence actions are supposed to be aimed at, and restricted to, achieving the repulsion of an attack, the expulsion of an invader and the restoration of the territorial *status quo ante bellum*.[347] A 'change in leadership' was not strictly necessary to repel the attack, to expel the invader or to restore the territorial *status quo ante bellum.*

It might be argued that once an action in self-defence has begun, the total defeat of the armed forces of the enemy may be necessary to achieve the legitimate end of restoring the security of the state.[348] Yet examples also exist where states have acted in purported self-defence, in the course of which they have effected a change of leadership in the target state, thereby provoking widespread condemnation.[349] It is contended that in the case of Afghanistan, the removal of the Taliban regime was not a proportionate response. That assessment is made on the basis of the existing norms of international law, which in 2001 (and in 2008) did not permit the overthrow of a government as a legitimate aim of a self-defence action; on the basis of the principles contained in Article 2 of the UN Charter; and on the basis of the *opinio juris* of states as evidenced by numerous precedents.[350] Had the US

346 Gardam, J., *Necessity, Proportionality and the Use of Force by States* (Cambridge: Cambridge University Press, 2004) 157, n. 89.

347 Higgins, R., *Problems and Process: International Law and How We Use It* (Oxford: Oxford University Press, 2004) 232; McDougal, M. and Feliciano, F., *Law and Minimum World Public Order: The Legal Regulation of International Coercion* (New Haven; London: Yale University Press, 1962) at 222–4; Gardam, ibid., at 156ff; Dissenting Opinions of Judge Higgins, *Legality of the Threat or Use of Nuclear Weapons*, supra n. 306 at 583–4.

348 For example, the use of force to repel Iraq's invasion of Kuwait and the UK's use of force in the Falkland Islands. With regards to Iraq, Dinstein argues that Kuwait (and the international coalition) 'could have chased the beaten Iraqi forces all the way to the last bunker in Baghdad': Dinstein, supra n. 170 at 211. Regarding the Falklands War, Greenwood argues that the UK had the right to use force not only to retake the Islands, 'but also to guarantee their future security against further attack': Greenwood, C., 'Command and the Laws of Armed Conflict' (1993) Strategic Combat Studies Institute *Occasional Paper No. 4* at 7–8. See discussion of this issue in Gardam, supra n. 346 at 162–7.

349 The examples of the US's use of force in Grenada and Panama are relevant. In the case of Panama, the US's invasion (*Operation Just Cause*) in December 1989 was specifically directed at, and resulted in, the overthrow of the *de facto* military leader, General Noriega. The justifications for his overthrow included his connections with drug trafficking. In the case of Grenada, the US's invasion (*Operation Urgent Fury*) on 25 October 1983 resulted in the overthrow of the Soviet-backed regime led by Bernard Coard and the installation of what the US described as a 'popular native government': Cole, R., *Operation Urgent Fury*, Office of the Chairman of the Joint Chiefs of Staff, 1997: <http://www.dtic.mil/doctrine/jel/history/urgfury.pdf> at 17 June 2008.

350 The limited use of force by states such as Israel and the US against targets in foreign states, in response to acts of terrorism, was largely condemned in the 1950s, 1960s

and the UK limited themselves to al Qaeda targets, then they *may* have satisfied the requirement of proportionality. They could have argued that their use of force was analogous with previous instances where limited missile strikes in response to terrorist attacks have attracted little or no condemnation from the international community.[351] Regime change was a step too far.

It is submitted that neither the US nor the UK adequately established the legal basis for removing the Taliban regime.[352] If the US–UK use of force was allowed to stand as a proportionate response, it would be difficult to deny that many other governments should not also be overthrown on the basis that they 'support' or 'harbour' suspected terrorists, or that they do not comply with US ultimatums to turn over suspected terrorists.[353] To allow the principle of proportionality to be stretched to such an extent that it condones the overthrow of regimes by individual states would completely undermine the principle's ability to limit the resort to force. It would also create a dangerous and unruly precedent.[354]

Immediacy

The third element of the right of self-defence requires that there must not be an undue 'time-lag' between the armed attack and the exercise of self-defence.[355] Discussion of this element is academic here since it is posited that even if there

---

and 1970s, but a change was evident in the 1980s and 1990s whereby states were much less inclined to condemn military strikes in those contexts, if they were limited in scope, carefully targeted and framed in the language of self-defence. However, neither Israel nor the US claimed that the terrorist threats they were facing entitled them to overthrow the governments of, *inter alia*, Jordan, Lebanon, Tunisia, Libya or Iraq. Furthermore, the US's involvement in Grenada and Panama to effect leadership change was widely condemned, suggesting that the majority of states do not consider this to be a legitimate objective when exercising the right of self-defence.

351 For instance, the US missile strikes on the Iraqi Intelligence Service in 1993 attracted no formal condemnation; the missile strikes against Sudan and Afghanistan in 1998 were met with some condemnation but no formal censure by the Security Council. These examples could possibly have served the US and the UK with evidence that the *opino juris* of states allowed limited, targeted missile strikes.

352 Gardam also concludes that 'to target the military forces of the State and overthrow the government in such circumstances seems unlikely to constitute a proportionate response': supra n. 346 at 183.

353 Israel or the US could argue that the government of Lebanon should be overthrown because it is either supporting or harbouring the leaders of Hizb-Allah, including Hassan Nasrallah; or that the government of the Syrian Arab Republic be overthrown because it either supports or harbours members of Hamas such as the exiled political leader, Khaled Meshaal. The ramifications for allowing the Afghanistan scenario to stand as an example of a 'proportionate' exercise of self-defence are considerable: see discussion in Chapter 7.

354 See Chapter 7 at 258–260 regarding the use of force against Lebanon in 2006.

355 Dinstein uses the term 'time-lag'; supra n. 170 at 184. Other scholars refer to the need for a 'temporal link': Gardam, supra n. 346 at 152.

was an 'armed attack' (and it has already been argued that there was not), the use of force would have been unlawful on other grounds because the requirements of necessity and proportionality were not met. The question at issue here would be whether or not there was an undue 'time-lag' between 11 September and 7 October 2001, or whether the employment of force in self-defence was 'instant, overwhelming, leaving ... *no moment for deliberation*'?[356] Stressing that there must not be a significant delay, Cassese has observed that traditional or 'classic' self-defence must be an immediate reaction to aggression; if the victim state allows time to elapse, self-defence must be replaced by action under the authority of the Security Council.[357]

Article 51 preserves the right of states to use force and act in their own self-defence if they are attacked, until the Security Council can take over and implement measures to restore or maintain international peace and security. To allow a state to delay its response for three weeks is perhaps in itself an acknowledgement that there is no instant, overwhelming need to respond with unilateral force. In the case of Afghanistan, there was more than a moment for deliberation; there were in fact 26 days and, within that time, there was adequate opportunity for the US and the UK to seek other solutions to achieve their objectives, such as seeking Security Council authorisation for a UN-sanctioned multilateral response to the threat (which the Security Council had already identified) to international peace and security.[358]

It is not entirely clear what sort of timeframe would enable a state to satisfy the principle of 'immediacy' without breaching the principle of 'necessity'. Dinstein has observed that 'a war of self-defence does not have to commence within a few minutes, or even a few days, from the original armed attack'.[359] He notes that a state under attack 'cannot be expected to shift gear from peace to war instantaneously'. The argument being explored here is whether the 26-day delay meant that force was not used 'immediately'. 'Immediacy' is a relative concept; it must surely be measured in terms of the context of the situation. A justifiable delay could be caused by prolonged attempts at amicable negotiations or due to the fact that the sheer distance involved requires 'lengthy preparations before the

---

356 'States are traditionally allowed a leeway of time in which to initiate their defensive action': Gardam, supra n. 346 at 150; '... [M]oving forward to a war of self-defence is a time-consuming process, especially in a democracy where the wheels of government move slowly': Dinstein, supra n. 170 at 212.

357 Cassese, A., 'Terrorism is Also Disrupting Some Crucial Legal Categories of International Law' (2001) 12 (5) *EJIL* 993 at 997–8.

358 S/Res/1368 (2001) and S/Res/1373 (2001): in both resolutions the Security Council recognised that this act of terrorism, like all acts of international terrorism, constituted a threat to international peace and security.

359 Dinstein, Y., *War, Aggression and Self-Defence*, 4th edn (Cambridge; New York: Cambridge University Press, 2005) 242.

military machinery can function smoothly'.[360] The Falkland Islands War of 1982 is an instance of the latter and the 1990 Gulf War is an example of the former.[361]

In the past, the international community has settled on 'cooling-off' periods of three years[362] and, in other instances, of three months.[363] One might argue that 26 days was really a very short period when compared to other instances in which force has been used. For instance, in relation to Kosovo, the timeframe before force was employed was measured in months, rather than days. On 31 March 1998, the Security Council, acting under Chapter VII of the UN Charter, passed a resolution effectively threatening the Federal Republic of Yugoslavia with collective measures if it continued to repress its Kosovar minority.[364] On 23 September 1998, another resolution was adopted, threatening military action against the Serbs unless they negotiated, a measure that was successful to some extent when it resulted in peace talks.[365] One might argue that such a precedent tends to show that negotiations may occur over many months, thus, using force within a mere 26 days would probably satisfy the element of 'immediacy'.

Perhaps a more relevant situation would be the use of force by the US in 1998 against Sudan and Afghanistan. On 7 August 1998, the US embassies in Nairobi, Kenya and Dar-es-Salaam, Tanzania were attacked. On 21 August 1998, the US responded with missile attacks against targets in Sudan and Afghanistan.[366] The use of force by the US was not condemned by the Security Council, and a number of states seemed to accept or at least understand the US's actions, even if they did not specifically endorse them on the pleaded grounds of 'self-defence'.[367] Perhaps it could be argued that the 'delay' there, of 14 days, which seemed largely acceptable to the international community, is roughly equivalent to the delay in the case of Afghanistan. If the use of force in 1998 was indeed a legitimate use of force in self-defence (and it is arguable as to whether it was), then it would seem plausible that the use of force in October 2001, after a delay of 26 days, would possibly have satisfied the requirement of 'immediacy'.

360 Ibid., 243.

361 Ibid. With regards to the Falklands, Argentina argued that its use of force was justified on the basis that Great Britain had illegally seized the Falkland Islands in the 1830s and that it had, since that time, been in wrongful possession of Argentinean territory. For background to the dispute, see Shaw, M., *International Law*, 5th edn (New York: Cambridge University Press, 2003) 452–3. Argentina 'invaded' the Falkland Islands on 2 April 1982. The British response to this act of aggression was swift: by 5 April 1982 there were a number of aircraft carriers, frigates, destroyers, tankers and supply ships steaming towards South America: Gibran, D., *The Falklands War – Britain Versus the Past in the South Atlantic* (New York: McFarland and Company, 1998) 73–5.

362 The Peace of Westphalia.

363 The Covenant of the League of Nations.

364 S/Res/1160, adopted on 31 March 1998.

365 S/Res/1199, adopted on 23 September 1998.

366 See discussion of this incident in Chapter 5 at 139–142.

367 Ibid.

The proposition that has been argued in the foregoing paragraphs is that even if there had been an 'armed attack' against the US on 11 September 2001, the use of force against Afghanistan most likely did not meet the requirement of necessity and almost certainly did not meet the requirement of proportionality; however, arguments exist which may support a finding that the requirement of immediacy could have been satisfied. This is a purely academic point, however, given the finding in the early part of this chapter regarding the preliminary question of whether an 'armed attack' had occurred.

When Did the Right to Use Force in Self-defence Expire?

If there was an armed attack,[368] and if it was adequately attributed to al Qaeda and the Taliban,[369] and if the elements of necessity, proportionality and immediacy were met,[370] one remaining question to be asked would be whether the right had 'expired' by the time that force was ultimately employed on 7 October 2001. Article 51 states that nothing in the Charter shall impair the inherent right of self-defence if an armed attack occurs, *until* the Security Council has taken measures necessary to maintain international peace and security.[371]

When the Security Council adopted Resolution 1373 on 28 September 2001, it was 'taking measures to maintain international peace and security'.[372] It stated that it was acting under Chapter VII of the Charter when it decided that *all states* should implement a list of 11 measures[373] and when it called upon states to implement a further seven measures.[374] In that resolution, the Security Council established provisions which obliged all states to, *inter alia*, criminalise assistance for terrorist activities, deny financial support and safe haven to terrorists and share information about groups planning terrorist attacks.

In themselves, those were measures taken to maintain international peace and security. Since the Security Council had taken control of the response, and had decided on a range of measures, some of which were mandatory, it is contended that the right to exercise individual self-defence thereby expired. If the US and the UK still retained a right to use force on 7 October subsequent to that resolution's adoption on 28 September, that would logically imply that Resolution 1373 (2001) did *not* contain measures to maintain international peace and security.[375]

---

368 See discussion above at 189ff.

369 See discussion above at 202ff.

370 See discussion above at 206ff.

371 Article 51 of the Charter of the United Nations.

372 See text of S/Res/1373.

373 S/Res/1373 (2001), para 1(a)–(d) and 2(a)–(g).

374 Ibid., paras 3(a)–(g).

375 The corollary is that if S/Res/1373 did *not* contain measures to maintain international peace and security, what was the purpose of those measures and why did the

In Resolution 1373 (2001), the Security Council indicated that it was ready and willing to consider options, which conceivably could have included the authorisation of force. The final two paragraphs hint at future Security Council involvement and demonstrate that it intended to retain control of the response.[376] Paragraph 8 indicates that the Council was willing to 'take all necessary steps' which could be seen as a veiled reference that it was not yet ready to authorise 'all necessary means', as it had done in relation to Iraq.[377] Nevertheless, it could have authorised the use of force if that had been necessary to implement the anti-terrorism measures in the resolution (including the measure which required states to deny safe haven to those who finance, plan, support or commit terrorist acts).[378] From 28 September 2001, the onus was on the US and the UK to seek the Security Council's authorisation to use force, an authorisation that it may well have granted had the case been made that force was necessary to implement Resolution 1373. One last aspect of the duration of the right of self-defence should be addressed. It was noted in Chapter 5 that once a self-defence action has begun, there is debate over when it should end, and especially as to whether it is for the individual state that is exercising the right, or the Security Council, to make that determination. Conte has argued that the right to exercise self-defence continues only 'for as long as the exercise of self-help is *necessary* to prevent further attacks against the victim State' (his emphasis).[379] He concludes that since the Taliban is no longer in power, it is 'highly questionable whether Afghanistan remains ... a base of al-Qaida operations' and therefore:[380] '[I]t is difficult to see how the continued international conflict in Afghanistan could be necessary to avert threats against the US and, thus, how it could be lawful.' That conclusion is based on the premise

Security Council expressly state that in adopting them it was acting under Chapter VII of the Charter?

376 S/Res/1373 (2001) paras 8 and 9.

377 S/Res/678 (1990), adopted on 20 November 1990, authorised Member States to 'use all necessary means' to uphold and implement Resolution 660 (1990) (which called for Iraq to withdraw from Kuwait) and all subsequent resolutions and to restore international peace and security in the area.

378 S/Res/1373 (2001), para 2(c). Paragraph 2(a)–(d) all contained provisions that might have applied to the State of Afghanistan. The argument could have been made that Afghanistan was not complying with those measures, therefore, the Security Council would have to authorise states to use 'all necessary means' to ensure their implementation. The parallels with the resolutions in 1990 and 1991 pertaining to Iraq are interesting. In Resolution 661 (1990), adopted in August 1990, the Security Council recognised the inherent right of self-defence under Article 51 and referred to the invasion as an armed attack. In a later resolution, 678 (1990), adopted in November, it then authorised the use of all necessary means to enforce the earlier resolutions. There was a clear precedent for states to go back to the Council to seek authorisation, *even* when the right of self-defence had been earlier acknowledged by the Council.

379 Conte, supra n. 231 at 65.

380 Ibid.

that the use of force was initially lawful, but at some point, after the apparent 'defeat' of the Taliban, it became unlawful. The premise that the use of force was *initially* lawful is in turn based on the presumption that self-defence aims to *prevent further attacks* against the victim state.[381] However, the widely accepted purpose of self-defence is *not* to prevent future attacks but to *repulse an existing attack*.[382] Once the scope of self-defence is extended, beyond halting or repulsing attacks to preventing future attacks, the entire nature of the right is altered. A self-defence action then becomes a potential pretext for a long-term occupation, on the basis that the threat of future attacks still exists.[383]

The more compelling interpretation is that the right to self-defence is limited to a response that repels or halts an existing attack, or prevents an imminent attack. In the case of Afghanistan, the use of force was unlawful from its inception because if there was an 'armed attack', the attack had ended 26 days before self-defence action was taken.[384] From the point at which the attack ended on 11 September, or at least from the point when the Security Council adopted Resolution 1373 on 28 September, the authorisation of the Security Council was thereafter required to legitimise any use of force against Afghanistan.

Pre-emptive Self-defence

In the previous two chapters, the concept of anticipatory or pre-emptive self-defence has been discussed.[385] In Chapter 5 it was concluded that under existing international law, anticipatory self-defence is not permissible, or at least not until

---

381 Ibid.: 'Put simply, self-defence is an exercise of military self-help in response to an armed attack in order to prevent further attacks against the victim State.'

382 See the Dissenting Opinion of Judge Higgins in the *Legality of the Threat or Use of Nuclear Weapons* case, supra n. 306 at 583–4; Judge Ago: 'the action needed to halt and repulse the attack ...', in Judge Ago's Eighth Report on State Responsibility to the International Law Commission, supra n. 309 at 245.

383 If Conte's interpretation of self-defence is correct, the US would be within its rights to argue that elements of the Taliban and/or elements of al Qaeda still remain active in Afghanistan, and until they are entirely removed, the threat of future attacks still exists. Media reports suggest that the leadership of al Qaeda remains in Afghanistan: see Syed Saleem Shazad, 'Inside the Anti-US Resistance', *Asia Times*, 11 July 2006, available at: <http://www.e-ariana.com/ariana/eariana.nsf/be77f8366cbd693387256b790077e1df/5964ed693d7b0534872571a8002a0590?OpenDocument> at 17 June 2008. That presence would then provide the US with the justification to keep its troops in Afghanistan, virtually indefinitely, on the basis that it is acting in self-defence to prevent further attacks.

384 Alternatively, the right to self-defence ended on 28 September 2001 when the Security Council adopted Resolution 1373 (2001), as argued above, since that was a demonstration of the Council taking measures to maintain international peace and security.

385 See Chapter 4 at 88–92 and Chapter 5 at 117–124.

the attack is 'imminent' in the *Caroline* sense.[386] Pre-emptive self-defence is relevant to the present inquiry by virtue of the justifications put forth in the US and UK's letters to the Security Council.[387] The US's intention to use force in pre-emptive self-defence was quite clear. The Authorization for the Use of Military Force resolution adopted by the US Congress on 14 September indicated the Congress' willingness to permit force to be used against 'nations, organizations or persons ... [to] ... prevent any future acts of international terrorism'.[388]

In its notification to the Security Council, the US stated that it was not only responding to the attacks of 11 September 2001, but it was responding to 'the ongoing threat to the United States and its nationals ...'[389] The US armed forces initiated actions designed to prevent and deter further attacks on the US. The US also indicated that in the future, force might be employed against other states: 'we may find that our self-defence requires further actions with respect to other organizations and other States.'[390]

The UK's letter to the Security Council was different in the sense that it did not justify the use of force as a direct response to the events of 11 September 2001 *per se*; instead, it stated that forces were deployed 'to avert the continuing threat of attacks from the same source'.[391] The UK made statements in other forums indicating that one of the key objectives of *Operation Enduring Freedom* was to effect a change in leadership in Afghanistan, 'to ensure that Afghanistan's links to international terrorism are broken', which underlines the anticipatory purpose behind the UK's decision to use force.[392]

One obvious problem with the above statements is that they assume that the right of self-defence permits force to be used in anticipation of future attacks, even though there is no apparent knowledge of when those attacks are likely to occur, where they are going to be launched from or what form they are likely to take. The US and the UK thereby indicated their intentions to use force in self-defence to prevent non-imminent future attacks from unspecified sources. It is submitted that this is a departure from the accepted, restrictive, interpretation of Article 51, which

---

386 See Chapter 5.

387 See Appendices 1 and 2, respectively, for the US and UK letters to the Security Council.

388 Supra at n. 28 and accompanying text.

389 S/2001/946: Letter dated 7 October 2001 from the Permanent Representative of the US to the UN, to the President of the Security Council, as reproduced in Appendix 1.

390 Ibid. The same types of statements were made by President Bush in addresses to the nation and to Congress, such as the address on 20 September 2001 when he stated that, 'Our war on terror begins with Al Qaeda, but it does not end there. It will not end until every terrorist group of global reach has been found, stopped and defeated': President Bush, Address to a Joint Session of Congress and the American People, 20 September 2001, supra n. 34.

391 S/2001/947: Letter dated 7 October 2001 from the representative of UK to the President of the Security Council, reproduced in Appendix 2.

392 Hoon, G., 'Operation Veritas' Speech to the House of Commons, London, 1 November 2001.

literally states that force is permitted in self-defence *if* an armed attack occurs. The US and the UK ostensibly tried to extend the timeframe within which self-defence can be exercised, so that they would be entitled to use force indefinitely to prevent future attacks. This interpretation of Article 51 should not be accepted and the evidence shows that states have, historically, not accepted it.[393]

The only compelling conclusion is that Article 51 confines states to exercising the right of self-defence *only* in response to an armed attack. If an armed attack is not yet on the horizon, a concerned state cannot launch an aggressive war in order to prevent future attacks before they are planned. However, a state which feels that future attacks may be launched against it does not have to stand idly by and wait for them, as Dinstein has noted:[394]

> [W]hen a country feels menaced by the threat of an armed attack, all that it is free to do – in keeping with the Charter – is make the necessary military preparations for repulsing the hostile action should it materialize, as well as bring the matter forthwith to the attention of the Security Council (hoping that the latter will take collective security measures in the face of a threat to the peace) ... *Regardless of the shortcomings of the system, the option of a pre-emptive use of force is excluded by Article 51.* (Emphasis added)

The pre-emptive doctrine advanced by the US and the UK in their respective letters to the Security Council (and confirmed in the US's 2002 NSS),[395] are plainly inconsistent with the letter and spirit of Article 51.[396] The interpretation of self-defence adopted by the US and the UK has only attracted support from a few other states, such as Israel[397] and Australia.[398]

The conclusion reached here is that neither international law nor state practice allows force to be used in pre-emptive self-defence, unless the threat is imminent and there is no choice of means and no moment for deliberation. The US and the UK purported to exercise a right of pre-emptive self-defence in the case of Afghanistan and, as such, the legality of that use of force is questionable. It is often

393 For instance, the use of force by Israel on the Osirak reactor in Iraq in 1981 stands out as an example of where the Security Council unanimously rejected the right of pre-emptive self-defence.

394 Dinstein, supra n. 170 at 167. Gardam also notes that '... to date, the fiction is generally maintained in practice that a right of anticipatory self-defence is not available to States': supra n. 346 at 147.

395 See Chapter 5.

396 See discussion of the 2002 National Security Strategy in Chapter 5.

397 As demonstrated by its long-standing conflict with its neighbours and particularly in relation to the attack on the Osirak reactor in 1981: see discussion in Chapter 5. Israel has also been making threats against Iran recently regarding Israel's intention to use force against Iran if the latter continues to develop its uranium enrichment programme.

398 See Chapter 5 regarding Australia's support 'in principle' for the doctrine of pre-emptive self-defence.

stated that 'hard cases make bad law'. In this case, the sympathy that quite rightly existed for the US allowed it and the UK to use force, and allowed them do so whilst advancing a wide-ranging doctrine of pre-emptive self-defence. If all states were permitted to act upon the doctrine espoused in the wake of 11 September, and employ force in 'self-defence' whenever they identify a source of future attacks, the list of potential targets could be endless. One could imagine that force might be employed against any of the states which possess nuclear weapons (and those states which have the potential to manufacture or acquire them in the future); against any state that has alleged 'terrorists' within its borders;[399] and against any state which could be assessed as constituting an 'ongoing threat' to any other state. Ultimately, the limitations on the use of force in self-defence would be undermined to such an extent that they would be rendered virtually meaningless.

Other Possible Justifications for the Use of Force Against Afghanistan

The above analysis has addressed whether or not the US and the UK were able to justify their use of force on the grounds of self-defence. That has been the focus of this chapter because that was the justification relied upon when the US and the UK notified their use of force to the Security Council. However, to round out the analysis, a brief reference is also made to three other possible grounds which the US and the UK might have expressly relied upon: humanitarian intervention, Security Council authorisation and intervention by invitation.

Humanitarian Intervention

Most scholars who discuss the legitimacy of the use of force against Afghanistan do not discuss the issue of humanitarian intervention.[400] That is understandable given that, in their respective notifications to the Security Council, the US and the UK justified the use of force squarely on the grounds of self-defence.[401]

---

399 On 20 September 2001, President Bush alleged that al Qaeda is linked to many organisations such as the Egyptian Islamic Jihad and the Islamic Movement of Uzbekistan. He also claimed that 'there are thousands of these terrorists in more than 60 countries': President Bush, Address to a Joint Session of Congress and the American People, supra n. 34. All of those states could potentially be the target of a US military intervention, if the Afghanistan precedent is followed.

400 For instance, Conte, supra n. 231 at 6: 'Humanitarian intervention is not considered, however, since it is beyond the scope of the relied upon or even arguable grounds of intervention in Afghanistan and Iraq.'

401 Conversely, the literature on humanitarian intervention seldom deals long on the use of force against Afghanistan: see Chesterman, S., 'Humanitarian Intervention and Afghanistan', in Welsh, J., *Humanitarian Intervention and International Relations* (Oxford: Oxford University Press, 2004) at 163: '... the military action was presented – and broadly

However, shortly after the terrorist attacks, there were frequent references by both President Bush and Prime Minister Blair to the Taliban's human rights record and to the humanitarian situation in Afghanistan. In his Address to a Joint Session of Congress and the American People, President Bush stated the case against al Qaeda and the Taliban. Between explaining that al Qaeda was responsible for the attacks of 9/11 and immediately prior to issuing an ultimatum to the Taliban, President Bush said this:[402]

> Afghanistan's people have been brutalized – many are starving and many have fled. Women are not allowed to attend school. You can be jailed for owning a television. Religion can be practiced only as their leaders dictate. A man can be jailed in Afghanistan if his beard is not long enough.
>
> The United States respects the people of Afghanistan – after all, we are currently its largest source of humanitarian aid – but we condemn the Taliban regime. (Applause) It is not only repressing its own people, it is threatening people everywhere by sponsoring and sheltering and supplying terrorists. By aiding and abetting murder, the Taliban regime is committing murder.
>
> And tonight, the United States of America makes the following demands on the Taliban …

The placement of the assertions regarding human rights and the humanitarian situation is significant when viewed in the context of the entire statement: the above extract is a crucial passage which links the paragraphs regarding al Qaeda to the ultimatum issued to the Taliban.[403] In its letter to the Security Council, the US stated that it would provide the people of Afghanistan with 'food, medicine and supplies'.[404] Similar statements were made by the British Prime Minister, who said that the operation in Afghanistan consisted of three parts, one of which was humanitarian.[405] Prime Minister Blair said that the UK was 'assembling a coalition of support for refugees in and outside Afghanistan'.[406] After 11 September 2001, there was a great deal of attention, in both the US and the UK, regarding the

---

accepted – as an exercise of the right of self-defence. Such an intervention seems ill-suited to discussion in a volume on humanitarian intervention.'

402 President Bush, Address to a Joint Session of Congress and the American People, supra n. 34.

403 Ibid.

404 Letter dated 7 October 2001 from the Permanent Representative of the US to the UN, Addressed to the President of the Security Council, UN Doc S/2001/946, reproduced in Appendix 1.

405 The other two parts being 'military' and 'diplomatic'.

406 Statement by Prime Minister Tony Blair, 10 Downing Street, 7 October 2001, cited in House of Commons Library, Research Paper 01/81, supra n. 335.

Taliban's human rights record, particularly focusing on women's dress codes, the lack of religious freedoms and the restrictions on educational opportunities for girls and women. A plethora of media articles about these issues sprung up simultaneously.[407]

For the international lawyer searching for the justifications for the use of force against Afghanistan, references to the Taliban's human rights record are irrelevant in one sense – since anything except the most serious human rights infringements arguably provides no basis for military intervention[408] – but relevant in another, as these references suggest that the Bush Administration and the Blair government needed an extra ground upon which to legitimise (if not exactly legalise) their use of force against Afghanistan, especially the objective of regime change. The frequent and overt references to humanitarian concerns were most likely not accidental: they may also have been an attempt to 'win the hearts and minds of the Afghans themselves, as well as to hold together an increasingly shaky international coalition'.[409]

Whether or not international law permits a right of unilateral humanitarian intervention is a moot point. There is now a voluminous body of literature in this area which addresses the fraught issue of whether or not a right exists for states – individually or collectively – to intervene in the internal affairs of other states, on humanitarian grounds.[410] It is beyond the scope of this work to determine whether

407 See, for example, US Statement of Defense, Craner, L., 'Human Rights and the Taliban', 6 November 2001: <http://www.state.gov/g/drl/rls/rm/2001/6339.htm> at 17 June 2008. Newspapers and magazines, such as *Time*, were very concerned about the plight of women, children and non-bearded men in Afghanistan under the Taliban.

408 One could argue that human rights violations do provide a basis for intervention based on the Kosovo precedent, but the human rights abuses that Bush referred to in his address were not akin to the nature or scale of those in Kosovo. It was argued that NATO had used military force in 1999 'to prevent an overwhelming humanitarian catastrophe': UN Doc, S/PV.3988 (1999) 12.

409 Chesterman, supra n. 401 at 163–75.

410 For instance, see Rodley, N. (ed.), *To Loose the Bands of Wickedness – International Intervention in Defence of Human Rights* (London: Macmillan Publishing, 1992); Scheffer, D., 'Toward a Modern Doctrine of Humanitarian Intervention' (1992) 23 *University of Toledo Law Review* 253; Heiberg, M., *Subduing Sovereignty – Sovereignty and the Right to Intervene* (London: Pinter Publishers, 1994); Téson, F., *Humanitarian Intervention: An Inquiry into Law and Morality*, 2nd edn (New York: Transnational Publishers, 1997); Abiew, F., *The Evolution of the Doctrine and Practice of Humanitarian Intervention* (The Hague: Kluwer Law International, 1999); Glennon, supra n. 345; Lepard, B., *Rethinking Humanitarian Intervention – A Fresh Legal Approach Based on Fundamental Ethical Principles in International Law and World Religions* (Pennsylvania: Pennsylvania State University Press, 2002); Zolo, D., Poole, F. and Poole, G. (trans.), *Invoking Humanity – War, Law and Global Order* (London; New York: Continuum, 2002); Wheeler, N., *Saving Strangers – Humanitarian Intervention in International Society* (Oxford: Oxford University Press, 2002); Holzgrefe, J. and Keohane, R. (eds), *Humanitarian Intervention – Ethical, Legal, and Political Dilemmas* (Cambridge: Cambridge University Press, 2003);

a right of humanitarian intervention currently exists under international law; even some of the texts which are entirely devoted to this issue do not seek to resolve the debate.[411] It can at least be said that the UK explicitly claimed the existence of such a right when justifying its actions in northern Iraq in 1991 and Kosovo in 1999.[412] However, neither the US nor the UK made such an explicit claim in 2001, perhaps because there was an anxiety about creating a precedent, perhaps because invoking humanitarian intervention would have limited the US's ability to use force, or perhaps because it was simply implausible.[413]

Although humanitarian intervention was not put forward as a justification *per se*, it was nevertheless referred to repeatedly by both administrations. It is the view of this author that this was neither accidental nor incidental.[414] The foregoing analysis has shown that although the US and UK might arguably have had legal grounds to launch limited strikes against al Qaeda targets,[415] their targeting of the Taliban was 'highly problematic'.[416] It was far more difficult to attribute responsibility for 9/11 to the Islamic State of Afghanistan than al Qaeda. The frequent references to the Taliban regime's human rights record, and the humanitarian situation in Afghanistan, could be interpreted as an attempt to legitimise the inclusion of the regime's removal as an objective of the US–UK military operations.[417] This proposition is supported by the fact that in key addresses by both President

---

Orford, A., *Reading Humanitarian Intervention – Human Rights and the Use of Force in International Law* (Cambridge: Cambridge University Press, 2003); Jokic, A. (ed.), *Humanitarian Intervention – Moral and Philosophical Issues* (New York: Broadview Press, 2003); Welsh, J. (ed.), *Humanitarian Intervention and International Relations* (Oxford: Oxford University Press, 2004); Breau, S., *Humanitarian Intervention: The United Nations and Collective Responsibility* (London: Cameron May, 2005); Nardin, T. and Williams, M. (eds), *Humanitarian Intervention* (New York; London: New York University Press, 2006).

411 Rodley, ibid., at 14.

412 Aust, A., Legal Counsellor, Foreign and Commonwealth Office, statement before the House of Commons Foreign Affairs Committee, 2 December 1992, *Parliamentary Papers* 1992–1993, House of Commons, Paper 235-iii, 85, reproduced in (1992) 63 *BYIL* 827; see also Greenstock, J., UK Permanent Representative to the United Nations, statement to the Security Council on 24 March 1999, UN Doc S/PV.3988 (1999).

413 Byers, supra n. 202 at 405: '[T]he apparent incongruity of invoking a humanitarian argument in response to terrorist acts probably precluded this justification from the outset.' See also Chesterman, supra n. 401.

414 Chesterman argues that the invocation of humanitarian concerns 'were, at best, coincidental to other motives'. He writes: 'The attribution of humanitarian objectives begs the question of why nothing had been done for the Afghan population *before* 11 September 2001': Chesterman, supra n. 401 at 163.

415 Possibly based on the *opinio juris* of states as demonstrated by, *inter alia*, the international reaction to the US bombing of Libya in 1986, the bombing of Baghdad in 1993 and Sudan and Afghanistan in 1998.

416 Paust, supra n. 252.

417 The frequent references to the opium trade was another example of how both administrations attempted to bolster their case against the Taliban, by linking the latter to

Bush and Prime Minister Blair, they repeatedly referred to human rights under the Taliban and the humanitarian situation in Afghanistan when outlining their intentions to use force in self-defence.[418] Their respective legal advisors would have been aware that such issues are entirely irrelevant if a state has been the subject of an 'armed attack'.[419]

Security Council Authorisation

The US did not argue that it was justified in using force on the basis of explicit Security Council authorisation, but at least one commentator has suggested that it *could* have done so.[420] Byers argues that in Resolution 1373, when the Security Council decided that all states 'shall ... *take the necessary steps* to prevent the commission of terrorist acts ...', that could have been interpreted as authorising the use of force. Byers concedes that the language used in Resolution 1373 differed from previous authorisation clauses (such as 'all necessary means'), but he maintains that it '*could* have provide[d] the US with an at-least-tenable argument ... that force is necessary to "prevent the commission of terrorist acts"'.[421]

The fact that the US did not rely on this phrase, buried in the midst of a list of anti-terrorism measures, was due to the realisation that other states, such as

---

criminal activity. This was somewhat disingenuous, given that the Taliban had acted to ban the opium trade.

418 President Bush, Address to a Joint Session of Congress and the American People, supra n. 34; see also 10 Downing Street, Prime Minister's Statement to Parliament on the September 11 attacks, 4 October 2001: <http://www.numberten.gov.uk/output/Page1606.asp> at 17 June 2008; Prime Minister's Statement at 10 Downing Street, 25 November 2001 <http://www.primeminister.gov.uk/output/Page1604.asp> at 17 June 2008; see also Prime Minister's Statement on Action in Afghanistan, 7 October 2001: <http://www.primeminister.gov.uk/output/Page1615.asp> at 17 June 2008. In a clear statement of the connection being made, Prime Minister Blair said on 13 November 2001: 'The Taliban regime are not yet fully dislodged from oppressing the people of Afghanistan and shielding Al- Qu'eda [sic]': see Transcript of the Prime Minister's Statement on Afghanistan, 13 November 2001: <http://www.primeminister.gov.uk/output/Page1664.asp> at 17 June 2008.

419 Even Cherie Blair, the wife of the former British Prime Minister, has focused on the so-called humanitarian objectives of the use of force against Afghanistan. In a recent interview on New Zealand's National Radio, she was commenting on her surprise that her husband would end up being a Prime Minister who took troops, *inter alia*, 'into, of course, Afghanistan, where the Taliban regime, which had been so brutal to women in particular, was overturned ...': interview by Kim Hill, available at: <http://www.radionz.co.nz/national/programmes/saturday> at 16 June 2008. The point emphasised here is that nearly seven years after the US–UK invasion of Afghanistan, which was supposed to be an intervention based upon the ground of self-defence, many people still seem to harbour an apparent misconception over the reasons for the intervention.

420 Byers, supra n. 202 at 401–3.

421 Ibid.

China and Russia, might also rely upon it in the future.[422] To those examples, one could also add states such as Israel against Lebanon, Ethiopia (potentially against Somalia or Eritrea), Turkey (potentially against the Kurdish forces in Iraq), Iran (potentially against the Kurdish forces in Iraq and Iran), India or Pakistan (potentially against nationals from the other), Japan (potentially against missile bases in North Korea)[423] or almost any other state facing what it might deem 'terrorist acts'. The US did not rely on that phrase in Resolution 1373, most likely because it was simply not an authorisation to use force, but also because to have relied upon it would have amounted to a ceding of authority to the Security Council. The US chose to rely on its interpretation of its own inherent right of self-defence and therefore had no need to argue that it was authorised to use force by the Security Council. If it had attempted to rely on the phrase 'take all necessary steps', it would most likely have failed since other authorisations of force have historically used much stronger terminology.[424]

Intervention by Invitation

The third and final possibility could have been based on an invitation to intervene from the Northern Alliance.[425] The US could perhaps have argued that the Taliban was not the legitimate government of Afghanistan; that it was a rebel group that was only recognised by three other states; and that the legitimate representative of Afghanistan was the Northern Alliance. The seat at the UN was held, throughout the Taliban's reign, by a member of the Northern Alliance. It was by no means clear as to which faction was the most appropriate one to represent Afghanistan in the UN General Assembly.[426] Intervention by invitation was never seriously advanced by the US and the UK, probably because the 'intervention by invitation' and self-defence arguments were mutually exclusive justifications for resorting to

---

422 Ibid.

423 Feffer, J., 'The Axis of Intervention', *Foreign Policy in Focus*, 27 July 2006: <http://www.fpif.org/fpiftxt/3389> at 17 June 2008.

424 Compare with the Security Council's resolution which authorised force against Iraq in 1990: the phrase 'all necessary means' was used and it was placed in a prominent position within the resolution: see S/Res/678 (1990).

425 See Article 20 of the ILC's Draft Articles: 'Valid consent by a state to the commission of a given act by another state precludes the wrongfulness of that act in relation to the former state to the extent that the act remains within the limits of that consent.'

426 In 1997, two sets of credentials were presented: one from Burhan-u-ddin Rabbani and the other from Alhaj Mullah Mohammed Rabbani. The Credentials Committee decided to defer a decision on the understanding that the current representative would continue in the meantime: see *Credentials of Representatives to the Fifty-Second Session of the General Assembly*, 'Report of the Credentials Committee', 11 December 1999, UN Doc A/52/719: <http://www.un.org/ga/52/credcomm/reporscr.htm> at 17 June 2008.

force.[427] The US opted for self-defence as the most plausible of the two to establish on the facts.

Conclusion

This chapter has traversed all aspects of the US and UK's justifications for using force against Afghanistan in 2001. It has deliberately focused on the official justifications for using force, as set out in their respective notifications to the Security Council on 7 October 2001, but it has also taken into account the 'unofficial' attempts to bolster the case for using force.[428] The evidence suggests that what occurred on 11 September 2001 was an act of terrorism, a criminal act, a terrorist attack, but it was not an 'armed attack'.[429] The proper and legitimate response to that act of terrorism, as with all acts of terrorism, ought to have been based on the law enforcement model and ought to have involved the arrest, extradition and prosecution of suspects. If this act of terrorism was indeed a 'crime against humanity' as was asserted on numerous occasions,[430] it would have attracted universal jurisdiction and any state would have had an obligation to prosecute or extradite suspects.[431] The US's legitimate objective to prevent further attacks from occurring ought to have been achieved not through stretching the concept of self-defence to pre-empt future acts of terrorism, but through the implementation of

---

427 When asserting the right of self-defence, the US had to maintain that the Taliban regime was in power in Afghanistan, in order to attribute the actions of al Qaeda to it and hence be able to target the Taliban and its military installations. The US could not have simultaneously argued that it was invited to intervene at the behest of the Northern Alliance, since that would necessarily have required recognition that the Taliban was not representing the state, creating further problems for attributing responsibility to the Taliban; see also Byers, supra n. 202 at 404.

428 'Unofficial' because the US and the UK did not refer to the human rights/humanitarian intervention aspect in their notifications to the Security Council, yet this ground was repeatedly referred to by both President Bush and Prime Minister Blair in public statements.

429 See statements from EU bodies, statements from the members of the Security Council and statements from Prime Minister Blair referred to above, that 'the murder of British citizens in New York is not different to the murder of British citizens in the heart of Britain itself'.

430 Virtually every member of the Security Council who spoke on 12 September called the terrorist attacks of 11 September an attack not just on the US but on all humanity: supra n. 177 and accompanying text.

431 See Kenny, supra n. 41 at 106, who pointed out that the UN High Commissioner for Human Rights also considered that what occurred on 11 September 2001 amounted to 'crimes against humanity', which meant that 'the individuals responsible would have nowhere to hide if intelligence services identify their whereabouts and if evidence as to their guilt is made available'.

the Security Council's anti-terrorism measures (set out in Resolution 1373 (2001)) as well as through a range of other domestic measures involving immigration, intelligence[432] and domestic security arrangements.[433]

That is not to say that force was a completely inappropriate response to the events of 11 September 2001. Military force may well have had a role to play in maintaining international peace and security. However, it was for the Security Council to make that determination, because it is the Security Council that is charged with determining whether there has been a threat or breach of international peace and security and with recommending measures to counter such a threat. On 12 September 2001 and again on 28 September 2001, the Security Council determined that there *was* a threat to international peace and security, and it showed that it was ready and willing to do what was necessary, not only to respond to the 11 September attacks, but to prevent future attacks.[434] Furthermore, when it passed a raft of anti-terrorism measures on 28 September 2001, it not only showed that it was in control of the response, but it had indeed 'taken measures to maintain international peace and security' which henceforth precluded the US and the UK from using force in self-defence.[435] The evidence cited above, including statements from members of the Security Council and the UN Secretary-General, support the inference that the events of 11 September were widely perceived as acts which required a global response, by all humanity, under the auspices of the UN Security Council.

This chapter has applied the international law pertaining to self-defence, as set out in the previous chapter, to the use of force against Afghanistan. The following conclusions have been reached. First, no 'armed attack' occurred, as that term is understood in Article 51 of the UN Charter. Second, if there was an 'armed attack', it had ended by the evening of 11 September 2001, 26 days before force was employed. However, even if those propositions are rejected, responsibility for the so-called 'armed attacks' was not adequately attributed to the state of Afghanistan, and hence the attacks on the Taliban and the stated objective of regime change were unlawful. Third, even if there had been an armed attack which was adequately attributed to Afghanistan, the reaction from the US and the UK breached the customary law principles of necessity, proportionality and

---

432 Note that the alleged mastermind of 9/11, Khalid Sheikh Mohammad, was arrested in Pakistan due to intelligence from the Emir of Qatar – not due to the use of force against Afghanistan: Suskind, R., *The One Percent Doctrine – Deep Inside America's Pursuit of its Enemies Since 9/11* (New York: Simon & Shuster, 2006).

433 The failures in all these areas were highlighted in *The 9/11 Commission Report*, supra n. 1.

434 Therefore, stretching the concept of self-defence to encompass pre-emptive self-defence was also unnecessary.

435 Article 51 of the UN Charter. The right to self-defence does not continue indefinitely; only until the Security Council takes measures to maintain international peace and security.

possibly immediacy: it was not absolutely *necessary* to use force in self-defence on 7 October 2001 as it was not the last resort open to the US and the UK; it was not *proportionate* in the sense that it included regime change in Afghanistan as one of its key objectives; and the use of force was possibly not *immediate*, there being a 26-day delay between the end of the attack and the use of force in response. Finally, even if there was an armed attack that gave rise to an initial right to use force in self-defence, the right had expired as of 28 September 2001 when the Security Council took measures to restore international peace and security.

If the use of force was *not* a legitimate exercise of self-defence, the only possible conclusion is that it was an unlawful use of force. It is apparent from the evidence presented in this chapter that there was a significant element of revenge and retaliation in the desire by the US to use force against Afghanistan. That was evident from President Bush's first reaction on 11 September 2001 when he stated that 'somebody's going to pay'.[436] It was reiterated in his speeches to the American people and in remarks made at the National Security Council Meeting on 11 September.[437] He spoke of the US response being more than just 'instant retaliation'.[438] He also warned the civilised world against allowing this act to go 'unpunished'.[439] It was also recognised in statements from the Parliamentary Assembly of the Council of Europe and some world leaders, who urged the US to respond in a way that did not merely seek revenge.[440]

Whilst a desire for revenge, punishment and retaliation are understandable, the use of force in self-defence is not supposed to have punitive elements. This is well understood and is regarded as a time-honoured notion.[441] The apparent motivation to punish the perpetrators of the attacks supports the conclusion reached in this chapter, namely that this was not a genuine example of self-defence; it was more akin to an unlawful reprisal. As discussed in Chapter 5, forcible reprisals were prohibited by virtue of Article 2(4) of the Charter. The use of force against Afghanistan bears striking similarities to past examples of forcible reprisals that have been condemned by the international community and/or the Security

436 Supra n. 16.

437 President George W. Bush said the US would '*punish* not just the perpetrators of the attacks, but also those who harboured them', supra n. 24. President Bush also said to an audience in New York: 'I can hear you. (Applause) The rest of the world can hear you. (Applause) And the people who knocked these buildings down will hear all of us soon. (Applause)': supra n. 25.

438 President Bush, Address to a Joint Session of Congress and the American People, supra n. 34.

439 Ibid.

440 For instance, see PACE Resolution 1258 (2001) Article 8, where the Council of Europe warned against using force to exact 'hasty revenge': supra n. 94.

441 See Judge Ago who cautioned against any suggestion that self-defence has a punitive character: see Gardam, supra n. 346 at 157.

Council.[442] The only real difference is that in the present case, the US and the UK not only used missile strikes to respond to an act of terrorism,[443] they also invaded a sovereign state, removed the governing regime and kept a substantial military presence in the country for (at the time of writing) nearly seven years thereafter, with no expectation of any termination of that military presence.[444]

In the aftermath of 11 September, one might assume that everything has changed, that we live in a dramatically different world,[445] that the Rubicon has been crossed.[446] But *has* everything changed? Terrorist acts occurred before 11 September and they have continued to occur since that day. Terrorist acts were called 'a threat to international peace and security' before 11 September and afterwards. In terms of responses, states resorted to force under the guise of 'self-

442 Compare with the use of force by Israel against Syria in 1955; the use of force by the UK against Yemen in 1964; the use of force by the US against North Vietnam in 1964; the use of force by Israel against As-Samu, Karameh, Es-Salt and the Beirut Airport in the 1960s; the use of force by Israel against Lebanon during the 1970s; the raid by Israel on Tunis in 1985; the missile attacks by the US on Libya in 1986; and, to a lesser extent, the use of force by the US against Iraq in 1993, the US missile strikes against Sudan and Afghanistan in 1998 and the US strikes against Iraq in 2001, all of which were discussed in Chapter 5.

443 As in, for instance, the use of missile attacks by Israel on Tunis in 1985 or by the US against Libya in 1986.

444 *Operation Enduring Freedom* (OEF) began on 7 October 2001. OEF is the official name given by the US to its military operation in Afghanistan (although there are other military operations with the same name and a country-specific suffix associated with its broader 'war on terror'). The International Security Assistance Force (ISAF) is the NATO-led security and development mission that was established by the Security Council on 20 December 2001 as per Resolution 1386 (2001). The last handover of power from US-led forces to NATO-led ISAF forces occurred on 5 October 2006. At the time of writing (June 2008) there are approximately 52,913 military and civilian personnel operating under ISAF leadership. Note that overall command of ISAF rotates, but in June 2008 both the outgoing and incoming ISAF commanders, Army General Dan McNeill and Army General David McKiernan respectively, were Americans. OEF continues to operate alongside ISAF. In May 2008, an announcement was made to increase US troop levels by 7,000 to 40,000: see *TimesOnline*, 5 May 2008, 'US "To Send 7,000 Extra Troops to Afghanistan"', available at: <http://www.timesonline.co.uk/tol/news/world/article3871915.ece> at 17 June 2008. An announcement was made approximately six weeks later to increase British troop levels to 8,000 soldiers: see *Aljazeera English*, 'UK Sends More Troops to Afghanistan', available at: <http://english.aljazeera.net/NR/exeres/08DD45B9-627D-4E3D-BA7C-8852697FCA32.htm> at 17 June 2008. After those troop increases take effect, there will be a greater US and UK troop presence in Afghanistan than at any time since the 7 October 2001 invasion began.

445 *United States Army in Afghanistan, Operation Enduring Freedom*, October 2001–March 2002, 'Introduction': 'The terrorist attacks on the World Trade Center and the Pentagon on 11 September 2001 dramatically changed the world in which we live.'

446 Maogoto, supra n. 231 at 115–19; also Lansford, supra n. 107 at 78–80.

defence' before 11 September and they have done so after 11 September. The only real difference, the only 'dramatic change', was the particular target, since the US had not been attacked on its territory before to such effect. The proposition being put forth here is that the 'change' is not so dramatic that it justifies a rewriting of international law to suit the security interests of a handful of states. This chapter, alongside the previous, has demonstrated that there are compelling reasons why self-defence is so tightly constrained in Article 51. Those states which seek to challenge the constraints by simply ignoring them do not change the law, they just violate it.

Chapter 7
Conclusion

This text has sought to demonstrate why the use of military force against Afghanistan, beginning on 7 October 2001, was unlawful. It was unlawful because there are currently only two circumstances in which a state may resort to force: in self-defence (individual or collective), or pursuant to a mandate from the Security Council. This use of force was neither an instance of legitimate self-defence nor was it authorised by the Security Council. As for the latter, although an opportunity certainly existed, neither the US nor the UK sought the Security Council's authorisation to employ force against Afghanistan. Even though the Security Council declared that the acts of terrorism which occurred on 11 September 2001 were a threat to international peace and security, it did not authorise force as a response. As for the former, this was not an instance of legitimate self-defence, despite the fact that both the US and the UK claimed to been acting pursuant to Article 51 of the UN Charter and even though they duly reported their actions to the Security Council.[1]

The justifications for using force against Afghanistan have been examined from several angles. In Chapter 2, the changing nature of conflict was analysed and it was found that, even taking into account acts of terrorism such as the one that occurred on 11 September 2001, the world is not operating in an entirely new security paradigm. What is evident from the analysis in Chapter 2 is that since the UN Charter was written, conflict has changed quantitatively and qualitatively. In the latter half of the twentieth century, the number and severity of inter-state conflicts have declined sharply and the threat which they pose to international security has been superseded by the threats posed by intra-state conflicts. Chapter 2 showed that the asymmetric threats posed by non-state actors have risen throughout the post-1945 period. However, instances of terrorism have tended to decline in the post-Cold War era. Indeed, it was noted that if the 11 September attacks – which were unusual in type and gravity – were taken out of the 2001 statistics, that year would have experienced some of the lowest casualty statistics for terrorism in the post-Cold War era. Chapter 2 showed that the al Qaeda form of terrorism is a new type of terrorism in some ways, since it is characterised by fewer attacks with greater civilian casualties per attack, but the analysis also showed that, whatever the death toll might be from such terrorist attacks, they cannot compare to the large-scale losses of civilian and military lives which were a feature of the large-scale inter-state wars so prevalent prior to 1945, and in comparatively fewer instances post-1945. Thus it may be said that conflict has changed in the latter half of the

1 See their respective letters to the Security Council, reproduced at Appendices 1 and 2.

twentieth century, but now that some time has elapsed since 2001, it is becoming clear that it has not changed so much that the landscape of international peace and security is unrecognisable. What is different is that the trans-national threats posed by non-state actors require trans-national solutions more than ever before. What has become clear is that no single state can secure security for itself, by itself:[2] '[E]nhancing security for one group in the world at the expense of another, or without the others, has always been inherently discriminatory and unfair. Now it is starting to look more like a contradiction in terms.'

The statistics presented in Chapter 2 showed that in the years since the events of 11 September 2001, the US has not been greatly affected by terrorism, relatively speaking. In 2005, according to US statistics, there were approximately 14,500 fatalities worldwide caused by terrorist acts.[3] Of that number, only 56, or 0.4 per cent, were American citizens.[4] That figure was a decrease on the previous year, where Americans made up 1 per cent of casualties. Since 2005, the percentage has fallen further still. The latest two years' worth of data from the US National Counterterrorism Centre (NCTC) suggest that whilst there may be more fatalities worldwide, there are fewer American fatalities. In 2006, there were more than 20,000 fatalities worldwide of which 28, or 0.14 per cent, were Americans.[5] It is noteworthy that those 28 American citizens were mainly killed in Iraq, a conflict that was initiated by the US amidst dubious claims of legitimacy.[6] The statistics for 2007, released in April 2008, mirror the 2006 findings.[7] The NCTC's statistics show that, despite perceptions, the US is one of the *least-affected* states in the world.

In terms of regions, the region that was the worst affected by terrorism in 2005 was the Near East,[8] both in terms of number of attacks and number of fatalities.[9]

---

2 Bailes, A., 'Introduction: Global Security Governance: A World of Change and Challenge', in *SIPRI Yearbook 2005 – Armaments, Disarmament and International Security* (Oxford; New York: Oxford University Press, 2005) at 1.

3 National Counterterrorism Centre (NCTC), 'Report on Incidents of Terrorism 2005', 11 April 2006, Chart 8, 17.

4 Ibid.

5 National Counterterrorism Centre, 'Report on Incidents of Terrorism 2006', 30 April 2007, 9–12; see discussion in Chapter 2 at 32–33.

6 Ibid., at 12: according to the US Department of State, there were 28 US fatalities as a result of terrorist attacks in 2006. Incidents in Iraq took the lives of 22 individuals, and another three died in Afghanistan. Three other incidents (one each in Israel, Pakistan and Thailand) claimed the lives of the remaining three victims.

7 In 2007, of the 22,685 deaths worldwide which the NCTC attributed to terrorist acts, 19 of those fatalities (0.08 per cent) were American citizens. Of those 19 fatalities, 17 died in Iraq and 2 in Afghanistan: see NCTC, '2007 Report on Terrorism', 30 April 2008, at 27; see also the discussion in Chapter 2 at 29–35.

8 This region encompasses North Africa, the Arabian Peninsula, the Levant, Iraq and Iran.

9 NCTC, 'Report on Incidents of Terrorism 2005', supra n. 3, 1, Chart 10.

Colombia was the only state in the Western hemisphere to be included in the list of the 15 worst-affected countries.[10] That trend continued in 2006: the worst-affected region by far was again the Near East,[11] followed by South Asia.[12] The list of the 15 worst-affected countries was dominated by states in the Near East, South East Asia and Africa.[13] In 2007, the same regions were reportedly the worst affected.[14]

The pattern that has emerged over the past few years is that terrorism, however that term is defined, is a phenomenon that seems to affect some regions, countries and citizens more than others. It is submitted that it would be unacceptable, morally and legally, if a state which is statistically one of the least-affected by terrorism were to be given the freedom to change international law to such an extent that the right of self-defence is reinterpreted to suit its current perception of its immediate security needs. Rather than accepting that international terrorism is a new and unusual threat to global peace and security, and particularly the US's security, international lawyers ought to be at the forefront of the debate in maintaining the authority of the UN Charter and the Security Council to constrain the resort to force.

In Chapter 3, the nature of 'terrorism' was explored from historical, political and legal perspectives. 'Terrorism' is a term that has continued to defy definition. That is because it is frequently used as a byword for 'enemy', and thus it has become at once self-fulfilling and meaningless.[15] The importance of examining the meaning

10 In terms of fatalities, the 15 worst-affected countries in 2005 (fatalities are indicated in brackets) were: Iraq (8,262), India (1,361), Colombia (813), Afghanistan (684), Thailand (498), Nepal (485), Pakistan (338), Russia (238), Sudan (157), Democratic Republic of the Congo (154), Philippines (144), Algeria (132), Sri Lanka (130), Chad (109) and Uganda (109): NCTC, 'Report on Incidents of Terrorism 2006', supra n. 5, 24.

11 In 2006, attacks across this region increased by 83 per cent on the previous year, rising to nearly 7,800 as compared with 4,222 in 2005. Fatalities rose by 57 per cent, from about 8,700 in 2005 to nearly 13,700 in 2006. The number of injured in this region doubled from 13,534 in 2005 to over 25,800 in 2006: ibid., 42.

12 In 2006, there were slightly fewer incidents than in 2005 (3,654 compared with 4,000) but there were 19 per cent more fatalities (3,600 compared with the previous total of 3,000): ibid., 15 and 76.

13 In terms of fatalities, the 15 worst-affected countries in 2006 were (fatalities are indicated in brackets): Iraq (13,340), India (1,256), Afghanistan (1,042), Sudan (716), Sri Lanka (627), Colombia (533), Thailand (520), Chad (518), Pakistan (387), Philippines (291), Nepal (261), Russia (115), Algeria (112), Nigeria (97) and Israel (83): ibid., 25.

14 In 2007, the worst-affected region was the Near East, followed by South Asia, and Africa was a distant third. The Western hemisphere was the least-affected region. In terms of fatalities, the 14 worst-affected countries in 2007 were (fatalities are indicated in brackets): Iraq (13,606), Afghanistan (1,966), Pakistan (1,335), India (1,093), Thailand (859), Somalia (767), Sudan (403), Chad (368), Colombia (364), Sri Lanka (241), Philippines (209), Algeria (192), Democratic Republic of Congo (178) and Russia (150): see NCTC, '2007 Report on Terrorism', 30 April 2008, 26, Chart 6.

15 The flexibility of the term was demonstrated recently when US President George W. Bush visited the UK. Protesters who objected to his visit called him a 'terrorist': see

of 'terrorism' is underscored by the formal justifications put forward by the US and the UK: their resort to force against a sovereign state in purported self-defence was undertaken as a response to 'terrorism', which was portrayed as an entirely new type of threat. Chapters 2 and 3 provided evidence that terrorism is *not* a new threat. The use of force by non-state actors against the state is a problem that has existed since antiquity. The difficulty of distinguishing between means adopted by the pirate/anarchist/terrorist to achieve their objectives and those chosen by states has been noted by scholars such as Cicero and St Augustine.[16] Chapter 3 discussed the ways in which modern states have attempted to meet the challenge posed by non-state actors, which has largely been through legal and judicial mechanisms, on the understanding that acts of terrorism are criminal acts, not acts of war.

Although an internationally acceptable definition would possibly assist in combating terrorism, one of the major obstacles to reaching consensus is the long-recognised right of people to use force against occupiers of their territory. In the past, many international agreements specifically protected that right and expressly excluded from the definition of terrorism the use of force when exercising that right. More recently there has been a shift towards condemning all acts of terrorism, regardless of motive. Another aspect of the definition which has created division is whether or not acts of the state (such as acts undertaken by members of the military during armed conflict) should be included in the definition of terrorism. It is submitted that the current drive towards excluding acts of the military from the proposed comprehensive international draft convention may be unwise in the sense that it will enforce the perception that states are immune from charges that they have engaged in 'state terrorism' when they carry out acts that would otherwise satisfy the definition of 'terrorism'. Arguably, continuing to uphold that distinction will create a feeling of resentment from those who are subjected to

---

Aljazeera.net, 'Protests greet Bush on UK visit', available at: <http://english.aljazeera.net/news/europe/2008/06/200861912280194590.html> at 18 June 2008. Bush has previously been accused of being 'the biggest terrorist in the world today' by Venezuelan President Hugo Chavez: see *ABC News Online*, 'Bush the "Biggest Terrorist in the World Today"', available at: <http://www.abc.net.au/news/newsitems/200605/s1639568.htm> at 18 June 2008.

16 Cicero recalled an exchange between a pirate and Alexander of Macedon: '[F]or when he [the pirate] was asked what wickedness drove him to harass the sea with his one pirate galley, he replied: "The same wickedness that drives you to harass the whole world ..."': Cicero, *De Re Publica* III, XIV (Keyes, C. trans.), Loeb Classical Library (London: Heinemann, 1928) at 203. St Augustine later quoted from Cicero in *De Civitate Dei*, Book IV, Chapter 4 (Bettenson, H. trans.) (Harmondsworth: Penguin Books, 1972) at 139, wherein St Augustine wrote: 'Remove justice, and what are kingdoms but gangs of criminals on a large scale? What are criminal gangs but petty kingdoms? ... For it was a witty and truthful rejoinder which was given by a captured pirate to Alexander the Great. The king asked the fellow, "What is your idea, in infesting the sea?" And the pirate answered, with uninhibited insolence, "The same as yours, in infesting the earth! But because I do it with a tiny craft, I'm called a pirate: because you have a mighty navy, you're called an emperor."'

acts of 'terrorism' by states and their armed forces. It is submitted that scholars such as Ganor and Wardlaw[17] who do not exclude state actors have provided more useful definitions. The question of how to treat state actors continues to trouble the negotiations for a draft comprehensive convention on terrorism. It is suggested here that 'terrorism' should be defined by the act, the target and the objective – not the status of the perpetrator as 'state' or 'non-state'. Even if an overlap *is* created between various sectors of international law, so that a member of the military forces of a state may theoretically violate provisions of humanitarian law as well as the proposed terrorism convention, that may not be an altogether negative development. It may not be as damaging as excluding state actors altogether from a charge of terrorism, by virtue of the definitions employed. It is the view of this author that an alleged breach of international humanitarian law may not have attached to it the same stigma and the same negativity in the public eye as a breach of a comprehensive convention on terrorism.

Chapters 4 and 5 addressed the evolution of limitations on the use of force from the League of Nations era through to the United Nations Charter until the present. An even more expansive historical inquiry could have been undertaken. Given that President Bush clothed his justifications for using force in phrases that echoed the just war doctrine,[18] the historical basis of that particular doctrine could also have been examined here. By tracing the modern development of limitations on the resort to force, on the use of force in self-defence, pre-emptive self-defence, on the use of reprisals and on the use of force in response to non-state actors, what became evident is that states have never agreed on when and why they may employ force. Even when the majority of nations seemed to have reached agreement and adopted the UN Charter which prohibited the resort to force, the reservation of the inherent right of self-defence, which was left undefined in Article 51, has allowed states to continue to interpret that right as they see fit. The 'inherent' right to self-defence is limited – first and foremost – by the wording of the Charter, as that has been interpreted by the International Court of Justice and applied by states.

Resort to Force: Undoing the Constraints

Taking a broader view of the analysis that has been presented in the foregoing chapters leads one to reflect that we are possibly entering an age when some states are attempting to undo the constraints that have been built up over time to limit the resort to force. Some general observations regarding the current position and the future direction are offered.

---

17 See discussion of the definition of 'terrorism' in Chapter 3.

18 President Bush: 'To all the men and women in our military – every sailor, every soldier … I say this: Your mission is defined, your objectives are clear, your goal is just': Presidential Address to the Nation, 7 October 2001: <http://www.whitehouse.gov/news/releases/2001/10/20011007-8.html> at 18 June 2008.

First, recent events suggest that the international community may be on the brink of returning to a situation which existed prior to the UN Charter, and probably even prior to the Covenant of the League of Nations, when states used force freely against their enemies (perceived or real), sometimes under false pretexts.[19] Many of the classical scholars wrote of the need to constrain the resort to force because, too often, states use force and attempt to justify it in the language of self-defence, when really it is nothing more than aggression. Cicero wrote that the only just wars were for revenge or punishment,[20] and even though those objectives are supposedly no longer acceptable reasons for resorting to force, recent events suggest that force is sometimes acceptable when the objective is quite plainly stated to be 'revenge' and punishment for 'evil-doers'. Drawing parallels between the current scenario and that of the Roman Empire is not merely indulgent hyperbole. During the height of the Roman Empire, military commanders enjoyed flexibility in deciding when force was employed, even when philosophers and scholars were attempting to restrict the resort to force. Parallels with the current security climate are evident in the sense that the strict letter of the UN Charter still purports to uphold the virtues of peaceful dispute settlement, and the Charter purportedly limits the resort to force as well as the threat of using force, whilst militarily powerful states seem quite able to resort to force (or threaten to resort to force) whenever they deem it in their security interests to do so.[21]

Secondly, there is a risk that the international community may be returning to a pre-UN Charter scenario where forcible reprisals are permitted. Although Article 2(4) of the UN Charter outlawed the use of forcible reprisals, the practice of a few militarily powerful states, if left unchallenged, may lead to a situation where force is routinely resorted to by states, in contravention of the UN Charter, as a method of dispute settlement, to achieve 'justice' or pursuant to the state's perceived security interests. Forcible reprisals were acceptable when Wheaton wrote the *Elements of International Law* in 1836[22] and the *Naulilaa* dispute in 1928 set out the conditions

19 Samuel Pufendorf (1632–1704) once wrote that men usually go to much labour to conceal the real causes of unjust wars: Pufendorf, S., *De Jure Naturae et Gentium Libri Octo*, Vol 2, Book Eight, Chapter VI, para 3 (Oldfather, C. and W. trans.), The Classics of International Law, microform, Scott, J. (ed.) (Dobbs Ferry, New York: Transmedia, 1934).

20 Cicero, *De Re Publica*, Book III, XXIII, 35 (Keyes, C. trans.), Loeb Classical Library (London: Heinemann, 1928) at 213.

21 Recently, Israel has made several threats to use force against Iran, with the Israeli Minister of Transport, Shaul Mofaz, stating that a strike against Iran is 'unavoidable' if Iran continues to press ahead with its uranium enrichment programme. Such threats are breaches of Article 2(4) of the UN Charter. For reporting of Israel's threats see, for example, *Telegraph.co.uk*, 'Israel Threatens to Strike Iran's Nuclear Plans', 7 June 2008, available at: <http://www.telegraph.co.uk/news/worldnews/middleeast/israel/2088964/Israel-threatens-to-strike-Iran's-nuclear-plans.htm> at 18 June 2008.

22 Wheaton: '[R]eprisals are to be granted only in case of a clear and open denial of justice': Wheaton, H., *Elements of International Law*, 8th edn. (Dana, R. ed.) (Boston: Little, Brown and Co, 1866) §291, 310.

which established the legitimacy of reprisals.[23] Historically, for a reprisal to be legitimate there had to have been a previous violation of international law by a state, an unsuccessful request for redress of the wrong and the measures adopted in response were not to have been excessive.[24] When one applies those conditions to the facts pertaining to the use of force in October 2001, it is plausible to argue that the use of force on the latter occasion may have been an attempt, conscious or otherwise, to revive the doctrine of reprisals as a form of self-help for states. If this is the case, it is unfortunate, since reprisals are plainly inconsistent with Article 2(3) of the UN Charter, which requires states to settle their international disputes by peaceful means, and Article 2(4), which prohibits the threat or use of force against another state.[25] Although a few scholars may argue in favour of a resurrection of the reprisal doctrine,[26] there has not been a groundswell of support for that notion, nor has state practice demonstrated that a change has already occurred in favour of the lawfulness of reprisals. Although the return of the reprisal doctrine in the context of responding to terrorist attacks may have 'found a mooring'[27] in the current Bush Administration, the fact remains that the majority of states have not followed suit. As at the date of writing, armed/forcible reprisals remain unlawful.[28]

Thirdly, it has already been noted that states have virtually always faced threats from non-state actors, whether they be pirates, anarchists or terrorists.[29]

---

23 See reference to the *Naulilaa* dispute in Chapter 4, n. 128.

24 Ibid.

25 That the UN Charter prohibits reprisals involving the use of force is universally accepted by scholars of international law. For example, see Brownlie, I., *International Law and the Use of Force by States* (Oxford: Clarendon Press, 1963) 281; Bowett, D., 'Reprisals Involving Recourse to Armed Force' (1972) 66 *AJIL* 1 at 1; Kwakwa, E., *The International Law of Armed Conflict: Personal and Material Fields of Application* (Dordrecht; Boston: Kluwer Academic Publishers, 1992) 132; Arend, A. and Beck, R., *International Law and the Use of Force: Beyond the Charter Paradigm* (USA and Canada: Routledge, 1993) 42–3; Gray, C., *International Law and the Use of Force*, 2nd edn. (Oxford: Oxford University Press, 2004) 163.

26 For instance, see O'Brien, W., 'Reprisals, Deterrence and Self-Defense in Counterterror Operations' (1990) 30 *Va. J. Int'l L.* 421 at 475, where he argues that it would be sensible to assimilate armed reprisals into the right of legitimate self-defence. See also Seymour, A., 'The Legitimacy of Peacetime Reprisal as a Tool Against State-Sponsored Terrorism' (1990) 39 *Naval Law Review* 221 at 224.

27 This argument is made by Kelly who asserts that the ultimatum issued by President Bush to the Taliban encompassed all the criteria that Afghanistan had to meet in order to avoid a military reprisal: see Kelly, M., 'Time Warp to 1945 – Resurrection of the Reprisal and Anticipatory Self-Defense Doctrines in International Law' (2003) 13(1) *Journal of Transnational Law and Policy* 1 at 21.

28 See discussion below, 'Unlawful Reprisal rather than Lawful Self-defence'.

29 Pirates existed in ancient Greece and Rome and are referred to in the works of, *inter alia*, Homer, Thucydides, Livy, Plutarch and Cicero. For a discussion of historical references to pirates, see Phillipson, C., *The International Law and Custom of Ancient Greece and Rome* (London: Macmillan and Co Ltd, 1911; reprinted in New York:

The parallels between piracy and terrorism and between anarchy and terrorism have been touched upon in earlier chapters. It is suggested that when looking for solutions to the threat posed by terrorism, the international community ought to reflect on the ways in which anarchism and piracy were subdued. Success in the 'war on anarchy' was perceived in the late 1800s to require trans-national co-operation through policing and intelligence exchange.[30] Piracy was brought under control by a variety of measures, including the categorisation of pirates as *hostes humani generis*; they came to be regarded as criminals whose acts attracted universal jurisdiction. It is worth noting that unilateral resort to force was not an option for states that were the victims of the criminal acts of piracy and anarchy. One of the key factors which led to the demise of piracy as a threat to the security of states was the decision by states to renounce, in a multilateral treaty, their resort to methods akin to piracy. When the Declaration of Paris was signed in 1856,[31] signatory states agreed that they would prohibit and outlaw privateering, which was tantamount to state-sponsored piracy.[32] An opportunity currently exists for all states to take a similar position with regards to terrorism: states are being given the option of defining it broadly enough in the draft comprehensive convention on terrorism that they can denounce all acts of terrorism, whether the actors involved be state or non-state, and they could choose to accept that terrorist acts can be carried out by the military forces of a state in situations of armed conflict.

Throughout this book the historical aspect of a current security threat, namely terrorism, has been emphasised. One of the conclusions offered is that it seems somewhat disingenuous to maintain that international terrorism is a 'new' threat to global peace and security, which belongs exclusively to the modern era, and which ought to entitle states to disregard or rewrite the Charter which belongs to a previous era. The arguments made by statesmen such as current US President George W. Bush and former Australian Prime Minister John Howard, to the effect

---

Williams S. Hein & Co, 2001); Zimmern, A., *The Greek Commonwealth*, 5th edn (London: Oxford University Press, 1931); and Rubin, A., *The Law of Piracy*, 2nd edn (New York: Transnational Publishers, 1998). Anarchists were a particular threat during the late 1800s and early 1900s: see discussion in Chapter 2 at 24–28.

30 See discussion in Chapter 2 at 24–26.

31 In 1856, a number of states signed the Declaration of Paris which declared for the first time in a multilateral treaty that: 'privateering is, and remains, abolished': Declaration of Paris, signed in Paris on 16 April 1856. The Declaration of Paris was signed by 51 parties including all of the major European maritime states, but not the United States.

32 The 1856 Declaration of Paris ended, amongst its signatories, the widespread practice of states using privateers. It has been described as 'a recognition of shared guilt' in the sense that the signatories formally accepted that granting letters of marque and reprisal was nothing but state-sponsored piracy and that the practice of piracy in general could only be brought under control if *states* relinquished the right to partake in such a practice: see Burgess, D., 'The Dread Pirate Bin Laden: How Thinking of Terrorists as Pirates Can Help Win the War on Terror' (2005) *Legal Affairs*: <http://www.legalaffairs.org/issues/July-August-2005/feature_burgess_julaug05.msp> at 18 June 2008.

that we are living in a new age which requires a new interpretation of the Charter, seem to this author to overstate the differences between the present and the past. International terrorism in the modern sense is not so far from the threats which states have always faced from non-state actors. Just as scholars considered pirates to be the common foe of all mankind (*communis hostis omnium*),[33] entitling states to arrest and prosecute pirates wherever they were found, so should modern states consider international terrorists to be criminals whose actions attract universal jurisdiction. The precise means by which the non-state actors seek to achieve their objectives may have changed, but it is submitted that the basic 'in group versus out group', or 'powerful state actor versus powerless non-state actor' distinction exists today as much as it did when it was described by St Augustine.

Only States are Capable of Waging War

Classical scholars all agreed that wars were fought by states, between sovereigns or princes – not between states and individuals. Plato referred to war as being a natural and inevitable condition, for *states*.[34] Cicero wrote that war was undertaken by states, which he famously defined as having a senate, a treasury, unanimity and concord amongst their citizens; all others he deemed brigands or pirates.[35] The early Christian scholars such as St Augustine assumed that war was declared by a proper authority: either God or a lawful ruler.[36] St Thomas Aquinas' definition of the 'just war' required that war be fought under the authority of a ruler or 'prince'.[37] The Spanish scholars such as Vitoria[38] and Suárez[39] wrote that war is carried on between states and that it must be waged by a 'legitimate power', as did

---

33 See Cicero, M., *De Officiis*, Book III, XXIX (Miller, W. trans.) Loeb Classical Library (London: Heinemann, 1913).

34 Plato, *The Republic*, Book V, 470C-D (Lee, D. trans.) (Harmondsworth: Penguin, 1987) at 258.

35 See Cicero, M., *De Officiis*, supra n. 33 at 385; see also Cicero, M., *Philippics* IV, VI, 14 (Ker, W. trans.) Loeb Classical Library (London: Heinemann; New York: G.P. Putnam's Sons, 1926) at 249.

36 St Augustine, *Contra Faustum*, Book XXII, 75, The Gnostic Society Library, available online at: <http://www.gnosis.org/library/contf2.htm> at 18 June 2008.

37 This was the first of St Aquinas' three conditions for waging 'just war', the principle of *auctoritas principas*; see *Summa Theologiae, Secunda Secundae*, question 40, reply to objection 1(literally translated by Fathers of the English Dominican Province) (London: R. & T. Washbourne, 1912–25).

38 Francisco de Vitoria., *De Jure Belli*, 417–22 (Bate, J. trans.) in Scott, J., *The Spanish Origin of International Law: Francisco de Vitoria and his Law of Nations* (Delran, New Jersey: Legal Classics Library, 1934).

39 Francisco Suárez, *The Three Theological Virtues: On Charity*, Disputation XII, 'On War', section IV, para 1 in Scott, J. (ed.), *Selections from Three Works of Francisco Suárez*, The Classics of International Law, microform (Dobbs Ferry, New York: Transmedia, 1944) at 824.

Gentili who emphasised that there must be sovereigns on both sides.[40] Vattel, too, confirmed that the sovereign alone has the authority to make war,[41] as did Grotius.[42] To those voices could be added other classical scholars including Zouche, who defined war as 'a lawful contention between different peoples or princes',[43] and Rachel.[44] Indeed, the requirement that war be fought between sovereigns or princes, between those who possessed 'royal or quasi-royal power',[45] was consistently held to be an integral element in defining 'just' wars. Textor pointed out that 'war-making belongs to Kings or those having like power'.[46]

The writings of classical scholars provide an important context for the contemporary debate regarding how states have responded, and ought to respond, to the use of force by private individuals. States and scholars have always regarded private individuals as being incapable of declaring war on a sovereign state and they have consistently maintained that any use of force by individuals should be treated as a criminal matter. The rationale for demanding that war be fought only between sovereigns can be traced back to Grotius' endorsement in 1625 of an even earlier statement from Demosthenes, that *war is made against those who cannot be controlled by the laws*, but *judicial decisions are rendered in the case of private citizens*.[47] Demosthenes' statement still makes perfect sense: private individuals can be restrained by laws – whether domestic or international or both – whereas states, which are above the law for they make the law, can only be constrained by force.

---

40 Alberico Gentili, *De Iure Belli Libri Tres*, Vol. II, Book I, Chapter II (Rolfe, J., ed.), The Classics of International Law (Dobbs Ferry, New York: Transmedia, 1993) at 12–13.

41 Emmerich de Vattel, *The Law of Nations or The Principles of Natural Law Applied to the Conduct and to the Affairs of Nations and Sovereigns* (Chitty, J. trans.) Book II, Chapter IV, § 71–8 digital edition (Philadephia: T. & J.W. Johnson, 1852).

42 Hugo Grotius, *De Jure Belli ac Pacis*, Book III, Chapter I, para 5 (Loomis, L. trans.) (Roslyn, New York: Walter J. Black, 1949) at 289.

43 Richard Zouche, *Juris et Iudicii Fecialis*, Part I, Section VI, The Classics of International Law, microform, Scott, J. (ed.) (Dobbs Ferry, New York: Transmedia, 1934).

44 Samuel Rachel, *De Jure Naturae et Gentum Dissertationes* §XLIV (Bate, J. trans.), The Classics of International Law, microform, Scott, J. (ed.) (Dobbs Ferry, New York: Transmedia, 1934) at 184–5.

45 Johann Wolfgang Textor, *Synopsis Juris Gentium*, Chapter XVI, paras 9–10 (Bate, J. trans.), The Classics of International Law, microform, Scott, J. (ed.) (Dobbs Ferry, New York: Transmedia, 1934) at 161.

46 Ibid.

47 Grotius concurred with Demosthenes who wrote that war was directed against those who could not be held in check by judicial processes, 'for judgments are efficacious against those who feel that they are too weak to resist', but 'against those who are equally strong, or think they are, wars are undertaken': *De Jure Belli ac Pacis*, Prolegomena, para 25 (Kelsey, F. trans., The Classics of International Law, 1925) at 18.

Another important rationale underlies the need to treat individuals differently than states and to require wars to be fought between sovereigns. As noted by Grotius in *De Jure Belli ac Pacis*, declaring war on behalf of a state 'makes it known for certain that the war was not a private undertaking but was to be waged by the will of both peoples or the heads of both peoples'.[48] Textor also noted that since 'war' can only be fought between those possessing 'royal or quasi-royal powers',[49] it could not be fought against a state which was split into factions because, in such a case, 'there is no right of sovereignty in the antagonists, individually considered, such as there is in an undivided State'.[50] This is one of the reasons why it has been argued here that the US could not declare war against the State of Afghanistan in retaliation for acts of terrorism that were carried out by individuals, none of whom were representing the State of Afghanistan. In October 2001, Afghanistan was what Textor might have described as a state that was split into factions; there was no sovereign with whom to wage 'war'. When states such as the US and the UK declare war, or more precisely, engage in an armed conflict, with a 'state' such as Afghanistan,[51] in response to actions carried out by individuals who were not acting on that state's behalf or even within its control, they are surely ignoring a fundamental and historically accepted aspect of international relations concerning the attribution of acts of private individuals to the state.

Moreover, as Gentili noted, it would not be 'just' if the 'delinquency' of private citizens brought harm upon the entire body of citizens 'since the wrongdoers do not seek the welfare of all'.[52] The argument here is that it is unjust for the wrongdoing of the individuals who flew the planes on 11 September 2001 to bring harm upon the entire body of citizens in Afghanistan. The members of al Qaeda who are alleged to have carried out the acts of terrorism were not 'seeking the welfare of all' in Afghanistan. Gentili required that war be fought by regular soldiers and undertaken by a regular army: the individuals who carried out these particular terrorist attacks were neither regular soldiers nor part of a regular army.[53] The nexus between those individuals and the state was not established, simply because it did not exist.

---

48 Grotius, ibid., para 11 at 293.

49 Textor, supra n. 45.

50 Ibid., chapter XVI, paras 25–6 at 165.

51 In response to a question about 'the precise legal basis of the campaign' against Afghanistan, the Parliamentary Under-Secretary of State of the UK's Foreign and Commonwealth Office stated that: 'The military coalition in [sic] engaged in an armed conflict in self-defence against those who perpetrated the terrorist attack of 11 September and those who harbour and sustain them.' However, 'No Formal Declaration of War has been Made by HMG': *BYIL* LXXII (2002) 697.

52 Gentili, supra n. 40, Book I, Chapter XXI at 99–103.

53 Indeed, that assertion has been a key element in the Bush Administration's argument that the individuals arrested in Afghanistan should not be accorded 'prisoner of war' status and are instead 'unlawful combatants', a discussion of which is beyond the scope of the present work.

The Use of Force against Afghanistan

The legality of the use of force against Afghanistan has been the issue at the heart of this work. In Chapter 6, the argument was made that the use of force was unlawful, for at least five reasons, which are summarised in turn below.

First and foremost, the US did not suffer an 'armed attack' as required by Article 51 of the UN Charter. The term 'armed attack', in both the UN Charter and the Washington Treaty, has always been understood to refer to attacks *by states, upon states*. That has been repeatedly confirmed by states, by the ICJ as recently as 2004 and by the Security Council, as demonstrated by its general stance of condemning the use of force in response to terrorism on most occasions. Providing territory for training camps of alleged terrorists or 'safe-haven', if that is what the Taliban regime could have been held responsible for, is not and has never been accepted as being legally equivalent to carrying out an 'armed attack'. The significance of NATO's invocation of Article 5 of the NATO Treaty – which was heavily relied upon by the US to bolster its claim of self-defence[54] – was discussed at length and found to be minimal. It was argued that Article 5 probably ought not to have been invoked. Doubts were expressed at the time by diplomats as to whether there had been an 'armed attack' warranting the invocation of Article 5. Proof that invocation of Article 5 was sought by the US essentially for cosmetic reasons is bolstered by the fact that after it was invoked, NATO officials awaited requests for specific assets, but it was evident that the US intended to remain in full control of the military operations.[55]

It is noteworthy that during the debates which took place in both the Security Council and General Assembly immediately after 11 September, there was no mention of the phrase 'armed attack' by *any state* in reference to the events of 9/11, not even by the US representative.[56] Furthermore, neither the Security Council nor the General Assembly ever referred to the 11 September hijackings as 'armed attacks' in their post-11 September resolutions. The US Congress, when it authorised the use of force, did not call the hijackings 'armed attacks', and neither the Council of Europe nor the OAU used the term 'armed attacks' either. Perhaps most significantly, the UK's letter to the Security Council, which purportedly justified the use of force on the grounds of self-defence, omitted reference to the term 'armed attack'.[57]

Secondly, the use of force against Afghanistan was unlawful because even if it could be established that the US suffered an 'armed attack', the attack was over

---

54 President Bush: 'Perhaps the NATO Charter reflects best the attitude of the world: An attack on one is an attack on all': Address to a Joint Session of Congress and the American People, 20 September 2001.

55 See Lansford, T., *All for One: Terrorism, NATO and the United States* (Aldershot: Ashgate, 2002) 79; see also Chapter 6.

56 See discussion in Chapter 6, esp 78–79 and 185–189.

57 Ibid., and see the original document as reproduced in Appendix 2.

by the time force was employed. There was simply no need – no *necessity* – to use force on 7 October 2001 to halt an attack, or to prevent an imminent attack from occurring. The attack was indeed over by the evening of 11 September, evidenced by statements from the White House that it was safe for the President to return to Washington DC, because the Administration regarded the threat of attack as having ended. From that point onwards, any use of force was designed to prevent a future unknown and apparently non-imminent attack – a right that is *not* presently recognised in international law.

Thirdly, even if there *was* an armed attack, the US and the UK failed to adequately attribute responsibility for it to the Islamic State of Afghanistan. The US even admitted in its letter to the Security Council on 7 October 2001, as it was launching air missile attacks on Afghanistan, that its inquiry was in its 'early stages' and that there was 'still much we do not know'.[58] The US alleged that 'al Qaeda had a central role in the attacks',[59] but it provided no evidence in its letter to the Security Council to link the individuals who hijacked the planes to al Qaeda, and in turn to the Taliban and the State of Afghanistan. Before resorting to force against Afghanistan, the US and the UK ought to have provided specific evidence to the Security Council directly connecting the individuals who carried out the attacks to the Taliban regime. Under the principles of state responsibility, which have been enunciated by the ICJ, the ICTY and are encapsulated in the ILC's Draft Articles, the Taliban had to have had control over the *specific operation*, or at least 'overall control, going beyond the mere financing and equipping of forces',[60] to be held responsible. However, neither the US nor the UK argued in their respective letters to the Security Council that the Taliban directed or controlled the acts of terrorism that occurred on 11 September 2001.

Fourthly, the use of force failed to meet the customary law requirements of necessity, immediacy and proportionality. Classical scholars always referred to war being 'just' if it was, *inter alia*, the last resort and there were no other options available. Here, there were other options available to the US and the UK, such as the measures adopted by the Security Council on 28 September 2001, as well as the use of diplomacy, the use of intelligence and the use of arrest and extradition procedures. The opportunity to negotiate further also clearly existed; the evidence shows that it was the US, rather than the Taliban, that was unwilling to negotiate.[61] The US stated that its ultimatum was *not* open to negotiation and *The 9/11 Commission Report* concluded that even as it issued the ultimatum, the Bush Administration 'knew' the Taliban would not comply. Since the option of negotiation or peaceful settlement had not been properly exhausted as a means of resolving the crisis, it is arguable that force was not the last resort; thus, force was not strictly *necessary* at the time that it was employed on 7 October 2001. Furthermore,

58 UN Doc. S/2001/946, reproduced in Appendix 1.

59 Ibid.

60 See *Prosecutor v Tadić*, as discussed in Chapter 6.

61 See Chapter 6.

the resort to force was arguably not *immediate*; it was delayed by 26 days after the so-called 'armed attack' had ended, and the need to employ force could not be said to have been 'instant, overwhelming, leaving no choice of means and no moment for deliberation' in the *Caroline* sense. As for *proportionality*, it has been argued in Chapter 6 that the objective of using force to remove the Taliban regime from power was a disproportionate response. Proportionality may be measured in various ways. It was acknowledged in Chapter 6 that one interpretation is that a roughly 'proportionate' number of civilians died in Afghanistan in the months following the American/UK invasion when compared to the number of civilians who died on 11 September 2001. However, that type of rudimentary comparison is unsatisfactory because, firstly, there have been an ever-increasing number of civilian fatalities since the commencement of the military campaign on 7 October 2001. Estimates of civilian deaths vary, with some studies suggesting that perhaps between 8,000 and 18,000 civilians may have been killed in Afghanistan as a direct and indirect result of the decision to use force in 'self-defence' by the US and the UK.[62] In addition, comparing figures of civilian fatalities may not be the most effective way of measuring 'proportionality'. To determine whether a response is 'proportionate' regard ought to be had to the *objectives* of using force. Here, the declared objectives (as evidenced in documents from both the US and the UK) were not, or perhaps not *just*, to achieve the arrest of Osama bin Laden and to destroy alleged terrorist training camps within Taliban-controlled territory. The wider objective from the outset was to completely remove the Taliban regime from holding any form of power in Afghanistan.[63] Pursuing that objective was made more palatable by frequent media references to the supposedly poor human rights record of the Taliban regime.[64] Yet no matter how unsatisfactory the Taliban's record on human rights may have been, it would never, on its own, have justified an invasion of Afghanistan and the complete removal of the Taliban regime from power. Examples were discussed in Chapter 6 which suggest that no state has ever been able to invade another sovereign state and remove the existing regime, thereafter replacing it with a more 'acceptable' regime, and been condoned for pursuing such a course of action.[65] The decision to include the goal of regime change in the US and the UK's stated objectives rendered what could, possibly,

62 See discussion in Chapter 6 regarding the estimates of civilian deaths in Afghanistan. The figure of 8,000–18,000 is from a study by Conetta in 2002, see Chapter 6 at n. 341.

63 Regime change was clearly enunciated as an objective of the use of force: see Hoon, G., *Operation Veritas*, referred to in Chapter 6.

64 See discussion in Chapter 6 regarding the frequent references to human rights under the Taliban regime and the humanitarian situation in Afghanistan.

65 See discussion of the use of force by the US against Grenada and Panama in Chapter 6.

have been a lawful act of self-defence (had it been limited in time and scope to purely al Qaeda targets) into an unlawful act of aggression.[66]

Fifthly, it is submitted that even if the right to use force in self-defence initially existed, the right had expired by the time that the US and the UK employed force on 7 October 2001. This line of argument assumes that the US suffered an 'armed attack' on 11 September 2001 which allowed it to respond with force in self-defence. When the Security Council adopted Resolution 1373 on 28 September 2001, it set forth a comprehensive array of measures to maintain international peace and security, some of which were compulsory for all states. Since those measures can only be interpreted as 'measures to maintain international peace and security', Article 51 dictates that the right to use force in self-defence thereby ceased to exist. This interpretation of the Charter is in keeping with the purpose for which Article 51 was first introduced. Reference was made in Chapter 4 to *les travaux préparatoires* to demonstrate that Article 51 was only ever intended to be an emergency measure, to allow states to act until the Security Council could take over, or in case the Security Council was unable or unwilling to act.[67] Article 51 was never intended to create an indefinite and infinite right of self-defence such as that advanced by the US in its letter to the Security Council, and amply illustrated in its statement that 'we may find that our self-defence requires further actions with respect to other organizations and other States'.[68] That interpretation of its alleged right is in contradiction with both the letter and spirit of Article 51.

Unlawful Reprisal rather than Lawful Self-defence

Reaching the somewhat controversial conclusion that the use of force against Afghanistan was *not* lawful self-defence begs the question: how should this use of force be understood in terms of international law? The current work has shown that the use of force by the US and the UK was either an act of revenge and retaliation, which, in the pre-Charter era would have been called a 'reprisal', or it was an act of anticipatory or pre-emptive self-defence.[69]

Reprisals, which were punitive by nature, were outlawed by the Charter. By contrast, self-defence is not an action that is intended to punish or avenge: the

---

66 Cassese, writing soon after 9/11, observed that if military force was employed, it would have to be proportionate and that, 'Force may not be used to wipe out the Afghan leadership or destroy Afghan military installations and other military objectives that have nothing to do with the terrorist organisations, unless the Afghan central authorities show by words or deeds that they approve and endorse the action of terrorist organisations': Cassese, A., 'Terrorism is Also Disrupting Some Crucial Categories of International Law' (2001) 12 *EJIL* 993.

67 See discussion of the history of the Charter in Chapter 4.

68 Letter dated 7 October 2001 from the US to the President of the Security Council, as discussed in Chapter 6 and reproduced in Appendix 1.

69 See discussion below regarding the use of force against Afghanistan as anticipatory self-defence.

resort to force in self-defence is supposed to protect the state in a moment when it is subject to armed attack. In the days following 11 September 2001, President Bush spoke openly and frequently of the need to retaliate and to punish the perpetrators.[70] In President Bush's Address to a Joint Session of Congress and the American People, he stated that the US's response 'involves far more than instant retaliation and isolated strikes'.[71] This telling admission overlooks the fact that all states surrendered the right to retaliate and exact revenge when they signed the UN Charter. That has been confirmed by both the Security Council and the ICJ.

Although analogies drawn from domestic law are not always helpful, one can justifiably be drawn between the right of self-defence in international law and the right of self-defence that is preserved in domestic criminal laws. An individual usually has a defence to the use of force against another citizen, which would otherwise be considered to be assault, if they are acting in defence of themselves or another, and they use reasonable force. However, no jurisdiction would permit the defence to be established if force was used in revenge or retaliation.[72] Individuals entrust the state, in the form of its police forces and its justice and correction systems, to perform those roles, in accordance with the rule of law. At the global level, states have entrusted the Security Council with the role of maintaining international peace and security and states must seek the mandate of the Security Council if they wish to use force once an armed attack has ended. That surrendering of the individual will of each state was what Kant referred to in 1795 when he surmised that the only way for states to find perpetual peace would be by giving up their freedom and by accommodating themselves to the constraints of common law, by establishing what he called 'a league of peace'.[73]

The assertion made herein, that the use of force against Afghanistan was an unlawful reprisal rather than a lawful act of self-defence, is further strengthened by an historical analysis. The historical evolution of forcible measures short of war suggests that there are strong parallels between what were previously called 'reprisals' and the use of force against Afghanistan. Prior to the UN Charter, reprisals were considered lawful. States were allowed to use force against other states to resolve issues in dispute, without declaring war and thereby bringing the international law on 'war' into effect. As mentioned above, the *Naulilaa* case set out the rules for engaging in reprisals, such as the existence of a wrong by a state, a request for redress from the victim state, and the subsequent refusal by that state to

70 See references cited in Chapter 6 at 162–167.

71 President George W. Bush, Address to a Joint Session of Congress and the American People, 20 September 2001, available at: <http://www.whitehouse.gov/news/releases/2001/09/20010920-8.html> at 18 June 2008.

72 In New Zealand criminal law it is accepted that 'actions by way of retaliation or out of revenge cannot be justified as self-defence': Robertson, B. (ed.), *Adams on Criminal Law* (Wellington, New Zealand: Brooker & Friend, 1992) at CA48.07.

73 Kant, E., *To Perpetual Peace: A Philosophical Sketch* (Humphrey, T. trans.) (Indianapolis: Hackett Pub., 2003).

offer redress. If the terrorist attacks which occurred on 11 September 2001 could have been adequately attributed to the Islamic State of Afghanistan, governed ostensibly by the Taliban regime, then the response to them appears to meet all the elements of a classic reprisal. There was a prior wrongful act (allowing the territory of Afghanistan to be used for training purposes by terrorist groups); there was a demand for redress (the ultimatum issued to the Taliban by the US); and there was, allegedly, a refusal to grant such redress.[74] When an adequate response to the ultimatum was not forthcoming, the US resorted to force. Thus, as noted above, it is submitted that the US's use of force was a reprisal against the State of Afghanistan.[75]

If the facts seem to fit the classic formulation of reprisals,[76] then the ramifications are troubling because forcible reprisals were outlawed by the UN Charter. States are supposed to resolve their differences, whatever they may be, by peaceful means. It was acknowledged in Chapters 5 and 6 that although forcible reprisals are unlawful, some states have continued to use them and some scholars have argued that some form of 'reasonable' reprisal should be recognised in international law. Some instances in which reprisals have been used by states were reviewed in Chapter 5. The analysis there showed that although reprisals may be strictly unlawful, the Security Council has taken a softer stance on them in recent years when compared to its consistent condemnation of them during the 1950s, 1960s and, to a lesser extent, 1970s. Some of the examples of reprisals from the 1970s and 1980s bear remarkable similarities with the use of force against Afghanistan in 2001. For example, a parallel can be drawn between the Israeli attacks on Lebanon during the 1970s and the use of force against Afghanistan in 2001 in so far as Israel often justified its attacks on Lebanon on the grounds that it was a base for terrorists. Israel attempted to justify the use of force in the Litani Raid on the grounds of 'self-defence', and Israel frequently used force to punish its neighbours for allowing terrorists to operate from those territories. The Security Council usually condemned the use of force by Israel on those grounds as unlawful reprisals.

The use of force against Afghanistan in 2001 can be compared with the use of force in the 1990s, in particular, when the US used force against Iraq (1993) and against Sudan and Afghanistan (1998). In both of those instances, the use of force was unpopular, and even though there was no formal condemnation by the Security Council, the general consensus was that those were not legitimate cases of self-defence as permitted under Article 51. Further examples from 2000–2006 were discussed in Chapter 5 where it was demonstrated that states are sometimes unwilling to publicly oppose the use of force, even though it is technically an

74 See discussion of the ultimatum in Chapter 6.

75 See discussion above at 239 n. 27 where it is noted that some scholars, such as Kelly, have observed that the ultimatum to the Taliban appeared to be an attempt to meet the pre-Charter criteria for lawful forcible reprisals.

76 Ibid., especially see Kelly, supra n. 27.

unlawful reprisal rather than a lawful act of self-defence. The use of force in 2001 demonstrates that this pattern appears set to continue. It is contended that the use of force by the US and the UK against Afghanistan, beginning on 7 October 2001, could be viewed as the most significant example of an unlawful forcible reprisal in recent years. It was a use of force that was plainly understood as an act of revenge and retaliation[77] and it bore all the hallmarks of an armed reprisal.[78]

Although there might have been considerable sympathy within the international community for a short, sharp response by the US, as suggested in the EU's references to a 'riposte',[79] the international community should not, and it is argued here, *did* not, sanction the use of force in either the manner or the scale in which it was eventually employed. It was noted in Chapter 5 that during the 1970s and 1980s, when the Security Council was frequently asked to respond to reprisals, the Council took the position that just as terrorism had to be condemned, so did reprisals in response to terrorism. In a Security Council debate in 1972, the Council stated that:[80] 'While we condemn acts of terrorism, we also condemn acts of reprisal since they flout the Charter and they are contrary to the purposes on which this Organization rests.' In 1972, it was reasoned that reprisals were equally worthy of condemnation as acts of terrorism: to try to justify one by the other would inevitably lead 'to the most deadly outbidding, to blind destruction of lives, to constantly increasing dangers to international peace and security'.[81] The wisdom that was demonstrated by the Council's members in 1972 seemed to have been conspicuously absent in the aftermath of the events of 11 September 2001, and in the debate, or lack thereof, regarding the lawfulness of the use of force by the US and the UK.

The issue of where reprisals currently stand in international law is integrally linked to the question of the lawfulness of the use of force against Afghanistan. If one can establish that reprisals, in some form or another, are once again lawful, then it does not matter whether the use of force against Afghanistan was a reprisal. But if one comes to the conclusion that reprisals were 'outlawed' by the UN Charter, and they remain unlawful, then if the use of force in 2001 can be classified as a reprisal, it will be held to be intrinsically unlawful. Some scholars have addressed this issue by arguing that the doctrine of reprisals has been resurrected, at least in some circumstances. Kelly has argued that President Bush's linkage of states to the terrorists they harbour, in an almost legal agency relationship, is not a resurrection

---

77 See discussion in Chapter 6 at n. 24, n. 25 and n. 34 regarding President Bush's statements.

78 See Kelly, supra n. 27 at 21: 'President Bush's ultimatum to the Taliban … encompassed all the criteria that Afghanistan had to meet in order to avoid a military reprisal.'

79 See Chapter 6 at 173.

80 UN SCOR 1662nd Meeting at 4, UN Doc S/PV/1662 (1872); see also discussion in Chapter 5.

81 Ibid.

of the reprisal doctrine against states *a priori*.[82] He argues that 'states are only on the receiving end of reprisals *through* the terrorists, who are the actual targets of the reprisals'. It seems to this author that that is a distinction without a difference.[83] The military reprisals by the US and the UK against the state and territory of Afghanistan were aimed not only at the alleged terrorists: they were aimed at the Taliban regime. The evidence presented in earlier chapters suggests that the US and the UK intended to direct the reprisals at the Taliban regime and to effect (and currently to retain) regime change in Afghanistan.[84] Thus, this was an instance in which reprisals were aimed at 'state actors' (not only non-state actors), and this is the basis for the submission made herein, that the use of force was unlawful.

One final point to note regarding the current status of reprisals in international law is that despite the occasional use of reprisals by states, and hence, breaches of international law by those states, the law itself may have been challenged but it has remained unchanged. An interesting demonstration of this is to be found in international law texts that have been written, or at least updated, post-11 September 2001: the texts do not suggest that the law on reprisals has changed as a result of the use of force against Afghanistan.[85] The conclusion which must be drawn from the foregoing is that forceful measures by way of reprisal are still unlawful under Article 2(4) of the UN Charter. Any state that engages in them is breaching international law.

---

82 Kelly, supra n. 27, 21–2.

83 Kelly concedes that the argument he is exploring, that reprisals are only aimed at the terrorists and not the state itself, is a 'distinction without a difference': ibid., 22.

84 See discussion in Chapter 6 regarding the justifications put forward by the US and the UK for the use of force. The military installations of the Taliban, and not merely al Qaeda, were clear targets for the use of force, as was regime change a stated objective. Even in 2008, the NATO-led ISAF forces are not only targeting al Qaeda – they are also targeting the Taliban forces.

85 For example, see Shaw, M., *International Law*, 5th edn (New York: Cambridge University Press, 2003) 1023–4: 'Those general rules [on reprisals] are still applicable but have now to be interpreted in the light of the prohibition on the use of force posited by Article 2(4) of the United Nations Charter. Thus, reprisals short of force may still be undertaken legitimately, while reprisals involving armed force may be lawful if resorted to in conformity with the right of self-defence' (footnotes in original omitted). A leading text on public international law from an Australian perspective is also informative on this point. The section on 'reprisals' which was published in the first edition, in 1997, is repeated word-for-word in the updated second edition, in 2005: see Blay, S., Piotrowicz, R. and Tsamenyi, M. (eds), *Public International Law – An Australian Perspective* (Melbourne: Oxford University Press, 1997) 255–6; and compare with Blay, S., Piotrowicz, R. and Tsamenyi, M. (eds), *Public International Law – An Australian Perspective*, 2nd edn (Melbourne: Oxford University Press, 2005) 238–9.

Anticipatory Self-defence and the Use of Force against Afghanistan

It was noted earlier in this chapter that the use of force against Afghanistan could be characterised as either an act of revenge and retaliation, that is, a reprisal, or as an act of anticipatory self-defence.[86] As has been discussed in Chapter 6, the US and the UK explicitly justified their resort to force against Afghanistan on the basis that it was aimed at preventing *future* attacks of the kind experienced on 11 September 2001.[87] Because of those justifications, the standing of anticipatory self-defence in international law has been discussed and its evolution charted, from the pre-Charter period through to the present. Two key points are reiterated here.

First, the notion of using force in anticipatory self-defence is restricted by the wording of Article 51 itself, which only permits force to be used in self-defence 'if an armed attack occurs'.[88] Academic arguments have long been raised in support of expanding the plain, literal meaning of Article 51,[89] and there has

86 It is noted that, throughout this book, the terms 'anticipatory self-defence' and 'pre-emptive self-defence' have been used interchangeably. This is consistent with the usage adopted by other scholars such as: Shaw, supra n. 85 at 1028; Gray, supra n. 25 at 95; Cassese, A., *International Law* (Oxford; New York: Oxford University Press, 2001) at 307; Malanczuk, P., *Akehurst's Modern Introduction to International Law*, 7th edn. (New York; London: Routledge, 1997) at 311–12; Kelly, supra n. 27 at 22–4. It is acknowledged that some scholars perceive clear differences between 'anticipatory' and 'pre-emptive' self-defence: see Shah, N., 'Self-Defence, Anticipatory Self-defence and Pre-emption: International Law's Response to Terrorism' (2007) 12(1) *JCSL* 95 at 111; and also O'Connell, M., 'The Myth of Preemptive Self-Defence', *ASIL Task Force on Terrorism* (2002) 1–22 especially n. 10, available at: <http://www.asil.org/taskforce/oconnell.pdf> at 18 June 2008. The view adopted here is that it matters little whether one uses the term 'anticipatory self-defence' or 'pre-emptive self-defence'; the main point of distinction is how imminent the threat is that is to be averted. However, the author acknowledges in Chapter 1 that there is a difference between 'anticipatory self-defence'/'pre-emptive self-defence' on the one hand, and the Bush doctrine of 'pre-emption' on the other. The latter division seems, to this author, to be the more important distinction to make. It is also noted that another interpretation of the notion of 'pre-emption' has recently been put forth by an American academic. Philip Bobbit argues for 'preclusion' which in his conception appears to be 'pre-emption' on a much grander scale: see Bobbit, P., *Terror and Consent: The Wars for the Twenty-First Century* (New York: A.A. Knopf, 2008).

87 See the US and UK's letters to the Security Council of 7 October 2001, reproduced in Appendices 1 and 2 respectively. The US's letter, signed by John Negroponte, states that 'United States armed forces have initiated actions designed to prevent and deter further attacks on the United States'. The UK's letter, signed by Stewart Eldon, states that its forces were employed 'to avert the continuing threat of attacks from the same source'.

88 See Article 51 of the UN Charter.

89 See discussion in Chapters 5 and 6 regarding the interpretation of 'armed attack' and the use of force in anticipatory or pre-emptive self-defence; for arguments in favour of a liberal or 'counter-restrictionist' interpretation of Article 51, see especially Bowett, O'Brien and McDougal, discussed therein.

been a particular increase in the amount of scholarly debate on this issue since 11 September.[90] The range of views span from, at one end of the spectrum, those who would allow force to be used in self-defence to prevent terrorist capability before it is employed, and even before it is acquired,[91] to those who argue that no state can lawfully engage in pre-emptive self-defence under international law as it currently stands.[92] Despite the continuing debate amongst academics, it is fair to conclude that the majority of academics and the majority of states remain balanced in favour of an interpretation that force may not be used, and should not be used, in anticipation or pre-emption of an armed attack, unless the attack is imminent.[93]

---

90 A significant number of articles on this issue have recently been published in, inter alia, the *Journal of Conflict and Security Law*, the *American Journal of International Law*, the *European Journal of International Law*, the *Washington University Journal of Law and Policy* and the *Cornell International Law Journal*. There is a plethora of articles and comments on various aspects of the use of force against Afghanistan, available on the *European Journal of International Law*'s Discussion Forum, The Attack on the World Trade Centre: Legal Responses, available at: <http://www.ejil.org/forum_WTC/index.html> at 18 June 2008.

91 For example, see Wedgwood, R., 'The Fall of Saddam Hussein: Security Council Mandates and Pre-emptive Self-defence' (2003) 97 *AJIL* 576; Yoo, J., 'Using Force' (2004) 71(3) *University of Chicago Law Review* 729.

92 For example, see Paust, J., 'Post-9/11 Overreaction and Fallacies Regarding War and Defence, Guantanamo, the Status of Persons, Treatment, Judicial Review of Detention and Due Process in Military Commissions' (2004) 79 *Notre Dame Law Review* 1335 at 1343: '… there is nothing preemptive about nipping an armed attack in the bud. The point is that you need a bud. Self-defence cannot be exercised merely on the ground of expectations, anticipations, and fear. You have to prove that the other side is already embarked on an inevitable course of action.' See also Glennon, M., 'The Fog of Law: Self-Defence, Inherence and Incoherence in Article 51 of the United Nations Charter' (2003) 22 *Harv. J.L. & Pub. Pol'y* 16 at 20; Gross, E., 'Thwarting Terrorist Acts by Attacking the Perpetrators or their Commanders as an Act of Self-Defence: Human Rights Versus the State's Duty to Protect its Citizens' (2001) 15 *Temple International and Comparative Law Journal* 195 at 213; Greenwood, C., 'The Legality of Using Force Against Iraq', Memorandum to the UK Government on 12 October 2002, available at: <www.publications.parliament.uk/pa/cm200203/cmselect/cmfaff/196/2102406.htm> at 18 June 2008.

93 See Arend and Beck, supra n. 25 at 138–73; and compare with, *inter alia*, Shaw, supra n. 85 at 1028–30; Cassese, supra n. 86 at 307–11: 'In the case of anticipatory self-defence, it is more judicious to consider such action as *legally prohibited*, while admittedly knowing that there may be cases where breaches of the prohibition may be justified on moral and political grounds and the community will eventually condone them or mete out lenient condemnation'; Gray, supra n. 25 at 130: 'It is only where no conceivable case can be made that there has been an armed attack that they resort to anticipatory self-defence. This reluctance expressly to invoke anticipatory self-defence is in itself a clear indication of the doubtful status of this justification for the use of force.' See also Paust, Glennon, Greenwood, Gross, ibid. See also Bothe, M., 'Terrorism and the Legality of Pre-emptive Force' (2003) 14(2) *EJIL* 227 at 238–9: 'a change in the law to the effect of opening up broader possibilities for anticipatory self-defence is not desirable.' See also the legal opinion

This author agrees with the conclusion reached by Shah, that 'the arguments for pre-emptive self-defence are not persuasive and the notion seems too broad and fraught with risks to be accepted as a norm of international law'.[94] The author also agrees with the prescient observation of Bothe, that:[95]

> [I]f we want to maintain international law as a restraint on the use of military force, we should very carefully watch any attempt on the part of opinion leaders to argue that military force is anything other than an evil that has to be avoided. The lessons of history are telling. If we revert to such broad concepts, such as the just war concept, to justify military force, we are stepping on a slippery slope, one which would make us slide back into the nineteenth century when war was not illegal.

The second point is that, as other scholars have also observed,[96] the US and the UK both purported to use force against Afghanistan to prevent and deter future, unknown and unplanned attacks.[97] As discussed above and in Chapter 6, international law does not, at present, allow the use of force to prevent future, non-imminent attacks. Therefore, the use of force, if indeed it was employed on the basis of anticipatory self-defence as asserted here and elsewhere, was unlawful on this ground as well. So, whether the use of force is characterised as a reprisal or as an exercise of anticipatory self-defence, the same conclusion is reached regarding its legality.

---

of Attorney-General Lord Goldsmith to Prime Minister Blair: 'Force may be used in self-defence if there is an actual attack or imminent threat of an armed attack … The concept of what is imminent may depend on the circumstances … However, in my opinion there must be some degree of imminence': Goldsmith, L., 'Iraq: Resolution 1441', Secret Memo to the Prime Minster, 7 March 2002, available at: <http://www.ico.gov.uk/upload/documents/library/freedom_of_information/notices/annex_a_-_attorney_general's_advice_070303.pdf> at 18 June 2008.

94 Shah, N., 'Self-Defence, Anticipatory Self-Defence and Pre-emption: International Law's Response to Terrorism' (2007) 12(1) *JCSL* 95 at 117.

95 Bothe, supra n. 93 at 238.

96 For example, see McCormack, T., 'The Use of Force', in Blay, Piotrowicz and Tsamenyi, supra n. 85 at 230: 'However, once the attacks of 11 September 2001 had occurred, it was no longer possible for the USA to respond in self-defence to those specific attacks. The deployment of military force in Afghanistan … was clearly undertaken *to defend the USA against future attacks … The aerial bombardment of Afghanistan … was an anticipatory action* based on the likelihood of future attacks' (emphasis added); see also Bothe, supra n. 93; Cassese, supra n. 66.

97 See the US and UK's letters to the Security Council, reproduced in Appendices 1 and 2 respectively.

Repercussions and Ramifications

The ramifications of the use of force against Afghanistan in 2001 for international law, and for international peace and security, can be summed up as follows. This was an instance of an unlawful use of force in response to a criminal act, whether it is classified as an unlawful reprisal or as an instance where force was used in anticipatory self-defence where the future threat was not imminent. There should be no doubt that acts of terrorism are *criminal acts* – the evidence is overwhelmingly in favour of that conclusion. All multilateral and regional conventions, as well as domestic legislation, treat acts of terrorism as criminal acts – not acts of war. Since antiquity, states have regarded pirates, anarchists and terrorists as individuals who ought to be dealt with through criminal processes. Scholars have long understood that the sins of private individuals cannot be visited on the entire population, unless the state expressly accepts responsibility for those individuals' actions. After 11 September 2001, the Council of Europe was one organisation which was prepared to state that this act of international terrorism was a criminal act, and a matter for a body such as the International Criminal Court. The fact that both the US and the UK repeatedly called for 'justice', whilst simultaneously preparing for the use of military force, would tend to suggest that 'justice' can be attained by bombing approximately 200 pre-selected targets from the air, followed by a full-scale land invasion and occupation which has so far lasted more than seven years and shows no signs of ending in the near future. Cicero's rhetorical question in *De Re Publica* seems pertinent; he wrote: 'Remove justice and what are kingdoms but gangs of criminals on a large scale?'[98]

The position being advocated here is that 'justice' can only be attained by following the recognised course of response to criminal acts, namely, providing the evidence to pursue the processes of arrest, extradition and, if warranted, prosecution and ultimately punishment. Cassese suggested, rather optimistically, in late 2001 that there was 'much merit'[99] in the proposal that the alleged perpetrators be handed over to the Hague International Criminal Tribunal for trial, after promptly revising its Statute. He noted that 'an international trial would dispel any doubt about a possible bias' (if such trials were held in, say, New York) and in addition, 'an international trial would give greater resonance to the prosecution and punishment of the crimes allegedly committed by the accused'.[100] That suggestion has much to commend it.

It is timely to observe that no such international trials ever took place and that many individuals who were arrested in Afghanistan subsequent to the US–UK invasion, who then became detainees at Guantanamo Bay, have recently been released without being charged with any offence (although many remain in custody and still have not been charged with any offence). It is also significant

98 Cicero, also cited by St Augustine, supra n. 16.

99 Cassese, supra n. 66.

100 Ibid.

that several individuals who have been tried for terrorist offences in US courts have been acquitted. If some semblance of delayed 'justice' has been achieved in those cases, at least in so far as they now have been released or acquitted, no such 'justice' was offered for the several thousand Afghan civilians who died, and continue to die, as a direct or indirect result of the US–UK decision to employ force. It would be an unfortunate development for international peace and security if any state were permitted to use force against any other state, after the occurrence of a terrorist attack, in order to achieve 'justice'. The use of force in this instance by two militarily powerful states makes a mockery of the many statements that were delivered in the Security Council and in the General Assembly that this was *not* an attack just on the US, but an attack on more than 60 nations, and an attack on all of humanity. If those statements had held any weight and if they had been acted upon, the response would have been sanctioned by the only organisation that represents 'all of humanity'.

The second significant repercussion relates to the fact that the international community (except the US, Israel and perhaps recently the UK) had never previously sanctioned the unilateral and unconditional use of force by individual states against another state, including regime change, in response to an act of terrorism. There is some precedent in state practice for isolated military strikes in response to an act of terrorism,[101] but there is no precedent which would suggest that the international community is willing to support the unlimited and illimitable invasion and destruction of another state in response to acts of terrorism allegedly committed by individuals who were not acting for or on behalf of that state but who may have had some connection to persons within that state's borders.[102] This particular use of force was unusual and unlawful, and it is contended that if it is

101 For example, the US's use of force against Baghdad in 1993 and the missile strikes against Sudan and Afghanistan in 1998, as discussed in Chapter 5.

102 One might argue that there is a precedent, namely, the invasion of Algeria by France in 1830. The use of force by France was justified on numerous grounds, including the elimination of piracy. Parallels have been drawn throughout the historical analysis between piracy and terrorism. However, the elimination of piracy as a ground for invasion in that instance was only declared later and it was not the main reason for France's conquest and occupation. The main reasons why France decided to invade Algeria were related to the restoration of French honour following a personal insult upon the French consul in Algiers (the 'fly-whisk' incident), the redress of trade-related grievances, the protection of French property and in pursuit of the ideals of French imperialism. The elimination of piracy and the abolition of Christian slavery were not relevant considerations prior to 1830: see Falls, N., 'The Conquest of Algiers' (2005) 55(10) *History Today* 44. Other scholars have also noted that it would not be persuasive to argue that the invasion and conquest of Algeria was motivated simply, or even mainly, by a desire to repress acts of piracy; French imperialism was seemingly a much more important factor in the expansionist policies pursued in 1830 and thereafter: see de Tocqueville, A., *Writings on Empire and Slavery* (Pitts, J. trans.) (Baltimore: Johns Hopkins University Press, 2000).

allowed to stand as an example of a lawful act of self-defence, the repercussions for each state's sovereignty, and for international peace and security, are grave.

Moreover, the international community, and the Security Council in particular, failed to challenge the US's claim that it may, in the future, use force against other organisations and other states.[103] The wisdom of allowing such a claim to stand unchallenged was amply demonstrated by the ease with which the US was able to move from its use of force against Afghanistan in 2001 to its use of force against Iraq in 2003. It is submitted that the latter could not have been achieved without the former, and the former was achieved because the international community did not question the legitimacy of using force in self-defence in those undoubtedly tragic circumstances, due in large part to an overwhelming feeling of sympathy for the US within the international community.

It is submitted that the proper response for the US and the UK in 2001 would have been to bring the issue before the Security Council, and to discuss within the Council the objectives of identifying the suspected individuals and the options available for bringing them to justice through the normal means. If the Security Council had found that limited missile strikes were necessary, perhaps targeting al Qaeda specifically, it could have authorised them. It was never given the opportunity to do so. Furthermore, the Security Council has, on previous occasions, acted pursuant to Chapter VII and authorised the use of military force against regimes which it considers to be a 'threat to the peace'.[104] It could, had it been given the chance and had it considered it justified, authorised the use of 'all necessary means', including the use of force, against the Taliban regime in 2001. It was not given the opportunity to exercise its authority.

US intervention in Iraq – 2003 It is clear that the international community was overcome with a sense of sympathy for the US after 11 September 2001 but it ought not to have allowed that sense of sympathy to overtake the responsibilities of ensuring that states, even the most militarily powerful states, act within the bounds of international law. By refusing to submit its will to that of the Security Council, the US demonstrated that it can use force when and where it wants, regardless of its legality. The danger in standing by and keeping silent was amply demonstrated in 2003. The use of force against Afghanistan, which was virtually unchallenged

103 See the US's letter to the Security Council, reproduced in Appendix 1.

104 In 1994, military enforcement measures were authorised to reverse the military coup against the democratically elected government of Haiti: S/Res/940, 31 July 1994. See also the discussion in Franck, T., *Recourse to Force – State Action Against Threats and Armed Attacks* (Cambridge; New York: Cambridge University Press, 2002) at 42–4, where he notes that the UN has deployed military and/or police force in Congo, Somalia, Haiti, East Timor, Namibia, Cambodia and Mozambique to neutralise or disarm factions.

in 2001, paved the way for an even more conspicuous breach of international law in 2003.

The lawfulness of the use of force against Iraq in 2003 is not the topic of the current work.[105] However, it is arguable that the use of force in Afghanistan eased the way for the use of force against Iraq in an indirect sense, by preparing public and international opinion for further uses of force, and in a direct sense by means of the statement made by the US in its letter to the Security Council on 7 October 2001 when it indicated that, 'we may find that our self-defence requires further actions with respect to other organizations and other states'.[106] It was discussed above, and in Chapter 6, that anticipatory self-defence was a key plank in the US and UK's justifications for the use of force against Afghanistan. Again, anticipatory self-defence was put forward as one of the key justifications for the use of military force against Iraq in 2003.[107] In March 2003, when the US reported to the Security Council on the legal justifications for using force against Iraq, there was once again a reference to using military force in order to pre-empt future threats.[108] It is argued that such a contentious claim was able to be made and acted upon in 2003 by virtue of the fact that it had been put forward and acted upon in 2001 without any, or any significant, objection from the international community or, especially, from the Security Council.

Israel's intervention in Lebanon – 2006 The ramifications of allowing the 2001 precedent to stand were further demonstrated in July 2006 when Israel invaded

105 For a discussion of the legal basis for the use of force against Iraq, see, *inter alia*, Maogoto, J., *Battling Terrorism* (Aldershot: Ashgate, 2005) especially 111–24; McGoldrick, D., *From '9-11' to the Iraq War 2003 – International Law in an Age of Complexity* (Oxford: Hart, 2004); Kelly, supra n. 27; Conte, A., *Security in the 21st Century: The United Nations, Afghanistan and Iraq* (Aldershot: Ashgate, 2005) especially at 139–61; McCormack, supra n. 96; and Wall, A., 'The Legal Case for Invading Iraq and Toppling Hussein' (2002) 32 *Israel Yearbook on Human Rights* 165.

106 UN Doc S/2001/946, Letter dated 7 October 2001 from the Permanent Representative of the US to the UN addressed to the President of the Security Council, reproduced in Appendix 1.

107 Anticipatory self-defence was not the *only* justification put forward. It was alleged that Iraq was in material breach of its disarmament obligations under Resolution 1441 (2002), and it was also alleged that the military action was authorised by earlier UN Security Council resolutions, namely, Resolutions 678 (1990) and 687 (1991): ibid.; see also Goldsmith, supra n. 93.

108 UN Doc S/2003/351, Letter Dated 20 March 2003 from the Permanent Representative of the United States of America to the United Nations Addressed to the President of the Security Council (21 March 2003). The letter, signed by John Negroponte, asserts that: 'The actions that coalition forces are undertaking are an appropriate response. They are necessary steps to defend the United States and the international community from the threat posed by Iraq and to restore international peace and security in the area.'

Lebanon, again on the pretext of 'self-defence'.[109] The use of force by Israel in 2006 is particularly alarming in terms of providing an insight into how the Afghanistan intervention may be used in the future. Israel alleged that it was acting in self-defence when it used military force against southern Lebanon. The Israeli Prime Minister, Ehud Olmert, said Israel was using 'the basic elementary right of self-defence'[110] when it launched its military offensive. It referred to the 'barrage of heavy artillery and rockets into Israel' and the alleged kidnapping of two Israeli soldiers by non-state actors from Hezbollah as a 'belligerent act of war'.[111] Israel alleged that responsibility lay with the government of Lebanon, 'from whose territory these acts have been launched', and also with the Islamic Republic of Iran and the Syrian Arab Republic, 'which support and embrace those who carried out this attack'.[112] Israel described those governments as 'an Axis of Terror'[113] and alleged that they had 'opened another chapter in their war of terror'.[114] Israel claimed that its response was an act of self-defence in accordance with Article 51 of the UN Charter, and it alleged that it was entitled to 'exercise its right of self-defence when an armed attack is launched against a Member of the United Nations'. [115]

Israel's justification for using force against Lebanon seems to have been inspired by President Bush's National Security Strategy of 2002, discussed in Chapters 5 and 6, which itself was the policy underpinning the use of force against Afghanistan.[116] The parallels between Afghanistan in 2001 and Lebanon in 2006 are evident in the sense that, in both cases, isolated terrorist attacks were alleged to have been 'armed attacks', and governments whose territory was allegedly used by the terrorists were themselves directly implicated as being legitimate targets for military reprisal. One scholar who has directly connected President Bush's National Security Strategy to Israel's use of force against Lebanon, Anthony D'Amato, argues that:[117] 'The community of nations quickly reached consensus as to the validity of this strategy under international law. Hardly any nation has voiced an objection. We may safely say that the Bush Doctrine is Israel's legal

---

109 See Identical Letters dated 12 July 2006 from the Permanent Representative of Israel to the United Nations addressed to the Secretary-General and the President of the Security Council, signed by Dan Gillerman.

110 Reuters, Associated Press, Telegraph Group Ltd, 'Self Defence Is Our Right', *The New Zealand Herald*, 26 July 2006, B1.

111 Identical Letters dated 12 July 2006 from the Permanent Representative of Israel to the United Nations.

112 Ibid.

113 Ibid.

114 Ibid.

115 Ibid.

116 See discussion of the US National Security Strategy in Chapter 6.

117 D'Amato, A., 'International Law Aspects of the Mideast "War"', JURIST – Forum 18 July 2006, available at: <http://jurist.law.pitt.edu/forumy/2006/07/international-law-aspects-of-mideast.php> at 18 June 2008.

justification for the bombardment it is inflicting upon Lebanon.' Whether D'Amato is correct when he asserts that the Bush doctrine of pre-emption is considered a 'valid' strategy under international law is open to debate. What is clear is that Israel essentially relied upon the justifications for the use of force which the US and the UK relied upon when they invaded Afghanistan in 2001. Had Israel been mindful of the precedent set by the US and the UK in relation to Afghanistan, Israel could arguably have legitimately targeted the governments of Lebanon, and potentially also Syria and Iran. Israel could have relied upon the invasion of Afghanistan as a precedent for a military invasion of those sovereign states, had it had the desire and the means to do so, since those states allegedly had terrorists operating from within their borders just as the Taliban had supposedly 'allowed' terrorists to operate from the territory that it controlled prior to 11 September 2001, and according to Israel they had 'supported' or 'embraced' those alleged terrorists, as had the Taliban regime.

Israel's intervention in Syria – 2007 A further example of Israel's interpretation of its Article 51 right of self-defence was evident on 6 September 2007, when its aircraft violated Syrian airspace and then launched air strikes at a target within Syria, in an operation referred to as *Operation Orchard*.[118] One possible reason for Israel's unilateral resort to force on that occasion was that Israel reportedly suspected Syria of having nuclear installations that were being developed with the assistance of North Korea, although that was not the only possible explanation.[119] Whatever the real reason behind the air strikes, and regardless of arguments over the reliability of the intelligence presented by Israel, and more recently by the US, the key point to consider from an international law perspective is that a militarily powerful state considered that it was within its rights to unilaterally employ force against a neighbouring sovereign state, supposedly because it wanted to pre-empt

118 For analysis of the air strike, see The James Centre for Non-Proliferation Studies, Weitz, R., 'Israeli Airstrike in Syria: International Reactions', 1 November 2007, available at: <http://cns.miis.edu/pubs/week/071101.htm#fnB37> at 18 June 2008. For media reports, see, *inter alia*, *New York Times*, 'US Confirms Israeli Strikes Hit Syrian Target Last Week', 12 September 2007, available at: <http://www.nytimes.com/2007/09/12/world/middleeast/12syria.html?fta=y> at 18 June 2008.

119 Suggestions included Israel wanting to discourage the US's policy of engaging North Korea over its nuclear ambitions, to Israel wanting to send a message to Iran over the vulnerability of its planned nuclear facilities, to Israel wanting to destroy Iranian ammunition bound for Hizbollah forces that were being stored in Syria: see, for example, *The Jerusalem Post*, 'IAF Targeted Iranian Weapons in Syria', 11 September 2007, available at: <http://www.jpost.com/servlet/Satellite?pagename=JPost%2FJPArticle%2FShowFull&cid=1189411388088> at 18 June 2008. The lack of clarity over the reasons for the strikes was due in part to the fact that Israel was initially silent, even denying that a strike had taken place at all, and was not prepared to engage in a public discussion on the reasons for its strike. The US also initially denied any knowledge that a strike had occurred and there was also initially a muted response from Syria.

a future, non-imminent attack from either that state, or from another neighbouring state (perhaps Iran), or because it wanted to prevent weapons from Iran passing through Syria into the hands of non-state actors who might, at some future time, use those weapons against Israel. There were also claims that Israel was trying to undermine the peace process, and Syria's role in it, ahead of the regional peace summit that took place in November 2007.[120] The allegation that Syria had been secretly developing a nuclear reactor was only formally made to the International Atomic Energy Agency (IAEA) in April 2008 when the US provided the IAEA with intelligence information supporting its claims. The IAEA 'deplored the fact' that such information had not been made available in a timely manner, given that Israel had destroyed the alleged site in September 2007.[121]

Another significant point for international lawyers to note was that Israel did not send a notification to the Security Council pursuant to Article 51, which suggests one of two things: either Israel did not consider that it was acting in legitimate self-defence or, alternatively, it considered that it was acting in self-defence but it did not, for some reason, believe that it had to comply with the notification provisions in Article 51. Syria did not respond with force (although it would arguably have been within its rights to do so)[122] but the Syrian President, Bashar al-Assad, signalled that his country reserved the right to respond to the attack.[123] Syria submitted a letter to the UN Security Council protesting at Israel's use of force and its 'flagrant defiance of international law'.[124] The letter was circulated to the 15 members of the Security Council but the Council did not take any action. This may have been because the Syrian letter to the Security Council did not seek any particular course of action,[125] but surely the Security Council ought to have

---

120 See, for instance, Jalal Ghazi, 'Arab Media See Israeli Raid on Syria As More Psy-War Than Proxy-War', 21 September 2007, available at: <http://news.newamericamedia.org/news/view_article.html?article_id=57acd649faf9ebc8a2df05785eba7ec7> at 18 June 2008.

121 IAEA Press Releases, Press Release 2008/06, 'Statement by IAEA Director-General Mohamed El-Baradei, 25 April 2008', available at: <http://www.iaea.org/NewsCenter/PressReleases/2008/prn200806.html> at 18 June 2008.

122 If the use of force by the US and the UK against Afghanistan in 2001 is considered to be 'lawful' use of force, either in self-defence or as a resurrection of the doctrine of reprisals, then Syria would have been able to justify a military response against Israel on the same grounds. Indeed, its case for resorting to force would have been even stronger given that it suffered an attack from what were clearly state actors: members of the Israeli Air Force.

123 See *BBC News*, 'Assad Sets Conference Conditions', 1 October 2007, available at: <http://news.bbc.co.uk/2/hi/middle_east/7021986.stm> at 18 June 2008.

124 UN SC Doc S/2007/537 (9 September 2007) Identical Letters Dated 9 September 2007 from the Permanent Representative of the Syrian Arab Republic to the United Nations addressed to the Secretary-General and the President of the Security Council.

125 This was the explanation given by French diplomats, as reported in the *Jerusalem Post*: supra n. 119.

discussed the unilateral use of force by one of its members, and it ought to have issued a statement indicating that this was an unacceptable and unlawful act. The Security Council was sitting in early September 2007 when the Israeli attack on Syria occurred: it issued a statement on 7 September 2007 deploring a terrorist act in another Member State, which makes its silence on the use of force by Israel even more confounding.[126] Thus, perhaps even more significant than the actual use of force by Israel was the international community's lack of condemnation of that use of force which may not be easily excused merely on the basis that Syria requested its statement to the Security Council to be 'circulated'. The concern, from an international law perspective, is that there seemed to have been a tone of virtually tacit approval for the use of force. There was a 'synchronised silence' in the Arab world;[127] the only states to condemn Israel were Russia, Iran, Turkey and North Korea, although there was a tentative denouncement from the Arab League.[128] There was even an accusation that condemnation of the use of force was akin to an acknowledgement of guilt.[129]

Although the Security Council did not discuss the issue, the Director-General of the IAEA did state that it viewed the unilateral use of force by Israel as 'undermining the due process of verification which is at the heart of the non-proliferation regime'.[130] The latest development at the time of writing is that Syria agreed to allow a delegation from the IAEA to inspect the Al-Kibar site that was attacked by Israel; with Syria's co-operation, IAEA inspectors conducted a site visit to Al-Kibar in June 2008. Following that visit, 'the IAEA asked the Syrian

---

126 The first meeting of the Security Council for the month of September 2007 took place on 7 September. The statement referred to was S/PRST/2007/32, 7 September 2007, in which the terrorist attack in Batna, Algeria that took place on 6 September 2007 was condemned.

127 See Moubayed, S., *Al Ahram Weekly Online*, 'With Friends Like These ...' 20–26 September 2007, available at: <http://weekly.ahram.org.eg/2007/863/re63.htm> at 18 June 2008.

128 The Arab League's Secretary-General, Amr Moussa, referred to the Israeli Air Forces's actions as 'unacceptable maneuvers': see *People's Daily Online*, 'AL Chief Says Alleged Israeli Violation of Syrian Airspace "Unacceptable"', 8 September 2007, available at: <http://english.people.com.cn/90001/90777/6257854.html> at 18 June 2008.

129 In an interview with the Israeli media, former US Ambassador to the UN, John Bolton, implied North Korea's culpability in the alleged Syrian nuclear facilities when he posed the question: 'Why would North Korea protest an Israeli strike on Syria': see Horowitz, D., *The Jerusalem Post*, 'Bolton: Why Would North Korea Protest Syria Raid?', 16 September 2007, available at: <http://www.jpost.com/servlet/Satellite?pagename=JPost%2FJPArticle%2FShowFull&cid=1189411406670> at 18 June 2008. The more important question from a legal point of view is: why didn't all states protest the Israeli raid on Syria?

130 See IAEA Press Releases, Press Release 2008/06, 'Statement by IAEA Director-General Mohamed El-Baradei, 25 April 2008', available at: <http://www.iaea.org/NewsCenter/PressReleases/2008/prn200806.html> at 18 June 2008.

authorities to provide access to additional information and activities'.[131] Samples were taken by the IAEA during the visit and the latest information available is that no evidence of nuclear material has been found.[132] Although the IAEA's assessment is yet to be completed, present indications suggest that Syria's explanation for the site's existence is more plausible than Israel's. That conclusion must be left open to challenge until the IAEA's work is completed, but if it is correct, the international community's reluctance to challenge the use of force by Israel is of even greater concern.

Afghanistan/Pakistan border – 2008 The interpretation of the right of self-defence has arisen again recently in relation to the use of force on the Afghanistan/Pakistan border. The Afghan President, Hamid Karzai, warned that Afghan troops may be sent across the Afghanistan–Pakistan border to fight Taliban forces and to target Taliban leaders if those Taliban forces came over the border to launch attacks in Afghanstan. Karzai reportedly said that it was Afghanistan's right to 'self-defence' to respond by mounting cross-border raids into Pakistan.[133] Pakistan has responded by stating that it will not allow anyone to interfere in its internal affairs.[134] These border clashes in the name of self-defence were ongoing at the time of writing.[135]

Allowing the use of force against Afghanistan to stand as an example of the legitimate exercise of self-defence is unfortunate for international law, for the enduring role of the United Nations and especially the Security Council, and also for civilians who happen to live within states whose territory – or part thereof – might be used for training purposes by private individuals who later commit acts of international terrorism. More than anything, this use of force, if left unchallenged, would seriously undermine international peace and security and the UN Charter's ability to prevent states from unilaterally resorting to force. If President Bush was correct when he claimed that there are 'thousands of these terrorists in more than 60 countries',[136] and that al Qaeda is 'linked to many other organisations including

---

131 IAEA, 'Board Begins September Deliberations', 22 September 2008, available at: <http://www.iaea.org/NewsCenter/News/2008/board220908.html> at 12 January 2009.

132 IAEA, Al-Baradei, M., 'Introductory Statement to the Board of Governors', 22 September 2008, available at: <http://www.iaea.org/NewsCenter/Statements/2008/ebsp2008n007.html> at 12 January 2009.

133 See *Telegraph.co.uk*, Coughlan, T., 'Afghanistan Threatens "Self-defence Raids" into Pakistan', 16 June 2008, available at: <http://www.telegraph.co.uk/news/worldnews/asia/afghanistan/2135765/Hamid-Karzai-threatens-cross-border-revenge-raids.html> at 18 June 2008; see also *Aljazeera.net*, 'Karzai Threatens Pakistan Raids', 15 June 2008, available at: <http://english.aljazeera.net/news/asia/2008/06/200861912283818O458.html> at 18 June 2008.

134 Ibid.

135 February 2009.

136 President George W. Bush, Address to a Joint Session of Congress and the American People, 20 September 2001, available at: <http://www.whitehouse.gov/news/

the Egyptian Islamic Jihad in Egypt and the Islamic Movement of Uzbekistan',[137] the virtually unlimited potential for the unilateral resort to force under the pretext of 'self-defence' is as equally significant as it is disconcerting. The potentially unlimited nature of the use of force in self-defence following Afghanistan was reiterated by President Bush when he stated that the 'war on terror ... will not end until every terrorist group of global reach has been found, stopped and defeated'.[138] Thus, the US has indicated its intention to exercise a virtually unlimited right to self-defence. The Security Council must engage itself actively to maintain peace and security or its role will be further undermined.[139] As other scholars have observed, 'inaction by the Security Council will lead to further erosion of its regulation of the use of force'.[140]

As discussed earlier, the use of force has been held up by some publicists, such as Michael Kelly, as an example of the resurrection of the reprisal doctrine. In the interests of enhancing global peace and security, all members of the international community must reiterate that all uses of force which are undertaken outside of the parameters of the Charter are unacceptable and unlawful: acts of terrorism must be condemned but so also must acts of reprisal in revenge. The use of force in pre-emptive self-defence, when the attack is non-imminent, must likewise be consistently condemned as unlawful.

One of the recurring themes throughout this book has been the need to be both aware of, and to learn from, the past. This is by no means a novel idea[141] but its importance deserves reiteration. Recently, calls have emanated from Israel with increasingly provocative language that it is considering a pre-emptive strike against Iran in order to remove its nuclear weapons capability.[142] Israel's pre-emptive strike against the Iraqi nuclear reactor, 'Osirak', in 1981, was discussed in Chapter 5; it was universally condemned by the international community as an unlawful use of force. Given that the Security Council has demonstrated an increasingly permissive attitude towards the use of force by states since that time, it is difficult to determine whether the international community would act to prevent another unlawful use of force by Israel, or whether, in the event of history repeating itself, the Security Council would again unanimously condemn any such resort to force.

---

releases/2001/09/20010920-8.html> at 18 June 2008.

137 Ibid.

138 Ibid.

139 See Myjer, E. and White, N., 'The Twin Towers Attack: An Unlimited Right to Self-Defence?' (2002) 7(1) *JCSL* 5 at 16.

140 Ibid.

141 See, for instance, Ago, R., 'The First International Communities in the Mediterranean World' (1982) 53 *BYIL* 213, cited in Chapter 1. See also Bothe, supra n. 93 at 238; Kelly, supra n. 27.

142 See comments of Dr Zvi Shtauber, director of Tel Aviv University's Institute for National Security Studies. Shtauber was quoted as saying that, 'You don't have to attack all the sites ... you can attack a couple of them': Silver, E., 'Analyst Fuels Talk of Pre-emptive Strike', *The New Zealand Herald*, 9 January 2007, B2.

Given the precedent set in Afghanistan, followed by the use of force against Iraq in 2003, against Lebanon in 2006, and against Syria in 2007, it is submitted that the international community must immediately address the unlawful and unilateral use, or threat, of force by states which consider that their security is threatened.

It seems clear to this author, and to others, that the Security Council has failed to 'engage itself actively to maintain peace and security'.[143] Thus, although the Security Council's authority and the rule of law are no doubt under threat from militarily powerful states, the Council itself must shoulder some of the responsibility for neglecting its primary duty which is to restore and maintain peace and security.[144] The Security Council must reassert its power by taking a clear position on the use of force by states in purported self-defence. As Myjer and White have observed, the current trend is towards a simultaneous erosion of the Security Council authority under chapter VII and a purported widening of the exceptions to the prohibition on the use of force embodied in Article 2(4) of the Charter.[145] These two developments are a real and present danger, not only to the future role and authority of the Security Council, but also consequently to global peace and security.

This book has focused mainly upon the legality of the use of force against Afghanistan. It has been argued that this was an unlawful use of force which breached existing rules of international law, rather than an instance in which a new development in international law was instantly forged. Although it is perhaps still too early to definitively conclude whether 2001 will mark the beginning of a new era in international law, the current signs are that it possibly will not. Since 2001, there have been several other significant terrorist attacks which have come to the attention of the Security Council.[146] In each instance, the Security Council has condemned such acts of terrorism as a threat to peace and security, and, where appropriate, *international* peace and security, just as it did post-9/11.[147]

---

143 Myjer and White, supra n. 139 at 16.

144 Ibid. Myjer and White argue that: 'Erosion of Security Council authority to deal with situations that fall within chapter VII appears to have become, either by accident or design, part of the policy of powerful states, particularly the United States.'

145 Ibid.

146 For instance, the bomb attacks in Bali, Indonesia on 12 October 2002; the hostage-taking in Moscow on 23 October 2002; the bomb attack in Kikambala, Kenya, and the attempted missile strike on Arkia Israeli Airlines flight 582 departing Mombassa, Kenya on 28 November 2002; the bomb attack in Bogota, Colombia on 7 February 2003; bomb attacks in Istanbul, Turkey on 15 and 20 November 2003; bomb attacks perpetrated by ETA in Madrid, Spain on 11 March 2004; the terrorist attacks in London on 7 July 2005; and terrorist attacks in Iraq during 2005.

147 For instance, see UN Doc S/Res/1438 (2002), condemning the Bali bombings; UN Doc S/Res/1440 (2002), condemning the Moscow hostage-taking; UN Doc S/Res/1450 (2002) condemning the incidents in Kenya; UN Doc S/Res/1465 (2003) condemning the Colombia bombings; UN Doc S/Res/1516 (2003), condemning the attacks in Turkey; UN Doc S/Res/1530 (2004), condemning the attacks in Spain; UN Doc S/Res/1611 (2005)

It is significant that in not one of those resolutions since 2001 has the Security Council referred to the 'inherent right of self-defence', the phrase to which so much significance was attached in the context of justifying the use of force against Afghanistan.[148] This may be interpreted as a sign that the Security Council does not consider that a state which has been affected by an act of terrorism has a right to use force in self-defence, as a matter of course.[149] It may also be interpreted as a deliberate attempt to soften the perception that in September 2001 new international law was instantly created whereby any state that suffers a terrorist attack is entitled to retaliate by using force in exercising its 'inherent right of individual or collective self-defence'. This series of post-9/11 resolutions underlines the point which has been made here: that the use of force against Afghanistan purportedly in self-defence was not a legitimate exercise of that right, nor was it an instance in which new customary law was created, despite the 'recognition' and 'reaffirmation' by the Security Council that the right to self-defence exists. The Security Council's resolutions confirm that there is no new right to use unilateral force in response to a terrorist attack, be it international or otherwise, and furthermore, states have not exercised such a right in the intervening years. On the contrary, the Security Council resolutions which have been adopted since September 2001 regarding the threat posed by terrorism confirm that this is a threat to international peace and security, that states ought to find and bring to justice the perpetrators, organisers and sponsors of such attacks[150] and that the primary responsibility for maintaining international peace and security lies with the Security Council.[151]

The UN Charter is the culmination of hundreds (or, arguably, even thousands) of years of evolution and development in inter-state relations. At least since the time of the ancient Greeks, states have used force for a variety of reasons, but

condemning the London bombings; and UN Doc S/Res/1618 (2005) regarding the attacks in Iraq. Compare those resolutions with the wording of UN Doc S/Res/1368 (2001) and UN Doc S/Res/1373 (2001): in each of the latter resolutions, there was a preambular paragraph respectively 'recognising' and 'reaffirming' the inherent right to self-defence.

148 Recall the argument canvassed in Chapter 6 where it was discussed that many scholars consider the references to the inherent right of self-defence in S/Res/1368 (2001) and S/Res/1373 (2001) as proof that the US and the UK were entitled to use force against Afghanistan.

149 Gray has observed that: 'This failure to refer to self-defence … seems significant. It may be an indication that the right to use force in self-defense against past terrorist acts may remain exceptional, perhaps available only in cases of attacks on territory rather than on nationals abroad': Gray, C., 'A New War for a New Century?', in Eden, P. and O'Connell, T. (eds), *September 11, 2001 – A Turning Point in International and Domestic Law* (New York: Transnational Publishers, 2005) 113.

150 See UN Doc S/Res/1438 (2002); UN Doc S/Res/1440 (2002); UN Doc S/Res/1450 (2002); UN Doc S/Res/1465 (2003); UN Doc S/Res/1516 (2003); UN Doc S/Res/1530 (2004); UN Doc S/Res/1611 (2005); and UN Doc S/Res/1618 (2005).

151 For instance, see UN Doc S/Res/1624 (2005), third preambular paragraph; UN Doc S/Res/1735 (2006), second preambular paragraph.

have shown an enduring desire to justify the resort to force, to make it seem 'just'. Tribes, ethnic and religious groups, and states have long recognised that peace is the ultimate objective for mankind, but they have struggled over the way in which force ultimately remains an option, reserved for use in limited circumstances. President Bush, operating under a different paradigm to statesmen of the past, nevertheless showed a desire to be on the side of 'justice' when he expressed the US's intended response to the terrorist attacks of 11 September 2001.[152]

The Charter represents the most recent embodiment of that historical desire to restrain the resort to force. However, the use of force against Afghanistan, and the justifications which were put forward by the US and the UK to support that use of force, challenges the basic tenets of the Charter. The hard-won gains that limit the resort to force essentially to two situations (when sanctioned by the Security Council or in self-defence) are being directly challenged. If the Charter's prohibitions on the resort to force *are* outdated, as alleged, somewhat unconvincingly, by some statesmen,[153] then there ought to be an open debate on proposed amendments to the Charter. As it stands, the use of force against Afghanistan, followed closely by the use of force against Iraq, then Lebanon and Syria, amongst other examples, suggests that Athenian imperialism may not have been consigned to history after all. We may be entering a new age when, once again, 'the strong do all they can and the weak suffer what they must'.[154]

152 'Freedom and fear, justice and cruelty, have always been at war, and we know that God is not neutral between them … Fellow citizens, we'll meet violence with patient justice – assured of the rightness of our cause, and confident of the victories to come': President George W. Bush, Address to a Joint Session of Congress and the American People, supra n. 136.

153 See Chapter 5 at 121–124.

154 Thucydides, *The History of the Peloponnesian War*, Book V, Chapter XVII; see Chapter 1, n. 1.

Appendix 1
S/2001/946

Letter dated 7 October 2001 from the Permanent Representative of the United States of America to the United Nations addressed to the President of the Security Council

In accordance with Article 51 of the Charter of the United Nations, I wish, on behalf of my Government, to report that the United States of America, together with other States, has initiated actions in the exercise of its inherent right of individual and collective self-defence following the armed attacks that were carried out against the United States on 11 September 2001.

On 11 September 2001, the United States was the victim of massive and brutal attacks in the states of New York, Pennsylvania and Virginia. These attacks were specifically designed to maximize the loss of life; they resulted in the death of more than 5,000 persons, including nationals of 81 countries, as well as the destruction of four civilian aircraft, the World Trade Center towers and a section of the Pentagon. Since 11 September, my Government has obtained clear and compelling information that the Al-Qaeda organization, which is supported by the Taliban regime in Afghanistan, had a central role in the attacks. There is still much we do not know. Our inquiry is in its early stages. We may find that our self-defence requires further actions with respect to other organizations and other States.

The attacks on 11 September 2001 and the ongoing threat to the United States and its nationals posed by the Al-Qaeda organization have been made possible by the decision of the Taliban regime to allow the parts of Afghanistan that it controls to be used by this organization as a base of operation. Despite every effort by the United States and the international community, the Taliban regime has refused to change its policy. From the territory of Afghanistan, the Al-Qaeda organization continues to train and support agents of terror who attack innocent people throughout the world and target United States nationals and interests in the United States and abroad.

In response to these attacks, and in accordance with the inherent right of individual and collective self-defence, United States armed forces have initiated actions designed to prevent and deter further attacks on the United States. These actions include measures against Al-Qaeda terrorist training camps and military installations of the Taliban regime in Afghanistan. In carrying out these actions, the United States is committed to minimizing civilian casualties and damage to civilian property. In addition, the United States will continue its humanitarian efforts to alleviate the suffering of the people of Afghanistan. We are providing them with food, medicine and supplies.

I ask that you circulate the text of the present letter as a document of the Security Council.

(*Signed*) John D. Negroponte

Appendix 2
S/2001/947

Letter dated 7 October 2001 from the Chargé d'affaires a.i. of the Permanent Mission of the United Kingdom of Great Britain and Northern Ireland to the United Nations addressed to the President of the Security Council

In accordance with Article 51 of the Charter of the United Nations, I wish on behalf of my Government to report that the United Kingdom of Great Britain and Northern Ireland has military assets engaged in operations against targets that we know to be involved in the operation of terror against the United States of America, the United Kingdom and other countries around the world, as part of a wider international effort.

These forces have now been employed in exercise of the inherent right of individual and collective self-defence, recognized in Article 51, following the terrorist outrage of 11 September, to avert the continuing threat of attacks from the same source. My Government presented information to the United Kingdom Parliament on 4 October which showed that Usama Bin Laden and his Al-Qaeda terrorist organization have the capability to execute major terrorist attacks, claimed credit for past attacks on United States targets, and have been engaged in a concerted campaign against the United States and its allies. One of their stated aims is the murder of United States citizens and attacks on the allies of the United States.

This military action has been carefully planned, and is directed against Usama Bin Laden's Al-Qaeda terrorist organization and the Taliban regime that is supporting it. Targets have been selected with extreme care to minimize the risk to civilians.

It is important to underline that these operations are not directed against the Afghan population, or against Islam. The United Kingdom is proud to be a multicultural, multiracial country, and Prime Minister Blair has made clear the anger of the United Kingdom, and the anger of the vast majority of Muslims, to hear Usama Bin Laden and his associates described as 'Islamic' terrorists. They are not: they are just ordinary terrorists.

I ask that you circulate the text of the present letter as a document of the Security Council.

(*Signed*) Stewart Eldon
Chargé d'affaires a.i.

Index